WHO LIVES? WHO DIES?
ETHICAL CRITERIA IN PATIENT SELECTION

ETHICAL CRITERIA
IN PATIENT SELECTION

Who Lives? Who Dies?

JOHN F. KILNER

YALE UNIVERSITY PRESS · NEW HAVEN & LONDON

Published with assistance from the Louis Stern Memorial Fund.

Grateful acknowledgment is made to the following for permission to reprint material from previously published articles: the *American Journal of Public Health*; The Hastings Center; the *Journal of Health Politics, Policy and Law*; *The Annual of the Society of Christian Ethics*; *the Archives of Internal Medicine*. Grateful acknowledgment is made to the following for permission to reprint: the Wadsworth Publishing Company, for excerpts from *Intervention and Reflection*, 2d ed., by Ronald Munson, ed. © 1983 by Wadsworth, Inc. Reprinted by permission of the publisher; the MIT Press, for excerpts from *Ethics in Medicine,* by Stanley J. Reiser et al., eds. © 1977 by MIT Press; Purdue University Press, for excerpts from *Muted Consent,* by Jan Wojcik, © 1978, Purdue University Press by Purdue Research Foundation; The Hastings Center, for a case study adapted from "In Organ Transplants, Americans First," a case study with commentaries by Jeffrey M. Prottas, Olga Jonasson, and John I. Kleinig, *Hastings Center Report* 16:5 (October 1986), 23–25; Robert M. Veatch, for case studies adapted from *Case Studies in Medical Ethics,* © 1977 Robert M. Veatch; Shana Alexander, for material from "They Decide Who Lives, Who Dies," *Life* 53 (November 9, 1962).

Set in Times Roman type by Brevis Press, Bethany, Connecticut. Printed in the United States of America by Book Press, Inc., Brattleboro, Vermont.

Library of Congress Cataloging-in-Publication Data
Kilner, John Frederic.
   Who lives? who dies? : ethical criteria in patient selection /
John F. Kilner.
      p.   cm.
   Bibliography: p.
   Includes index.
   ISBN 0–300–04680–4 (alk. paper)
         0–300–05220–0 (pbk.)
   1. Medical ethics.   2. Medical care—Moral and ethical aspects.
I. Title.   II. Title: Ethical criteria in patient selection.
   [DNLM: 1. Decision Making.   2. Ethics, Medical.   W 50 K48w]
R724.K54   1990
174′.2—dc20
DNLM/DLC
for Library of Congress   89–16542

The paper in this book meets the guidelines for permanence and durability of the Committee on Production Guidelines for Book Longevity of the Council on Library Resources.

10   9   8   7   6   5   4   3   2

To Connie Kilner,
a mother whose love has never been a scarce resource

CONTENTS

Contents

INTRODUCTION

It is hard to imagine a more agonizing choice than deciding which persons should live and which should die. Yet the burden of this choice is the inescapable result of recent lifesaving breakthroughs in medicine. Many lives can now be saved which in an earlier day could not have been. Sometimes, however, the means are simply not present to save all in need.

The dilemma of deciding who shall live has long been acknowledged as a "terrifying question," but the struggle to answer it looms ahead for the most part.[1] In the words of one observer, "The battle has just begun and the war is yet to be fought."[2] In fact, the selection of recipients of limited lifesaving medical resources is widely recognized as one of the crucial ethical issues of the day.[3] The need for broadly acceptable criteria for making these selections has been underscored in the fields of medicine, public policy, law, sociology, ethics, religion, industry, and journalism, to name a few.[4] There is a similarly broad recognition that people in all walks of life must become more aware of these decisions, wrestle with them, and help to formulate acceptable selection criteria.[5]

This book is designed to facilitate this process for professional and lay readers alike by gathering in one place the full range of ethical arguments, pro and con, relevant to each major patient selection criterion. Extensive citations (with page locations where applicable) are provided for most arguments in order to encourage further investigation. The notes, however, may be disregarded by those interested only in an overview of the issues. Readers should be able to formulate a viewpoint on any criterion after reading the relevant chapter. By the time readers reach the final chapter, in which an overall approach to patient selection is put forward, they should be well equipped to evaluate the proposal.

Surprisingly, this subject has received only limited in-depth analysis, significantly less than comparable issues in the field of medical ethics.[6] Why is this so? It may be that some people are unaware of how widespread life-and-death patient selection decisions are today, and those who are aware may not want to face the stark tragedy of making decisions that leave certain people to die.[7] In many cultures, death is not something easily prepared for, and to plan for decisions that lead to death for some (even if to life for others) can make a person appear coldhearted.[8] Others, though, may neglect patient selection dilemmas because they are more impressed with the scope or seriousness of other issues, such as the broad budgetary decisions that cause some patient selection predicaments in the first place.[9]

Although none of these reasons justifies the lack of comprehensive attention patient selection decisions have received, the last is perhaps the least objectionable. There are many ways to reduce health care costs and to make available more resources to treat all in need. For example, wasteful expenditures can be trimmed, preventive and other basic health measures can be favored over expensive use of advanced technology, and greater political priority can be placed upon funding health care in general.[10] Equitable resource allocation to health care and within health care is, in a sense, essential before the ideal nature and scope of patient selection decisions can be identified.[11] Indeed, considerable scrutiny must be devoted to the perplexing macroallocation questions confronting health care today.[12]

Recognition of the vital significance of broad allocation decisions and of meeting the basic health care needs of all does not mean that life-and-death patient selection decisions must be neglected in the process. Despite all of the measures noted above, medical resources—financial and otherwise—will almost certainly remain limited relative to need.[13] In fact, countless health professionals and selection committees are having to make difficult patient selection decisions right now (see chapter 1). They must regularly cope with the frustrations of those who cannot obtain a needed lifesaving resource as well as with the joy mixed with guilt of those who can. To observe that these decisions should not have to be made offers little consolation. They do have to be made, and there is a pressing need to determine how best to deal with them, even though the tragic nature of the decisions cannot thereby be escaped.[14]

Ironically, facing patient selection decisions squarely may ultimately prove one of the best strategies for minimizing their frequency. It is much easier to make broad budgetary decisions without having to determine which particular people among those equally in need must be left to die as a result. When the tragedy and complexity of patient selection are kept clearly in view, however, there is a great incentive to minimize resource scarcities.[15] The attempt to avoid patient selection decisions only ensures that they will persist unexamined.

Some people describe the decisions as triage or rationing.[16] I have chosen to avoid the first term, in part because the military and other contexts from which it is borrowed are not exact parallels to patient selection predicaments.[17] In its traditional contexts, moreover, *triage* has a utilitarian bent (for example, toward discarding that which is lesser in quality) that can bias the consideration of which selection criteria are ethically acceptable.[18] The term *rationing* is similarly inappropriate and biased in some people's minds.[19] I prefer to employ the more neutral and descriptive language of *patient selection*. Patient selection includes any stage at which classes of people (for example, nonresidents or the elderly) are barred from further consideration or individual patients are selected for treatment.[20] I have also chosen to refer to chronic as well as acute interventions as *lifesaving*, for two reasons. Not only is the term more familiar than alternatives such as *life-sustaining*, but it emphasizes that the alternative to the treatments in view here is death.

Although many of the illustrations in this book are from the United States—and patient selection is indeed an issue there—the problem is manifestly worldwide.[21] References, accordingly, are often made to the situation in countries throughout the world. Indeed, patient selection decisions do not presuppose a governmentally funded national health care system. They arise at all levels of authority, from the individual health care setting through local, regional, and national governmental jurisdictions. The selection procedure ultimately proposed here is designed to be relevant at all levels. Selection criteria have been formulated broadly enough that they can usually be applied to the complete range of lifesaving resources. Where important issues unique to a particular resource arise, they are noted.

This book should not be construed as in any way welcoming or encouraging patient selection decisions. On the contrary, such decisions are to be energetically avoided whenever it is possible to treat all in need. Some selection decisions, however, are unavoidable. That is why making such decisions and preparing for them by evaluating possible selection criteria do not involve "playing God." Such an accusation implies that there is an alternative to deciding. There is not. Even to "make no decision"—that is, to let all die when some can be saved—is to choose one alternative from among possible approaches. Playing God is unavoidable, if what is meant by that phrase is deciding who among those in need will be given medical treatment.

My arguments here consistently reflect this conviction. The book opens with two foundational chapters, the first documenting the unavoidable necessity of patient selection in the United States and around the world. The second chapter is devoted in part to explaining the need for having criteria upon which to base patient selection decisions. How the criteria examined in this book have been identified and analyzed is explained in the remainder of chapter 2.

Each of the next fifteen chapters is devoted to a single criterion (or cluster of closely related subcriteria). The chapters are grouped according to the nature of the criteria. The first group are labeled social criteria because they seek to promote some particular or general social good as a result of the selection decisions made. The second group I have designated sociomedical criteria since they are similar in many respects to the social criteria but are often given medical justifications. Next come medical criteria, so named because they are medical on their face—having to do with medical benefits and prognoses. The last group are called personal criteria because their justifications are rooted in personal values such as liberty and the worth of the individual.

Since this book is intended in part as a resource for those who want to evaluate the various criteria on their own, the heart of each of these fifteen chapters is devoted to identifying the justifications and weaknesses of the major selection criterion at issue. Discussions of justifications and weaknesses are generally preceded by a definition of the criterion and documentation of instances in which the criterion has been employed. No criterion examined here is merely theoretical: each plays an important role in contemporary patient selection. Concluding each of these chapters are two features: observations as to the aspects of the criterion most likely to be widely recognized in society at large as ethically acceptable, and a case study (with discussion) that illustrates how the need to consider the criterion may arise in a health care setting.

Two additional chapters complete the book. Chapter 18 examines how the acceptability of the fifteen selection criteria is altered when the resources involved are experimental. In the context of this discussion a sixteenth possible selection criterion is introduced and assessed. The final chapter has three components. First, the criteria most likely to meet with widespread approval are identified through an overview of the concluding sections of the preceding sixteen chapters. The sixteen criteria are next critically evaluated, with ethically sound criteria being assembled into a proposed patient selection procedure. How this procedure may be adapted to include other criteria with potentially widespread support is noted. Finally, two important challenges jeopardizing the prospects for a widely acceptable, ethically sound selection procedure are examined.

In the assessment of the various selection criteria I have attempted to be as comprehensive as possible. As explained in chapter 2, the criteria themselves have been identified first through an original study of the criteria that many physicians actually use today. A somewhat different original study of criteria employed in Kenya provides cross-cultural perspective. Literature relevant to patient selection in a broad range of fields (such as medicine, economics, philosophy, religion, sociology, psychology) has been extensively reviewed so that issues not uncovered in the original studies might be identified. All of the justifications and weaknesses of each criterion discovered in these various ways have then been gathered to enable the reader to assess each criterion as thoroughly as possible.

Beyond a massive collection of the views of others, though, this book contains a significant amount of original work. I have noted the original U.S. and Kenyan studies. Numerous justifications and weaknesses of various criteria throughout the book have not been identified elsewhere in the literature—though even in such cases sources are occasionally cited where tangential ideas might prove stimulating for further reflection. The section "Possible Common Ground" at the end of the analysis of each criterion, moreover, is an original assessment of the forms of the criterion (if any) that are most likely to meet with widespread support in today's pluralistic setting. Finally, in the closing chapter I contrast an overall selection procedure incorporating only the most easily supportable selection criteria with an original proposal argued for on ethical grounds. The two procedures are similar in many respects, though there are crucial differences. My conviction is that this original proposal, too, can receive widespread support if the issues it raises are thoughtfully and publicly examined.

As a person formally trained in ethics rather than medicine, I do not venture to make strictly medical judgments in this book. Rather, my purpose is to clarify the social-ethical context within which medical decisions are made. Nevertheless, I am grateful to the many colleagues, particularly those in medicine and medical ethics, who have responded so constructively and encouragingly to presentations of some of this material at various universities (Harvard, Yale, Brown, Kentucky) and in numerous professional settings (National Kidney Foundation, Washington, D.C., and Ann Arbor; American Hospital Association, Chicago; American Society of Nephrology, Washington, D.C.; Society of Health and Human Values, Chicago; Cleveland Clinic, Cleveland; Children's Hospital, Boston; Chandler Medical Center, Lexington). These colleagues have helped me make the book as true-to-life as I can make it, as have the many hundreds of U.S. and Kenyan physicians and healers who participated in the original patient selection studies discussed here.

Nancy Cummings of the U.S. Department of Health and Human Services warrants special note for her amazing page-by-page analysis of the manuscript. Her insights were consistently helpful, as were the astute comments of Kathleen Nolan of the Hastings Center and Arthur Dyck of Harvard University regarding the overall manuscript. A special word of thanks is also reserved for Gerald Winslow, Sissela Bok, Ralph Potter, Stanley Reiser, David Cowen, and Robert Bunge, who raised probing questions during the formative stages of this book; for Cherlene Brant, Shelley Bandy, Elizabeth Collins, and Maribeth Jennings, who tirelessly labored with pens and word processors through the various drafts of the manuscript; for Edward Tripp and Lawrence Kenney, whose editorial expertise was a joy to experience; and especially for Suzanne Kilner, my wife, who cheered me on throughout while graciously serving as my strictest critic.

PART ONE

The Predicament

CHAPTER ONE

Limited Resources

A popular myth today holds that a prosperous country like the United States need not worry about the problem of patient selection since there are resources sufficient for all. Some may believe even that this sufficiency extends throughout the world. This myth is less than a half truth. The truth in it is that the financial resources exist to eliminate many of today's scarcities. Will such resources be made available to meet the medical needs of all? Unfortunately, such a development is not likely, even within the United States. Other nonfinancial resources like organ transplants are also scarce relative to need. New scarcities, moreover, are inherent in the march of technology. In other words, patient selection criteria are desperately needed everywhere today and will continue to be so in the future. Nevertheless, before serious effort is devoted to wrestling with the criteria themselves, the need for them must be clearly established. The purpose of the present chapter is that single task.

The Problem in the United States

No nation, including the United States, is free from patient selection dilemmas. Health care has always been rationed in the United States in that a lack either of physicians or of the ability to pay for their services has constantly afflicted some.[1] In many situations particular treatments have been scarce, at least for a time.[2] Prominent examples include blood supplies in special cases, iron lungs for the treatment of polio, and lifesaving drugs such as insulin, polio vaccine, and streptomycin, all of which were in short supply after they first became generally available.[3] Wars and natural disasters have similarly created situations in which limited resources forced decisions as to who would be saved and who would be left to die.[4]

The classic modern high-tech example of a scarce lifesaving medical resource in the United States is chronic hemodialysis for kidney failure.

The first dialyzer, or artificial kidney, constructed for animal trials in 1913, had received some use in humans by 1946, but maintenance dialysis for chronic kidney disease was not available until 1960, when an indwelling cannula was developed.[5] The benefits of this technology are limited, for it cannot cure kidney disease or restore kidney function; but dialysis is at least life-sustaining (see chapters 14 and 15 for a discussion of relevant quality-of-life issues). By the mid-1960s, only 800 people were receiving hemodialysis, although those recognized as suitable candidates for it numbered 10,000 or more.[6] Within another two years as many as 10 percent of those needing hemodialysis in order to live were able to receive it.[7] However, this figure likely represents only the ideally suited candidates. Those treated were probably only 3 percent of all those whose lives potentially could have been saved by hemodialysis.[8] Estimates of the number of suitable candidates denied treatment grew during the early 1970s, with figures over 20,000 being cited for 1972.[9]

Such scarcity, involving staff as well as machines, rendered inescapable extremely difficult choices about who could make use of the lifesaving resource.[10] Since there were no national decision-making guidelines, each facility devolved its own method of deciding. Swedish Hospital in Seattle, one of the largest hemodialysis facilities in the country, received extensive (and often adverse) publicity when some of the decision procedures used by its Admissions Advisory Committee were revealed.[11] By 1972, feeling the political pressure, Congress largely funded the treatment of end-stage renal disease for Medicare patients.[12] Although 90 percent of the U.S. population were thereby covered, 7 percent or more do not meet the eligibility requirements and others have difficulty gaining access to available resources.[13] Only a small number of patients needing dialysis qualify for coverage by the Veterans Administration. Accordingly, medical directors of renal facilities estimate that 1,000 people a year still die in the United States for lack of dialysis alone.[14] At the same time, ironically, others may be receiving dialysis who should not. It is possible to prolong the dying process without truly benefiting the patient (see chapters 10, 14, and 15).

The congressional funding decision was a response to various factors, including the progression of dialysis beyond the experimental stage and the lobbying of the nephrology community.[15] Yet, curiously, no congressional hearings were held on the matter, and less than thirty minutes of debate took place on the Senate floor.[16] Federal funding apparently presented a way of avoiding uncomfortable life-and-death patient selection decisions altogether, especially those involving evaluations of the social worth of patients.[17] The arguments voiced by a majority of the senators during the brief floor debate confirm this interpretation.[18] As a result, the opportunity to develop carefully considered approaches to medicine's inevitable patient selection decisions was lost.[19]

Federal funding has made dialysis available to the vast majority of those in need, but the supply of other lifesaving treatments continues to be limited.[20] The necessity of making patient selection decisions, accordingly, remains inescapable.[21] In many health care settings personnel have found it necessary to establish committees to help them make such decisions.[22] Although funding and trained personnel limitations contribute to the scarcity, certain resources themselves are not available to all in need.[23] One major arena in which patient selection decisions are commonplace is that of organ transplantation.[24] Kidney transplants, for example, perhaps the most familiar of the lifesaving transplant operations, have been performed for well over thirty years but remain scarce relative to need. Many hundreds—perhaps thousands—of patients a year still die for lack of an available organ (under circumstances in which dialysis, if available, will not sustain them).[25]

More recent developments include heart and liver transplantation. According to all estimates, a significant selection problem exists in the arena of heart transplantation.[26] Public studies place the number of potential recipients at 32,000 to 75,000 per year but the number of available hearts at only 1,000 to 2,000.[27] Even if the extremely strict patient selection criteria employed at Stanford University are applied, over 750 ideal candidates die each year for lack of a donor heart.[28] From this perspective, selection criteria are doubly needed—to identify the ideal pool of candidates and to make the final selections. Considering the diversity of estimates, a study by the National Heart, Lung and Blood Institute has concluded that no more than one-fourth of the acceptable candidates can receive transplants because the number of suitable organs will always be insufficient.[29] The high costs and limited facilities and personnel also contribute to mortality that could be prevented through heart transplantation.[30] Liver transplantation has only recently received a comparable degree of national attention. Estimates indicate that the scarcity of organs and need for selection criteria are as pressing here as in heart transplantation.[31]

Another arena in which patient selection decisions have become commonplace is intensive care. When space is not available patients are generally turned away, though sometimes someone is removed to make space.[32] Such denial or removal is not always fatal.[33] However, there is always a significant risk, and deaths as a result have indeed been documented.[34] Sometimes the scarcity is a matter of available beds (and the funds for acquiring more); sometimes it is due to a nursing shortage.[35] The impact on the patient is the same either way if the resource cannot be provided. Neonatal intensive care is particularly prone to life-threatening scarcities.[36] Especially during periods of budget cutbacks, specialists have cited cases in which babies die while waiting for an intensive care bed to become available—with estimated numbers as high as 15 cases per month in one state.[37]

Other current examples of scarce lifesaving resources compelling patient selection decisions tend to reflect limitations in dollars made available to health care rather than a shortage of a resource per se. In that sense, they bring into question the legitimacy of the ability-to-pay selection criterion (see chapter 16) in particular rather than merely establishing a need for a whole set of criteria. Examples of this type include expensive surgeries and special forms of administered nutrition, especially parenteral nutrition.[38] Emergency room and other basic care for poor patients without insurance is another case in point. The refusal of such care to the poor creates major risks to life and health, and numerous cases have resulted in premature death.[39] The need to select patients and to develop criteria for wise decision making, as we have seen, is striking. Before looking at what the future will likely hold, though, we would do well to place the United States' predicament in broader perspective. The ethical dilemmas involved have long been around. But the advent of lifesaving health care has magnified the problem vastly.

A Worldwide Shortage

Through the centuries, the need to decide whose life to save when not all can be saved has arisen in various settings.[40] Cicero, for example, records an early Stoic discussion of the case of two floundering men and a floating plank only large enough to support one of them.[41] Lactantius mentions a similar dilemma posed by Carneades in ancient Rome, but in this case one man is stronger than the other.[42] Such questions troubled the early Christians too. As Ambrose notes, they were concerned about the presumption that a wise man ought to take a plank away from an ignorant sailor.[43] In Jewish tradition the somewhat different case of two men traveling through a desert with enough water to sustain only one of them seems to have been a major paradigm.[44]

From the seventeenth to the nineteenth centuries, numerous ship-wreck cases requiring life-and-death decisions received wide publicity, particularly when legal trials followed.[45] The best-known case, *United States v. Holmes*, involved the sinking of a ship near Newfoundland.[46] When it became apparent twenty-four hours after the disaster that a leaking lifeboat carrying survivors could not remain afloat unless it was significantly lightened, fourteen people were selected and thrown over-board by the crew. In *The Queen v. Dudley and Stephens* three men and a boy were stranded in a small boat far from land; but their dilemma involved the apparent necessity of one member having to be killed and eaten if the three remaining members were to have enough food to survive.[47] During the trial, earlier parallel cases were introduced and debated, especially a Dutch account of a Caribbean disaster.[48]

Today, vital allocation decisions must be made throughout the world with respect to various resources,[49] but in no area is the decision-making problem more widespread than in medicine. Scarce lifesaving medical resources must be allocated in more developed and less developed coun-tries alike.[50] However, the resources to be allocated are somewhat dif-ferent in the two settings. In many less developed countries, the most pressing problem is a lack of resources that would be considered basic in a more developed country. More than 14 million children die every year owing to malnutrition and infection. Some lack food; others lack oral rehydration therapy, an inexpensive means of treating the majority of cases involving diarrhea-caused dehydration, which kills over 5 million children annually.[51] Another 3.5 million suffer vaccine-preventable deaths, over half attributable to measles.[52] Lacking access to antibiotics, over 3 million children die annually from acute respiratory infections.[53] Millions more children die because parents do not have access to information about healthy lifestyle practices and medical precautions.[54] Unstable eco-nomic and political conditions make improvement in the above scenario difficult.[55]

Health care personnel persistently remain in short supply all over the world.[56] The tragedy of this shortage was graphically portrayed by one physician interviewed as part of the Kenya study (see chapter 2). She confessed that at least one night every week she is caring for a critically ill child when another critically ill child is brought in for treatment. She is working alone—the only intensive care available. If she leaves the one she is with long enough to care for others more than superficially, he or she dies. However, if the new arrival does not receive almost constant attention throughout the night, the latter dies instead.

In more developed countries intensive care units have been introduced to help avert such crises. However, the technology involved is expensive and not always available to everyone in need. Numerous technologies are becoming increasingly available, sometimes creating patient selection dilemmas where none existed before: all in need simply would have died. Organ replacement and other expensive surgeries are typical instances.[57] This is not to imply that technological shortages do not plague less developed countries as well. The resources just noted—not to mention such widely applicable technologies as fetal monitoring equipment—could meet a great deal of need there. Often, however, a recently invented or very expensive resource in a developed country will not exist in a less developed country, where primary care is the leading issue. If it does exist, it will be in radically short supply.[58]

A good example of a developed country in which advanced technological capability has collided with financial constraints is Great Britain. Some patients are denied lifesaving resources available to others because the government has decided to limit significantly the resources available for health care.[59] Intensive care, coronary artery surgery, and total parenteral nutrition are cases in point.[60] The epitome, though, seems to be resources for the treatment of renal disease. Annual "unnecessary" deaths due to renal failure are variously estimated in the hundreds or even thousands.[61] Part of the problem is the lack of transplantable kidneys; part is the result of government decisions to restrict funding (and thus staff as well as equipment) for dialysis.[62]

The Challenge Ahead

The massive number of life-and-death patient selection decisions identified in the preceding pages is but a foretaste of what is to come. Consider, for example, the future confronting the United States in such areas as organ transplantation.[63] Although legislation has helped to increase the supply of available organs, cultural barriers and improved highway safety laws will continue to constrain organ donation, and the great cost of transplantation remains an imposing obstacle.[64] In fact, improvements in transplant technology such as the control of organ rejection (and perhaps also the artificial heart as a temporary bridge to transplantation) will continue to make organ transplantation a viable option for more patients.[65] The drug cyclosporin as well as a whole family of drugs, monoclonal antibodies, have already had this effect.[66] In the face of better success rates, more physicians will refer their patients for transplantation, thereby exhausting the available transplantation facilities and personnel.[67]

A similar scenario characterizes other resources, such as intensive care space. Expanding medical indications for the use of this resource are increasingly pushing demand beyond levels mandated by cost containment policies.[68] Persistent shortages of artificial organs, newly developed drugs, and specialized nursing and other medical personnel are also likely—not to mention the resources needed to treat massive casualties in disasters such as the long-anticipated San Francisco earthquake or the aftermath of a nuclear attack.[69] The need for acceptable patient selection criteria will only become greater with time.

As previously suggested, some of the resource scarcities will be due to financial constraints. Demands upon available resources are expected to be unusually great for decades to come due to the swelling of the ranks of the elderly as the baby boom generation ages.[70] The cost of their health care will continue to grow as success in preventing early death leads to the increased incidence of chronic illness.[71] Meanwhile, the cost of particular technologies will continue to escalate—such treatments as dialysis, neonatal intensive care, and coronary bypass surgery already cost over \$2 billion a year each.[72] The mushrooming of health care costs will not be confined to the United States—nor has it ever been[73]—yet rarely has another nation allowed health care costs to consume more than 10 percent of its gross national product. Such a prospect has concerned some observers since this rise cannot continue indefinitely.[74] Nevertheless, the figure for the United States has reached 11 percent (well over \$450 billion), with the rate of medical inflation far higher than that of other goods and services.[75] Many patient selection dilemmas have been obviated in the past by the funding of treatments for all in need—an approach still worthy of every effort.[76] However, in the face of increasing medical costs, this solution is likely to become less and less available.[77]

The financial pressures have become so great that even funded treatments, such as those for renal disease, are targets of economizing efforts.[78] Limited restrictions upon the availability of dialysis resources have already been imposed.[79] Moreover, physicians themselves indicate that patient selection decisions have again become a part of their dialysis practice.[80] Although the abandonment of the entire federal funding program is not likely, the imposition of cutbacks currently suggests that more may follow—as unwelcome as that prospect may be.[81] The United

States is not the only country under increasing financial pressures, for many countries are presently reevaluating their level of funding for the treatment of renal disease.[82]

Part of the problem in the United States is that the costs of the end-stage renal disease program were greatly underestimated in the planning stage,[83] skyrocketing in the first decade of funding from $229 million (for 11,000 people) in 1972 to $2 billion (for 73,000) by 1983.[84] Projections suggest that the present growth curve will continue into the next century.[85] As early as a year after federal funding began in 1972, official reports were acknowledging that patient selection decisions for other life-saving resources could not possibly all be avoided through similar funding.[86] The same conviction has repeatedly been voiced since that time—"once burned, twice shy."[87] To make matters worse, many of the technological developments that lie ahead may be even more costly than treatment for renal disease.[88]

A good example of a resource that is not likely to be fully funded in light of the renal experience is the artificial heart.[89] The idea of an artificial heart has long captivated the public imagination and received much attention in the medical community as well.[90] Research began on it as early as the 1950s, and by 1963 the National Heart Institute's Advisory Council had decided to give its development a high priority. Within three years the National Heart Institute had established a full-fledged Artificial Heart Program to define goals and coordinate research activities.[91] Since then, considerable resources have been devoted to developing the artificial heart.[92]

Such an investment of time and money has given the program momentum, despite the poor quality of life recipients have experienced. Costs are expected to outstrip even those of the end-stage renal disease program. A federal study has suggested that the annual price tag could approach $5 billion, while other estimates are higher.[93] In addition, the availability of specialized medical personnel is expected to limit the number of qualified patients who will receive an artificial heart.[94] The use of artificial hearts to sustain patients temporarily while they await heart transplants will likely compete with longer-term use. Add to these constraints the arguments of some that limits on the supply of artificial hearts are to be welcomed in the face of higher medical priorities, and it is easy to understand why the artificial heart is typical of tomorrow's limited resources.[95] Since such scarcity relative to need is likely to persist indefinitely with regard to the artificial heart, the importance of developing acceptable patient selection criteria cannot be overemphasized.[96]

Indeed, technological advance insures that the making of selection decisions will remain unavoidable. Sometimes discoveries solve scarcity problems by eliminating the need for a particular treatment.[97] More often, though, new technologies create new access problems and the ethical dilemmas that go with them.[98] The technologies themselves are wonderful. Uncomplicated cancer cures, artificial lungs, and cell modification to enable the body to grow new organs, for example, would be spectacular even if expensive.[99] But the expense is not irrelevant vis-à-vis the entire range of human need and desire. In the words of one commentator, "Prometheus has met Malthus. Unbounded aspirations must confront scarcity."[100]

To acknowledge this clash is not to welcome or approve of it.[101] The United States and other more developed nations arguably have the wealth to meet the basic life-threatening needs of their people, yet priorities are such that even now people are left to die while massive resources are devoted to goods considered frivolous by most.[102] How much more will this be so as the costs of medical technology escalate.[103] Escalating costs will hopefully prompt greater attention to the efficacy of preventive care relative to expensive technologies that sustain rather than cure. But the need for greater use of the latter than can be afforded almost certainly will persist. Another worthy goal is the elimination of waste, but such economizing can only temporarily delay the full impact of resource limitations; there is only so much waste to be trimmed.[104] Some difficult patient selection decisions have already become a fact of life, and the magnitude of the problem will necessarily grow for the foreseeable future as technological capability expands.[105]

Even if there were no monetary constraints, acceptable criteria for distributing scarce lifesaving resources would remain a critical need. Every major technological development is followed by an extensive period during which the treatment is genuinely scarce.[106] This period ranges from the point at which a treatment is no longer experimental to that at which enough of the resource in question has been produced and distributed so as to be available to all in need.[107] Dialysis followed this course, and the same is anticipated (though distribution to all may never be realized) with such resources as the artificial heart.[108] Even if lag periods are brief, difficult patient selection decisions will be necessary for a while.[109]

Wealthy countries like the United States are passing from one technological era to another. The old was a "low-tech" era, one still experienced by many nations of the world in which people must be left to die for lack of such medical resources as vaccines and antibiotics. The need for patient selection criteria under such circumstances is apparent. Emerging from this first era, a nation understandably rejoices that these agonizing choices—perhaps never faced publicly or systematically—have been left behind. But the reprieve is short-lived, for a high-tech era of equally tragic patient selection decisions is at hand. The *National Heart Transplantation Study* paints the picture starkly: "Instead of an unidentified mass of individuals being denied access to a needed resource, persons whose names have become known to the public will be declared ineligible for a treatment or service they are known to require. Perhaps this scenario is inhumane, but it is undoubtedly a true representation of reality."[110] The need to make difficult decisions will not go away simply because people avoid them. Rather, such decisions will demoralize and undermine a nation unprepared to meet the challenge they pose. So every effort to obtain needed resources must be joined by the crafting of sound patient selection criteria to equip people to make the unavoidable decisions that lie ahead.

CHAPTER TWO

Plentiful Approaches

Two different types of response to the unavoidability of selecting patients are common. One is to assess possible selection criteria and assemble all those found acceptable into an overall approach to patient selection. Such a response is the one adopted in this book. The other type of response is to avoid such criteria altogether. There are, in fact, six major ways to avoid selection criteria. Although not one is ultimately satisfactory, they must be examined individually because each reflects an important sensitivity. The first three are not widely supported, but even they contain an element of truth that must be kept in view.

Avoiding Selection Criteria

The first way to avoid selection criteria is to assert that criteria are not required because all should be treated.[1] Indeed, whenever possible all in need (as defined in chapter 10) should be treated, but as we saw in chapter 1 some situations rule out this choice. Admittedly, this realization may discourage the energetic search for imaginative ways of treating all in a desperate situation. Innovative ways of meeting the needs of all are always to be pursued first,[2] and only when these fall short—and they will at times—are patient selection criteria necessary.

A second occasionally voiced argument against selection criteria is that they claim to "solve" a problem that cannot but remain a tragedy. Proponents assert that a criteria approach fails to take responsibility for the tragedy that some must be left to die because this approach yields an "answer" to scarce resource dilemmas.[3] As a criticism of some discussions of criteria to date this assertion is on target; but the weakness is not inherent in the approach. Every patient selection decision is indeed a tragedy, for someone is always being consigned to death. The tragedy is intensified for those who perceive that resources to treat all exist but have been misallocated to less worthy pursuits. No approach to patient selection can change these realities. However, additional problems can be generated if selection decisions dehumanize people or disregard basic moral values. Selection criteria can protect against this, as long as the tragedy inherent in the selections is kept clearly in view.[4]

A third questionable outlook dismisses commonly supported selection criteria as inappropriate in the experimental settings (such as dialysis in its early years) in which they have been advocated.[5] An important insight inheres in this stance, as long as its implications are not extended too far. Identical criteria do not apply in experimental and nonexperimental situations, as will be explained in chapter 18. Nevertheless, some criteria are relevant even in experimental situations; and there remain the various situations in which nonexperimental resources are limited relative to need.

The fourth method of avoiding selection criteria involves the outlook that medical judgments are sufficient to make any patient selection decision.[6] One argument to this effect holds that when resources are limited the criterion of medical need can simply be tightened until the number who qualify for the resource match the resources available. However, a genuine criterion of medical need is no longer being applied under such circumstances—a fact to be explored later in relation to the medical-benefit criterion (chapter 10). Another way to reduce patient selection to medical judgment is to support ranking patients simply according to degrees of medical suitability. This approach subtly incorporates considerations beyond the purely medical, as explained later in the analysis of the likelihood-of-benefit criterion (chapter 12). In other words, medical judgments may indeed play a central role, but other ethical considerations necessarily come into play either explicitly as additional criteria or implicitly as criteria for deciding between different types of medical criteria. In either case they need to be openly examined.[7]

The fifth outlook on patient selection that is antagonistic to the use of selection criteria is that which favors leaving all to die when all cannot be saved. Espoused most forcefully in legal analyses of the shipwreck cases cited in chapter 1, this position takes a radical approach to equality.[8] If life itself is at issue, proponents argue, there is no basis whatsoever upon which to choose one person's life over another's. Many writers dismiss this view as invalid[9] or summarily reject it as "morally grotesque"[10] or as an "erroneous absurdity."[11] Even those who pay attention to it assign such labels as "unrealistic,"[12] "preposterous,"[13] and "irresponsible."[14] What is more, it is claimed even that the medical profession would not give the approach a moment's thought[15]—that it is universally counterintuitive.[16]

Although in the end it may be wrong to leave all to die, the approach is not unthinkable for moral persons. It is not counterintuitive, for instance, to the legal scholars mentioned, nor was it unimaginable to at least two U.S. hospitals that refused dialysis in the 1960s to all in need rather than treating only some.[17] In fact, there are entire cultures in which the radical egalitarianism in view here is quite intuitive. An example is the Akamba people of Kenya, as reported in the Kenyan study introduced later in this chapter.[18] When faced with a choice between using the last dose of medicine to save one person's life and dividing the dose between two patients (knowing from experience that a half-dose is almost certainly not enough to save anyone), many Akamba healers choose the latter out of an egalitarian commitment.[19]

A strong disposition toward equality, though, does not by itself necessarily translate into a particular approach toward allocating scarce resources. Because of cultural differences in outlook, countries such as England, Italy, and the United States, which uphold equality, often do not adopt the same allocation policies.[20] Not surprisingly, then, what really predisposes Akamban healers to view resource allocation as they do is their traditional religious perspective. As a Bantu people, the Akamba consider every person's life to be precious because it belongs to God.[21] Medicine for them is ultimately just a vehicle God uses in order to heal, and thus a healer's responsibility is to divide whatever is available among all those who need it and then leave the healing to God.[22]

What are we to make of this Akamba view—shared by some in other cultures—that it is better to treat all equally (even if it appears all are likely to die) than to try more actively to save some? It has definite strengths from certain perspectives. Egalitarians especially appreciate the equal regard for life that it champions—a regard that protects against frivolous distinctions between people in the face of death.[23] Others appreciate the way it preserves people from the moral taint of selecting some people to die.[24] Some would also commend the way it takes seriously God's power to heal and its concern to save all of the lives in jeopardy (rather than assuming too quickly that only some can be saved). Such considerations at least underscore the value of considering this perspective.

However, critical problems with this approach in the end render it morally deficient. Rather than treating all well by treating them equally, it wrongs all by leaving all to die.[25] Insufficient attention is paid here, ultimately, to the preservation of the human race. The very nature of the situation is one in which every effort is being made to save lives. If this responsibility cannot be carried out completely, it should nevertheless be carried out as fully as possible.[26] Concern for the well-being of others requires this.[27] In other words, there is more at stake morally than equality; and when equality prevents the upholding of more basic values, it must give way.[28] Such an outlook need not conflict with the will of a life-affirming God. Even then, however, equality may remain instructive. A more life-affirming understanding of equality, in fact, underlies one of the selection criteria to be examined later (random selection, chapter 17). From another perspective, it is fortunate that this approach is so flawed. Were it to be followed, newly developed but scarce resources would not be given to anyone. As a result they would not as likely be improved and made less expensive so that eventually they could be provided for all in need.[29]

The sixth and final approach to patient selection that strives to avoid using selection criteria is "ad hockery,"[30] in which the individual or group selecting patients has few if any constraints upon the values that direct the selection decisions.[31] The approach has been widely employed,[32] often out of despair over the prospect of finding any ethical "solution."[33] Its use was most widely publicized during the pre-1972 dialysis patient selection era, when as many as 57 percent of the centers acknowledged employing it.[34] The most notorious instance involved Swedish Hospital in Seattle.[35] Many authors have condemned those involved[36] and one has suggested that the response they received in the literature should have been much more harsh.[37] Such assessments are more easily made with the benefit of hindsight. At least those involved were willing to act so that some could be saved.[38] However, the question for today wherever resources are scarce is, With the advantage of hindsight, is an ad hoc approach to patient selection wise? For a host of reasons the answer is no.

Absent any standards, patient selection decisions are arbitrary at best[39] and at worst reflect the nonobjective point of view of those doing the selecting.[40] Even the best people will be influenced by self-interested considerations when patient selection decisions are left to their judgment.[41] Ad hoc decision making opens the door wide to the rule of personal bias.[42] Just as the decisions of the Seattle committee reflected the middle-class values of the committee members,[43] so any ad hoc decision will depend upon the decision maker's attitude toward various characteristics of the patients being considered.[44] Overall, the chosen will tend to resemble the choosers.[45] Not surprisingly, then, when physicians were asked which thirty out of forty described patients they would select, only thirteen patients were consistently selected and none were consistently rejected.[46]

In other words, ad hoc selection is unfair.[47] It has no built-in consistency, and Who shall decide? completely eclipses the matter of How shall they decide? The question of power replaces the concern for justice.[48] The receiving of treatment hinges upon who the patients are and how persuasively they can present their case for being treated.[49] As a result, mistrust and tension build between physician and patient,[50] and the value society places upon human life and the equal worth of persons is eroded.[51]

The Seattle committee hoped to avoid some of these social demoralization costs by keeping the basis for each selection decision secret.[52] But after a while, any patterns in decision making will generally emerge even when a committee's or individual's deliberations are secret. Once this happens, the social demoralization costs will be incurred, but the decision makers and patients will have been cheated of the opportunity to have the decision-making criteria publicly reviewed and refined.[53] If no pattern in decision making emerges, then charges of arbitrariness, bias, and inequity are all the more justified.[54]

Assessing Selection Criteria

The alternative to the various attempts to avoid patient selection criteria is to employ those criteria that are ethically justifiable to guide patient selection decisions. Assessing such criteria is the purpose of the remainder of this book. Many criteria have been advocated, most of which have at least indirect relevance to good decision making. Sixteen of these are examined here in detail, with related subcriteria sometimes being considered together under a common name. These sixteen criteria have been identified through an original study of U.S. medical directors and are critically evaluated here by means of such tools as an original cross-cultural (Kenyan) study and a particular method of classifying ethical arguments. The U.S. study, the Kenyan study, and the classification system, though, first need a brief introduction.

THE U.S. STUDY[55]

Questionnaires were sent to the medical directors of every kidney dialysis facility and kidney transplantation facility in the United States (according to an amended "National Listing of Providers" published by the Health Care Financing Administration) to gather information on the current level of support for a range of patient selection criteria. Demographic data were also collected. Although medical directors are not the only ones who make the many thousands of patient selection decisions in view here, they do constitute the group most frequently involved in them.

In order to identify the frequency with which various criteria are employed—or would be under conditions of future scarcity—transplantation directors were given a list of sixteen defined and illustrated criteria and asked to rate each criterion twice: once with regard to the criterion's importance in present patient selection decisions, and once with regard to similar decisions in the future (assuming continued scarcity). Possible ratings ranged from 1 ("not at all important") to 5 ("decisively important").

Since dialysis resources are not presently subject to major scarcity, dialysis directors were asked to assess these sixteen criteria only in terms of their relevance were dialysis resources ever to be severely restricted in the future. Through consultations with physicians in the Boston area, a smaller list of criteria more relevant to the "unlimited" resource of dialysis today had also been developed. Dialysis directors were asked to identify which of these (or other) criteria they currently employ. As this list essentially corresponds to five of the sixteen scarcity-oriented criteria, it is possible to ascertain some of the impacts that limitations upon available resources would have upon patient selection.

Questionnaires were returned, after a single mailing and limited telephone follow-up, by 373 dialysis directors (representing a little over 40 percent of their listed number) and 80 transplantation directors (representing a little over 50 percent of their listed number). Sixteen returned letters ("addressee unknown") and the discovery that some facilities on the provider list no longer have telephone numbers suggest that a number of facilities have merged or closed. So the percent of nonresponders is actually somewhat lower than the above percentages indicate. Moreover, participants in the study appear to be representative of renal medical directors as a whole, at least in terms of demographic data.

Because all the sets of sixteen ratings given by dialysis and transplan-

Table 1.   Importance Attached to Selection Criteria

Average Importance-Scores*	Percent Who Would Consider Criterion
Very important	*Virtually all would consider*
Medical benefit: 4.2 (1.0)	Quality of benefit: 97
Likelihood of benefit: 4.0 (1.0)	Psychological ability: 97
Quality of benefit: 3.8 (1.0)	Likelihood of benefit: 96
Willingness: 3.7 (1.3)	Length of benefit: 96
Length of benefit: 3.6 (1.0)	Medical benefit: 95
Somewhat important	*Very large majority would consider*
Psychological ability: 3.2 (1.0)	Willingness: 89
Age: 2.7 (1.1)	Age: 88
Special responsibilities: 2.5 (1.3)	
Slightly important	*Majority would consider*
Resources required: 2.2 (1.1)	Special responsibilities: 69
Progress of science: 2.0 (1.1)	Disproportionate resources: 66
Social value: 2.0 (1.0)	Supportive environment: 61
Supportive environment: 2.0 (1.0)	Progress of science: 58
Ability to pay: 1.8 (1.1)	Social value: 56
Random selection: 1.7 (1.1)	
Virtually unimportant	*Very large minority would consider*
Favored group: 1.4 (0.8)	Ability to pay: 43
Sex: 1.0 (0.3)	Random selection: 31
	Favored group: 27
	Virtually none would consider
	Sex: 1

*Criteria are scored on a 5-4-3-2-1 scale, reflecting decreasing importance. Standard deviations in parentheses.

tation directors turn out to be similar, they will be grouped here. However, this grouping does not imply that the various criteria are employed identically by the two types of directors. Three of the criteria—age, random selection, and psychological ability—are given slightly (about half a point) greater emphasis on average by the transplantation directors. Moreover, the precise considerations involved in such criteria as "medical benefit" differ between the two treatments. Yet the ratings are similar enough and the ethical issues involved basic enough that the two sets of data can meaningfully be considered together.

The importance that the medical directors attach to the various selection criteria examined is displayed in table 1. The criteria are grouped in the first column according to the mean score given to each criterion and the nearest whole number to that average. The number of directors who would employ each criterion in at least some cases (that is, they rank it higher than 1) is then noted in column two.

The impact that restrictions upon dialysis resources would have upon

Table 2.   Impact of Scarcity upon Dialysis Selection Criteria

	Percent who would consider criterion	
Criterion	If resources unlimited	If resources limited
Length of benefit	71	96
Quality of benefit	44	97
Ability to pay	4	45
Medical benefit	62	95
Age	10	85

patient selection is indicated in a comparison of how many directors would employ five of the selection criteria under conditions of "unlimited" vs. "limited" resources. The results of this comparison are displayed in table 2.

As table 1 illustrates, fifteen of the sixteen patient selection criteria considered in this study are employed by a substantial number of directors. Moreover, the range of scores given to each criterion and the standard deviations noted in table 1 are quite high. These facts alone underscore the need for energetic scrutiny of the medical and ethical justifications for each criterion, in that some criteria are in direct conflict with others and the lives of identifiable persons hang in the balance.

Each of the fifteen criteria with significant support will be examined in detail in later chapters, as will another criterion that was added by a significant number of the directors: an imminent-death criterion (see chapter 11). Data from the U.S. study will be cited throughout the book wherever relevant.

THE KENYAN STUDY[56]

In order to obtain a different cultural perspective on patient selection decisions I traveled to the Machakos District of Kenya to interview healers among the Akamba people. Akamba healers are of two types: traditional healers (witchdoctors, herbalists, and midwives) and health workers, who work in government or mission health care facilities. A sample population of 132 persons was randomly selected, with equal representation from both groups. An Akamba research assistant, Daniel Ngwala, provided invaluable relational and linguistic assistance during lengthy personal interviews with these healers.

Since the Akamba think in terms of stories, it seemed appropriate to ask questions in the context of a series of stories.[57] The stories focus mainly on a healer named Mutua and two patients, Mbiti and Kioko.

Resources are so scarce that only one of the two can be saved. In each situation, Mbiti arrives earlier, which, according to the Akamba, is a presumptive reason for treating him before Kioko. But different facts about the two people are also stated in successive questions—for example, Kioko is helping many people in his area, whereas Mbiti is not— in order to see if the Akamba ever view such considerations as more important than order of arrival.

Though I was eager to understand the full range of Akamba perspectives on the allocation of scarce lifesaving medical resources, I was especially interested to learn what significance, if any, they attach to four basic values frequently invoked in the U.S. allocation debate. Informal preliminary research revealed that the Akamba explain their treatment decisions by referring to these values in the following particular form:

EQUALITY: All people are fundamentally equal when life itself is at stake, so the first to arrive should be treated when only one life can be saved.

USEFULNESS: The most important goal in deciding whom to treat is to achieve the greatest social benefit possible.

NEED: Whoever is in the greatest danger of dying right away should be saved.

LIFE: The most important goal in deciding whom to treat is to save as many lives as possible.

To determine the significance that the Akamba attach to these values, study participants were asked twenty-four questions, and their answers were assigned value-significance points according to the values they expressed. Participants could earn a point for equality on twenty-three of the questions. Six questions pertained to usefulness; three to need; three to life; and others to a variety of values such as choice. For example, if a healer maintained that Mbiti, who arrives first, is to be treated rather than the patient Kioko, who is involved in projects to benefit the community, then the healer received an equality point. However, to receive this point the healer had to justify her or his choice with some sort of reference to the notion that people equally warrant treatment when life-threatening health problems are concerned. The implicit idea expressed here is that treatment should do nothing but proceed according to the natural lottery: first-come, first-served. (As noted previously, a significant number of healers were so strongly egalitarian that they never chose one patient over another. These healers automatically received a high number of equality points.)

Where Kioko rather than Mbiti was chosen because of his greater

Table 3.   Average Value-Significance Scores by Education

Type of healer	Level of education	Average scores			
		Equality	Usefulness	Need	Life
Health workers	None-Standard 7	15.5	1.6	2.3	2.1
	Standard 8-Form 2	14.1	2.1	2.4	2.7
	Form 3-Form 4	9.8	3.8	2.4	2.9
Traditional	None-Standard 8	15.2	1.8	2.4	2.2

social usefulness, then the healer received a usefulness point rather than an equality point. Other questions presented the possibility of receiving, say, a need or life point as against an equality point. In nearly all of the questions it was possible to accumulate either an equality point or a point of some other type—the three categories mentioned here being the major ones. That virtually every question involved a possible equality point does not mean that equality is in some sense more important than the other values but merely reflects the manner in which the moral choice typically arises for the Akamba healers. They must choose between their adopted norm of first-come, first-served and some competing moral claim arising from the particulars of the case before them.

Once assigned in this manner, points of each type were added up for each person. The resulting equality scores ranged from 3 to 23 (average 14.3), usefulness scores from 0 to 6 (average 2.1), need scores from 0 to 3 (average 2.4), and life scores from 0 to 3 (average 2.3). In each case the highest score reflects the number of questions pertaining to that category.

What accounts for a healer's particular set of value-significance scores? Whether a person is a health worker or a traditional healer appears to matter for equality, usefulness, and life scores. But what, more precisely, accounts for the difference between the two groups? To attempt to answer this question, personal information was gathered at the start of each participant's interview. Identified were each person's sex, age, marital status, length of marriage, number of children, level of education, length of (medical) training, job responsibility, years worked, and religion. Potentially significant relationships between the ten personal factors and the value-significance scores could then be examined.

No consistent correlation emerged between nine of the ten personal items and the value-significance scores. Only education appeared to make a difference. The health workers were divided as evenly as possible into three groups according to the highest level of education completed (table 3). (Kenyans complete the "standard" grades and then the "forms" before becoming eligible to enter a college or university.) Because none of the traditional healers interviewed had more than a primary education, they are treated here as a separate group and serve as a check upon the other results.

Statistical analysis of the scores suggests that the importance health workers attach to equality, usefulness, and life (not need) is significantly influenced by their education. In fact, all three correlations are statistically significant at well above a 99 percent confidence level. The more education one has received, the lower her or his equality score. This drop corresponds to a rise in both usefulness and life scores. However, when the weight ascribed to equality is changing most rapidly—beyond the primary educational level—the rise in usefulness scores is the primary change associated with the drop in equality scores. These conclusions have been confirmed in two ways. First, average scores for the traditional healers correlate almost perfectly with their low level of formal education as a group (see table 3). Second, highly educated Akamba physicians interviewed after the initial interviewing was completed received scores that in all cases are consistent with the trends documented in this study.

The Kenyan study will contribute to the analysis of this book in several ways. The scoring trends discussed above will provide a helpful perspective in the concluding chapter. The refusal of many Akamba to make patient selection decisions has already figured prominently in an earlier part of this chapter. Finally, Akamba perspectives on particular criteria such as special responsibilities (chapter 6) and age (chapter 7) will be included wherever they help to expose questionable cultural assumptions that have a critical bearing upon the acceptability of those criteria.

CLASSIFYING ETHICAL ARGUMENTS

While the various justifications and weaknesses in the chapters that follow speak for themselves, arguments will be further characterized, where relevant, as productivity oriented or person oriented. A productivity oriented argument is one that is concerned with promoting the achievement of some good such as efficiency or happiness. A person oriented argument, on the other hand, is one that is concerned with respecting people in their own right, irrespective of the goods they produce.

Those schooled in ethics will recognize a resemblance here to the classical teleological vs. deontological and utilitarian vs. egalitarian/libertarian contrasts. Indeed, many have suggested that patient selection criteria and arguments for and against are best categorized according to these classical contrasts.[58] The problem with these categories is that many egalitarians and libertarians approve of the pursuit of utility to some degree, and many utilitarians approve of basic values like equality and liberty to some degree. Consequently it is difficult to categorize most justifications or refutations of a selection criterion as, for example, utilitarian, egalitarian, or libertarian. Recognizing this difficulty, many others venture only so far as to categorize selection approaches as a whole. They focus upon whether an approach favors making most selections on the basis of social value or randomness, once medical distinctions have been exhausted.[59] For critical purposes, a classification more ethically discerning than the latter is needed—if one less ambiguous than the former can be found. The categorization of arguments as productivity oriented and person oriented serves that purpose well. Even so, some arguments do not fall neatly into one category or the other, and where such is the case, no attempt will be made to stretch the categories to fit. This means of classification will prove helpful in making some of the broad assessments called for in the final chapter.

PART TWO

Social Criteria

CHAPTER THREE

Social Value

The common element of decisions involving social-value criteria is a concern for the impact that selection decisions will have on society at large. Which patient will be of greatest value to society if saved? Which patient will leave the greatest burden on society if not saved? Such a concern for the social value of patients plays a limited role in many of the criteria examined in this book. But a social-value criterion allows this concern a more definitive place in patient selection decisions.

Social value may be assessed through consideration of a variety of factors, including income, net worth, educational background, community service, and occupation.[1] The last of these may be valued in its own right or included as part of a vocational rehabilitation factor measuring the scope and likelihood of the patient's future contribution to society.[2] A social-value criterion is sometimes confused with a criterion that identifies the moral worth of a person, but the two notions need to be distinguished.[3] Social value does not measure the goodness of persons but merely how useful they are to society.

One apparent manifestation of social-value criteria at work is the preferential treatment of one sex over the other. Such favoritism is only rarely advocated explicitly.[4] Yet the selection of candidates for heart transplantation, coronary artery bypass grafting, dialysis, and kidney transplantation has significantly favored men over women.[5] Another such manifestation is race. In the same four treatment areas whites have been favored over other groups, such as blacks, as long as resources have remained scarce, though rarely is such favoritism explicitly defended (but see the discussion of a favored-group criterion in chapter 4).[6] It is not clear whether gender and race favoritism originates with patient selection or merely reflects prior medical or social differences, but some evidence points to the former.[7] Facility with the English language may be another example of a rarely defended but sometimes invoked form of social-value criterion.[8] The common link among various forms of a social-value criterion is the concern to save those patients who will be most valuable to society in the future. A concern to save those who have contributed most to society in the past is closely related to this concern and so will be examined in this chapter as well. The justifications given for the latter are sufficiently unique, though, to require separate attention.

A social-value criterion has been widely employed in the selection of patients to receive lifesaving treatment. An international study involving thirty countries, for example, has concluded that it "plays a very significant role in the selection process."[9] Additional studies have documented its sizable role in such places as Rumania, Scandinavia, Great Britain, and Australia.[10]

This criterion has also received much attention in the United States since the dialysis patient selection decisions of the late 1960s and early 1970s. At that time social-value criteria were widely applied in order to separate the social leaders from the "social leeches."[11] According to a study of dialysis centers during this time, 42 percent employed a social-value criterion per se, while 76 percent considered job rehabilitation potential, a factor often justified on social-value grounds.[12] The most heralded examples of social-value selection took place at the Seattle Artificial Kidney Center,[13] but other instances are reported in such locations as San Francisco General Hospital, Chicago's Michael Reese Hospital, Boston's V.A. Medical Center, Houston's Ben Taub General Hospital, and a number of hospitals in Los Angeles.[14]

Social-value assessments have not been confined to the realm of dialysis in the United States. They have long exercised significant influence in patient selection decisions generally.[15] Several studies have found indications, for instance, that those whom physicians consider more valuable to society are more likely to receive not only lifesaving but other treatment as well.[16] Specifically, a social-value criterion sometimes influences who receives treatment in emergency rooms and intensive care wards.[17] It plays a similar role in the selection process for recipients of transplantable organs, such as hearts and livers.[18]

My study of renal directors (see chapter 2) confirms the existence of widespread support for a social-value criterion. While directors on the average do not consider the criterion to be especially important (mean score 2.0 out of 5), more than half (56 percent) consider it to have a legitimate place in patient selection. If anything, this figure may be understated.[19] Such a finding is not surprising in light of the strong influence of utilitarian thinking in the United States and other countries today (see chapter 19). Indeed, social-value assessments are thoroughly utilitarian in their exclusive concern to achieve the greatest good for society.[20] Indications are, however, that patients are less supportive of the criterion than are physicians.[21]

Justifications

Because of this affinity with utilitarian thinking, most of the arguments made on behalf of a social-value criterion are productivity oriented. Sometimes this orientation is not apparent owing to the brevity of the discussions of social-value assessments,[22] and occasionally it may be masked, as when social-value and medical arguments are intertwined.[23] But for the most part the productivity oriented nature of the criterion is explicit.

Selection in accordance with social value may be considered a most rational approach in that it accepts responsibility for the decision and makes it possible to tackle several problems simultaneously.[24] It not only provides a way to choose patients but also produces additional social benefits by preserving those who are most valuable to society. Since society has invested its resources in a patient's treatment—or in developing the possibility of that treatment—it is entitled to the sort of return on this investment that a social-benefit criterion can provide.[25] Absent this criterion, then, there would be an unnecessary waste of some of society's most gifted people.[26]

While recognizing that many people are leery of the practical difficulties involved in identifying and applying social-value standards, proponents of this criterion see no serious workability problems. They note the broad agreement suggested by the similarity of the various proposals that advocate social-value selection.[27] Standards reflecting the values of the majority of the people can, in the view of some, be identified rather simply through polls.[28] Alternatively, a democratic process can be preserved by establishing patient selection committees made up of people who are representative of the various types of persons in the community.[29] Other observers, concerned that societies as well as individuals may desire what is not truly in their best interest, favor a more select group of committee members, one that could identify standards and choose patients in accordance with society's true interests.[30] For some, these deciders should all be physicians—though the advice of additional persons may be welcome.[31] In other words, proponents of social-value selection have devised a number of detailed plans for putting the criterion into practice.

It may be possible to discount other workability problems as well. That a criterion is difficult to apply in practice is arguably no reason for not attempting to apply it if it is warranted on other grounds.[32] Even if a person's social value cannot be precisely determined, it can be estimated closely enough to produce more value for society than if estimations were not made.[33] At least clear cases of differences in social value should be considered.[34] People make decisions all the time based upon calculations of consequences that are anything but certain.[35] In fact, lifesaving medical resources have always been made most available to those judged most likely to benefit society in the future.[36] Someday even better ways may be developed to quantify and computerize the complex matter of people's value to society.[37]

For those who are concerned about some of the potentially harmful aspects of a social-value criterion, proponents note that these harms will not necessarily occur. There is no reason, for instance, why the criterion need be considered arbitrary or capricious. It is a means to a worthy end—the good of society as a whole—and should not be merely the expression of whim or fancy.[38] After all, the decision at issue is not whether a patient is "worthy" of treatment; rather, it is an assessment of where in society a resource can most productively be used.[39] Furthermore, creative nonconformists who will ultimately prove important to society need not be excluded by a social-value criterion, for if it is operating properly it should give some priority to such people. Besides, society has always tended to reject nonconformists, so a social-value selection criterion is instituting no new problem for society.[40]

Although most of the arguments on behalf of this criterion are productivity oriented, person oriented justifications can be offered as well. In most cases the aspects of a person which make that person valuable to society are the result of personal choices and effort on the part of the person involved. Perhaps someone has decided to sacrifice a great deal of money and convenience to obtain the training necessary to become a physician who is useful to others. A social-value criterion affirms the autonomy of human beings by affirming the significance of the choices that they make.[41] Further, a social-value criterion may respect the dignity of persons. It can be very degrading to live without being gainfully employed. Social-value selection tends to keep alive only those who will be gainfully employed, at least in the sense that those chosen will be actively contributing to the well-being of others.[42]

As noted previously, a related but distinctly different form of social-value criterion is that which rewards past contributions rather than anticipated future ones. This form of the criterion might encourage people to be more productive in the future so as to obtain better access to lifesaving treatments if needed.[43] But for the most part, this form of the criterion is supported on grounds other than productivity.

One such rationale is that of justice. Although there are many different understandings of what justice entails, one important dimension of it is that all persons should receive their due.[44] A possible implication of justice, then, is that those who have been destructive of society (for example, through criminal activity) or have not assumed socially important responsibilities should have less claim on society's limited resources than do others.[45] There is an issue of equity here as well. If those who will make contributions in the future will be rewarded, then it is only fair that those who have made contributions in the past likewise be rewarded.[46]

Past, like future, contributions should also be considered in selection decisions because of the importance of respecting the autonomous choices of people. Each person should be free to make choices and then be responsible for the consequences of those choices.[47] Alternatively, rewarding past contributions to society can be conceived of as showing appropriate gratitude by giving back something to those who have given.[48] Even medical considerations may come into play here. It may be appropriate, for instance, to give lower priority to a drug addict or an alcoholic not only for some of the reasons just noted but also because continued substance abuse will render treatment ineffective.[49]

Weaknesses

A host of objections have been raised to a social-value criterion. Because objections to many other criteria hinge upon some of the difficulties most clearly evident in a social-value criterion, these difficulties will be examined in detail here. Justifications of the criterion will first be criticized, and then ways in which the criterion is unfeasible, biased, and harmful will be separately considered. Most of the objections to be raised are person oriented in nature, although questions of feasibility and harm, at least, may also be productivity oriented. Where separate attention is not given to the significance of future and past contributions, both are in view.

Justifications   First to be critically evaluated, then, are the rationales for selecting patients according to their social contributions. Consider, to begin with, the matter of future contributions. While it is plausible to suggest that society should reasonably expect a return for its investment in developing and perhaps producing critical medical resources, that return is arguably not the kind envisioned by social-value proponents. A legitimate return may entail nothing more than people benefiting medically from treatment.[50] Moreover, if all are members of a society that has corporately invested in scarce resources, all should have access to those resources without reference to their social status.[51]

The idea that there is a consensus among many people concerning a workable form of social-value selection is equally questionable. Those who do support social-value selection may have radically different ideas as to exactly who is valuable to society, for such specifics are virtually never provided. Moreover, wholehearted supporters may in fact be a small minority. Throughout the history of medicine, social-value selection criteria have generally been condemned as unethical.[52] Official bodies in the United States and abroad have rejected them.[53] Even when they were employed most frequently in the United States—during the early days of dialysis—they were sharply criticized by physicians and nonphysicians alike.[54] If any consensus exists, it would seem that it is against considering social value in patient selection.

Justifications for rewarding past contributions are also open to serious question. For instance, while it is true that people would want to be in the best possible position to obtain lifesaving resources if needed, they are unlikely to make significant social contributions simply to protect against the small chance that they will need a scarce resource.[55] The appeal to justice is also dubious. Although a society may decide that destructive (criminal) behavior merits punishment, it is inappropriate that denial of health care should be the form that the punishment takes— particularly when denial means death and the courts have not deemed the death penalty warranted.[56] And what of those whose lack of past contributions is due to unjust discrimination against them? Their situation would seem to be decisively different from that of persons who have made autonomous choices for which they may be held accountable.[57] Persons unjustly discriminated against generally have a just claim to preferential rather than inferior treatment. Yet giving them priority access to lifesaving treatment would again be to misuse access to health care as a corrective for broader social problems.[58]

Two other justifications for a retrospective social-value criterion have been identified earlier in the chapter. The equity argument—that past contributions should be counted if future ones are—hinges on the ac-

ceptability of considering future contributions. If considering future contributions in the selection of patients is wrong, then equity may even
mandate refusing to consider past contributions. Equally questionable is
the gratitude argument, according to which an individual's relationship
to society is to be conceived of as analogous to one person's relationship
to another. If so, then before a person merits a resource to which virtually all in society have contributed that person must have done something to benefit virtually all in society—a rare occurrence. Moreover,
gratitude merits an appropriate degree of response. This thesis suggests
that providing someone priority access to lifesaving treatment would be
warranted only if the person involved had made a contribution of lifesaving proportions to society. Such reasoning has convinced many that
there is inadequate justification to support priority treatment for those
who have contributed most to society in the past.[59]

Feasibility   The second way that a social-value criterion is weak concerns the feasibility of implementing it. Practical considerations always
have some relevance in the assessment of a selection criterion, but they
are particularly relevant when a criterion depends so heavily upon the
gathering and evaluating of large amounts of data (as is necessary if the
criterion is to be applied accurately).[60] They are also particularly troublesome when social-value standards are to be regularized rather than
left up to the ad hoc judgments of decision-makers (see chapter 2 on
the unacceptability of ad hoc patient selection).[61]

Consider first the form of social-value criterion that is concerned with
future contributions. There is bound to be little agreement regarding
what sort of potential contributions should be considered when patients
are assessed.[62] Even supporters of the criterion have shied away from
addressing this issue.[63] Should a list of relevant contributions somehow
be compiled, a thorough ranking of them would be virtually impossible.[64]
Proponents of a social-value criterion tend to despair at this point as
well.[65] People's values in many countries, such as the United States, are
so diverse and intangible that they simply cannot be quantified or otherwise compared.[66] Studies in countries such as Switzerland and Great
Britain document that physicians considering the same pool of cases
make different selection decisions based on a variety of social considerations.[67]

Were it possible to overcome all of the preceding difficulties, one
would still be left with the problem of assessing tomorrow's contributions
on the basis of today's values. What is required is unachievable fore-
knowledge regarding that which will definitely be considered important

in the society of the future. Since we have no such knowledge, those most needed in the future might not receive scarce resources today on the basis of current values.[68] The foregoing difficulties suggest that only quite general statements of value standards are possible to direct social-value selection. As experience has shown, however, such vague guide-lines are little better than the lack of explicit guidelines characteristic of ad hoc selection.[69]

If the identification of accurate social-value standards is problematic, applying them is no easier. In order to determine what sorts of contri-butions people are likely to make, everything must be known about them. Even given an abundance of time the research required is massive; but in many life-threatening situations little time is available. There are also intangible aspects to people that are always difficult to assess, quan-tify, and compare.[70] Only after people's deaths is it really possible even roughly to gauge their contribution to their times.[71] From any earlier point in life it is very hard to predict with confidence exactly how much of their potential people will end up fulfilling.[72] The difficulty of pre-dicting the degree of rehabilitation patients will achieve following rig-orous operations or treatments only complicates matters further.[73]

Several additional matters of feasibility weaken the selection system as a whole. Even if social-value standards could be identified and persons could be accurately assessed in relation to those standards, the resulting selection of patients might be far from optimal in terms of social value produced. An optimal society requires an optimal mix of different types of people (for example, vocationally) rather than a concentration of whatever type of person is ranked highest on the social-value scale.[74] Furthermore, the costs to society of gathering and evaluating the exten-sive information necessary even to approximate accurate social-value assessments of people would be so great as to eliminate any social value gained.[75] In some cases, information gathering and legal appeals in be-half of patients who are not selected would likely consume too much time, the health of the patients involved thereby being jeopardized.[76]

Most of the same problems of feasibility that beset a social-value criterion based upon future contributions also beset its backward-looking counterpart. A definitive ranking of all types of past contributions and a thoroughly accurate assessment of each person's past value to society seem impossible—even were the government to establish an Office of Assessment of Social Contribution for this purpose.[77] Additional prob-lems would also need to be resolved. For instance, what is morally significant about past actions: effort, achievement, or some combination of the two?[78] Also, what about situations in which someone has been the kind of person or behaved in such a manner that would normally lead to a low ranking on the social-value scale—but has since dramatically changed for the better? Is there to be any practical way to demonstrate that past wrongs have been righted?[79]

Bias Closely related to the unfeasibility of a social-value criterion is its third area of weakness, its vulnerability to bias. Bias can easily intrude on social-value assessments of either type at a variety of points. The initial public formulation of social-value standards would likely be mired in the pressure politics of special interest groups.[80] Further, those responsible for providing the decision makers with the information they need to select patients—often physicians—might unconsciously insert their own biases. In such cases not only would biases intrude but the physician's writing or speaking ability would probably have a great influence upon whether or not the patient under consideration is selected.[81]

One last opportunity for bias to intrude is during the final deliberations of the decision makers. Again, the intrusion may be unconscious, but it is almost inevitable given the subjectivity involved in making overall evaluations of people's lives.[82] Social-value selection for dialysis in the United States before federal funding generated graphic examples of the ways that patient selection can be skewed by the personal biases of selection committee members.[83] One of these examples is featured in the case that closes this chapter.

Several factors account for the distorting effect of personal biases. When selection committees are involved, the committee may not be representative of all the values and interests society considers important.[84] Alternatively, the values and interests represented may not be properly balanced, as when the judgments of physicians are accorded undue weight even where social-value assessments alone are in view.[85] The problem is that people tend to favor treating patients who are most like themselves.[86] Accordingly, the identity of the decision makers is a critical issue. So too is the matter of who selects the selectors,[87] for the personal biases of these people can have a profound impact upon who ultimately gets chosen for treatment. If there is no consideration of social value a scoundrel may occasionally be selected for treatment; but perhaps better a scoundrel sometimes saved than a scoundrel deciding the fate of all.[88]

Harmfulness The openness of a social-value criterion to personal and societal biases begins to suggest some of the dangers inherent in it. Before the criterion's harmfulness is examined directly, however, the

origin and nature of the criterion's harms may be made more understandable if we note the debatable views of people and health care that
underlie it.

A social-value criterion essentially views patients as mere means to
improving the well-being of society rather than as entities with intrinsic
worth. According to this perspective, the ultimate value of something—
or someone—lies in what it can contribute to society. In presuming that
people think this way, social-value selection tends to strip them of their
character. They are portrayed as ready to acquire new convictions and
goals, and even to abandon loves and commitments, when such behavior
promises life with a higher social-value ranking.[89] Such a view offers a
new twist on the cynical maxim Every person has a price.[90] The problem
with this view is not that people should be treated alike in every circumstance, but that the intrinsic value of each person should be considered
an overriding factor when life is at stake.[91] (For an elaboration of this
view, see the Justifications section in chapter 17.) If justice entails giving
all their due, then can anyone rightfully claim to deserve life itself more
than another person?[92]

Accompanying this problematic view of people is an arguably mistaken
understanding of the institution of health care. Health care has traditionally involved physicians in assessing their patients solely with a view
toward what will benefit the patients themselves. Medical science has
stood not as the judge of people's merits or value, but as a practice
devoted to preventing their physical and psychological sufferings. Patient
selection according to a social-value criterion would radically alter that.[93]

Flowing from these debatable views of people and health care are
several harmful aspects of social-value selection. These harms are often
stressed by opponents of the criterion, for even the criterion's supporters
have acknowledged that such harms can nullify any benefit to society
produced by the criterion.[94] Most prominently, a social-value criterion is
unfair.[95] It gives certain types of people better access than others to a
desperately needed resource.[96] In the case of people born with different
levels of ability, these disparities are bad enough. However, when precisely those who have been most unjustly discriminated against in the
past are denied life itself because they have not achieved and will never
achieve equally with others, then something is not right.[97] A social-value
criterion compounds whatever unwarranted social discrimination already
exists. Particularly where past deficiencies can be remedied, there is
arguably better reason to remedy them than to disadvantage patients
further because of them.[98]

A number of groups in society are especially victimized by such compounded discrimination. One is the poor. Simply because they have been born without wealth, class privilege, or opportunities to develop their natural abilities, some poor people are also denied lifesaving medical resources by a social-value criterion.[99] Those unfortunate enough to be denied a good education or who are unable to find a job fare similarly.[100] Where social services have been made available, some people have been able to overcome their disadvantages. Those who have not had the benefit of such services in the past are precisely those most likely to be denied lifesaving resources in the present.[101] Even if the poor were to benefit along with everyone else from the social benefits generated by a social-value criterion, what benefit would that be to the poor who died because they were denied access to lifesaving resources?[102]

The mentally and physically handicapped constitute another group that would likely rank low on most social-value scales.[103] So would members of minority racial groups and foreigners—perhaps women also if society (or the group deciding) does not value them as much as men.[104] Even those with little political power might well lose out where social-value standards are designed, perhaps unconsciously, to benefit those with control over designing them.[105] Other losers would be the creative nonconformists like Socrates and Thoreau, whom society, to its eventual detriment, is always eager to be rid of.[106] (Those with genuinely destructive life styles are discussed in chapter 15.)

While these various forms of unwarranted discrimination stem from future- and past-oriented social-value selection alike, other forms are unique to one orientation or the other. For example, selection according to likely future contributions discriminates against the elderly, who are relatively limited by frailty and age.[107] On the other hand, selection according to past contributions discriminates against the young, who have had little opportunity to contribute.[108] It also gives low priority to criminals, even when they have fully paid the penalty for their crimes.[109] A particularly troublesome form of double jeopardy is involved: being convicted and punished more than once for the same crime.

In addition to being unfair, a social-value criterion demeans human dignity. It robs people of any unconditional worth and defines them purely in terms of their usefulness to others.[110] It is degrading in that it reduces the incommensurable worth of persons to the calculable worth of things.[111] People become mere objects of bartering—mere machines that are best left unrepaired when it is no longer efficient to fix them.[112] In cases in which this criterion has been applied, observers have been appalled at the callous way patients have been handled.[113] Curiously, proponents of the criterion have claimed that it promotes human dignity, for example, by keeping alive those who can work, rather than the unemployed. Leaving the poor to die, however, is a strange way to respect their dignity, and it takes from them the last precious thing they have—life itself.[114] In addition, it imposes on them assessments of their lives rather than allowing them to determine when their lives are not as worthy of sustaining as the lives of others (see chapter 15).[115]

Social-value selection is also destructive of the physician–patient relationship. Over the years a great reservoir of trust has built up in patients toward the medical profession because patients have seen that physicians (and other health care professionals) have consistently made decisions on a medical basis for the patient's own good.[116] This trust has enabled the profession to provide health care much more effectively. However, where a social-value criterion is applied, the medical profession seeks not the good of the patient alone but begins to consider whether or not treating a patient would be beneficial to others. Such an approach is hardly conducive to maintaining the patient's trust.[117]

Other problems with a social-value criterion stem from the way that the practice of ranking people according to their social contribution tends to spread beyond the bounds of scarce resource allocation. Having begun selecting dialysis patients on the basis of their social value, for example, various U.S. medical centers continued to select kidney transplantation and dialysis patients on this basis—even after resources for the treatment of end-stage renal disease were made much more available through federal funding.[118] Once people are reduced to their social value when life is at stake, that way of viewing them cannot help persisting in a variety of contexts.[119] Over time society may develop an expertise in ranking lives, but in the process, society will be scarred by power struggles, suspicion, and insensitivity to people's needs.[120] In the attempt to maximize the value in the community, the value (and integrity) of the community will suffer.[121]

Subjecting people's lives to social-value assessment in the context of patient selection may also be the first step in a much more serious erosion of moral values.[122] Even the first step is alarming since it involves depriving certain people of their lives without all of the legal safeguards that are a standard part of capital offense court trials.[123] Once it is permissible to save only the most valuable lives, it may next be acceptable to kill the less valuable in order to obtain body parts to save the more valuable.[124] Then no particular benefit except general social well-being may become necessary in order to justify the elimination of people who are considered a burden on society.[125] Some have noted that Hitler's Germany followed such a course from relatively innocuous beginnings characterized by a disregard for the intrinsic worth of every person.[126] In response it has been suggested that a selection committee choosing patients with regard to society's genuinely best interests rather than society's desires at the moment would avoid another Nazi Germany.[127] But it is hard to imagine a government-established committee that would not have considered racial purity to be genuinely in Nazi Germany's best interests.

Possible Common Ground

The prospects of finding common ground for proponents and opponents of a social-value criterion is rather bleak because of the basic premise that underlies the criterion. That people's value ultimately resides in their contribution to society is a very different notion from the view that their value is fundamentally intrinsic to them as persons. Because people differ on this issue there are many for and many against this criterion.

Even some of those who generally take a productivity oriented approach to patient selection, though, have serious doubts about this particular criterion. For instance, they may find that the practical difficulty of identifying widely accepted social-value standards and evaluating patients in relation to them is overwhelming.[128] Or they may suspect that so explicit a renunciation of equal regard for persons would do serious damage to public morality and social policy generally.[129] The greatest hope for consensus, then, would seem to lie in the direction of rejecting a social-value criterion; and in fact, such a consensus may already be emerging.[130]

The prospects for this consensus would be even greater if a way to recognize some of the exceptional cases of greatest concern to supporters of the criterion could be found. Several possibilities involving justifications other than social value suggest themselves. For example, sometimes people are so critically indispensable that the lives of others actually depend upon them. Such cases might be accounted for by a special-responsibilities criterion (see chapter 6). Where socially harmful behavior such as substance abuse seriously impairs the prospects of effective treatment, a medical-benefit criterion (see chapter 10) might warrant exclusion if the abuse cannot be corrected. If patients are a medical or social threat to others, special settings may need to be provided for their care.[131] Even patients who have little to contribute to society might be excluded if they themselves decide that they want to forego treatment for the good of others. Such a scenario represents one—though not the most common—application of a willingness criterion (see chapter 15).

An Illustrative Case

Swedish Hospital in Seattle, Washington, was a pioneer in the provision of dialysis to patients with end-stage renal disease. In those early days there were many more patients in need of dialysis than there were machines available to dialyze them. A committee of people representing the community at large was established to decide which patients would be treated. A typical meeting ran as follows:

LAWYER: The physicians have told us they will soon have two more vacancies at the Kidney Center, and they have given us a list of five candidates. Are there any preliminary ideas?

MINISTER: Let's start with the housewife from Walla Walla. How can we compare a family situation of two children, such as this woman in Walla Walla has, with the family of six children belonging to the aircraft worker?

STATE OFFICIAL: But are we sure the aircraft worker can be rehabilitated? I note he is already too ill to work, whereas the chemist and the accountant are both still able to keep going.

HOUSEWIFE: If we are still looking for the people with the highest potential of service to society, then I think we must consider that the chemist and the accountant have the finest educational backgrounds of all five candidates.

SURGEON: How do the rest of you feel about the small businessman with three children? I am impressed that his physician took special pains to mention that he is active in church work. This is an indication to me of character and moral strength.

HOUSEWIFE: Which certainly would help him conform to the demands of the treatment.

LAWYER: It would also help him to endure a lingering death.

MINISTER: Perhaps some people are more active in church work than others because they belong to a more active church.

BANKER: We could rule out the chemist and the accountant on economic grounds. Both do have substantial net worth.

LAWYER: Both these men have made provisions so that their deaths will not force their families to become a burden on society.

STATE OFFICIAL: But that would seem to be placing a penalty on the very people who perhaps have been most provident.[132]

Although this committee discussion regarding who should receive dialysis took place in the United States before federal funding of dialysis in 1972, it is included here for two reasons. First, it is a classic example of the struggle to decide whose life to save—cited more than any other in the literature.[133] Second, it represents a particularly explicit example of what has continued to recur up to the present when access to a variety of limited resources is being decided.

Most of the factors considered by the selection committee in this case are essentially social-value considerations and cannot readily be accounted for by other criteria. The number of the patient's children and the spouse's likelihood of remarrying are issues that concern the well-being of a small unit of society, an individual family. (See chapter 6 for an examination of the special significance of the family.) The patient's educational background and ability to return to work may affect the welfare of society at large as well as the family involved. These factors stand or fall based upon the analysis of this chapter.

In fact, the committee discovers some of the problems with a social-value criterion in its own attempt to apply it. Moral character may be something worth saving, but it may also make the dying process more endurable. Moreover, indicators of character like church work may not be indicators of character after all. Patients who have financially provided for their families can be left to die without economically burdening their families; but such a practice would encourage a morally irresponsible society. In light of these and the many other serious problems surrounding a social-value criterion, many people have understandably concluded that it is simplest and wisest to avoid the criterion altogether.

CHAPTER FOUR

Favored Group

In deciding who will receive scarce lifesaving resources, medical facilities may take a patient's group identity into account in two major ways. First, the geographical location of one's residence: residents of specified areas closest to the facility (for example, the immediate county, state, or country) are given priority. Second, the social group into which one falls: members of a particular group (for example, children or veterans) are given priority.[1]

A favored-group criterion is not widely supported by the medical directors in my U.S. study (see chapter 2). It is considered to play a legitimate role in patient selection decisions by only 27 percent of the directors, with the directors as a whole rating it as relatively unimportant (mean score 1.4 out of 5). Certain forms of the criterion, though, do receive more support in practice than others. In the United States, for instance, a transplantable organ has sometimes been given to a patient in the local community rather than being shipped to another location where a different patient is more likely to benefit medically from it. The viability of the organ is an important issue; even with the latest methods of preservation, there are limits as to how far an organ can be transported. Yet, the preference for transplanting organs locally sometimes reflects nonmedical considerations.[2] Similar state and regional priorities have also traditionally existed with regard to organ transplantation and dialysis.[3] Many U.S. transplant centers and professional organizations favor U.S. residents as well, though policy in this area is evolving.[4] An offshoot of this policy is that transplantable kidneys are generally not shipped overseas unless no acceptable recipient can be found within the United States.[5] Analogous residential standards are employed in other countries.[6]

Some lifesaving medical care is provided according to social rather than geographical groupings. Particularly prominent is the health care system of the U.S. Veterans Administration, which provides extensive care for the service-related and in some cases non-service-related medical problems of veterans.[7] Occasionally a favored-group criterion of this sort functions in a negative way—to exclude one group of patients from a lifesaving treatment provided to others. A case in point is the discontinuation of U.S. government payments for kidney dialysis required by native American Indians. Funding for this treatment and others was temporarily ended despite the fact that the government provides similar coverage for most other U.S. citizens in need.[8]

Justifications

Some people have objected to the way that favored-group considerations have been employed without explicit acknowledgment that this is being done.[9] There is certainly no lack of rationales that might be given for the criterion. Some justifications are productivity oriented and essentially pragmatic in character, whereas others tend to be person oriented.

To begin with several justifications of the productivity oriented variety, health care (along with many other services) is commonly provided to particular groups of people by particular facilities. It is convenient and cost-effective to continue this practice where scarce lifesaving resources are in view.[10] Ideally, perhaps, there would not have to be any restrictions concerning who could receive what lifesaving care. However, such restrictions are understandable until a consistently open system—for example, of organ sharing among all facilities—is established.[11]

Significant costs result from opposing a favored-group criterion. Specialized institutions generally resist efforts to tamper with their ability to focus upon a particular type of patient.[12] Without such focused care, they argue, the patient is the loser.[13] An entire national health care system may be the loser, on the other hand, if national residents are not given priority over foreigners.

A case in point is the provision of transplantable kidneys to nonresidents of the United States that could have gone instead to U.S. residents. Those not receiving transplants must take the more expensive and less rehabilitative route of dialysis, at substantially higher costs to Medicare and the Social Security disability program.[14] In late 1986 the Office of the Inspector General put the Medicare savings alone—were U.S. residents to be given priority for a year—at well over $37 million (spread over five years).[15]

Other justifications are explicitly oriented toward both productivity and persons, for they have to do with maximizing the number of lives saved. For instance, certain favored-group constraints may be needed in order for treatment to be as effective as possible. If extensive travel will inhibit the medical effectiveness of a particular outpatient treatment, a facility may want to restrict patients to those within a certain geographical radius.[16] If organ transplants are not as successful when lengthy shipping times are involved, a similar geographic restriction may be appropriate.[17] Where effective follow-up care is essential—again, as in the case of organ transplantation—nonresidents of the country where treatment is being provided perhaps should receive lower priority. The rationale for this priority is strongest when it is most likely that these patients will return soon after treatment to countries where adequate follow-up care is unavailable to them.[18] In addition, in the absence of priorities for national and even local residents, people may not be as inclined to donate lifesaving organs.[19]

The two remaining sets of justifications tend to be person oriented and pertain specifically to veterans and national residents. Priority medical care for veterans involves two somewhat different circumstances, for they may require care for service-related or non-service-related disorders.

If disorders are service-related, there is broad agreement about giving veterans priority treatment. The justification may be prudential—that without such care people will be unwilling to serve in the armed forces. More likely, however, the appeal will be to paternalism or justice. In the former case health care is a necessary corollary of the fact that the armed forces completely take over their members' lives for a period of time.[20] In the latter case health care is required to compensate the veteran for a disorder incurred in the process of serving in the military—a social good.[21] The social obligation may be seen as the reverse side of one form of the willingness criterion examined in chapter 15. Just as those who freely smoke cigarettes (knowing the risk) arguably assume personal responsibility for health care needs that result, so a society assumes responsibility for the health care of anyone whom it knowingly puts in risky situations.

When a non-service-related medical disorder occurs, however, the situation is different in the eyes of some. But others suggest that there may still be reason to give special care to the veteran. Although eventually children grow beyond the period when they can rightfully claim to be provided for by their parents, parents even then may choose to continue some level of material support. The armed forces' continuing provision of health care for veterans may be justified similarly. Such provision is particularly understandable in light of the fact that those who receive non-service-related care are often patients who do not have other medical coverage.[22] Alternatively, such care may be viewed as deserved because of past contributions to society.[23]

The final set of justifications applies specifically to the case of national residents. One may argue on the grounds of fairness that national residents should have first priority in receiving treatment. The example of U.S. residents receiving first access to organ transplants in the United States will be employed here, but the argument applies in principle to other resources and other countries as well. Canada, for instance, is one of many other nations that are publicly wrestling with such questions.[24]

The foundation for the priority that U.S. residents can claim when recipients of organ transplants are being selected at U.S. facilities is that U.S. residents have provided the means to make the whole enterprise possible. The organs themselves are donated by U.S. residents— whereas some other governments have forbidden their citizens to donate organs.[25] Furthermore, $100 million or more of public money and the efforts of over a thousand people are involved in educating the public about organ donation and actually obtaining the organs.[26] Under such circumstances, U.S. residents may claim a moral right to have first access to these organs.[27] Although wealthy nonresidents have occasionally obtained priority access to organs by paying extra,[28] this practice is open to question. Unless certain privileges such as first access to scarce lifesaving resources accompany membership in a national community, nations arguably may not be able to survive.[29]

Priority in access to organ transplants is so important because when lifesaving organs are provided to nonresidents at U.S. or foreign transplant centers, U.S. residents often must go without.[30] It is dubious to suggest that all such cases involve organs unacceptable to U.S. residents—unless some transplant centers with the organs are not inclined to share organs with other centers in the United States.[31] As one transplant surgeon in Great Britain has observed, the fact that U.S. organs have been sold overseas rather than given away suggests that they have not been useless to U.S. patients.[32] Not only must some U.S. patients go without, but when organs go to patients who leave the country soon after transplantation, valuable follow-up information on the effectiveness of the transplant is also lost.[33]

Other examples of nonresidents receiving resources in place of U.S. residents could also be cited. For example, judging from the extremely high percentage of kidney transplants in the District of Columbia that go to foreign nationals (22 percent), one might suppose that the incidence of dialysis there (and thus the incidence of U.S. patients awaiting kidney transplants) is low. However, the district has a higher incidence of dialysis than any state in the nation. At the same time that so many foreign nationals have been receiving kidney transplants in the District of Columbia, a military hospital there has been forced to close its kidney transplant waiting list (for U.S. residents) for lack of available kidneys of all types.[34] In short, U.S. residents have gone without, while some nonresidents have been transplanted. Particular attention has also been focused upon the large percentage of organs that at one point were being transplanted into foreign nationals at centers such as the University of Pittsburg (28 percent) and the hundreds of organs annually being sent overseas by such organizations as the South-Eastern Organ Procurement Foundation (Richmond, Virginia) and American Medical International (Beverly Hills, California) for more than purely medical reasons.[35]

Humanitarianism in general and in the medical realm in particular is generally commendable on the part of a nation. But it typically entails sharing out of a society's abundance, not giving in a way that is self-destructive to the point of being fatal to some of its members. The generosity of some at the expense of others is suspect. It is one thing if specific individuals decide to accept the rigors of dialysis or even forgo life itself so that foreign nationals may be saved, but it is arguably another matter when a medical facility or governmental body makes that decision for them.[36]

Weaknesses

Needless to say, opponents of a favored-group criterion do not accept many of the justifications just given. In fact, some forms of a favored-group criterion are merely group versions of the more individualized social-value criterion and are subject to its many weaknesses (see chapter 3). Other arguments against the criterion are really responses to the justifications described above. So the arguments against the criterion will be introduced here in the same order as the justifications to which they respond. Although there are a few ways that rejecting a favored-group criterion might prove more productive in the long run, as will soon become evident most of the arguments against the criterion are largely person oriented in nature.

To begin with, there is little question that a favored-group criterion is a simple and convenient extension of the way much health care is practiced. However, what is acceptable in much of health care is not necessarily acceptable when treatment is lifesaving and scarce. When lives are at stake the situation may be essentially similar to that surrounding treatment in an emergency room, where traditionally lives are saved without reference to social group or place of residence.[37] That treatment is scarce, moreover, means that patients rejected at one facility cannot necessarily obtain treatment at another. To make people's lives depend upon where they happen to live or what social group they happen to be a part of seems little more than arbitrary,[38] and may be unjustly discriminatory.[39] Poor communities often end up with relatively less access to lifesaving resources. The reasons for their poverty and inferior health care resources may have little to do with their own merit and much to do with public decision making, which can be insensitive to the politically weak.[40]

As suggested earlier, there is broad agreement that the imposition of a favored-group criterion falls short of the ideal.[41] Nevertheless, pragmatic considerations move some to argue in favor of certain forms of the criterion, as explained earlier. That an ideal is difficult to achieve, though, is a weak reason for not attempting to achieve it, as even some supporters of the criterion acknowledge.[42] The benefits of allowing facilities to focus upon the particular health care needs of specific groups of people can be retained even if this practice is opposed where scarce lifesaving resources are involved. While this limited opposition in the end may indeed have some pragmatic costs, some such costs are bearable as the inevitable price of pursuing ethical policies.

Potentially more serious are the arguments that rejection of this criterion will lead to additional loss of life. Although it is true that some organs will perish if they must be transported long distances, others (for example, kidneys) can survive long enough to be transported throughout the country (and to many additional countries as well).[43] Another stated reason for the additional loss of life without a geographical favored-group criterion is that treatment is not likely to be as effective when patients travel long distances for treatment or follow-up care. The problem here, however, may be more a matter of the patient's finances than anything else. Given the financial resources, the patient might be willing and able to live near the treatment center for the required time. When such is the case, the criterion at issue is really a questionable form of an ability-to-pay criterion (see chapter 16).[44]

Additional loss of life, alternatively, may result if the rate of organ

donation decreases because organs are made available to foreign nationals or nonlocal recipients. Yet, it is far from clear that people's
willingness to donate hinges upon this consideration.[45] In fact, the evidence suggests that donations from resident ethnic communities will increase when nonresidents of similar ethnicity are allowed to receive
transplants.[46] Moreover, local organ donation may be hurt more by requiring that organs be transplanted locally in a mediocre facility than if
they are allowed to be transplanted with greater success elsewhere.[47] If
the real concern is to save as many lives as possible, the widest possible
organ sharing is desirable to obtain organs for highly sensitized patients
and to obtain the best donor–recipient matches (see chapter 12).[48]

The weaknesses of the justifications remaining to be examined are
related to specific forms of the favored-group criterion. The first has to
do with veterans, in whose case special access to treatment for non-
service-related disorders is primarily at issue. Even supporters of special
access admit that veterans really have no fair claim to such favoritism.
It is a bonus that the government may simply want to provide.[49] While
this generous attitude is commendable, it may well be out of place when
there is not a sufficient abundance of resources available to benefit some
without thereby seriously harming others. Everyone's life arguably
should be valued equally by society irrespective of the positions they
have held in society or the contributions they have made to it (see chapter 3).[50]

The final set of justifications introduced in the previous section supports giving priority to national residents in the distribution of scarce
lifesaving resources. Organ transplants in the United States provide a
widely debated case in point. Some have argued that since U.S. residents
have contributed the organs, labor, and funds (including the technology
resulting from funded research), they should have first access to the
transplants. Advanced technology today, however, is virtually always the
product of international cooperation, at least to some degree.[51] A developed country like the United States, moreover, has benefited extensively from the inexpensive raw materials and labor obtained from other
countries. In fact, U.S. nationals frequently obtain medical care while
abroad, sometimes traveling abroad specifically for the purpose of obtaining such care. The immediate contributions of U.S. residents to the
enterprise of organ transplantation may admittedly give them as a group
a special interest in that enterprise, but this interest may best be understood at most as a right (or responsibility) to determine who should

receive transplants—not an automatic claim to priority access to treatment.[52]

Were it left to them, U.S. residents would not necessarily favor having absolute priority when it comes to organ transplantation.[53] They would undoubtedly expect some special benefits to accompany their residency status, but they would probably prefer benefits that would not prove fatal to nonresidents. It is unlikely that most would oppose emergency care for foreign nationals who have heart attacks or auto accidents while in the United States. Similarly, they would probably look for a way to make some scarce lifesaving resources available to nonresidents if the latter cannot obtain them elsewhere.[54] U.S. residents would be particularly concerned to make available the many organs that they themselves are not using.[55] Such, they would likely conclude, are the requirements of compassion and humanitarianism, which may be directed first—but not exclusively—toward "one's own people."[56]

Consider the predicament of foreign nationals seeking lifesaving organ transplants in the United States. Unable to survive in their own countries, they have left home and family, often using up every asset they own, to come to the United States in search of an organ transplant. Many of those with kidney diseases do not have access even to dialysis—unlike their U.S. counterparts, who generally can remain alive on dialysis if they do not receive kidney transplants. These foreign nationals are like the seriously wounded man in the Good Samaritan story, who is not helped by "his own" and so must be cared for by someone of a different cultural group.[57]

To give foreign nationals the organs that remain after all U.S. residents possible have been treated is a first step. But the help this provides is so limited that it leads foreign nationals (some of whom are actively recruited) to come to the United States in the false hope of obtaining a transplant.[58] Such an absolute favored-group criterion is arguably too restrictive.

To think in terms of an analogy, the United States has not waited until poverty in the United States has been eliminated to give foreign economic aid. In fact, U.S. medicine in particular has a long tradition of generously sharing its skills and technology with other nations and various of their citizens. To exclude them from scarce lifesaving treatments would seem inconsistent.[59] And the sharing of organ transplantation technologies as well as transplantable organs can provide an excellent opportunity to engender international goodwill.[60] Patients everywhere,

including those in the United States, ultimately benefit as a worldwide
pool of patients and donors develops and physicians gain the opportunity
to learn from a more diverse caseload.[61] Far from being mandated by
fairness, then, a favored-group criterion based upon national residence
is broadly objectionable.

Possible Common Ground

The widespread support that exists for the notions that medical facilities
should normally treat certain types of people and that physicians should
be able to select whom they will have as patients does not appear to
extend to situations in which the lives of other people are jeopardized
as a result. But lives are at stake when a favored-group criterion is
employed to select patients to receive scarce lifesaving medical resources, and patients excluded from a given facility often cannot obtain
treatment elsewhere. There are two exceptional circumstances, however,
that are widely accepted. The first involves cases in which medical selection criteria cannot be met unless some sort of geographical or social
constituency considerations are allowed. For instance, perhaps an organ
must be shipped so far or a patient must travel so far for treatment that
it is unlikely the treatment will prove successful; or a foreign national
may plan to return home immediately following an organ transplant and
therefore lack essential follow-up care. In such cases neither a medical-
benefit nor a likelihood-of-benefit criterion may be satisfied (see chapters
10 and 12 for the importance of these criteria). Even so, however, a
favored-group criterion per se is not really justified. Rather, these are
cases in which medical criteria come into play because of geographical
considerations.

Despite the legitimacy of considering a patient's group when assessing
medical selection criteria, it is important to keep in view the general
undesirability of constituency considerations. Otherwise every possible
effort may not be made to avoid them by finding ways to alter the circumstances of individual patients. Transportation assistance, for example, or financial support to make relocation possible can eliminate the
distance a patient must travel for treatment as a reason for exclusion
from treatment; perhaps adequate follow-up care can be arranged in the
home countries of foreign nationals.

The second exception to people's usual reluctance to allow favored-group considerations acknowledges the acceptability of employing the criterion when others are not hurt as a result. As discussed near the end of chapter 16, there appears to be broad support for allowing people to purchase their own scarce lifesaving medical resources if new resources are thereby produced and the supply available to other persons is not adversely affected. A group of people could do the same thing under the same conditions and restrict use of the newly produced resources to members of that group.[62]

For instance, if partial U.S. government support for a scarce lifesaving treatment is present, an individual state may decide to devote some of its tax revenues to making additional treatment resources available. Seemingly little problem exists in restricting the use of these additional treatment resources to those who have paid the taxes responsible for them.[63] This judgment assumes, however, that people in other states are not harmed by the policy. If sufficient harm can be demonstrated, this exceptional use of a favored-group criterion is not warranted. Accordingly, restricting access to organ transplantation exclusively to residents of particular states is problematic in that millions of federal tax dollars were spent to develop the technology involved.[64]

Special access to scarce lifesaving resources by veterans for non-service-related disorders would not seem to be justified by this exception. In this case, the national government would be devoting resources to a particular group of people rather than to others without a compelling special rationale such as is arguably present in relation to service-related disorders.[65] Any proposed exception in which non-service-related disorders are in view is rendered even more problematic by the fact that service in the armed forces and subsequent veteran status have not traditionally been open to all social groups, such as women.[66]

This exceptional justification for allowing patients special access to newly produced resources may, however, apply in the case of some foreign nationals. Where foreign nationals (or anyone—see chapter 16) can provide organs for transplant that would not be available to any other patient, organ transplantation of foreign nationals is not objectionable in terms of the use of organs.[67] In the past foreign nationals coming to the United States for kidney transplantation have usually provided living related donors in order to fulfill this condition. More recently, however, 90 percent of the foreign nationals transplanted in the United States have received kidneys removed from a cadaver.[68] If such kidneys are not medically appropriate for any U.S. residents, then again the exceptional justification would apply. People (that is, U.S. residents) outside of the group being specially considered would not be harmed significantly if group members receive the organs.[69]

The case of foreign nationals receiving organs that national residents also need is more complex and requires special attention. Arguments on both sides are convincing. Ideally, in the minds of many, medical care should be available to whoever needs it. Yet, at least in the case of organ transplantation in the United States, national residents have been largely responsible for producing the limited resources that exist.[70] Allowing nonresidents to pay extra has not appeared to be sufficient to offset this consideration, and it adds all of the ethical difficulties of an ability-to-pay criterion (see chapter 16).[71] The greatest hope for common ground seems to lie in establishing a quota system that will both insure and limit the supply of organs going to foreign nationals. Under such a system, foreign nationals would be allowed to receive only a certain percentage of the organs available in a country. To the extent feasible (perhaps resembling in some ways the U.S. immigration system), an equitable means of distributing access to treatment among countries and among medically needy patients within countries would be devised.

Such compromise is well suited to the problem area highlighted earlier—organ transplantation in the United States. The approach accurately reflects that the resources are largely a product of U.S. contributions but not completely so.[72] It also gives a small measure of responsibility for meeting the world's health care needs to the entity (nation) most capable of doing so.[73] Finally, it appropriately locates the moral responsibility of humanitarianism somewhere between a matter of rights owed to all and privilege owed to none.[74] Most people, though, will not accept a so-called humanitarianism that involves obligations which meet the needs of others by creating the same need in the givers, so it probably will prove most widely acceptable to restrict the quota system in the United States to organs such as the kidney, for which there is a lifesaving alternative (for example, dialysis) to organ transplantation. Then at least there is some means of keeping alive those national residents who must go without a transplant so that a certain number of foreign nationals can receive one.[75]

What should the size of the quota be? The most widely supported options appear to be 5 percent and 10 percent. The former has been proposed by the American Society of Transplant Surgeons, among others, and the latter most notably by the U.S. Department of Health and Human Services' Task Force on Organ Transplantation.[76] The 10 percent figure, however, prompted eight members of the Task Force on Organ Transplantation to oppose the idea of allowing any quota at all—a dissent later supported by a report of the U.S. Office of the Inspector General.[77]

Accordingly, the lower figure is probably more likely to receive widespread support. Its acceptableness is further enhanced by the fact that even supporters of the 10 percent figure recommended by the task force have expressed their preference for a figure falling somewhere in the 5–10 percent range.[78] Moreover, concern about foreign nationals receiving U.S. organs reached its peak at a time when 5.2 percent of the cadaver kidney transplants taking place in the United States involved foreign recipients,[79] which suggests that any level above 5 percent is too high. To be sure, though, public concern was most aroused by revelations that as many as 22 percent or more of the kidney transplants in some locations were for the benefit of foreign nationals.[80]

A widely sanctioned 5 percent quota system might operate as follows in a national setting. Since there is to be a limit on the number of foreign nationals who will receive these transplants, some way of deciding which foreign nationals will receive these transplants must be determined.[81] The simplest method is probably to put all candidates into the same pool irrespective of nationality. All would then be selected according to whatever medical and other criteria are deemed acceptable.[82] If the national organ transplant network is able to keep track, day by day, of how many residents and nonresidents are receiving kidney transplants, then nonresidents could receive such transplants until their percentage of the total reached, say, 5.5 percent. At that point, nonresidents would not again be considered for transplants together with residents until the percentage of nonresident kidney transplants dropped to, say, 4.5 percent. Then they would remain equally eligible with residents until the nonresident percentage again reached 5.5 percent, etc.

If up-to-date information is not nationally available, then this process would be applied at whatever level the information is available. Perhaps each transplant center would have to abide by this quota, but such a restriction would be unfortunate because nonresidents are likely to congregate in certain locations of the country (for example, the national capital). Implicit in the above suggestions is the idea that any kidneys which for whatever reason cannot be transplanted into any national residents would always be available to nonresidents.

Several potential outcomes are specifically not intended by this hypothetical scenario. One is the freeing of other governments from their financial responsibility for their citizens. Wherever possible, a nonresident's own government should be required to pay for an organ transplant done in another country such as the United States.[83] The approach is also not necessarily designed to encourage particular transplant centers to give more transplants to foreign nationals.[84] It is instead simply intended to encourage selection of kidney transplant recipients without reference to favored-group considerations—whatever impact that has on patient selection, within limits. Finally, although donations to a specified nonresident might be allowed in accordance with similar carefully defined provisions governing any such designation (see end of chapter 16), restricted donations of this sort should be discouraged. They reflect the prejudices of the donors and therefore disadvantage certain social groups in a life-threatening way.[85]

A quota system, though, is far from an ideal answer to the kidney transplant needs of nonresidents and does nothing to help meet other transplant needs. What nations must work toward is an international network within which organs can be shared internationally whenever medically appropriate.[86] There must also be a sharing of the necessary technology, skills, and finances so that residents of one country will not perpetually have to travel to another to use the other's organs and expertise.[87] Limiting the organs available to nonresidents in the United States by maintaining a quota system should have the beneficial effect of encouraging other nations to seek needed resources to develop the treatment programs required by their citizens.[88]

An Illustrative Case

Luiza Magardician, a twenty-year-old Rumanian citizen, arrived in New York in the hope of obtaining a kidney transplant and returning home. According to Reverend Dumitru Viorel Sasu of the Rumanian Orthodox Church of St. Dumitru in Manhattan, before her arrival here all available methods of treatment were tried unsuccessfully in her country.

The director of the National Kidney Foundation of New York-New Jersey says Ms. Magardician's chances of finding a kidney donor are bleak since there is a severe shortage of donors in the United States, and U.S. citizens would usually come first. At some facilities state residents are also given a special priority. In addition, Ms. Magaradician has reportedly exhausted her funds and could not afford hospital costs even if a donor were found.

Should the decision to offer Ms. Magardician a transplant be made strictly on the grounds of her medical needs or should her country of origin and financial situation influence the decision?[89]

Had a national quota system been in place when this case arose, the prospects for Luiza Magardician might have been clearer: she could have determined even before traveling to the United States whether or not organs were presently being made available to patients irrespective of residency. Given the absence of such a system, she would have needed to contact perhaps many individual transplant centers, but at least she could have learned if there were any that were below their quota for nonresidents. As it is, she can only come to the United States and hope that her case will happen to get the attention of the right people who can aid her in obtaining the needed organ. State residency requirements may also prove to be a hurdle, though an unwarranted one unless the strict conditions explained earlier have been satisfied.

Assuming an acceptable and available organ can be located, other obstacles must be cleared. The woman's eagerness to return home following transplantation suggests that she may not receive the follow-up care that is necessary if the transplant is to have a significant likelihood of benefiting her. Before she receives a transplant a facility would likely require her either to establish that she can receive adequate follow-up care in her home country or that she is willing and able to remain in the United States for the necessary care. In other words, favored-group considerations sometimes function best not as an easy means of excluding patients but as indications of circumstances in patients' lives that must be altered in order for essential medical criteria to be met.

Another obstacle in Luiza Magardician's way is that of paying for treatment. Funding should be sought first from her own government, and apparently interest in her case was shown before she left home. Since such funds are not always available, the need for international sharing of funds (in addition to organs and expertise) becomes evident. Lacking either of these sources, Magardician would be dependent upon the good will of others. If the U.S. government proves unwilling to grant a limited amount of money to help finance transplants received by nonresidents within the limits of a quota system, she would need to appeal to various groups and individuals. The Rumanian community in New York or elsewhere would be a natural starting point, with more public appeals perhaps to follow. If publicity obstacles could be overcome, she might well discover firsthand that people in the United States are not greatly enamored of a favored-group criterion.

Resources Required

A resources-required criterion is designed to favor those who require relatively little of a limited resource over those who need much more of it. Curiously, this criterion has not received as much attention as other selection criteria, partly because the possibility of a major disparity in the amount of resources required by various patients does not arise in relation to many treatments. Those who need a kidney transplant, for instance, all alike need a kidney. Once a kidney has been received by one person it cannot be used by another later.

In other circumstances, however, a resources-required criterion has played an important role. Before the large-scale production of penicillin in the United States, for example, the criterion was employed to determine whose lives would be saved by this wonder drug. As many lives as possible were thereby saved with the limited supply available.[1] In wartime the criterion has been one of the reasons medical personnel set aside the seriously injured to die. Their treatment consumes the time and resources that otherwise can be devoted to saving many more lives.[2] The criterion has been applied in the selection of patients to receive dialysis, as in the case described near the end of this chapter. Both in the United States and in other countries patients suitable for kidney transplants have been given first access to dialysis on the grounds that their need for the resource is only temporary.[3] Alternatively, patients with acute renal failure who need dialysis only temporarily have been preferred over those with chronic renal failure.[4] Of the medical directors in my U.S. study (see chapter 2), 66 percent affirm the legitimacy of a resources-required criterion; on average they rate it as slightly important (mean score 2.2 out of 5).

Justifications

Although a resources-required criterion has received relatively little attention, the attention it has received comes from a wide range of sources.

Its broad support is due mainly to its many possible justifications, a number of which are essentially productivity oriented. In fact, the criterion has been labeled purely utilitarian because it seeks to maximize the number of people who will benefit from the use of a limited resource.[5] From the perspective of getting the most out of the resources available, it does seem absurd to save a few lives rather than many.[6] Favoring those who require few resources is simply a matter of efficiency.[7]

From a person oriented perspective the criterion may seem equally obvious.[8] Since human life is uniquely precious, many lives must be saved before few.[9] In the realm of personal morality it may be sufficient to talk merely of the worth of the individual, but when society as a whole is in view, a sort of statistical morality is unavoidable.[10] Each life may be accorded a great and equal weight, but the weights of larger and smaller groups must be compared if many people are involved.[11]

This justification is related to, but different from, the rationale underlying practices of triage, as explained in the Introduction. It is also distinctly different from a more explicitly utilitarian justification in which all considerations are reduced to the same unit of utility. Only one consideration is in view here—human life—and so comparisons do not involve putting life on the same scale with other concerns. Rather, an equal and unique concern for all lives requires that as many lives as possible be saved. Two ways of selecting patients may equally use up the available resources and both save lives. But the point of the selection is to save specific human lives, not to use up resources or save "life" in the abstract. When the proper purpose is kept clearly in view, it will impel the saving of as many lives as possible.[13]

The concern for life may be advocated in other person oriented ways as well. It could be more aggressively argued, for instance, that even killing people is morally and legally justified if a larger number of lives can be saved as a result.[13] An alternative perspective is the social contract approach. Imagine what people would agree to were they to come together to formulate a selection policy without knowing what their places in society are. They would want to have as high a probability of being selected as possible, but would want to make sure that no one was significantly disadvantaged in the process for irrelevant reasons (such as race or sex). A resources-required criterion would therefore suit their purposes well.[14] Even from behind a veil of ignorance, more patients would prefer the criterion than oppose it, because it respects more patients' wishes to be treated than would otherwise be respected.[15]

Admittedly it would be difficult psychologically to leave those requiring disproportionate amounts of resources to die. But ethically the more important consideration, it can be argued, is saving the most lives (and thus not needing to leave an even larger number of patients to die).[16] Similarly, while the feelings of those excluded by a resources-required criterion are important, the more important consideration from a person oriented perspective is arguably the number of lives at stake (and thus the number of people who do not presently need to suffer through death).[17]

Weaknesses

The arguments against a resources-required criterion also emerge from both person oriented and productivity oriented perspectives, though the former predominates. The strongest opposition centers around the aggressive notion that it is acceptable to kill a person if more people can thereby be saved. This contention can be viewed, first of all, as irrelevant to the debate over a resources-required criterion, for the criterion involves only choosing among those who can be treated—not causing anyone's death. If the distinction between causing death and allowing death to occur is not accepted, though, one might still consider the killing involved here to achieve the desired end at too costly a price: the ultimate infringement upon the liberty and well-being of the minority.

An equal concern for all persons involved can be invoked in another way. Even if no intentional killing is involved, a resources-required criterion focuses on saving the greatest number of lives possible, not providing all candidates for treatment with an equal opportunity to be selected. This practice may constitute an unacceptable violation of the equal respect due all persons.[18]

Moreover, the drive to save as many lives as possible is arguably rooted in a mistaken understanding of medicine's purpose. Physicians have a duty to save life with the resources at their disposal, but this duty does not dictate which lives in particular are to be saved. When many need a treatment that a physician cannot provide for all, the physician must exhaust all of the available resources. No individual patients, however, can claim that treatment is rightfully theirs and not someone else's. Accordingly, no one is wronged if the resources are given to a smaller rather than a larger number of patients.[19]

Many people, as noted earlier, are suspicious of any selection criterion that attempts to maximize benefits. A moral perspective, they insist, entails recognizing basic human rights and not allowing any calculation of beneficial consequences to outweigh these rights.[20] People are unique; they are not quantifiable or measurable. When life itself is at stake calculations are simply out of place.[21] To compare groups of human beings merely on the size of their numbers is to reduce them to mere things.[22] Interestingly, virtually the opposite argument can also be made against a resources-required criterion if a productivity oriented perspective is adopted. One problem with the criterion is that it takes the numbers of people into account but none of their other important characteristics. It considers quantity but neglects quality. But it may be preferable to treat one outstanding person rather than to save two who are mediocre.[23]

Possible Common Ground

Although arguments can be made both for and against a resources-required criterion, those explicitly examining the criterion predominantly favor it. Its greatest public strength lies in the fact that it is the least objectionable of the social criteria. Its adoption allows those concerned to maximize the effectiveness of limited resources to do so—but in a way that does not blatantly undermine the notion that human life has a unique value shared by every person. Admittedly, some conclude that even this criterion does not do justice to the value of persons. Their line of reasoning, though, as we have seen, tends to support only the moral neutrality of saving more or fewer people. It does not necessarily lead to the conclusion that a policy favoring many lives over few would be morally wrong per se.

If a resources-required criterion is to be adopted, several forms of it should probably be avoided. One is the version that would exclude all long-term use of a resource so that it could be made available exclusively to those needing it only temporarily.[24] The classic instance is when dialysis is scarce, and the choice is between those needing dialysis "temporarily" (sometimes months or even years) while awaiting transplants and those needing it longer-term. A resources-required criterion need only give priority to temporary uses of scarce resources, not exclude long-term uses entirely. Total exclusion of chronic patients might leave resources sitting idle for extended periods in cases where temporary uses do not require all of the resources available.

A second dubious form of the criterion is one that would allow patients a fixed amount of a limited resource, irrespective of their needs. In other words, all would be given access to temporary treatment, for example, two weeks of intensive care or a year on an artificial heart—but no more.[25] Although this idea does explicitly respect equality and multiplies the number of people eligible for treatment, it conflicts with traditional medical practices. For instance, physicians become not caregivers but the proximate causes of death when they discontinue dialysis or remove artificial hearts from patients who are doing fine. In place of the long-standing provision of treatment on the basis of need is the questionable idea that people have less and less claim upon (or right to) health care the more care they have received.

A related drawback is that this form of the criterion replaces a focus on people with one on life-weeks or life-years (see the discussion of this issue in relation to an age criterion in chapter 7). Weeks of life or years of life may indeed be consistently saved, but no lasting commitment is made to caring for particular persons. The caregiver–patient relationship greatly suffers as a result. The discontinuing of treatment violates the implicit commitment of the caregiver to continue to treat once treatment is begun. If patients are informed at the outset that they will receive only temporary treatment, then no explicit commitments will be violated. But the damage to the relationship thereby simply shifts from the later period, when resources are discontinued, to the earlier point at which the temporary nature of the treatment to be provided is disclosed.

In light of the foregoing concerns, it is probably not a good idea to invoke a resources-required criterion to deny repeat treatments (for example, organ transplants) when the first is not successful.[26] Because treatments in such cases are separable events—though it may plausibly be argued otherwise—previously treated patients need not be given any special priority. They are no more being abandoned than any other patient who must wait for an equally needed organ transplant—particularly if they have been advised of this policy at the time of their first transplant.[27]

If their lives are indeed equally in jeopardy with those who have not been treated previously, however, their claim on resources should not be diminished either, especially not when the resources they have received have not been beneficial. Fairness does not demand that all in need receive one transplant before anyone else receives two. To impose such a requirement would be to shift the basis of (this) medical care radically away from medical need. Those who have been the neediest in the past would be most likely to be denied in the present. (See chapter 10 for a discussion of the importance of preserving medical need as the basis of medical care.) For a resources-required criterion to be applicable, it is necessary to predict which patients will need multiple transplants—an impossible task. If there are backup or alternative treatments (for example, dialysis in many cases of kidney transplantation), the foregoing assessment does not necessarily apply in whatever cases the resource in question is not strictly lifesaving.[28] Similarly, opposition to prioritizing those receiving first transplants disappears if there are medical grounds for doing so (for example, perhaps if repeat transplantations are sufficiently riskier).[29]

As long as these forms of a resources-required criterion are avoided, the criterion can provide a widely accepted way to save many lives. Some additional cautions are in order, though. First, it may not always be clear whether or not a particular patient falls within the group being accorded lesser priority by this criterion. In such cases the patient probably should not be given lesser priority, since the stakes are so high.

Another caution relates to a situation in which one or more patients should receive priority. A predicted difference in the amount of resources required by candidates for treatment is not sufficient in itself to establish the priority of some over others. Predicting this difference—like predicting a difference in the likelihood of who will benefit from treatment (see chapter 12)—is imprecise. Therefore only major disparities in resources required should be employed as a basis for patient selection.

In fact, although a further stipulation may not be theoretically necessary, the criterion is easiest to apply if the disparity between candidates is manifestly a matter of life and death. A choice between someone needing a resource long-term and one needing it only temporarily is one example. There the choice is between saving one chronic patient and saving many patients with temporary needs.[30] Patients are more likely to accept being excluded if they can see that the lives of more than one other person can be saved by the same resources they themselves require. The more specifically these other persons can be identified, the more persuasive the rationale.[31]

To conclude, a resources-required criterion will not be relevant to all patient selection decisions. Only in cases of major disparities in the resources required by various patients will the criterion have a place.

An Illustrative Case

The medical center at a U.S. state university found itself in a financial crunch during the 1960s. Its dialysis program had received heavy federal support, but the funds were drying up. The center had long favored kidney transplantation over dialysis as the treatment of choice for renal failure. Some patients, though, were unsuitable for transplantation, and the others needed dialysis temporarily until a transplant became available. An administrative meeting was called to explore ways to deal with the center's financial difficulties.

Bob Parsons suggested that the center cut down on the number of non-paying cases it accepted. Citing the center's long-standing service to the local community, Catherine Walker preferred to see anyone in need receive treatment at least for a year. At that point, she argued, many would have obtained transplants. Dialysis for the others would then be continued only if they could pay for it. Bill Corsini expressed his concern over the prospect of having to drop some patients "mid-flight" from the program; but he agreed with the importance of preventing a few patients from using up all the limited resources still available. In the end, a policy of providing dialysis only to those who were good candidates for transplants was adopted.[32]

This case not only recalls the past but also proves a source of insight for the present and future. Dialysis has been federally funded in the United States, but not in numerous other countries. Moreover, dialysis funding may fall victim again to cutbacks even in the United States, as explained in chapter 1. Such a potentiality raises issues that will attend many emerging technologies such as the artificial heart. Debates have already begun over the relative claims of temporary vs. long-term use of an expensive resource like the artificial heart in the context of limited health care dollars.

The problem in the present case is a combination of limited dialysis space and the lack of funds to obtain more—or perhaps even to continue operation of all machines currently owned. The ability-to-pay issue will be examined in chapter 16. If the poor are not excluded on the basis of their inability to pay, one is left with the danger that nonpayers may tie up the available machines long-term. Short-term nonpayers do not pose as serious a threat in that they will soon be replaced by others, many of whom will be payers.

A resources-required criterion, then, turns out to be doubly beneficial in this situation: it protects the financial solvency of the program and at the same time ensures that more people will obtain access to the program. The financial argument may or may not be compelling, depending upon what is at stake for the medical center, as explained in chapter 16. Thus it is important to be clear about the primary justification of a resources-required criterion. It is not essentially a medical or financial criterion.[33] Rather, it provides what is probably the least controversial basis upon which to save as many lives as possible when resources are limited.

Although the medical center was wise to adopt some sort of resources-required criterion, the policy as stated—only good candidates for transplantation are to be considered for dialysis—may well be too rigid. The policy is fine as long as there are more of these candidates than dialysis machines; but if such is not the case, it is better simply to grant priority to transplant candidates. Leaving open the possibility of treatment for noncandidates is important for reasons explained previously, as long as these patients are appraised realistically of their prospects for treatment.

CHAPTER SIX

Special Responsibilities

Even people who reject a social-value criterion (chapter 11) suggest that exceptional circumstances may call for a special selection criterion. Some people have special responsibilities toward others or toward society in general. The most common form of a special-responsibilities criterion is one that would favor patients who have family dependents—especially dependent children—over those who have not. This version has significant support in both the United States and Great Britain,[1] and was commonly employed to select U.S. dialysis patients before federal funding began in 1972.[2] Even since then the familial impact of a patient's undergoing dialysis has remained a crucial consideration in the decision to institute treatment.[3] Family responsibilities play a similarly important role in the selecting of organ transplant recipients.[4] The criterion is sometimes explicitly invoked, although it may instead be merely implicit in the way a selection decision is described.[5] One study has reported family considerations as very important in the intensive care unit admission decisions made by the majority of physicians surveyed.[6]

A special-responsibilities criterion has more rarely been applied in a way that involves the patient's responsibilities toward persons outside the family.[7] These responsibilities are generally perceived as being special in some way that distinguishes them from the full range of considerations involved in a social-value criterion.[8] Typically, the lives of other people are dependent upon a particular patient being saved. For instance, penicillin and other scarce treatments in wartime have been given to those able to return most quickly to battle so that the killing being done by the enemy may be stopped as soon as possible.[9] In an earthquake, it is generally agreed, those with medical expertise should be treated first if they can quickly be restored sufficiently to be able to treat others.[10] Of the medical directors surveyed in my U.S. study (see chapter 2), 69 percent affirm the legitimacy of a special-responsibilities criterion, with directors on average rating it as somewhat important (mean score 2.5 out of 5).

Justifications

Arguments in support of a special-responsibilities criterion may be either productivity oriented or person oriented. Many of the productivity oriented justifications, first of all, apply specifically to the family dependents aspects of the criterion. Favoring those with family dependents may be seen as being broadly beneficial to society.[11] Society saves the expense of having to support the family members who would otherwise be left unsupported.[12] The family is undergirded since it is enabled to remain intact,[13] and dependent spouses, parents, grandchildren, and especially children are preserved from potentially great suffering.[14] Finally, patients may fare better if there are large families to support them.[15]

Productivity oriented arguments may also be made on behalf of a more generic form of special-responsibilities criterion. Again, its general utilitarian value may be cited.[16] Unless certain people are saved in certain circumstances (such as war), there may be an increased loss of property and life.[17] A special-responsibilities criterion may instead be viewed as a particularly stringent form of social-value criterion, with all of the latter's justifications.[18] Considerable suffering may also be avoided when people who are emotionally dependent upon particular patients (a social worker or a member of the clergy, for example) are spared the traumatically permanent separation from them that the death of those patients entails.[19]

A more general way of stating these arguments is that in rare cases a normally diverse society becomes focused upon a particular concern that may involve the very survival of the community—though a massive threat to life is not a prerequisite in this rationale.[20] Under these circumstances it may be appropriate to impose a utilitarian triage system in which those who are essential to furthering the community's focal concern are saved.[21] Key military personnel, scientists, and politicians, for example, might be favored according to this version of the criterion.

Other ways of justifying a special-responsibilities criterion are person oriented. Some of these justifications address the particular importance of saving patients with family dependents. Such patients, by virtue of their family responsibilities, may be considered the most needy patients; and their dependents may be considered particularly vulnerable. Justice requires that the most needy be helped and the most vulnerable be protected.[22] It can also be argued that some family members, especially children, are so dependent upon a certain patient that their lives are psychologically (if not physically) at stake in a patient selection decision.[23]

These propositions may also be advanced in the case of persons other than family dependents, as can additional person oriented justifications. The basic concern in either case is for an escape valve to be available in exceptional circumstances—for some way of acknowledging the lesser of two evils.[24] In rare cases more than the lives of patients may be at stake in patient selection decisions: the lives of others may literally depend upon a particular patient being saved. A wounded physician in a natural disaster and a military leader in time of war are commonly cited examples. In such cases fairness requires that the life-threatening needs of all be weighed equally. According to this perspective, patients must be selected in a way that minimizes loss of life.

Although many people argue for a special-responsibilities criterion as a means to save more lives, its fairness is a matter of dispute. It may be viewed as unjust to the patients—since they are not given the kind of equal opportunity to receive treatment that some form of random selection would provide—and yet right nevertheless since it saves more lives.[25] However, justice need not be construed in so rigidly egalitarian a manner. Equal consideration is usually important because it protects everyone's interests; but in some cases the interests of all patients under consideration may be best served by giving priority treatment to those (for example, physicians in a disaster) who, by surviving, may be enabled to save additional lives (for example, before medical personnel arrive). It may be contended that such an exception is just in that it best protects the interests of all.[26]

This rationale may lead to the odd conclusion that patients who will donate money to produce more resources (thereby saving additional lives) should be favored according to a special-responsibilities criterion. Any apparent injustice in this outcome, though, probably lies not in the selection criterion, but in a society that leaves people to die for lack of health care funding. Under such circumstances, those with wealth will necessarily have an advantage.[27] Admittedly, it may be future rather than present patients who benefit from the additional resources that become available. But this outcome may be justified as a sort of just savings provision whereby present patients forego certain selection opportunities in order that future patients may have better prospects.[28]

Weaknesses

Since a special-responsibilities criterion is designed to provide special benefits, not surprisingly most arguments against it are person oriented in nature. Consider first the family dependents form of the criterion. Whereas most people would agree that families and family relationships are quite important, the priority of these considerations over the very lives of patients is more debatable. Children indeed experience a significant loss when a parent dies; but the greater loss is that of a patient who must die if the parent is selected.[29] If people were ignorant of family circumstances, they would probably agree that preserving everyone's chance at living is more important than lessening the generally temporary grief of family members, whose lives will go on.[30] Besides, favoring those with the most dependent families penalizes those who worked hardest to make their families financially independent and emotionally stable.[31]

The favoring of those with family dependents is also questionable in that such favoritism is essentially a form of social-value selection, with all of the problems attending that criterion (see chapter 3).[32] Some people are benefited, but at the unacceptably high moral cost of violating the basic right to life of others.[33] Those who have not yet had children, either because they are not old enough or for other reasons beyond their control, are unjustly discriminated against.[34] The scenario in view here has been described as an updated version of Rubens's portrayal of the Last Judgment: on one side are the people aspiring for dialysis, with the committee sitting on top; on the other side are the unemployed, divorced, and childless, going down to hell.[35]

A final difficulty with giving priority to patients with family dependents is that it takes for granted a particular cultural understanding of families, despite the viable alternatives. Implicit in the standard is the idea that taking families seriously entails favoring those with dependent children. But it is possible to place great value on families and yet affirm a very different approach to patient selection. African cultures such as the Akamba people of Kenya provide a particularly illuminating alternative, for they value family relationships highly.[36]

The Akamba view a person not merely as an isolated physical, mortal being, but rather as a physical representation of the dead, the living, and the unborn. Each person embodies a name that reaches through time. Consequently, the most miserable event that can befall a person is to die without having left children behind to perpetuate one's name: to do so is to undergo "total annihilation."[37] To ensure against annihilation, the Akamba traditionally marry early and have children as soon as possible thereafter. As they see it, the unborn are "in the loins of the living."[38] The death of a person who has no children accordingly entails the death of the unborn as part of the extinction of the living person's name and the severe diminishing of the family as a whole.

This view of the individual and the family has implications for resource allocation that differ markedly from those affirmed by supporters of a family dependents form of special-responsibilities criterion. In my own Kenyan study (see chapter 2), Akamba healers were asked the following question: If there is not enough medicine available to treat two dying patients, who should be saved, a man with five children or a man with none? Many Westerners would favor saving the man with children if the children are financially or psychologically dependent upon him. The Akamba, on the contrary, though they value children, maintain that higher moral mandates govern here. First, as this is a case of potential annihilation, many Akamba insist that the man without children must be allowed to live, so that he can "raise up a name" for himself by having children. Only in this way can a man "maintain his name" and thereby "remain."[39] At the same time, the lives of numerous *unborn* are also at stake. Thus, both an intergenerational "name" as well as the lives of the many individuals who make up this name are at issue here.

Commitment to family, then, by no means necessarily leads to a family dependents form of special-responsibilities criterion. Quite the opposite, taking families seriously includes viewing them as corporate and inter-generational entities, not merely as collections of individuals. From this point of view, much more harm can be done to a family (including its various individual members) than depriving children of a parent they depend upon. Acknowledging this in no way diminishes the seriousness of such deprivation. It only draws attention to the narrow cultural assumptions upon which the family dependents standard is based.

The more general form of special-responsibilities criterion is also open to criticism on a number of grounds. Most significant, it is often worded so vaguely that it seems to open the door to a wide range of dubious social-value considerations. Exactly what constitutes a focused community and how it is determined when the conditions for such an entity are met, for example, are never explained.[40] Particularly problematic in this regard is that a person's future actions are never certain. Whether or not patients, if selected, will actually live and go on to carry out those actions for which they were given preference in the first place is a matter of judgment and likelihood. Many of the drawbacks attending a likelihood-of-benefit criterion come into play here.[41]

A final set of difficulties is that the beneficiaries of a special-responsibilities criterion may turn out to be not the patients needing the scarce resource in question, but someone else. The chances of the former being selected are diminished when a person who is expected to benefit others in some critical way is chosen. Unselected patients will not benefit either from the potentially lifesaving work that a scientist will soon complete if treated now or from the money donated by the preferred wealthy person to produce more of the scarce resource in the future.[42] In other words, the neediest people at present—those who will die without a particular treatment—must be disadvantaged even further for the benefit of other persons.

Possible Common Ground

Notwithstanding the substantial support for some sort of exceptional special-responsibilities criterion in principle, there are many serious objections to the vague way in which it is commonly formulated and to the substance of the family dependents form of the criterion. Such difficulties can probably be avoided if the criterion is more precisely and narrowly defined. Three basic standards and five procedural guidelines commend themselves.

1. The person to be preferred according to the criterion must truly be indispensable. People are special in a variety of ways, but they are rarely indispensable. Usually there is another way to provide for whatever need a person is meeting—not in the same way, perhaps, but in a way that largely meets the need.[43]

2. Patients selected according to a special-responsibilities criterion must actually be able to fulfill their critical role once they are treated.[44] People judged indispensable may be so weakened by their illness or so incapacitated by their treatment that they will not be able to perform their critical service to others even if they are selected for treatment.

3. Serious moral harms—not simply the foregoing of benefits—must be anticipated if a particular person's life is not saved. The distinction between harms and benefits is crucial, for herein lies a most important difference between this criterion and a social-value criterion (chapter 3).[45] People not

selected for treatment will die, so something of equal moral significance must be at stake in order to justify compromising the selection chances of all but the favored patients. Various benefits and increased well-being are insufficient. In fact, a likelihood of saving the lives of others is really the only clear justification, unless something of greater significance morally can be agreed upon by society.[46]

Some have suggested that the justification must be strong enough to warrant stopping the treatment of patients already being treated.[47] However, if this stipulation adds a requirement any stronger than would otherwise apply (for example, because an implicit commitment to continue treatment once begun is being violated), then it is stronger than necessary. The crux of the matter is deciding between candidates for available resources, not reallocating all resources in use every time another person has need of them.[48]

To the three standards must be added five procedural guidelines in order for a special-responsibilities criterion to be widely accepted.

1. Each case must be considered on its merits rather than be automatically approved because of its type.[49] A politician, a physician, or a military leader may or may not meet the standards of the criterion; parents may be child abusers and not at all indispensable to their children's existence.

2. The person or persons who carry out this case by case assessment must be deemed appropriate for the task. Since the decisions entail making value judgments rather than strictly medical judgments, they are probably best made by a committee consisting partly of medical personnel and partly of people from other walks of life.[50]

3. The burden of proof in the application of this criterion should be upon those who would justify treating some patients specially because of their relationships with others. The lives of all patients being considered are in jeopardy without treatment. So the initial presumption in favor of giving all an equal opportunity to receive treatment must be overcome by demonstrating that more important relevant considerations also apply.[51]

4. Realistically there is no way to be certain that any of the three standards mentioned above apply in any given case. As a result, some such guideline as a "reasonable likelihood" that each of the standards can be met is necessary. Admittedly, judgment is necessary at this point. It is to be hoped that the involvement of a committee will prevent this guideline from being unreasonably lax or unreasonably stringent.

5. The exceptional nature of the criterion must be recognized. Because the three standards are so demanding, cases in which a special-responsibilities

criterion applies will be rare. If it is frequently applied, the committee may want to reexamine the strictness with which it is applying the three standards. The notion of exception is a tolerable moral concept only if it truly can remain exceptional.[52] Perhaps requiring unanimity within the committee before giving a patient special access to treatment according to this criterion would be a helpful restraint.[53]

These standards and guidelines make it easier to evaluate some of the commonly proposed examples of persons who should be preferred according to a special-responsibilities criterion. One such example is the soldier in wartime.[54] It is held that those who can be returned to the battle quickly should be treated first. The appropriateness of this example hinges upon its rationale. If the example is justified on the grounds of a focused purpose for the entire community, it is weak and not likely to be widely acknowledged.[55] As suggested in the third standard, the fact that lives are at stake needs to be cited explicitly. The prospect of its saving more lives is what gives this example its force.

A second common example is the important politician. It would come as no surprise if a national head of state or other top leaders were given special priority in the distribution of scarce lifesaving resources.[56] Again, though, the rationale needs scrutiny. If the contention is that those with the most power will get whatever they want, it may be descriptively true but morally wrong. To be justified, this example must satisfy the conditions outlined above. In particular, the circumstance must be such that absolutely no one could take that politician's place without there being loss of life (or another equally serious loss) in the process. Certain essential persons in time of war are the most likely candidates.[57] Yet, even then the serious loss reasonably likely to occur must be specified.

Scientists and physicians are also often singled out for special treatment.[58] But danger lies in assuming that every scientist and physician is of vital concern to society, and a selection committee made up not solely of medical personnel would help to protect against this assumption. Under certain conditions, however, exceptions may be warranted—for example, if a scientist is on the verge of making a major lifesaving discovery that others cannot accomplish in her or his absence. Physicians, nurses, and other medical professionals may also warrant priority treatment in the face of a disaster or other personnel shortage.[59] However, it must be reasonably likely that once treated they will still be both indispensable and in fact able to save the lives of others.

As for the case of the wealthy person who will provide more resources for others, the difference between theory and practice may prove decisive. In theory, saving the person with wealth would be potentially justifiable, as noted earlier, if more lives would be saved due to the wealth donated. Consider, however, the circumstances in which this case might arise. If money can produce additional supplies of the resource in question, then the wealthy person could simply purchase the resource privately, outside of the public distribution system (see chapter 16 on ability to pay). If money cannot produce additional supplies of the resource— that is, if it is limited by natural scarcity, as with organ transplants— then the wealthy person's money cannot provide resources to save additional lives. Another possibility is that increased supplies of the resource cannot be produced quickly enough to benefit the wealthy person, but can be made available to others in the future if sufficient funding is provided. Even in this very limited case, special priority for the wealthy person is not warranted unless it is reasonably likely that the person's funds are indispensable to the funding of the resource. In other words, it must be unlikely that government or private funding sources will be sufficient.

A final example concerns the matter highlighted in the case that follows.

An Illustrative Case

George Burnham and Donald Mattison were patients in adjoining rooms in the rehabilitation division of a state medical center. George was a thirty-three-year-old, severely retarded man who had lived in state institutions since the age of three. His family had had no contact with him for over twenty years. George had been trained to feed himself and to keep himself reasonably clean, but at the age of twenty-five he had suffered a cardiac arrest that left him with some paralysis. After rehabilitation he only occasionally lacked bowel control.

Donald Mattison, a forty-eight-year-old businessman, active in community and church affairs, married, and the father of four, had suffered a minor stroke, which left him slightly paralyzed. In his six weeks on the rehabilitation ward he had regained almost total use of his arm and leg. His prognosis for full recovery seemed excellent.

The hospital has at least one cardiac-arrest team on duty twenty-four hours a day, and one crash cart in every patient area at all times. The possibility of simultaneous cardiac arrests seemed remote. If it were to happen, there would not be time to transfer an additional crash cart from another patient area, since the rehabilitation ward is served by an extremely slow elevator.

But in this case the improbable happened. George had a cardiac arrest at 3:00 one morning. Within four minutes the cardiac team had arrived in his room and was ready to begin work. At that very moment Donald also had a cardiac arrest. Knowing of the simultaneous cardiac arrests, every team member hesitated. Two also knew both patients' family situations; the others, including the team leader, did not. After a moment, the team leader said, "First come, first served. Let's go to work." With no further hesitation, the team began to resuscitate George.

Without the emergency aid, Donald died. George was resuscitated, but suffered yet another cardiac arrest at 8:20 the next morning. This time another team was unable to revive him, and he too died. Did the team leader make the right decision in resuscitating George instead of Donald?[60]

When a choice must be made between two people, the chooser's first inclination usually is to search for significant differences between them. In the present case, Donald appears to have a somewhat better prognosis with treatment than George. Donald's ability to appreciate the benefits of treatment seems to be superior, in light of George's mental retardation. Perhaps the most striking difference, though, concerns the family situations of the two men: one is married and the father of four, the other has had no contact with family in decades. George, far from having others who depend upon him, is himself dependent. The big question, though, is whether or not such differences as family dependents are sufficiently significant to warrant consideration when people's lives are at stake.

Some patients have family members who are financially or emotionally dependent upon them. While the loss of someone close can be tragic, it rarely if ever meets the three suggested standards of a special-responsibilities criterion. Seldom is a person truly indispensable. At least minimally sufficient financial support may well be obtainable elsewhere, and emotional support, even though rarely the equal of that provided by the lost relative, is often available from another source as well. In many cases, patients are no longer able to provide support (or at least not the same level of support) even if they receive treatment. Of supreme import is the recognition that life itself will almost certainly be denied to a different patient who must go without treatment whenever one patient receives special priority. Whether the support that family members must do without is as morally significant as the loss of life that another patient must suffer is dubious.

Such matters are appropriately weighed by diverse committees rather

than individual decision makers. Had the issue been considered beforehand by a committee in the hospital where George and Donald were
being treated, the medical team answering the emergency would have
known whether or not the family situations of the two were even conceivably relevant to the decision about whom to treat. Assuming they
were, more must be known than the bare fact that Donald has a wife
and four children, whereas George has neither. Case-by-case consideration is important precisely because relationships do not necessarily imply meaningful dependencies, much less critical dependencies. The
burden of proof is on those who suspect that such a dependency exists.
In the absence of such proof it is best assumed that a special-responsibilities criterion does not apply.

PART THREE

Sociomedical Criteria

CHAPTER SEVEN

Age

An age criterion, usually intended to exclude the oldest patients from treatment, currently directs many patient selection decisions in the United States.[1] National and state surveys confirm public support for this practice.[2] Medical studies controlling for physiological differences among patients indicate that even nonscarce resources tend to be provided on the basis of age.[3] When resources are limited—for example, in the treatment of renal disease—an age-related pattern of patient selection is particularly evident. Before dialysis was federally funded, the use of an age criterion to screen out the old and very young alike was prominent, though exceptions were occasionally made.[4] Such a criterion has also been employed to exclude the elderly from receiving kidney transplants.[5] Even today, my study (see chapter 2) suggests that 88 percent of renal directors consider age a legitimate consideration. In the overall selection process it is held on average to be somewhat important (mean score 2.7 out of 5). Moreover, there is evidence indicating that these figures may understate physician support.[6]

Heart transplants have followed a similar route. Many centers usually accept only candidates who are less than fifty years old; others favor a cutoff of fifty-five.[7] Generally, age in excess of fifty years is considered to be a relative contraindication to heart transplantation, while for those over fifty-five the contraindication is absolute.[8] The difficulty of obtaining a heart transplant for those over fifty is one of the reasons pioneer artificial heart recipients Barney Clark and William Schroeder wanted the new device.[9] The upper age limit then being placed upon artificial heart recipients was sixty-five.[10]

Age criteria in the United States are also employed in the provision of intensive care.[11] One study of physicians found that 57 percent consider age a very important consideration in deciding which of two patients is to receive the last available bed in the ICU (with a much higher percentage according the criterion at least some importance).[12] Other studies document that the intensity of the medical intervention recommended correlates directly with age, after controlling for long-term prognosis and functional ability.[13]

The use of an age criterion is widespread outside of the United States as well. An international study of patient selection criteria has discovered that, of the countries with formal selection criteria who cannot provide treatment for all with renal disease, 60 percent employ an age criterion.[14] A few non-European countries like Singapore and Malaysia are on record as using an age criterion in the selection of renal patients, but its support in Europe is much more evident.[15] According to one study, 92 percent of the European renal transplant centers and 30 percent of the dialysis centers employ this criterion.[16] East Germany tops the list, with nearly 80 percent of its dialysis centers considering age and the majority of its renal transplant centers accepting no one over forty-five. Age criteria as they respect various lifesaving resources in other European countries such as Sweden, Norway, the Netherlands, France, and Rumania have been independently documented as well.[17]

The most publicized European supporter of an age criterion, though, is Great Britain, where the criterion is most evident in the exclusion of the elderly from dialysis, though other instances could be cited.[18] Although some suggest that the exclusion of the elderly is official national policy, it is really the unofficial result of referral patterns.[19] Physicians know that dialysis facilities can handle only so many patients, given a national allocation of resources for dialysis that is insufficient to treat all in need. At some age—with estimates ranging from forty-five or fifty to sixty or sixty-five—many medically qualified candidates simply cannot obtain dialysis.[20] The most common assessment is that few over fifty-five can obtain this treatment.[21] As these figures reflect, the impact of the age criterion is in fact gradual, with those at the higher ages being more rigidly excluded than those at the lower.[22] Overall, between fifteen hundred and three thousand medically qualified candidates in Great Britain alone are denied dialysis each year due to their age—a predicament not likely to change soon.[23]

The prevalence of an age criterion, particularly in Great Britain, suggests that the criterion may well become more prominent in the United States during the next few decades. If resources devoted to dialysis are restricted, then the British parallel will be particularly influential.[24] In fact, whereas only 10 percent of dialysis directors in my U.S. study employ an age criterion today, 85 percent indicate that they would do so under conditions of greater resource limitations. Beyond the realm of dialysis, too, the elderly are likely to fare less and less well in patient selection decisions for a variety of reasons.[25] Because the elderly require a disproportionately large amount of medical resources, the greatest potential savings lie in excluding them from treatment.[26] The lack of assertiveness on the part of many elderly plus the cultural value placed upon youth also make an increasing emphasis upon an age criterion likely.[27]

Justifications

Many arguments can be made on behalf of an age criterion. Some of them essentially equate this criterion with another, the latter having its own justifications. For instance, some argue that an age criterion is legitimate because it screens out the elderly, who are in no physical condition to benefit from treatment.[28] An age criterion, in other words, can be seen as a form of medical-benefit criterion (see chapter 10).[29]

Similar arguments can be made tying an age criterion to other forms of benefit criteria. Age may be one indication of the likelihood of medical benefit (see chapter 12), in that older people statistically do not do as well as the young undergoing most lifesaving treatments.[30] They certainly do not on average live as long as their younger counterparts, so a length-of-benefit rationale (see chapter 13) may be involved here.[31] Quality-of-benefit and psychological-ability arguments (see chapters 14 and 8, respectively) are also relevant to the extent that the elderly will not enjoy as high a quality of life or mental ability following treatment as do the young.[32] Viewed from another angle, the benefit that society will receive if an elderly person is saved is likely to be less than if a young patient is preferred. An age criterion, then, may serve as a convenient (though often hidden) form of social-value criterion (see chapter 3).[33] These and other rationales for considering age typically have chronological age in view. Parallel arguments can be constructed with reference to physiological age, but it is even more likely that the latter would reflect concerns (especially medical) other than age considerations per se.

Age criteria, though, can indeed be justified in their own right. To many they seem obvious—often apparently for productivity reasons.[34] Explicit productivity oriented justifications are of several types. One includes many of the considerations raised in the previous paragraph—that is, that an age criterion will help to ensure the best possible return on the investment of resources.[35] Another type focuses upon the convenience of an age criterion. Unlike uncertain and somewhat subjective medical judgments, a patient's age is a comparatively objective and pre-

cise basis for selection.[36] Moreover, an age criterion can be applied with
little resistance from the elderly, who as individuals (even if not collectively) can be relatively unassertive. Finally, the financial savings that
can be achieved if the elderly are excluded are also noteworthy, as mentioned earlier. For example, if only those over fifty-five years of age were
excluded from treatment for renal disease in the United States, 45 percent of the costs of the renal disease program would be saved.[37] In other
areas such as intensive care, the elderly use such a disproportionate
amount of resources that there is a great financial gain when they are
excluded. After all—though it is tragically stark to acknowledge—death
is the ultimate economy in health care expenditures.[38]

From a more person oriented perspective an age criterion may also
have great appeal. Part of its appeal, interestingly, stems from what it
is not. In the face of some lifesaving medical care today that is prone to
dehumanize people by trying desperately to forestall death at all costs,
an age criterion recognizes that it is appropriate to accept death when
old age arrives.[39] Furthermore, although "ageism" is sometimes asserted
to be as discriminatory as racism and sexism, an age criterion actually
avoids much of the criticism directed against racism and sexism. Everyone (if death does not intervene first) is subject to old age. The evil of
racism and sexism lies largely in the fact that only certain people are
penalized by deprivations attached to race or sex.[40]

Rather than promoting inequality, an age criterion may actually be
seen as promoting equality. The most important equality at issue here
from this perspective is the equal opportunity to live to the same age as
others.[41] Some notion of a prima facie right to a minimum number of
life-years may be involved.[42] This argument has a less person oriented
form as well, that in which each year of life rather than each person per
se is equally valued. From this viewpoint the concern is to maximize the
number of life-years saved by employing an age criterion.[43]

A variation of the equal-opportunity justification has to do with the
concept of life span. According to this view, there is a natural life span
(perhaps seventy or eighty years) that is normative rather than merely
a statistical average at the present moment in history. Once people have
reached this age, medicine should generally no longer be concerned with
saving (extending) their lives. They have lived a full life, and resources
should be devoted instead to those who still have important life projects
ahead of them.[44]

Another egalitarian proposal is that people should be treated equally
not so much in the present moment as over a lifetime. Health care should

be provided in a way that enables all people to live as long as possible.[45] To achieve this end, the resources available must be distributed throughout each person's lifetime so as to protect against early death. Expensive lifesaving resources, then, might be made available only to the young, with personal care services enhanced for the elderly (and preventive as well as other basic care perhaps provided to all).[46] Alternatively, all resources might be channeled to the young to increase their prospects, with the elderly encouraged to commit assisted suicide.[47] Unlike a utilitarian concern to maximize the total number of life-years saved—often helping some at the expense of others—this outlook adopts the perspective of the typical individual and seeks the most prudent distribution of limited resources throughout that person's lifetime.[48]

To this point the arguments made have focused upon an age criterion that would exclude the oldest people from having access to a given resource. Age criteria have been advanced in two other forms as well. One, prompted by many of the preceding justifications but shying away from excluding any group of people altogether, would establish relative quotas that would favor the young while providing at least some access to the old.[49] The other form would exclude the very young from treatment. Such a criterion frequently has been employed, for example, in selecting patients to receive dialysis. There the concerns have been that children lack the extreme self-discipline required for undergoing dialysis and that dialysis would inhibit the onset of puberty.[50] Even more so than in the context of the elderly, age criteria to exclude the young tend actually to be medical criteria (for example, medical benefit or quality of benefit), albeit applied to a specific age group. Unlike the elderly, the young do not usually have a diminished potential for economic productivity and they have not had the opportunity to live a long life.

Weaknesses

The foregoing justifications for an age criterion are far from universally accepted.[51] In fact, in circumstances where the criterion is most commonly employed—such as the provision of dialysis in Great Britain—physicians appear reluctant to admit using it. When confronted with medically suitable patients who are over the unofficial maximum age, British physicians often will not refer them to a nephrologist, telling them that nothing of medical benefit can be done.[52] Rarely do these patients question their physician's judgment. If they do apply to a clinic for dialysis, though, they will often be treated.[53] Some British physicians justify their deception with the half-truth that everyone over fifty-five is "a bit crumbly," but others admit to some deception.[54] Sensing the unacceptability of excluding patients on nonmedical grounds, these physicians disguise their use of an age criterion. Such deception is objectionable in the eyes of many.[55] British physicians are hardly unique in this respect—they are merely the most publicized case. The problem is more general to contemporary medicine.[56]

Many physicians around the world enunciate specific reasons why an age criterion is morally unacceptable. The justifications of the criterion just elaborated, for instance, may be unconvincing—largely for person oriented reasons. Consider first the productivity oriented justifications. Excluding the elderly will indeed ensure a better return on the investment of health care resources, but it may in the process demean people—as if the only concern is to get the most life-years out of a group of machines.[57] An age criterion is admittedly convenient as well. It is objective, but so are many characteristics of persons. The objectivity of a selection criterion does not necessarily make it appropriate. An age criterion is also convenient in that the elderly may well be the weakest and easiest to exclude from treatment; but some find this reason for special care, not less care.[58] Proponents cite the disproportionate cost savings that may result from employing an age criterion, but disproportionate spending on an age group is not necessarily a reason for cutbacks if legitimate needs vary by age groups. The appropriateness of spending educational dollars disproportionately on children may be a parallel.[59]

Person oriented justifications may also be questioned. For instance, the need to accept death when it cannot be avoided can be seen as a good reason to adopt a medical-benefit criterion. However, it is not necessarily relevant just because a person is elderly, for that person may have decades left to live if treated. On the other hand, the difference between an age criterion and selection by race or sex may be simply acknowledged without saying anything one way or another about the justification of an age criterion. The evil of racism and sexism, though, does seem related to more than the fact that only certain groups in society are subject to it: the evil also involves disadvantaging people for illegitimate reasons. In this respect, ageism may need to be guarded against as fastidiously as racism and sexism, particularly when the victims are already in the vulnerable condition of being sick.[60]

The three remaining justifications for excluding the oldest patients from treatment focus upon equal opportunity, life span, and prudence.

EQUAL OPPORTUNITY

An equal-opportunity justification defends giving people an equal opportunity to live long, thereby maximizing the life-years saved. That life-years rather than lives (persons) are valued, however, is highly controversial. In the eyes of many, persons are more than sums of life-years that are accumulated like property.[61] They are entities of equal value who must be treated as such.[62] Drawing an insight from the legal arena, some note that murderers are not generally punished less for killing sixty-five-year-olds than for killing twenty-five-year olds.[63] A life is equally precious at any age. Although it is indeed better to preserve someone's life for a longer rather than a shorter time, such preservation is arguably a different matter from preserving one person's life for a long time at the price of denying any chance of living to another.[64]

An age criterion seeking a maximum savings in life-years would also have the curious effect of saving fewer lives in certain cases. (The assumption here is that an expected minimum length of benefit—for example, a set number of months, as explained in chapter 10—would be required before a patient was treated.) When long-term, reusable resources like dialysis and intensive care are in view, an age criterion would save fewer people for a longer time rather than more people of various ages. The latter would, on average, reach old age and death sooner than the former, thereby freeing up the resources sooner to save more lives. In other words, the benefits of scarce resources would be confined to a few young rather than distributed to many of various ages.

Two problems unrelated to maximizing life-years are also involved in attempting, by means of an age criterion, to equalize the opportunity people have to live a long life. Compare, first of all, two women, one of whom is a year older but has recently spent longer than a year in a coma. Should the younger woman really be saved over the older comatose woman on the grounds that the younger has had less opportunity to experience life? It would appear, rather, that the younger is the one who has experienced more. But if this is admitted, then a problematically large number of imprecise qualitative considerations need to be included in any assessment of who has had the least opportunity to experience life. One supporter of this approach admits that such assessments would be "an overwhelmingly complicated task," calling it "procedurally and administratively a nightmare."[65] Perhaps other factors, such as one's socioeconomic or spiritual condition, have much more to do with one's lifetime experience of well-being than does age. Age provides too rough an approximation of lifetime well-being (or present physical health for that matter) to be used when something as important as life is at stake.[66]

The other problem related to equalizing opportunity to live long concerns the past access of patients to resources. Perhaps a younger person has already received a great deal of medical care, while an older person has received little. It may not be accurate to say that the younger person should be saved because she or he has not been given as great an opportunity to live as the older person. It would appear that the opposite is the case.[67]

LIFE SPAN

No more attractive is the variation of an equal-opportunity justification that limits lifesaving care to those who have not yet reached their natural life span. The very notion of a normative life span is debatable.[68] Even granting a theoretical biological limit to the human life span, the actual life span has grown through the years as life-extending care for the elderly has improved. An age criterion of the sort envisioned here would hinder medicine from extending even good-quality years at the end of life.

Further, such an age criterion demeans people who live beyond the natural life span. One supporter candidly admits this problem, given the world as it presently is.[69] But the problem is intrinsic to the justification. The justification's supporters assume that life-extending care beyond the natural life span is not warranted because everything of significance by that time has been "accomplished" and "achieved."[70] An implicit productivity orientation is revealed here: what matters is what one succeeds in doing. The meaning of life, however, is arguably as much a matter of being as of doing—it consists as much of relating to others as of completing tasks. Also, life goals are repeatedly altered to reflect different values at different ages.[71] To suggest that people at a later stage of life usually have no goals left is to assume wrongly that the (often productivity oriented) life goals of earlier years are the last word.

While the productivity bias of this justification is not generally perceived by supporters, its quality-of-life orientation is readily acknowledged. In fact, the justification may in the end really support a quality-of-life criterion rather than an age criterion. One supporter admits that an age criterion to exclude elderly patients would not be warranted unless their quality of life was low.[72] Whether a quality-of-life or age criterion is in view, the application of the criterion in practice is problematic. Assessing another person's quality of life accurately is no easier than determining if people have essentially completed their life goals—that is, without relying on patients' own statements. There is little reason to assume that all elderly persons will value their continued life less than younger persons will value their own.[73] Moreover, neither group is likely to be forthright about the degree to which they no longer value their lives when their very lives are at stake. The alternative, of course, is to withhold resources only from those who voluntarily forgo treatment—but that is to impose neither an age nor a quality-of-life criterion.

PRUDENCE

Is it truly prudent to distribute health care resources throughout life so that only certain resources are available at each stage of life? If the concern is to make more personal care services available to the elderly, an age criterion for acute care is not necessary. All that is needed is to place greater priority on personal care services when macroallocation decisions are being made. If an age criterion does have any warrant on prudential grounds, the comparing of individuals in order to favor the younger is not thereby sanctioned. Only the exclusion of entire age groups from consideration for a scarce resource is justified; but even this idea is open to question because of its idealism and harmfulness.

Ideally the proposal looks good, but even proponents admit the impropriety of introducing it in one health care setting and not in another.[74] They also admit that it may be politically unacceptable in any setting.[75] The potential strength of the proposal lies in its envisioning of the resource problem as distributing resources throughout an individual's lifetime. However, politically the issue is perceived in terms of which groups will gain greatest access to the most resources. Moreover, were the proposal applied throughout an entire nation such as the United States, injustices in the system could cause the application of an age criterion to make things worse.[76] These disadvantages are so compelling that one theoretical supporter of age rationing frankly concludes, "This is in no way a recommendation for the introduction of such practices in our present world."[77]

Apart from such concerns, however, an age criterion of the sort envisioned could prove harmful in its own right. Though not as thoroughly discriminatory as racism or sexism, it *is* subtly discriminatory. It assumes that all persons move through all age categories, but many people are born with congenital, genetic, or environmental conditions that ensure they will not live as long as most.[78] The age criterion in view here is seemingly discriminatory on its face, too, in that it would put elderly persons who had never required health care but were now being denied needed lifesaving treatment at odds with younger persons who may or may not have used other medical resources in addition to the scarce lifesaving treatment now available to them. The proposal would also impose constraints on liberty and welfare during the elderly stage of life that would probably be experienced as unbearably harsh by some, even if they were in fact objectively prudent.[79] In a sense the scheme is very paternalistic in that it adopts one understanding of what prudence entails and imposes it upon all. No personal discretion is allowed regarding whether or not to pursue lifesaving therapies in later stages of life.

At the same time a serious injustice would seem to be done in the first generation of the proposal's adoption. The elderly would be denied lifesaving resources without having previously received the special benefits accorded younger generations in order to justify denial of these resources in old age. Moreover, in their youth they would have paid for lifesaving resources for the elderly, only to find that when they become old the youth would not provide such resources for them.[80] It would hardly be prudent for them to support such a system. Some members of this generation of elderly would be forced to give up their lives for the good of all generations—a classic utilitarian form of injustice. To compensate them fairly during a transitional period would seem to require shifting resources that belong elsewhere, thereby creating new injustices. The problem is not merely a theoretical one. When Social Security legislation was first passed, the idea of giving the then-current generation of elderly less income support than future generations was soundly rejected—even though the contemporary elderly had not paid into the system from which they would be receiving.[81] A similar problem would occur every time a new lifesaving technology is introduced. The current elderly would be given no access to it—though the justification of this exclusion apparently requires that they previously have had priority access to it.[82] In the end, the prudential proposal assumes a level of stability in the health care system over a person's (actually, every person's) lifetime that is unrealistic.[83]

The approach may be still less attractive if it entails active (even if voluntary) euthanasia for the elderly. The specter of doctors, not to mention society in general, encouraging people to die so that health care resources can be saved is a potentially ominous one.[84] For euthanasia decisions to be truly voluntary, proponents admit, some of the savings generated when many older persons choose to be killed would have to be made available to provide decent health care for the elderly who choose not to be killed.[85] However, in that case the approach becomes self-defeating, since fewer and fewer patients would opt to die if they still had decent health care available. In fact, it is far from obvious that most people would opt for death over illness, even if supportive services were limited.[86]

OTHER JUSTIFICATIONS

The remaining justifications for an age criterion noted earlier in the chapter concern two forms of the criterion that do not exclude the elderly. One form would select patients from different age groups with different frequencies. Actually, the few who consider this approach admit that it is unworkable. For example, not many would agree on exactly which age groups should be preferred by how much over other age groups.[87]

The other form of the criterion, also viewed with suspicion by some, is that which has been used to exclude children from dialysis. At the same time it was being advocated with regard to dialysis in the United States, physicians in Italy were reporting that children on dialysis were doing as well as adults.[88] Even if children's lack of self-discipline had made it difficult for most to adhere to the treatment requirements, a medical-benefit criterion would have been sufficient to exclude them. As for the arrested development of children undergoing dialysis, this is always a tragedy—but arguably not nearly as tragic as leaving them to die.[89] Perhaps the people who would gain most from such a use of the criterion are not the patients but the rest of society, who would not have to bear the discomfort of seeing such children. This is a poor rationale, though, for denying life itself to these children. The children (or the guardians acting in their behalf) are the proper ones to make quality-of-life judgments, not society at large (see chapter 14 on a quality-of-benefit criterion).[90]

Implicit in the foregoing responses to possible justifications for an age criterion—and going beyond them—are two basic critiques. One has to do with values and the other concerns the matter of rights.

VALUES

An age criterion in most of its forms, first of all, reflects certain non-medical values.[91] Among these, the value of youth is prominent. In the

United States, for example, such a high view is placed upon youth that
it affects the practice of medicine generally.[92] Research indicates that the
older patients are, the less likely they are to be treated—even resuscitated—under the same medical circumstances.[93] So it is not surprising
to learn that some people originally supported funding dialysis for all
because it looked as if primarily young adults would be the beneficiaries.[94] No more surprising is the enthusiasm for allocating health care
resources generally on the basis of maximizing the quality-adjusted life-
years to be saved—an approach necessarily biased toward funding treatments that are beneficial mainly to the young.[95]

Youthfulness is attractive for various reasons, but especially for the
productivity that normally accompanies it. Economic productivity is
highly prized in many countries—so much so that those like the elderly,
who in many cases are less economically productive, are stereotyped
and looked down upon.[96] Such devaluation translates directly into reduced medical care generally from the medical profession.[97] It also undergirds an age criterion for patient selection that is largely a form of
social-value criterion (see chapter 11).[98]

The limited value placed on the elderly, and their corresponding limited access to certain lifesaving medical resources, is ultimately the product of various cultural and religious values.[99] This point becomes clearer
when the common view taken of the elderly in a country like the United
States is contrasted with that characteristic of, say, the Akamba people
of Kenya (though Western influences are now altering the Akamba view
somewhat). According to the Akamba, persons are much more than
economic beings. A poor person in old age deserves as much respect as
a rich or otherwise socially important person. In fact, old age calls forth
a unique veneration.[100] (An elaboration of the status of the Akamba
elderly may be found in the notes.)[101]

The high level of respect accorded older people in Akamba society is
intimately bound up with that culture's view of the relationship of the
individual and the community. Whereas the utilitarian view common in
the United States conceives of the social good atomistically in terms of
individual (mainly job-related) contributions summed over the breadth
of society, the Akamba view presupposes a social network of interper-
sonal relations within which one becomes more and more an essential
part the older one becomes. The more personally interwoven a person
becomes with others through time, the greater the damage done to the
social fabric when that person is torn away by death. This extended-

kinship social system commands a sort of spiritual loyalty and is cere-
monially celebrated in various practices and rituals.[102]

A different set of cultural values surrounding old age leads many
Akamba to make decisions about age-related resource allocation that
are very different from those generally supported in the United States.
As part of the Kenyan interviews (see chapter 2) I asked Akamba medical personnel whether an older or a younger man should be saved when
there are resources enough to save one only. Faced with such a dilemma,
many Akamba argue that the older man should be saved because he,
not the young man, "has more responsibilities" and "is a father to many
people."[103] The latter expression, though often literally true in the po-
lygamous Akamba society, here evokes a broader thought. The older
man is a leader, a wise counselor, and an inspiring figure worthy of
respect within his community.

There are viable alternatives, then, to the economic, individualistic,
youth-oriented outlook adopted by many in countries such as the United
States. Other countries, such as Sweden, could also be cited as examples
of places where great respect for the elderly leads to age criteria (when
they exist at all) that are much less restrictive than those in the United
States.[104] Opponents of an age criterion employ such observations to
argue that alternative attitudes toward the elderly are possible.

In fact, these opponents argue further that for a variety of reasons
any society should resist the temptation to discard its elderly. The first
reason is that if economic productivity is important, then the elderly are
more deserving of reward than anyone for their lifetime of contribution.[105] Second, their crowning lifetime achievements may still be before
them.[106] Third, the elderly are important to society for reasons other
than their economic productivity. They often have wisdom to share,
patient love to bestow, and various (though perhaps unspectacular) services to provide.[107] Even claims about their diminished mental abilities
have been challenged by recent studies.[108] Should they be penalized simply because their society overlooks, perhaps inadvertently, the true value
of their contribution? But the very attempt to justify the continued existence of the elderly in terms of their social contributions may itself be
misplaced. People have different *worths* in a social sense, but many see
their worth as persons as intrinsic to their personhood (this subject is
discussed further in chapter 19).[109] From this perspective, the proposal
to engineer such intrinsic valuing out of society (by systematically cul-
tivating in people a sense of obligation to die when they are first thought
to be terminally ill)[110] is quite distressing.

RIGHTS

The notion of intrinsic worth is really foundational to the second overall critique of an age criterion mentioned earlier: An age criterion may be weak not only because of the mistaken values that undergird it but also because it is a direct violation of basic human rights. A person's life, it can be argued, should be preserved simply because it is a human life. From this perspective, the age attached to that life would be irrelevant.[111] Otherwise one's right to life would diminish with every day that one lives. Basic human rights, however, are not so variable. They are attached to personhood per se. A year of life at any stage of life can be equally precious.[112] It has been suggested that the elderly have a right to humane termination procedures rather than a right to continue living.[113] Such a point of view, though, appears to be more concerned about conserving society's resources than it is about how persons themselves are treated.

Since an age criterion is often applied by excluding all patients above a certain age,[114] it also can be seen as violating basic rights in discriminating between patients when there is no just basis for doing so. Elderly patients do not fare well with certain treatments. Yet, a particular elderly person may be in better physical condition to undergo treatment than a younger person.[115] Certain elderly patients also have a strength of mind and heart that make them better candidates for treatment than some half their age.[116] Although some may have a low quality of life, many others do not.[117] Part of the problem involves the method of assessing quality of life (see chapter 14). Studies indicate that physicians and elderly patients differ markedly in their assessment of these patients' quality of life, in part because "objective" indicators of quality and subjective experience of quality sometimes differ so significantly.[118] In fact, some caregivers assume a diminished quality of life in the elderly even in instances in which objective indicators suggest otherwise.[119] Needless to say, then, finding a magic cutoff age beyond which people do not warrant receiving lifesaving treatment because of their age is necessarily problematic.[120] Any such cutoff is arbitrary and unfair.[121]

The terminology of "rights," however, may be misleading in cases where the resources necessary to honor fully those rights do not exist or have not been made available. Under such circumstances the language of equal *respect* may be more precise (especially in the context of equal needs). In these terms, an age criterion may be very disrespectful of the elderly as persons. Not only are they excluded from treatment as a class, but individual differences that would make some better candidates for treatment than others are not recognized.[122] In the process of showing such disrespect to an entire group of people, society itself can become brutalized. Even under schemes that advocate not age criteria per se but some other goal, such as distributing limited resources prudently throughout people's lifetimes, an important symbol may be at stake. When the elderly are left to die with no access to lifesaving treatments that are available to others, people actually practice abandoning the elderly and in that sense exclude them from communal care. Although philosophical justifications for such action might be offered, the damage to society's sense of responsibility for all of its members would be done.[123] What is arguably needed instead in some societies such as the United States is a distinct welcoming back of the elderly as full members of the community.[124]

These criticisms may lose some of their force when the resources in view are not at least potentially lifesaving. Where life is at stake, one can argue that the same fundamental human need for and thus rightful claim on available resources comes into play.[125] In fact, should the very young or the elderly have some difficulty making use of needed resources, then need itself can be seen to dictate that special efforts be made to overcome these difficulties (especially if the need is in some measure society's fault).[126] Special need—if it can be compensated for—is hardly a basis for offering less care. So, for instance, in cases in which the elderly have found it difficult to withstand the immunosuppressive regimen employed with kidney transplants, a frequent response has been to try different immunosuppressive regimens on them until workable treatments have been found, rather than simply to exclude them from consideration.[127]

Possible Common Ground

The foregoing discussion might imply an uncrossable chasm between those who are for and those who are against an age criterion. Such a gap may indeed exist if an age criterion is espoused on social-value grounds. However, many of those who favor an age criterion do so for medical reasons, in the belief that critical resources should not be wasted if the elderly (or the very young) cannot benefit from them. Opponents of an age criterion share this concern.

The challenge, then, is to find a way to pursue this concern that is so widely acknowledged. Perhaps the best way is to be careful about how we use language and identify as medical only those matters and criteria that are in fact medical. As noted earlier, age per se is not a medically relevant factor in that medical problems which make one elderly person a bad candidate may not affect another. Even a short life expectancy for any given elderly person cannot be taken for granted.[128] For this reason age is probably best not referred to as a medical criterion or supported as a criterion on those grounds.[129] The medical liabilities commonly associated with old age are themselves the potential reasons for exclusion—not age itself. Many elderly, for example, are so physically weakened that they make poor candidates for organ transplantation or intensive care; but others bear up fairly well in these circumstances.[130] In fact, studies show that a considerable number of elderly do well even with dialysis, from which they are so often excluded.[131]

Accordingly, age is best not identified as a separate patient selection criterion at all. Rather, its most widely acceptable role is probably as one of many "symptoms" to be looked for by the physician making the medical assessment required by a medical-benefit criterion. Like any observed symptom, age can be an indicator of a possible medical problem. It may serve as a tool the physician uses in applying a medical criterion, not as a criterion in its own right. From this perspective it is inappropriate to single out age during a discussion of selection criteria in a way that implies it is more than just one among many symptoms considered in the medical assessment. It is more a rule of thumb for this assessment than for patient selection in general.[132]

Even in such a restricted role, age considerations must be carefully handled to ensure that they are not accorded more influence than is warranted medically. It is easy to underestimate the ability of some elderly to endure treatment when life is at stake; and technological developments repeatedly make treatments all the more endurable.[133] In the end, the only way to be assured of how the elderly will bear up under a given treatment may be to treat them in large numbers, as was done during the early days of dialysis in Italy.[134] Whenever possible, a therapeutic trial can be employed to facilitate individualized assessments.

An Illustrative Case

As Fred Horn thought ahead to the Heart Transplant Patient Selection Committee meeting scheduled later that morning, he was reminded of some of the patient selection decisions he had been involved in during the early days of kidney dialysis. Once medical factors like tissue and blood typing had been accounted for, he mused, the two types of decision were rather similar. In fact, he had heard talk that patients might again be excluded from dialysis on the basis of old age, even as the present committee sometimes barred older patients from heart transplants.

Fred's mind wandered to a particularly disturbing decision he had been a part of, one in which the age of a potential dialysis patient was very much in question. He could remember the committee chairperson, Paul Sims, picking up the first of five applications from patients who were hoping to be given the opportunity to take the place of a patient who had just elected to discontinue dialysis. . . .

"Robert Algers," Mr. Sims announced. "He's a fifty-three-year-old lawyer with three grown children. His wife is alive and he's still married to her. He's a member of the Rotary Club and the Elks, and a former scoutmaster."

"From the practical point of view," said Dr. Crane, "he would be a good candidate. He's intelligent and educated and understands what's involved in dialysis."

"I think he's definitely the sort of person we want to help," said Mrs. Langford. "He's a real asset to the community."

"Wait a minute," said Mr. Sims. "I don't think fifty-three is old—I'd better not, because I'm fifty-two myself. Still, his children are grown, he's led a good life. I'm not sure I wouldn't give the edge to some younger fellow."

"I agree," nodded Mr. Brewster. "His contributions to the community are history. Let's save someone who can remain active for a long time. Besides, his age might hamper the effectiveness of his treatment. . . ."

Fred recalled how hard the selection decision had been on that occasion. He knew that with fifty-four-year-old Bill Dever among those to be considered later that morning for a heart transplant, the present decision would not likely be any easier.[135]

This disagreement over the merits of selecting the "aging" Mr. Algers is indicative of current disputes over the place of an age criterion in patient selection—whether involving heart transplants, dialysis, or other resources. The contributions for which Algers is appreciated in the community are largely in the past, and others are taking over many of his responsibilities. Such considerations in support of an age criterion appeal to standards of social value, over which there is little agreement. Other supporting arguments here appeal to a more egalitarian perspective (equality of opportunity) that is itself controversial even among egalitarians. The best hope for a broadly supported inclusion of age-related considerations, as we have seen, lies in the medical arena.[136]

But the common form in which the medical justification arises in this case is misleading. It is not the man's age that might hamper his treatment, as implied here; rather, it is the kind of physical limitations to which a man of fifty-three or fifty-four is prone. The difference is important. Were age per se a selection criterion, then a younger candidate could rightfully be preferred on the spot. If age is only a symptom, though, then the man's age should serve only as a reminder that a careful medical assessment is needed. If exclusion turns out to be medically warranted, then it should be justified solely upon medical grounds, without appeal to considerations of age.

CHAPTER EIGHT

Psychological Ability

The issue of psychological ability is complex. It may involve the intellectual and emotional capacity to cope with treatment or with life in general (in the latter context it raises more a social than a medical consideration);[1] it may involve the willingness to cooperate with treatment (see chapter 15 regarding the relevance of life style choices). In fact, the criterion may encompass not only mental capabilities of the patient that are more or less fixed, but also capabilities whose impairment may be removed by the very treatment under consideration.

In light of the potentially close relationship between the use of this criterion and the ability of treatment to fulfill its purpose, it is perhaps not surprising that 97 percent of the medical directors in my U.S. study (see chapter 2) indicate that they favor the criterion. On average, though, they rate it only somewhat important (mean score 3.2 out of 5). Studies done during the days before dialysis was federally funded have also documented extensive support in the United States for such considerations as intelligence and willingness to cooperate with treatment.[2] Another area of U.S. medicine in which use of a psychological-ability criterion has been widely acknowledged is organ (for example, heart and kidney) transplantation.[3] Even more common treatments for acute illnesses (including intensive care) are commonly governed by a psychological-ability criterion, according to surveys of U.S. physicians.[4] International studies too have identified support for the criterion.[5] It is particularly prominent internationally in decisions concerning who will receive limited dialysis resources.[6]

Justifications

Special reasons for employing a psychological-ability criterion may apply when a resource is experimental (see chapter 18), but many reasons for including it as a part of normal patient selection procedure may also be advanced. Sometimes it is listed, without explanation, as if it were a criterion separate from a medical criterion.[7] However, where justifications are made more explicit, they commonly involve considerations of medical benefit. Patients who are relatively unstable psychologically are judged unlikely to be able to benefit from treatment. As suggested in chapter 10, such considerations may be supported from either a person oriented or a productivity oriented perspective.

Psychological instability may inhibit a patient's ability to benefit from treatment in numerous ways. For instance, it may undermine the patient's motivation to live and thus to cooperate with any treatment.[8] Alternatively, it may render the patient unwilling or unable to follow medical instructions.[9] The problem may also be specifically related to the treatment under consideration. Perhaps the patient does not have the intellectual ability or emotional fortitude to cope with the demands of a particular treatment (as assessed, ideally, following a therapeutic trial).[10] The treatment itself (for example, necessary drugs following organ transplantation) may engender potentially debilitating depressive or psychotic disorders.[11]

The implications of disregarding such considerations are serious. Either the treatment may end up not working or the patient may end up committing suicide while being treated. Some treatments, such as dialysis, are so demanding that the suicide rates of patients undergoing the treatment may be as much as one hundred or more times that of the general population.[12] When a treatment fails or the patient commits suicide, not only is the scarce resource wasted but another patient perhaps more stable psychologically is left to die untreated.[13]

Justifications other than strict medical benefit may also be given for a psychological-ability criterion. For instance, relative likelihood of medical benefit may be invoked (see the justifications in chapter 12). The greater the psychological inability of patients, the lower the priority they may be given on the grounds that they are less likely than others to benefit medically from treatment.[14] On the other hand, medical considerations may be masking another, rarely explicit issue: psychologically unstable persons are arguably among those of least value (and perhaps greatest danger) to society. Whether they are in fact or not, people often view them as such. Because of their special needs, caring for them entails unusually great expenditures of money and effort as well. They would appear to be prime examples of the sort of persons who would be most readily excluded from selection according to a social-value criterion (see chapter 3).

Weaknesses

Many of the objections to a psychological-ability criterion reflect neither a person oriented nor productivity oriented outlook, but rather address the difficult of applying the criterion in practice. Part of the problem has to do with the imprecision of psychological testing, which may prove helpful in revealing a patient's present condition but is less accurate in predicting how patients will respond to future stresses.[15] The history of dialysis, for example, is filled with the frustrating experiences of those who attempted in vain to employ the criterion effectively.[16]

Hard data confirming that undesirable psychological characteristics lead to a patient's inability to comply with and therefore benefit from treatment are scarce. A court of law has ruled that even when employment is at issue, psychological tests cannot rightly be used to exclude certain individuals if only psychological theory rather than conclusive data indicates that they will perform poorly.[17] The stakes are even higher when life is at stake.[18]

Using psychological assessments to predict accurately a patient's ability to comply with and thereby benefit from treatment is problematic for two basic reasons. One is that it is often uncertain exactly what stresses a patient will have to endure with a particular treatment.[19] Some stresses may be anticipated, but others vary from case to case. Second, even when certain stresses can be anticipated, it often is not clear what psychological characteristics will render a patient unable to cope.[20] The human ability to cope with adversity has persistently defied exhaustive analysis.[21] Many a patient has responded well to treatment despite psychological assessments that predicted the contrary.[22]

When insulin first became available for treatment of diabetes mellitus, its supply was limited, and there was great pressure to formulate a rational way of determining whom to treat and whom not to treat. The theory that sufficient strength of character is needed to maintain the treatment regimen provided just such a way. However, what might have been anticipated at that time has since been demonstrated: most people whose lives depend on taking insulin and reducing sugar consumption can do so. The insulin experience suggests that a psychological-ability criterion can be illegitimately used to provide a seemingly reasoned basis for making patient selection decisions.[23]

Similarly, many of the studies describing the often severe psychological stress of patients undergoing treatments such as dialysis do not necessarily support the legitimacy of a psychological-ability criterion. To be relevant, the stress must stem from patients' psychological inability and be consistently predictable. As it is, the difficulties these studies cite are in some cases due more to the quality of care the patients received than to their psychological problems.[24] Many of the studies themselves acknowledge their inconclusiveness in that they provide no foolproof predictors of future treatment-related psychological trauma.[25]

Several other practical difficulties also undermine the validity of a psychological-ability criterion. One is that any disorder involved may itself be the source of a patient's psychological problems. If treatment is provided, the problems may disappear. This scenario is especially characteristic of kidney failure because the psychological impairment accompanying uremia can generally be relieved through dialysis.[26] Psychological problems may instead be the result of stress that can be relieved through counseling on the illness involved and the lifesaving potential of the treatment.[27] Second, it is difficult in such cases to establish what counts as instability. An unemotional response to something like kidney failure and the resulting life prospects is likely abnormal.[28] Yet normal reactions to a diagnosis of kidney failure—denial, depression, and so forth—may also be indicators of instability.[29]

A last practical difficulty remains. The application of certain common indicators of psychological inability to some groups of people is simply inappropriate. For instance, job instability or antisocial behavior may exclude patients from such treatments as heart transplantation.[30] Yet these indicators may be inaccurate in the case of handicapped persons. If patients are handicapped, these "problems" may be more a reflection of the difficulties people have relating to the handicapped than indicators that handicapped persons are psychologically unstable.[31] Similarly, there is a danger that unfounded judgments of psychological instability may be made on the dubious basis that a patient has seen a psychiatrist in the past or has a personality that strikes the evaluator as disagreeable.[32]

The remaining objections to a psychological-ability criterion are largely person oriented and have to do with the nature of the criterion itself. For instance, some of the central justifications for it are open to serious question. Though some argue for the criterion on the basis of its widespread support, such support may reflect one of its most dubious aspects. The psychologically unstable are among those least able to protect their own interests. Accordingly, they are among the most vulnerable when some must be excluded from treatment.[33] Were those selecting patients to select without knowing if they themselves were among the psychologically unstable in society's eyes, they might be much less quick to deny treatment based upon psychological ability.[34]

The alleged appropriateness of denying treatment to uncooperative patients is also open to question. General uncooperativeness does not always entail an unwillingness to cooperate with medical treatment; and uncooperativeness in lesser medical matters does not necessarily indicate that a patient will not cooperate when life itself is at stake.[35] In light of the high stakes involved, unappreciative and somewhat uncooperative patients should arguably be tolerated as long as they meet the require- ment of the willingness criterion (see chapter 15).[36] In some settings, the United States, for example, this caveat already has the support of law.

Implicit in the foregoing discussion is potentially one of the weakest dimensions of a psychological-ability criterion. The criterion is often a cover for at least five other, more questionable rationales, one of which is convenience. The presence of unruly, noncompliant patients may make the treatment of other patients more difficult. Moreover, the medical staff may prefer not to have to expend the greater effort necessary to care for patients whose psychological stability is impaired.[37] Accordingly, one British study shows some patients being excluded from dialysis be- cause they speak no English or are "mentally subnormal."[38] The study has provoked outraged responses from those who argue that the basis for such exclusions is mere convenience rather than the prospects of benefiting the patient medically.[39]

A second, slightly different perspective on a psychological-ability cri- terion is that it is more a cover for personal bias than a legitimate se- lection criterion. The concern here is that physicians' judgments about the coping abilities and cooperativeness of patients is much more a sub- jective matter than the physiological assessments they engage in.[40] Like everyone else, physicians find that they can work best with those most like them.[41] In fact, to some all forms of psychological impairment may be suspect, particularly in the ways that they appear to limit the patient's quality of life.[42] These considerations at least suggest the importance of involving specialists in making the psychological assessments involved in employing a psychological-ability criterion. However, even such special- ists are subject to the sorts of personal bias noted above, as evidenced by the degree to which assessments of the same patient can vary.[43]

A third rationale that may be hidden in a psychological-ability crite- rion is the pursuit of social value. In other words, the criterion can provide a means of excluding socially undesirable persons in a way that is not as obvious as it is with the problematic social-value criterion (see chapter 11).[44] Persons who are limited in their abilities to interact with others, perhaps due to some social deviancy or handicap, are particularly vulnerable to such exclusion.[45] A psychological-ability criterion appears to have often functioned in this way during the years of dialysis scarcity before federal funding, with the Swedish Hospital in Seattle being the most publicized example.[46] There, when social assessments of candidates were ended in favor of strictly medical selection criteria, psychological testing was also ended.[47]

Objections to this use of a psychological-ability criterion include most of the objections raised against a social-value criterion, such as the way mentally and otherwise handicapped individuals are unfairly subjected to the ultimate discrimination—the denial of life itself.[48] Ironically, precisely on social grounds a psychological-ability criterion may not be as warranted as at first appears, for history is replete with evidence that very unstable persons have made major social contributions. Additional concern may be voiced regarding the way that social considerations are smuggled in under the "medical" guise of psychological stability. Even strong critics, though, may grant exceptions when it can be shown that patients' social-psychological problems severely reduce their ability to benefit medically from treatment.[49]

Two of the five hidden rationales for a psychological-ability criterion remain. The fourth rationale concerns the patient's support system. Psychologically unstable patients are particularly dependent upon the support of others if they are to do well during treatment. However, denying some people any chance at life because others are not providing sufficient support raises serious questions of fairness, as discussed later in relation to a supportive-environment criterion (see chapter 9).[50] Fifth, the rationale behind a psychological-ability criterion may really be the likelihood of medical benefit (see chapter 12). The particularly serious problems with the psychological version of a likelihood criterion include the difficulty of measuring, predicting, and ranking psychological conditions precisely.[51] These problems are compounded by issues of fairness where statistical likelihoods are inaccurately applied to certain individuals.[52]

For all of the reasons noted above in opposition to a psychological-ability criterion, it might be argued that psychological problems should be corrected or compensated for, not used as a basis for preventing patients from receiving scarce lifesaving resources. Occasionally psychological instability in certain candidates may be treatable prior to or in conjunction with the lifesaving treatment being sought.[53] In other cases special treatment programs or provisions within programs can be established to provide the special care necessary to enable the lifesaving treatment to be effective.[54] Psychological assessments would then generally serve to identify patients needing special care rather than be used as a means of identifying patients to exclude from treatment.[55]

Possible Common Ground

The clearest and broadest support for a psychological-ability criterion appears to be restricted to those cases where the inability is so great that the patient in all probability will not benefit medically from treatment.[56] Experience with dialysis and heart transplantation in particular has shown that there are such cases and that it is possible to distinguish them from more objectionable applications of a psychological-ability criterion.[57] Strictly speaking, though, these acceptable cases are already identifiable by means of a medical-benefit criterion (see chapter 10) and do not require a separate psychological-ability criterion. Invoking this latter criterion separately mistakenly implies that these cases involve considerations other than medical benefit. One should consider psychological ability as merely one of several factors that are to be assessed in determining whether or not a patient meets the medical-benefit criterion.

Even understood in this limited way, psychological considerations would rarely prove definitive in excluding patients from lifesaving treatment. Seldom are psychological problems so severe and hopeless that they cannot be treated in a way that renders a lifesaving treatment workable.[58] The lifesaving treatment itself, as in the case of dialysis, may alleviate the problems. Moreover, in light of the life-or-death nature of the patient selection decision, the burden of proof should probably fall on those who would exclude a candidate from further consideration.[59] Questionable cases probably should not be excluded. One way of protecting against an overuse of psychological considerations is to apply them no more stringently than they would be if the lifesaving resource in question were unlimited in supply.[60] Under such circumstances, medical benefit would be the decisive consideration.

A few additional guidelines may help to insure that the psychological dimension of a medical-benefit criterion is implemented properly. Because technology is constantly changing, the relevance of individual psychological factors must regularly be evaluated. For instance, as a demanding treatment regimen is improved and becomes less demanding, a patient's capacity to cope with such stress becomes less relevant.[61]

Other guidelines have to do with questionable cases. When there is reasonable doubt that a patient will be able to benefit medically from lifesaving treatment, it may be possible for the patient to undergo an experience similar to the treatment needed in order to test the patient's ability to cope with it. Dialysis candidates, for example, are often placed on the strict diet required of dialysis patients months before commencing dialysis. Whether or not they can understand and handle the discipline can sometimes thereby be ascertained (while at the same time kidney deterioration is perhaps being limited and dialysis postponed).[62] Where substantial doubt remains and the resource in view is reusable (for example, a dialysis machine or intensive care space as opposed to a transplantable organ), a patient can then undergo a trial period of treatment both to test the patient's ability to cope with it and to determine if the patient is willing to continue treatment.[63]

Outside of those cases in which psychological instability is so great that it is taken into account by a medical-benefit criterion, a psychological-ability criterion is not likely to receive widespread support. Political and economic forces, as in the early days of insulin discussed earlier, may in fact create irresistible pressures to adopt some selection criterion such as psychological ability when a medical-benefit criterion is insufficient. However, such a decision is not likely to be made on widely acceptable ethical grounds, for the various reasons previously noted. There is one possible exception. Psychological ability can be employed as one of several indicators that some patients are more likely to benefit medically from treatment than others. In other words, psychological considerations may play a role in selection decisions as part of a likelihood-of-benefit criterion. Support for that criterion, however, is somewhat controversial (see end of chapter 12). Also, the psychological component of that criterion is particularly problematic, as noted above. Making accurate comparative assessments involving two or more patients is especially difficult.[64] So this method of employing psychological-ability considerations may not in the end be widely supportable. Even if it were, psychological ability would be serving as one factor to be considered in the application of another criterion, not as a criterion valid in its own right.

An Illustrative Case

Oliver Johnson, a fifty-seven-year-old black man, was admitted to Methodist Hospital intensive care unit after suffering seizures. He was found to have high blood pressure and impaired kidney function. Mr. Johnson had worked as a steeplejack until he was thirty-six, when he was dismissed from his job, and since then he had been unemployed. He was on welfare and was partially supported by his wife.

His significant medical history had begun at age fifty-one, when he entered another hospital for six months with a subarachnoid hemorrhage. While the hemorrhage was successfully treated, Mr. Johnson's full mental capability was never restored. His course of treatment was prolonged by congestive heart failure, urinary retention, and arthritis. In addition, he had a history of alcoholism. After recovering from that admission, he had limited his activities to his apartment. He went out only to a local tavern and only with his wife, who was a nurse in a children's psychiatric ward. Three days prior to the present admission Mr. Johnson became lethargic and lost his appetite. Soon thereafter he stopped urinating.

On admission, his seizures were initially controlled with drugs. A psychiatric consultant noted indications of a severe brain disorder. The record indicated that Mr. Johnson "couldn't cope." His first course of peritoneal dialysis was begun and successfully cleared some of the manifestations of uremia. His mental status improved dramatically, and he was able to answer simple questions.

Following Mr. Johnson's dramatic improvement and further evaluation of his condition, an attempt was made to find a hemodialysis program for him. He and a medical resident at the hospital traveled by ambulance to the clinic of a major teaching hospital in the city, where they were told that only ambulatory patients who could carefully follow instructions were considered for their program. At that time Mr. Johnson was able neither to move about on his own nor to demonstrate motivation for hemodialysis.[65]

Although other facilities may or may not take patients like Oliver Johnson (at least for a therapeutic trial), the hospital in the present case would not. The appropriateness of considering psychological ability is thereby brought into question, whether a lifesaving therapy like dialysis is funded for "all" (as in the United States) or it is not (as in many countries throughout the world).

In assessing a specific case such as that of Johnson, it is important to identify the real rationale underlying any appeal to psychological ability. In Johnson's case, the clinic considers his psychological difficulties definitive because they undermine both has ability to move about on his own and his willingness to cooperate with treatment. Both of these rationales are problematic. The mobility problem could conceivably be overcome with help from outside and inside the clinic. The clinic's unwillingness to seek or provide such help subjects Johnson's life to the dubious criteria of environmental support and convenience. At least some effort on the part of the clinic to overcome the mobility problem is warranted, unless the clinic knows of other facilities accessible to Johnson that will accept nonambulatory patients. In the United States today, sufficient nursing, social work, and other resources are generally available to help compensate for the disability of patients such as Oliver Johnson.

The problem of motivation is genuinely medical, in that at least minimal cooperation is required from patients if dialysis is to prove successful. But evidence in this case suggests that the lack of motivation is a product of the medical condition and at least partly correctable by the dialysis itself. This is precisely the sort of case in which a trial period of treatment may well be called for in order to establish whether or not the patient can attain sufficient motivation for the treatment to prove effective. If such motivation is not forthcoming, then it is important to note that the resulting rejection is on the basis of medical benefit, not psychological stability per se. The allowing of psychological ability as a criterion in its own right implies that other factors such as social value or personal preference are being considered.

CHAPTER NINE

Supportive Environment

A supportive-environment criterion basically favors those patients who will have a supportive environment during and following treatment. The criterion may also have a comparative dimension, such that those with the most supportive environment receive the highest priority access to treatment, all other considerations being equal. The environment at issue here includes the care provided by family, friends, and health care personnel[1] and also the facilities and other material resources available to patients.

The well-publicized Baby Jesse case examined at the end of this chapter is only one of a long list of instances in the United States in which a supportive-environment criterion has figured prominently. During the days of scarce dialysis before federal funding, the criterion was frequently employed.[2] One study showed that 64 percent of the dialysis centers made use of it.[3] A patient's immediate family situation was considered so critical that marital status became one of the selection criteria—a situation that persists in current selections of heart transplant recipients.[4] Leading university heart transplant centers including Stanford, Pittsburgh, and Arizona consistently emphasize the importance of at least some support person, if not spouse or relative, who is committed to providing the long-term emotional and physical support that a heart transplant patient needs.[5] In fact, environmental criteria are employed in organ transplantation generally, as well as in selecting some patients for intensive care.[6] In my U.S. study (see chapter 2), 61 percent of the medical directors indicate that a supportive-environment criterion should be considered in selecting patients, though on average the criterion is rated as only slightly important (mean score 2.0 out of 5).

Other countries also employ a supportive-environment criterion in the selection of patients. Usually a general form of the criterion is favored, though occasionally marital status per se is the focal concern.[7] Patients with renal disease being considered for dialysis or a kidney transplant are a case in point. In Singapore, for instance, an evaluation of the renal patient's social environment plays a prominent role.[8] A similar practice is implicit in a study of selection decisions in Great Britain, where a high percentage of renal patients are on home dialysis. British physicians were asked which ten of forty renal patients described to them they would reject if all could not be treated: The nine patients most frequently rejected all evidenced the lack of a supportive environment.[9]

Justifications

Like some criteria already considered, this one may take on special significance in situations where the resource in question is experimental, a topic examined separately in chapter 18. The circumstance presently in view is that in which patients are being selected to receive accepted therapeutic procedures.

A supportive-environment criterion is often justified not on its own terms but rather in terms of some other selection criterion. For example, justifications often appeal to medical benefit (see chapter 10). The lack of a supportive environment is a major contraindication to treatment because without it the treatment will stand little chance of proving medically effective.[10] One study of dialysis patients documents better compliance with crucial features of the dialysis regimen when patients have good social support.[11] A treatment such as a heart transplant may result in even a worse death than no treatment at all if sufficient postoperative care is not available.[12] Families and individuals can be very different in their ability to provide such care.[13] Curiously, even when the issue is broached in these terms, a supportive-environment criterion is generally referred to in a context separate from that in which medical criteria per se are discussed.[14] The implication is that more is involved in this criterion than merely medical considerations.

Medical benefit, though, is not the only form of medical justification that may be given for a supportive-environment criterion. Likelihood of benefit (see chapter 12) may be the appeal. Patients with favorable environments may be selected rather than those with poorer environments because the former have better survivability generally and are more apt to be able to adhere to any medical regimen prescribed.[15] Alternatively, the quality of medical benefit (see chapter 14) may be the real issue. Those with better environments are not only better able to cope with the demands of treatment but also most assured of an acceptable quality of life overall.[16] When the underlying appeal appears to be to a nonmedical criterion, the criterion in view is rarely identified. As explained later, opponents of a supportive-environment criterion suspect that considerations of social value (see chapter 3) come into play, and indeed, those with a poor home environment tend to be those of least value to society.

Justifications of a supportive-environment criterion that are spelled out in detail tend to be productivity oriented. A frequent goal is to achieve the best possible results with the limited resources available.[17] To invest the time and energy of more than one hundred people in a heart transplant operation like that of Baby Jesse seems a tragic waste if the few persons necessary to support the patient after the operation are not available.[18] Familial support enables the patient and family alike to benefit from treatment.[18]

Weaknesses

A supportive-environment criterion is subject to a number of weaknesses, not the least of which are pragmatic. The criterion is very difficult to apply, for several reasons. For instance, there is no agreement as to exactly what environments facilitate effective treatment.[20] Little intensive study has been devoted to pinpointing the relation between a variety of environmental factors and the medical benefit that a patient receives from treatment.[21] One study, in fact, has discovered that certain types of strong families may even be a hindrance to effective treatment because of the high level of stress they experience when a family member is threatened by serious illness.[22] Not surprisingly, then, when environmental criteria are employed they usually claim no more than that unspecified environmental supports are generally necessary for treatment to be effective.[23] Such imprecision is problematic enough when the existence or nonexistence of medical benefit is being established; it is virtually paralyzing when the relative likelihood of various patients benefiting must be accurately assessed.

The vagueness of the link between environmental and medical considerations is troublesome for additional reasons. Although some connection may exist, to overgeneralize it is to exclude certain people from treatment unfairly for reasons that do not apply to them individually. Children from a two-parent home may automatically be considered more suitable candidates for treatment than children from a one-parent home, even though some of the former settings are more unstable and unsupportive than some of the latter.[24] Homes in which one person is a reformed alcoholic may be assumed to be relatively unstable, whereas in reality the opposite may be true.[25] Many individuals who appeared to be poor candidates for treatment according to a supportive-environment criterion have fared quite well with treatment.[26]

If the application of this criterion is erratic in the context of a treatment center selecting patients to receive scarce lifesaving medical resources, it becomes even more so in other, related contexts. Once a referral center decides to employ a supportive-environment criterion, physicians begin to screen out patients whom they judge inappropriate to refer for treatment because of questionable home environments. Such judgments, though, may be even less well founded than the uncertain assessments made by the treatment center.[27]

The criterion also tends to spread to classes of patients for whom resources are not scarce. A case in point is dialysis in Great Britain. Although dialysis is not readily available there to patients over fifty or fifty-five years of age (see chapter 7), it generally is to young adults. However, environmental considerations have become so widely employed in distributing limited resources that a twenty-three-year-old might conceivably be rejected for so tenuous a reason as being an orphan.[28]

Additional weaknesses of a supportive-environment criterion tend to be person oriented. One concern is that the criterion may be a cover for other criteria, social value and quality of benefit being prime examples.[29] An environmental-support criterion can provide a means of screening out those patients whose life circumstances make it more likely that they will be a burden to society and will have to endure a low quality of life. The imprecise relationship between environmental supports and medical outcomes invites this concern, for the poor environment appears to be more central than its exact medical implications.[30] The weaknesses of such social-value and quality-of-benefit considerations are detailed elsewhere (chapters 3 and 14, respectively). Similarly, an environmental-support criterion may be a cover for an ability-to-pay criterion, in that the poor may consistently lack the means to provide certain types of supportive care[31] (the problems attending an ability-to-pay criterion are examined in chapter 16).

Even if other criteria do not explicitly enter into the decision, personal bias is likely to influence assessments of patients' environments. Such influence is attributable in part to the difficulty of obtaining objective data with which to identify clearly inadequate environments—though evaluation instruments are constantly being improved.[32] Further, people show a propensity to consider life styles radically different from their own or those with less intellectual ability to be inferior and relatively unsupportive.[33] In particular, because the living patterns of certain racial and ethnic groups may vary considerably from predominant norms, these groups may be disproportionately excluded from access to scarce life-saving resources.[34]

Another form of unfair discrimination attends a supportive-environment criterion. Persons other than the patient (for example, the parents of a young patient) may be the ones responsible for the patient's poor home environment. It seems unfair to leave some patients to die because of deficiencies in other people or circumstances that are beyond a patient's control.[35] The injustice is perhaps clearest when particular standards of environmental support, such as "sufficient family support," are invoked. Such a requirement discriminates against people without families and those alienated from their families.[36]

Rather than being denied lifesaving treatment, persons with insufficient support arguably should be provided the support they need as part of their treatment.[37] The provision of such support may be categorized as medical when it is a vital part of treating a patient effectively. Even the most demanding needs of patients, including patients who are children, can be met by persons specially available for that purpose.[38] Such special provision is not at all uncommon in health care generally.[39] Another possibility is to find a treatment in which the patient's lack of environmental support is not so critical.[40] Admittedly, additional costs may be incurred by pursuing either of these alternative approaches, but such considerations arguably should not be definitive in a matter of life or death (see chapter 16 on ability to pay).

Possible Common Ground

The only likely consensus over a supportive-environment criterion apparently will involve those cases in which the ability of patients to benefit from treatment hinges upon the supportiveness of their environments. If this is the justification for the criterion, however, then a separate supportive-environment criterion is not needed. A patient's environment should simply be one of a variety of factors assessed in order to determine whether a patient meets the medical-benefit criterion.[41] The implication that more than medical considerations are involved can be avoided if a patient's environment is considered only within the explicit context of determining medical benefit. To a lesser but perhaps acceptable degree, this implication can also be avoided when medical benefit is conceived of in relative rather than absolute terms (see end of chapter 12).

Even as a component of a medical criterion, environment assessment needs to be subject to several guidelines in order to remain broadly acceptable. First, the relationship between various environmental factors and the medical outcome of the treatment in view must have been clearly demonstrated. The lack of such a clear relationship has resulted in certain factors not being considered in the assessing of candidates for organ transplantation.[42] Next, the unique features of any given case must be carefully weighed, for the level of personal support necessary varies significantly from individual to individual. According to one study of transplant recipients, the time and energy required of their families ranged from "a lot" to "a little," with at least 25 percent of the recipients at each end of this spectrum.[43] Finally, if there is doubt about whom to treat—for example, because the relevant difference between candidates for treatment is so minor—the imprecision of the assessments involved here suggests that a patient be neither excluded outright from treatment nor given lower priority on environmental grounds.[44] In fact, patients are probably best not denied treatment on environmental grounds unless they would be so even if the resource in question were not scarce.

An Illustrative Case

Jesse Dean Sepulveda was born with hypoplastic left heart syndrome, a congenital defect that is usually fatal. Neonatal specialists at Huntington Memorial Hospital in Pasadena, California, turned immediately to Loma Linda University Medical Center, which had performed more infant heart transplants than any other facility in the country.

Jesse's parents were soon interviewed by a Loma Linda psychiatrist, and the mother's records, including information she gave to social workers, was examined. The medical center's selection committee unanimously rejected Jesse as a candidate for a heart transplant.

Although the reasons for the rejection were never made public, the parents were told by their physician at Huntington that they were judged unlikely to provide the postoperative care required by Jesse because they were unmarried and young (the mother was seventeen, the father twenty-six). When they told this account to their priest, Michael Carcerano, Rev. Carcerano visited the physician to confirm the account and then expressed his concern over the matter to Susan Carpenter McMillan, California spokesperson for the National Right to Life Committee. She in turn alerted the press.

In the uproar that followed, Loma Linda continued to decline to make a full public statement for confidentiality reasons. Individual members of the selection committee, however, indicated that the mother's "substance abuse" problems were influential in the committee's thinking. Reports of the father's substance abuse also circulated in the press. Jesse was eventually accepted as a candidate for a heart transplant after his parents agreed to sign over custody of him to his paternal grandparents.[45]

In the well-publicized Baby Jesse case the patient's family situation appears to have been a pivotal consideration in his initially being turned down for a heart transplant. Throughout the public debate the exact nature of the relationship between medical and environmental factors was seldom made clear. Confusion at this point is probably responsible for the wide range of opinion as to the moral acceptability of a supportive-environment criterion.

In light of the analysis in this chapter, the application of the supportive-environment criterion in the case of Baby Jesse seems to have been problematic though well intentioned. The experimental nature of the treatment underscored the importance of the committee's being as certain as possible that Baby Jesse would receive substantial medical benefit from treatment (see chapter 18).[46] Experience indicated that supportive care—the administering of medication, the complying with dietary requirements, and so forth—was a prerequisite of such benefit. So the concerns that Baby Jesse have sufficient supportive care and that the family unit be reasonably strong seem to have been warranted.

Once these concerns are acknowledged in theory, however, their meaning must be precisely elaborated. What exactly constitutes a supportive environment? Apparently care from a young, unmarried couple in which at least one parent has engaged in substance abuse did not qualify according to the selection committee. Yet once the hospital accepted their child for transplantation, the parents expended great effort to obtain the needed organ.[47] Such effort suggests that the environmental factors considered by the hospital were not adequate predictors of the parents' capacity to rise to the occasion of their child's need. An article in Loma Linda's own newsletter recognizes that the selection committee may have been mistaken about the ability and commitment of Jesse's parents to care for their child after surgery.[48]

A second troublesome feature of the Loma Linda decision is that the medical center apparently denied the baby access to a transplant because of the inadequacy of his parents rather than try to remedy that inadequacy and thereby make the transplant possible. That the alternative of transferring custody of the child to his paternal grandparents was discovered only after pressure was applied from outside testifies to the fact that an acceptable remedy was available.

The medical center's reluctance to provide such an alternative at the outset left it vulnerable to charges that the selection committee was making social-value and quality-of-life judgments rather than merely medical ones. In fact, the major news account of the case in the *New York Times* summarized the committee's decision by noting that Jesse was rejected "not for medical reasons but for social reasons." The account went on to elaborate the "social guidelines" regularly employed by the committee.[49] The only way to avoid the appearance that such highly controversial considerations have been employed is not to speak of environmental considerations as independent criteria or guidelines but as factors explicitly confined to a narrow role as one component of strictly medical criteria. As Loma Linda has acknowledged, this was a valuable learning experience. In fact, the medical center set an example through its careful reflection following the event with a view to refining its patient selection criteria.

PART FOUR

Medical Criteria

CHAPTER TEN

Medical Benefit

A medical-benefit criterion is absolute in character. Unlike the medical criteria of chapters 12–14, it assesses patients on their own merits without reference to others. It includes for further consideration all (and only) those who will likely receive a significant benefit as a result of treatment. Many factors enter into the medical assessments implied by the criterion, and the results are not always clear-cut or uniform among physicians.[1] Consider the area of organ transplantation. Donor–recipient compatibility as to blood type, cytotoxic antibodies, and size of organ is considered essential by some physicians for there to be the potential for significant medical benefit from certain operations.[2] Such specifics must be matters of medical assessment; but when such factors are thought of as prerequisites to medical benefit, insistence upon them constitutes a form of medical-benefit criterion. As to resources such as dialysis and intensive care, sometimes the only way to determine if a patient will benefit from them is through a trial use. The point of the medical-benefit criterion is straightforward: to try to benefit anyone who can benefit. Not surprisingly, the criterion is widely employed and advocated[3] and even in my U.S. study receives a higher rating than any other criterion examined (see chapter 2). Considered on average very important (mean score 4.2 out of 5), the criterion is acknowledged to be legitimate by 95 percent of the medical directors.[4]

Justifications

A variety of rationales can be given in support of this criterion, some quite broad and common to most ethical perspectives. For instance, given the medical context, a medical-benefit criterion seems perfectly rational.[5] To select patients without reference to medical considerations would be simply irresponsible.[6] In fact, it would be inhumane in that some patients would be given false hope.[7] From a productivity oriented perspective, the matter may be put pragmatically: Any medical intervention that will not work is wrong, for it is a waste of potentially useful resources.[8]

Person oriented arguments, on the other hand, tend to appeal to the notion of human need.[9] When limited resources are available and some people need those resources in order to live, distributive justice mandates that these people receive priority access.[10] Need constitutes the major exception to the egalitarian presumption generally built into concepts of justice.[11] In such concepts need and equality often coexist either intuitively or on the basis that a social contract prevails (according to whose terms people devise their ethical standards out of protective self-interest under hypothetical circumstances in which they do not know their place in society).[12] Priority justly goes to those in need, with those equally in need (for example, all whose life could be saved by a resource in question) receiving equal priority.

The notion of need includes the ideas that some disease or injury condition is present and that a patient's life is thereby undesirably altered. What constitutes an undesirable alteration is a value judgment that requires careful examination in relation to each resource.[13] A need for a lifesaving resource implies that a patient's life is in jeopardy without it; no preferable alternatives remain.[14] Moreover, sufficient clinical data must be collected to establish the limits of what types of cases genuinely need how much of a specific resource.[15] For instance, the sickest patients may paradoxically not need a particular resource at all if they have deteriorated to the point where it is no longer of benefit to them (or their death is imminent from other unalterable causes).[16] Even with such limitations, though, the requirement of need has proven a helpful guide in the selection of patients.[17]

Weaknesses

Medical-benefit criteria in practice, however, do not always reflect an honest assessment of need. For better or worse, when resources are limited, standards of need are sometimes purposely tightened until the number of patients who satisfy the medical-benefit criterion is reduced to match the number of resources available.[18] Although this practice enables medical personnel to avoid explicitly denying lifesaving resources to some in need, it does so by distorting the medical-benefit criterion to communicate something to patients that is not accurate. Such distorting may be a matter of concern to people of any ethical persuasion.

This misleading use of the criterion has been well documented in relation to the provision of dialysis in Great Britain,[19] where the number of patients accepted for treatment has fallen far short of the number who are likely to have benefited from treatment on any reasonable assumption. The number treated has accordingly been substantially smaller than the number of patients accepted in most other Western countries. Nevertheless five out of nine directors of renal units interviewed in one study did not admit to any shortage of dialysis places for medically qualified patients.[20]

What is the explanation for this? Medical selection criteria have been altered to include considerations other than strictly medical ones. The altering is confirmed by an examination of selection criteria in different sections of Britain. Where resources are more plentiful, the criteria are looser and therefore more patients are accepted.[21] Some altering, though, has gone on before patients are even considered for dialysis by nephrologists. General practitioners, aware of the resource constraints, decide not even to suggest dialysis to some patients who would benefit medically from it.[22] This practice has been documented by a study which, utilizing a single descriptive list of potential dialysis candidates, compares the number of patients that general practitioners and renal specialists would consider medically acceptable. The number selected by the general practitioners is significantly lower.[23]

Apparently general practitioners find it painful to do less than the best for their patients (and correspondingly hard to inform them that they are doing so).[24] Moreover, these physicians see little help—only frustration—for their patients if they are referred for dialysis only to be confronted later with the harsh reality that resources are scarce and cannot be provided to them for nonmedical reasons.[25] Consequently,

> the physician, in order to live with himself and to sleep well at night, has to look at the arguments for not treating a patient. And there are always some—social, medical, whatever. In many instances he heightens, sharpens, or brings into focus the negative component in order to make himself and the patient comfortable about not going forward. He states the reason for not going forward in medical terms . . . but that formulation in many instances is in no small part conditioned by the fact that there really aren't enough resources to treat everybody, and there is a kind of rationalization.[26]

This rationalization is even less surprising when the predicament of the physician is seen in broader perspective. Although British society has restricted the available resources so that medically acceptable candidates must go without dialysis, it has not thought through and provided the physician with nonmedical criteria by which to exclude some patients. Physicians thus use the medical criteria that are available to them.[27] Some lose sight of the fact that they are engaged in rejecting medically acceptable patients by altering the medical-benefit criterion.[28]

While understandable, this application of a medical-benefit criterion is arguably quite harmful to patients. Unaware that they could benefit from treatment, they do not seek it from other, normally less accessible sources where it might be available. The physician's refusal to refer deprives them of the only lifesaving option they have.[29] They and others concerned about them are also precluded from efforts to make more resources generally available in the future. Some observers find such deception an immoral breach of professional duty as well as a violation of British law.[30]

Great Britain is not unique in its handling of the medical-benefit criterion. The British National Health System simply has been studied frequently, and its practices are well documented, but the same approach has been observed in numerous other countries as well, such as Canada.[31] One study of thirty countries reports that 23 percent claim to provide dialysis to all medically acceptable patients—a claim that probably reflects in many cases the same kind of criteria tightening that occurred in Great Britain.[32] In the period just after dialysis was introduced in the United States the medical-benefit criterion was in like manner manipulated at times.[33] The practice continues today at times in the intensive care setting and would almost certainly reemerge in the arena of dialysis if further economic restrictions were imposed.[34] In fact, some fear that this deceptive use of a medical-benefit criterion will become widespread in U.S. medicine under increasing financial constraints, for reasons akin to those identified in relation to British physicians.[35]

Another weakness of a medical-benefit criterion is that it can so easily mask judgments of a patient's social value.[36] Actual and hypothetical examples of this predicament abound.[37] Most of those who criticize the criterion on these grounds reject social-value assessments largely on person oriented grounds (see chapter 3). They also tend to see the physician's role as a purely medical one rather than as a vehicle for imposing society's nonmedical values.[38] Productivity oriented supporters of social-value assessments, though, may also be critical of hiding these assessments in medical garb rather than espousing them openly.[39]

The masking of social-value judgments occurs in a variety of ways. Medical assessments sometimes include such a complex of considerations that social judgments can slip in undetected.[40] For example, medical need may be assessed in terms of how articulately patients present their predicament or how well society or medical science will be served if certain patients are returned to functioning,[41] and medical criteria such as likelihood of benefit, length of benefit, and quality of benefit may be employed under the label of medical benefit. Unlike a true medical-benefit criterion, these three criteria engage in problematic close comparisons of candidates for treatment and seek to enhance the productivity of available resources by rejecting certain patients who would benefit from treatment (see chapters 12–14).[42] At other times medical assessments may not be based upon a fixed group of considerations at all, so that social values can subtly influence ad hoc medical judgments.[43] At issue in all of the illustrations just presented is the ease with which the decision maker's inevitable social biases can insert themselves into what purports to be an objective medical decision.[44]

Possible Common Ground

Since the justifications for some sort of medical-benefit criterion are so compelling and widely acknowledged, the challenge ahead is to formulate and administer the criterion in a way that guards against the distorting and masking tendencies identified above. A good place to begin is with the problem of hidden social-value judgments.

Even those who fear that social-value considerations will inevitably taint any medical-benefit criterion admit that some sort of need-related medical-benefit criterion is necessary.[45] To minimize the subtle influence of social judgments, physicians must be on their guard against such biases.[46] Safeguards can also be built into the assessment procedure itself. For instance, medical standards can be developed (by medical experts) with a view toward screening out social-value considerations and then be made public for review and comment.[47] Another possibility is to mandate the already common practice of involving several physicians—at least one in addition to the patient's own—in order to protect all patients under consideration from social bias.[48] In one study physicians who were asked independently to apply a medical-benefit criterion made the same basic assessment in only thirty-two of one hundred cases.[49] Cooperative assessments would help to eliminate some of this variability.

As previously noted, another hidden place of entry for social-value considerations is through the productivity oriented comparison of patients called for by likelihood-of-benefit, length-of-benefit, and quality-of-benefit components in a medical-benefit criterion. These three factors are indeed integral to medical assessment, but they do not necessarily entail comparisons between patients. As part of a medical-benefit criterion they should supply only minimal standards that any patient must meet in order to be considered further for treatment. (Their acceptability as independent, comparative criteria is a separate matter assessed in chapters 12–14.)

In other words, a medical-benefit criterion can minimize the influence of social-value considerations by assessing only *whether or not* a patient would have a significant likelihood of receiving a significant therapeutic benefit with treatment. The exact meaning of *significant* in this criterion would have to be worked out by the medical community in conjunction with society at large. The important idea for present purposes is the notion of a minimal rather than a comparative criterion.

Reasonable assessments of significant therapeutic benefit are common in health care and are already being employed in public formulations of medical-benefit criteria.[50] Strong public and private support exists for a minimal likelihood-of-benefit component.[51] The details of what constitutes (minimal) significance regarding likelihood of benefit, though, must be worked out resource by resource since critical factors are variable. For instance, a relatively high level of significance is necessary with regard to transplantable organs in order to justify the dangers of surgery and immunosuppressive therapy to the recipient.[52] The dangers of surgery to living-related donors must also be considered in these cases where applicable. However, it is important not to set the significance level so high that organs are wasted or patients who have a legitimate prospect of benefiting from transplantation are automatically excluded from consideration.[53] On the other hand, intensive care does not involve the same level of danger in every instance as does transplantation.[54]

The notion of significant therapeutic benefit also needs to be defined somewhat further in terms of length and quality if it is to serve as a practical guide. What constitutes a significant benefit when length of life is concerned? Some say more than a few months; others, a number of years.[55] The minimums suggested by the dialysis directors in my U.S. study average 28–33 weeks, or about 7 months. The comparable figure for kidney transplantation directors is 93–106 weeks, or about 2 years. The differences in figures to some extent reflect differences between the resources involved. While this is understandable, as noted in the previous paragraph in relation to the likelihood-of-benefit component, it may not be wise. If differences between resources can be sufficiently accounted for in the likelihood component, then a more consistent judgment as to what constitutes a significant lenghthening of life in the practice of medicine could be established.

A minimal quality-of-life standard, on the other hand, may not be possible at all, for reasons to be examined in chapter 14. Standards tend to be too subjective (for example, life must be "worth living") or conducive to hidden social-value considerations (for example, "rehabilitation" must be likely).[56] Patients themselves are probably the only ones who can assess whether or not their lives will be of sufficient quality to be worth living.

When setting the various standards that define a significant likelihood of significant benefit, those responsible should always keep in view the fact that the standards are minimal in nature.[57] No one who is thereby excluded should be able to claim justifiably that she or he could have benefited medically from treatment. If living a year longer, for instance, can reasonably be considered a significant benefit, then the length-of-benefit requirement of the medical-benefit criterion should not be longer than a year. Borderline cases should probably be included for further consideration in view of the imprecision of the judgments involved.[58] Even with so inclusive a medical-benefit criterion, patients with virtually no likelihood of significant benefit could be excluded irrespective either of their desires or those of their family.[59] At the same time, those who meet the standards but do not personally consider their expected likelihood, length, or quality of benefit to be sufficiently great could decline treatment either at the outset or following a therapeutic trial (see willingness criterion, chapter 15).

A medical-benefit criterion is probably best designed to exclude only those who should be excluded even for treatments that are not presently scarce.[60] Were there no financial constraints in any area of health care, there would be no need for even this sort of minimal criterion in many cases. However, as long as pressing needs go unmet, a significant likelihood of significant benefit is necessary before any medical resources are used. A thoughtfully developed medical-benefit criterion, then, will not only help to direct the distribution of scarce resources but will also help medical personnel decide when it is ethical to withhold resources such as respirators, resuscitation, and dialysis that often are not scarce.[61] It will help as well to direct decisions to discontinue treatment, whether scarce or not. In fact, it is doubly important to have such a criterion for discontinuing treatment (for example, following a therapeutic trial) if borderline patients are not to be excluded when first considered for treatment.[62]

An Illustrative Case

The infant intensive care unit at Lister Hospital has reached capacity. One of the infants, John, will in all likelihood die in the next few days. Although prognosis is sometimes difficult to establish with infants less than a year old, the physician in charge and his team are virtually certain that John's massive brain hemorrhage will soon be fatal.

At this very time, an urgent call has come to the intensive care unit to admit another infant named Peter as soon as possible. Peter has sustained multiple chest and head wounds in an automobile accident, but his prognosis with intensive care is good. The physician in charge of John and of the whole infant intensive care unit is inclined to take John off the respirator, now needed for someone else. John's parents, though, would like every effort made to save their son. There are few other units in the area and all are full. A transfer to a unit in a neighboring state would put either John's or Peter's life at serious risk.[63]

The case of John and Peter is perplexing not just because two infants are in competition for the same resource. One gets a nagging feeling that to continue to make the resources available to John is a waste—or worse, an actual harm to John. Under such circumstances the potential relevance of a medical-benefit criterion is particularly striking.

John is near death, and Peter desperately needs the intensive care resources John is now using. Much of the discomfort generated by this case is over the prospect of allowing Peter in effect to kick John out of the intensive care unit.[64] However, such a confrontation between patients can be avoided entirely. It is proper to consider discontinuing intensive care for John not primarily because of Peter's need but because of the dictates of a medical-benefit criterion. Such a criterion would provide an objective basis for the physician and others to resist any unreasonable demands by John's parents.

One can imagine all sorts of emotional and legal entanglements were John to be discharged today. But these problems would be due largely to the lack of a good medical-benefit criterion, not to its presence. Were such a criterion to be clearly formulated and publicly known, parental outrage and lawsuits would be less likely—especially if John's physicians promptly discontinued intensive care when medically unwarranted rather than waiting until another arrived who needed the resources. As always, carefully formulated criteria will provide helpful guidance, not simple formulas that obviate the need for good medical judgment.

CHAPTER ELEVEN

Imminent Death

All patients who require a lifesaving resource may need that resource, but do they all need it to the same degree? What if one patient needs a resource immediately, whereas another can live without it for a long time? If urgency is a legitimate consideration, can it justify even the removal from treatment of patients whose predicaments are not urgent? These important medical questions are not answered by a medical-benefit criterion (chapter 10).

In order to distinguish urgent from nonurgent cases, an imminent-death criterion is sometimes employed when length of remaining life is roughly predictable. Death may be considered imminent when it is expected within several days or weeks according to competent medical judgment.[1] Although this definition is not precise, it is the best that the circumstances will allow and has been found workable by many in clinical practice.[2] Two additional versions of the criterion have been adopted. Some resources require substantial lead time to prepare patients for treatment. This used to be true, for example, of dialysis,[3] but it is rarely the case with treatments today. Nevertheless, in such instances the time range covered by an imminent-death criterion must be broadened. Another version of the criterion breaks the time period when death is imminent into several subperiods, with those in the subperiod closest to death having the highest priority.[4]

According special priority to those closest to death has long been a standard practice in medicine.[5] An imminent-death criterion, for instance, partly determined the distribution of insulin in the days when it was still scarce.[6] It has also influenced the selection of patients to receive organ transplants, particularly kidneys and hearts.[7] In fact, a broad range of lifesaving heart operations have been made available first to those for whom death is imminent, when resources have been limited.[8] Analogous practices hold in the provision of intensive care.[9]

Justifications

To many the fact that preventable death is imminent for a patient is itself a reason to give that patient priority access to the necessary lifesaving resource.[10] The analogy may be drawn to the time-honored practice of triage in wartime, when conditions of scarcity and urgency have dictated that the pressing needs of some take precedence over the less critical needs of others.[11] What, though, is the underlying basis for the priority that urgency seems to generate? There are two major contenders, need and life.

Need is the same person oriented concern that undergirds the medical-benefit criterion (chapter 10). According to that criterion, some may be favored over others in the distribution of limited medical resources because only they truly need the resources. However, the question arises as to whether or not further discriminations are possible among those in need. Do some need access more than others? If life is not at stake, degrees of need may readily be employed to distinguish patients.[12] In lifesaving circumstances, though, all alike are in ultimate need. Nevertheless, need can still provide a basis for further unequal treatment.[13] Some patients who eventually will need a particular resource in order to live do not need the resource immediately. In that sense their need is not as great,[14] and they can legitimately be distinguished from those for whom death is imminent if they go without treatment.[15]

Another possible justification for an imminent-death criterion is life itself. This criterion can result in the saving of more lives. As in the case of a medical-benefit criterion, the saving of lives here may be advocated from either a person oriented or productivity oriented perspective. Since some patients can survive for a while without treatment, there is a possibility that a superior treatment may become available in the interim, permitting the treatment of all. Alternatively (and more likely), additional resources may be made available by individuals or the government in response to a tragic lifethreatening situation.[16] In fact, the scarcity itself may be only intermittent, as is the case in intensive care units.[17]

Interestingly, some supporters of an imminent-death criterion see even one of its potential weaknesses as a strength. The criterion is decidedly imprecise as to the dividing line between those with and those without priority access to treatment. Yet this lack of precision corresponds closely to the physician's inability to give exact medical prognoses.[18] In other medical contexts, such as the discontinuing of treatment for dying patients, the term *imminent* has been found to be ideally suited to the making of imprecise but essential distinctions between patients. The California Natural Death Act provides a good example in its requirement that the physician can withdraw life-sustaining procedures only "where [among other conditions], in the judgment of the attending physician, death is imminent whether or not such procedures are utilized."[19]

The California Medical Association and California Nurses Association, as well as the California Conference on Local Health Officers, have all supported the legislation.[20] It was also predicted from the moment of its passage—rightly as it turns out—that many states would follow California's lead.[21] In reviewing the imminent-death terminology in the California law, ethicists have concurred that the notion of imminent death is an objective condition that a physician can assess with reasonable accuracy.[22] So it is not surprising that *imminent death* has been adopted as a meaningful term of classification in hospital and legal contexts alike.[23] Even the American Medical Association and National Academy of Sciences have employed it.[24] Moreover, according to a national survey, it enjoys a broad measure of public support in the United States.[25]

Weaknesses

Despite being widely acknowledged, an imminent-death criterion has a number of weaknesses—some substantive and some pragmatic. Among the substantive difficulties, several are largely person oriented. For instance, unless a lottery is adopted as the primary means of patient selection, patients will have reasonable expectations (based upon the experience of formerly selected patients) as to how long they will have to wait to be treated. An imminent-death criterion interferes with these expectations by allowing some patients suddenly to jump into top priority position.[26] In fact, the very act of one patient's moving ahead of another after both have been waiting for a while is questionable if the person passed by dies as a result.[27] Another problem is that an imminent-death criterion invites unfair special treatment for some. Physicians may be tempted to move some patients into the imminent-death category more quickly than others.[28] There have even been complaints that some transplant centers illegitimately overstate the urgency of their patients' conditions in order to gain priority access to scarce organs.[29]

The justification of the criterion on the basis of need can also be questioned, from more than one perspective. An imminent-death criterion may be a disservice to patients in that it tends to make everyone wait until they have greatly deteriorated before they are treated. In fact, the condition of many may be so diminished by the time they receive treatment that they do not survive.[30] Patients are not helped and resources are wasted. Even if resources are not wasted in every case, the likelihood of medical benefit is reduced across the board by this criterion.[31] Such a reduction is especially serious when success rates are of central concern because the resource in question has not thoroughly proven itself.[32]

Saving life as a justification for an imminent-death criterion is also open to various rebuttals. It is one thing to apply the criterion to a lifeboat situation, which offers a reasonable expectation of rescue at any moment. It is another to claim that new or additional resources are likely to appear soon under most circumstances of selecting patients to receive scarce resources.[33] Not only is it unlikely that more lives will be saved, but this goal may not be desirable. Although the provision of treatment to all is much to be desired, the pool of patients must be restricted somehow if resources are limited. Letting some people die while waiting for treatment is a better means to this end in the eyes of many than excluding them by some imposed criterion.[34] An imminent-death criterion works at cross-purposes with this preference by keeping as many untreated patients as possible lingering this side of death.

In addition to these substantive weaknesses, several pragmatic problems should be noted. According to some, the criterion is too rigid in that it allows physicians relatively little leeway in deciding which patients should have priority on medical grounds.[35] For others, the criterion is too loose. Most medical conditions do not allow of a precise way to determine when death is imminent, so it is very difficult to decide who should be given priority in accordance with the criterion.[36] A third difficulty concerns the way that the criterion can be manipulated by patients. They cannot control their social value, age, or place on a waiting list, for example, but they can exercise control over how rapidly their condition deteriorates. Finally, when increasing priority is given to patients as the urgency of their condition increases (for example, starting at the point when they become homebound),[37] the criterion may become a cover for other criteria. Even if one patient is homebound and another is not, they may equally value their lives and desire treatment. To put one patient ahead of another may be to impose a questionable social-value or quality-of-benefit criterion (see chapters 3 and 14).

Withdrawal of Treatment

For those who find merit in an imminent-death criterion, despite the weaknesses identified, a further question arises, one that pertains to any acceptable criterion but arises most commonly when the death of a patient is imminent. That question concerns the moral acceptability of withdrawing treatment from a patient when a higher priority candidate comes along. It is always appropriate to consider withdrawal when continued treatment may not benefit the patient being treated. However, what about the case in which the rationale for withdrawal primarily concerns another patient's need for the limited resource already in use? When a second patient's death is imminent and no resources are available, is it ever acceptable to displace a patient already being treated?

Many physicians have thought so in the past. When adrenal cortical extract was limited, for instance, a patient might have been taken off it before being fully recovered if a patient in more critical condition needed it.[38] Patients have commonly been removed prematurely from intensive care as well when other patients with more pressing needs have arrived.[39] To some, such removal is standard medical practice.[40]

A number of rationales undergird this conviction, two of which can be productivity oriented. More patients can be kept alive longer in this way, or at least the likelihood of prolonging the lives of more patients is increased.[41] These gains, however, must outweigh the unhappiness generated by withdrawing treatment from some patients.[42] Accordingly, the case for withdrawal is strongest when the patient is an infant or an unconscious adult.[43] The quality of life of other patients who are undergoing treatment—and of the staff as well—could also be improved if it were acceptable to remove disruptive patients from treatment in favor of more agreeable candidates (though the legal issues involved are complex).[44]

A person oriented perspective shares the enthusiasm over the prospect of prolonging additional lives. As indicated in the preceding and following chapters, however, something more concrete than an improved likelihood of benefit is desirable. Perhaps someone in intensive care no longer genuinely needs treatment because it can no longer do any good or because other forms of care will suffice. Then withdrawal will make possible the saving of another specific life.

Withdrawal is equally acceptable in the eyes of many physicians, patients, and families when, for example, it is difficult to make an accurate diagnosis until a patient has undergone a therapeutic trial of a resource

such as intensive care. It may be in the best interests of the patient—
not to mention those of other patients needing access to intensive care—
to discontinue the treatment once a reliable diagnosis is available.[45]
Moreover, the patient may not be able to make a sufficiently informed
decision concerning whether or not to undergo extended treatment (for
example, an artificial organ) until experiencing that treatment for a
while. Treatment may restore a patient's ability to make informed decisions (for example, uremic dialysis patients who are comatose or dis-
oriented) or may simply enlighten the patient as to what the treatment
will entail. Withdrawal ought to be considered acceptable under these
circumstances so that therapeutic trials may more readily be employed.

To many, the idea of withdrawing a treatment that is still needed is
unthinkable.[46] Concern for the happiness and security of patients so
deprived, as noted earlier, may be in view here.[47] More often, though,
such person oriented considerations as the importance of abiding by
commitments are central.[48] Once treatment has begun, there is an implied contract (moral, if not legal) to the effect that it must continue as
long as it is needed.[49] A physician–patient relationship is created in which
the physician's loyalty is expected.[50] The patient should be able to trust
in that loyalty even if it has not been explicitly pledged by the physician.[51]

Those concerned about commitment are also apt to oppose withdrawal of treatment on the grounds that it is immoral to kill an innocent
person in order to save another.[52] Some fear that unless this moral
boundary is maintained, euthanasia against the will of the patient will
eventually result.[53] Even opponents of withdrawal acknowledge that it is
acceptable if treatment has become medically useless.[54] However, in such
cases a medical-benefit criterion rather than withdrawal is really at issue.
A medical-benefit criterion should always be applied whenever it is relevant. For this reason many physicians and observers are suspicious of
withdrawal decisions that are triggered by the arrival of another patient
who needs the same resources.[55] They suspect that more is in view than
the medical condition of the patient from whom treatment is being withdrawn.

Possible Common Ground

As suggested above, the imminent-death criterion (as opposed to the
idea of withdrawing treatment from patients) has widespread support in
the medical community and public at large. This support may well be

tied in part to the expectation that the supply of resources (for example, transplantable organs) is growing. Where such is clearly not the case, the criterion is more difficult to defend because additional patients cannot be benefited on account of it. Even then, though, other rationales appear sufficient to sustain general support for the criterion. In the more easily justifiable situations, some serious difficulties with certain forms of the criterion remain. For the most part, however, these forms can be avoided by a careful formulation of the criterion. For instance, if the criterion gives priority to those patients who are so far deteriorated that their lives cannot be saved, then the important medical-benefit criterion is being ignored (see chapter 10).[56] Instead, the criterion could give priority to those candidates who are within two weeks of being disqualified from treatment on the basis of the medical-benefit criterion. Such predictions are often difficult to make, especially when patients who are not very sick are nevertheless at significant risk of dying.[57] If a prediction cannot be made with reasonable accuracy, an imminent-death criterion cannot legitimately be employed.

Even before the last two weeks in which treatment may well be beneficial, a patient's likelihood of benefit may begin to decrease. The relevance of this consideration depends upon the legitimacy of the likelihood-of-benefit criterion. Only a major drop in likelihood of benefit relative to other candidates for treatment would call this criterion into play (see chapter 12), and even then, caution is necessary. Surgeons have noted that major surgery such as heart transplantation and liver transplantation can be done, with a reasonable likelihood of benefit occurring, much later in the course of a patient's deterioration than is commonly thought possible.[58] Likelihood-of-benefit considerations must not be invoked prematurely.

For those who are concerned that an imminent-death criterion involves categories that are unrealistically precise, three remedies are available. First, the degree of precision required can be minimized by not dividing the time period when death is imminent into subperiods. Patients would either be or not be in the imminent-death period. This provision would have the added advantage of guarding against the inclusion of social-value and quality-of-benefit considerations. Second, improper exclusions due to imprecision could be largely avoided by including all questionable cases in the higher priority category. In any case, research must continue to enable clinicians to determine more accurately when the death of a particular patient is imminent.[59] Third, sanctions could be imposed to discourage physicians and institutions from overstating the urgency of their patients' conditions.

One last problem involves the violation of some patients' expectations when others are allowed to skip over them in line. The seriousness of this problem is really a function of the other criteria that are being used to select patients. The problem is most serious if a first-come, first served approach is adopted, since patients generally have (or can obtain) a good sense of their place in line. It is less serious but still significant if criteria such as age or social value are employed, for people so ranked have only a vague sense of their priority in the waiting pool. Least problematic in this regard is a lottery because no patient in a lottery pool can expect to be selected before any other.

One way of eliminating the problem would be to allow a person whose death is imminent to receive a scarce lifesaving resource only if a certain requirement is met. The person who otherwise would have received the resource must be able to survive long enough to be reasonably assured of receiving treatment in time.[60] Unfortunately, this tactic does not solve the problem; it merely postpones it. Even if the person next in line by virtue of waiting time or age or social value is able to survive until the next resource becomes available, the person second in line may not be able to survive beyond that same point. In other words, the person second in line may perish if someone is given priority via an imminent-death criterion. In a lottery, the favored person whose death is imminent does use a resource that otherwise would have gone to someone else, but no particular person is denied treatment in the sense that no one had any higher claim on the next available resource than did any other person.

In contrast with the widely supported criterion of imminent death, the idea of treatment withdrawal is quite controversial. Its acceptance is unlikely as long as it entails the abandonment of patients with life-threatening conditions. However, permanent withdrawal of treatment need not be the issue here. If temporary withdrawal is stipulated instead, it becomes possible to save the life of an acutely ill patient who needs treatment only temporarily without entering into the controversies surrounding permanent withdrawal. The possibility of temporary withdrawal, of course, does not arise if a resource (such as a transplanted organ), once used, cannot safely be transferred to the use of a different person. However, imagine a person who has become significantly better while undergoing a repeated, long-term treatment such as dialysis. Suddenly an emergency patient arrives requiring only short-term use of the person's scarce treatment resources in order to be saved. Most would want to provide for the extreme need of the second person if it could be done without breaking any commitment to try to save the life of the first.[61] (Needless to say, if separate resources are available to handle acute cases, as is commonly the case with dialysis today in the United States, such a scenario would not occur.)

The foregoing approach steers its way between two other outlooks on withdrawal of treatment. It does not go as far as allowing one person to displace another simply on the ground that he or she has a better prognosis. Yet it does not confine the withdrawal of treatment to cases in which treatment would be withdrawn even under conditions where no scarcity existed. The governing notion is to help those who desperately need and would benefit from treatment, as long as patients currently being treated can also be protected from a greatly increased risk of harm.

Still, the major objections to withdrawal will remain unless withdrawal is not allowed without patient consent (or familial–surrogate consent if the patient is incompetent). To risk even minimally harming someone without the expressed or implicit consent of the one potentially harmed is morally unacceptable to many. If informed consent were not required, people would be forced to follow their physician's decisions when it is not clearly in their best interest to do so. Those who see such forced submission as a violation of the physician–patient relationship would insist that the suspension, even temporarily, of the agreement between physician and patient to initiate treatment must be mutually agreed upon.[62]

In light of the previous analysis, then, the temporary suspension of a patient's treatment would probably receive widespread support only if the following five narrow conditions were met:

1. the patient, or surrogate if necessary, has given informed consent (presumably at the outset of treatment rather than under the pressure of the moment when another person needs the treatment);
2. the patient's life is not jeopardized if treatment is temporarily withdrawn and the patient is sustained by other available means;
3. another person's death is imminent unless she or he receives use of the resources currently being used by the patient;
4. should the patient's life be jeopardized at any moment, the use of the resources would be immediately restored (the emergency patient would have to give informed consent regarding this fourth condition before being given the opportunity to supplant the patient; moreover, the policy would be publicly known);

5. only one patient at at a time may be kept suspended from a specific resource (for example, piece of equipment).

The temporary withdrawal of many life-sustaining resources may not be possible. In the rare cases when withdrawal *is* possible and would be justified, the risk to the patient would be minimal and the commitment to save his or her life preserved. Moreover, the life of the emergency patient would often be saved, or, in cases in which the patient needed the resource again, at least prolonged. Needless to say, withdrawal would not be sanctioned as an easy way out of continuing to provide expensive treatment, as it sometimes has been in the past.[63] When withdrawal does not fulfill the conditions specified here, the alternative is not to overload existing resources (for example, intensive care space)—at least not if the lives of all being treated are thereby jeopardized. The results can be tragic.[64] The maximum (reasonably safe) capacity of existing resources should be determined before crises arise.

An Illustrative Case

Mrs. Schade entered a New York hospital with congestive heart failure and various complications. She was elderly and given little chance of leaving alive; but she surprised the physicians. Little by little, during several weeks in the intensive care unit, her condition improved. Then the unexpected happened. One day all of the intensive care beds filled up and a young man arrived in critical condition, needing intensive care. Distressed, the doctors finally decided to move Mrs. Schade to a general ward, where instead of one nurse for two patients there were two nurses and a nurse's aide for forty patients.

In less than three hours Mrs. Schade was dead. The tube that carried air from a respirator to her lungs had become disconnected—as it often had in the past—and there had been no one there to reconnect it. She was found by her daughter-in-law, who had dropped by for a visit.

A few weeks later the situation got tense again when all except one of the intensive care beds became full. That evening an elderly man was brought to the emergency room by ambulance, the victim of a heart attack. Upon arrival CPR was being applied. No pulse could be detected. After some anxious moments and the efforts of numerous physicians and nurses, the man was revived. The physician in charge noted that the man belonged in the intensive care unit—that resuscitation would indeed be warranted if his heart should stop again. However, he decided to send him to one of the general wards instead because he had cancer (albeit with no evidence of metastasis) and was elderly. In particular, the physician did not want to block a bed in the ICU for a younger patient, who, he knew by experience, was bound to arrive soon.

A little more than two hours later the man was dead. His heart had stopped, this time without all of the special care at hand that had been available to him two hours before.[65]

The tragic failure to observe the conditions for temporary withdrawal suggested above is nowhere better illustrated than in these two examples. The examples may not represent normal medical practice. As true instances of what physicians have done under the pressure of limited resources, however, they can be quite instructive. Schade, having significantly improved in the hospital's intensive care ward, was transferred to a general ward because another person whose death was imminent had arrived. However, it was evident beforehand that this suspension from intensive care could not be done without seriously jeopardizing her life, since her respirator tube frequently became disconnected. Not surprisingly, she was dead three hours after being removed from intensive care. In the elderly man's case, emergency care had begun. Yet he was denied continuing care in the form of a place in the intensive care unit—although death was imminent without it—on the grounds that some younger candidate (whose death was imminent) might well arrive later. In the woman's case the first two conditions were violated, in the man's the second and third.

CHAPTER TWELVE

Likelihood of Benefit

When a likelihood-of-benefit criterion is invoked, usually without being defined, it generally implies that patients should be evaluated in terms of the probability that they will benefit medically from treatment. A patient with a greater likelihood would be preferred (all other relevant considerations being equal) over one with a lesser likelihood. Unless otherwise specified, I use this view of the criterion in the present chapter.

There are two alternative views, however. One is that likelihood considerations should constitute only a minimal requirement. To be a candidate for selection any patient would have to have a significant likelihood of benefiting medically from treatment. This view of the criterion is discussed in chapter 10 because it is really a component of a medical-benefit criterion rather than a separate consideration. The other view of a likelihood-of-benefit criterion is a compromise version, according to which only major disparities in likelihood are considered. This view will be examined in the final section of this chapter.

In the United States a likelihood-of-benefit criterion has long been widely supported.[1] When intensive care units are nearly full, for example, the criterion is often employed to determine who will receive the available beds.[2] Another area of medicine in which the criterion is commonly invoked is the transplantation of organs (for example, hearts and kidneys).[3] My own U.S. study (see chapter 2) confirms the popularity of this criterion, with 96 percent of the medical directors granting it a valid role in patient selection. In fact, on average the criterion is rated as very important (mean score 4.0 out of 5). If anything, the criterion is expected to play an increasingly important role in future patient selection decisions in the United States.[4] Evidence suggests the criterion is widely favored in many other nations of the world.[5] It may have special support and justification when the treatment in question is experimental. However, those cases will be considered separately in chapter 18. Perhaps the greatest evidence of the use of this criterion can be found in the way that it underlies justifications of many other criteria, as noted in previous chapters.

Justifications

The merits of a likelihood-of-benefit criterion may seem obvious. What could be more rational than giving scarce medical resources to those judged most likely to benefit medically from them?[6] Some suggest even that lifesaving resources should go temporarily unused if it is reasonable to expect that a patient more likely to benefit from treatment than the candidates at hand will arrive soon.[7]

Justifications for a likelihood criterion are usually offered in productivity oriented terms. More is involved with this criterion than merely medical assessment. The criterion assumes a particular set of values.[8] Primary is the assumption that a reasonable likelihood of medical benefit is not a sufficient basis for receiving scarce medical resources. Those with the greatest likelihood should be favored to ensure the most productive use of available resources. This outlook can be characterized as essentially utilitarian, in that selections are purposely made so that the greatest benefit on the whole will be produced.[9]

Such a concern for productivity can take several different forms. For example, the notion of the medical, therapeutic, or practical utility of this concern may be invoked.[10] The frame of reference may be the pool of patients or society at large, but the priority of utility in some form over an equal opportunity for all who could medically benefit from treatment is consistent. Alternatively, the language of payoff, economic benefit, and efficiency may be used.[11] Here again the idea is that use of scarce resources should generate as much benefit as possible, whether to patients alone or to people generally.

Success is another potentially overriding motif that points toward a likelihood-of-benefit criterion.[12] A successful distribution of resources may be considered one that fulfills the purposes of a given treatment in as many patients as possible. Since any treatment is likely to benefit some more than others, some may simply be considered more suitable for treatment. Predictions as to which patients can be successfully treated are not foolproof; but studies have provided helpful data upon which to base such predictions.[13]

A final justification, which can be advanced from more than one perspective, is an appeal to the additional lives that would be saved were a likelihood criterion to be regularly applied. From a productivity oriented perspective, this outcome is one of the greatest possible benefits achievable from a medical intervention.[14] From a person oriented perspective, a number of life-related justifications are possible. For instance, the value of life itself may directly commend a likelihood criterion.[15] Alternatively, were people to plan a fair distribution scheme, not knowing who among them would need scarce medical resources, they might well favor any criterion that would increase the chances that those receiving resources would actually benefit from them.[16]

Weaknesses

Sometimes when justifications for a likelihood-of-benefit criterion are given, the examples offered suggest that a likelihood component of a medical-benefit criterion rather than an independent likelihood criterion is in view.[17] Perhaps a patient is so ill that treatment almost certainly will not prove effective; or a patient may die of another medical condition soon even if the immediate illness is treated. A medical-benefit criterion alone (see chapter 10) is sufficient to rule out treating such cases.

Such extreme (and inapplicable) examples may be used to justify a likelihood criterion because they alone escape some of the more serious implications of the criterion. These implications tend to be most problematic from a person oriented perspective. For example, one implication of the criterion is that some patients who have a significant likelihood of benefiting from treatment are given no chance whatsoever of being treated. Those with greater likelihoods are automatically and unfairly preferred.[18] A productive use of resources may be applauded, but the loss incurred in achieving it is arguably too great. The loss would be great enough even if better productivity were in every case assured. However, the difference between patients' likelihood of benefit is statistical only. In any given case, the patient preferred might die even with treatment, while the patient left out might have survived if treated.[19]

Another implication of a likelihood criterion is the dehumanizing effect of its preoccupation with efficiency. In a way reminiscent of social-value considerations (see chapter 3), it tends to favor efficiency over equal regard for persons (especially equal regard for the value each person attaches to his or her own life).[20] There is more to the health of a society, however, than physical well-being. The fairness and humaneness with which people are treated, among other things, are also critical. A society that ignores such factors in its pursuit of efficient medical care may stave off for a while the effects of illness, but in so doing only paves the road to ill-health in the end.[21]

Even those who strongly support improving the statistical chances of benefiting as many patients as possible may admit that their goal is illegitimate if it can be achieved only through injustice.[22] There are various ways that injustice may taint a likelihood criterion, beyond the fact that certain medically acceptable patients are given no opportunity to receive treatment. The patients most likely to be rejected via a likelihood-of-benefit criterion are not a representative group. Rather, they are the poorest members of society, and they may already be suffering not only the results of unjust discrimination but the lack of Medicaid as well as private health insurance. They are the ones most likely to be in poor health generally and to have multiple illnesses—either of which conditions may reflect insufficient nutrition or inadequate health care beyond their control.[23] A likelihood-of-benefit criterion can serve as a way of medically rationalizing the exclusion of such socially undesirable persons.[24]

Three other groups may be treated unjustly by a likelihood criterion. One is a particular racial group, such as blacks. In the United States, blacks do not fare as well as whites, for example, when undergoing organ transplantation—for some of the same underlying reasons just outlined.[25] A second group is the handicapped. Often little is known about the effect that a particular handicap will have upon one's ability to benefit from treatment. In fact, handicaps can range from major to quite minor. Nevertheless, it is commonly but incorrectly assumed that most handicaps will reduce a patient's ability to benefit from treatment at least somewhat. Even when the assumption is correct, a likelihood criterion ends up disadvantaging the handicapped in their competition for resources on the questionable grounds that they are handicapped.[26]

The final group arguably treated unjustly by a likelihood criterion includes all who are least likely to benefit from treatment, whatever the reason. Earlier it was suggested that all people might agree to a likelihood criterion if they did not know their place in society, on the grounds that more lives would probably be saved. However, such a social contract perspective generally holds that people would not approve policies that disadvantage those already in the most precarious position, knowing that they themselves might end up in that position. So even the greatest overall benefits (lives, money, happiness, and so on) are unjustly gained if they come at the expense of those who are already in the least advantaged position.[27]

In the domain of patient selection, *least advantaged position* may be variously defined. If it means the least advantaged in society generally, then the criterion's discrimination against the poor, noted previously, becomes an even more serious fault. If it means the least advantaged among those who could benefit from the scarce resource in question, then those with the most devastating condition—that is, those relatively less likely to benefit from treatment—would be in view. Justice would then require that overall gains from the distribution of resources not be obtained by taking away even the limited opportunity to survive that those less likely to benefit still possess. A likelihood criterion would thereby be excluded.

The remaining weaknesses of a likelihood-of-benefit criterion have to do with particular forms of the criterion. In its most general form, the criterion can be used to compare any two candidates for treatment in order to determine which one has the higher likelihood. There are two difficulties here, the first being the difficulty of obtaining precisely accurate determinations of likelihood. Prognoses cannot be established with exactness, as would be necessary were a 10 percent likelihood of benefit to be legitimately distinguished from a 12 percent.[28] The clinical data necessary to make prognoses more than educated guesses is usually not available.[29] Even those who favor a general likelihood criterion tend to base their support upon the stipulation that it is possible to determine prognoses exactly.[30]

Detailed comparisons of all candidates for treatment are also problematic because they interfere with medicine's basic responsibility to the patient. Rather than directing the health care providers to pursue treatment for any patient who will benefit medically from it, a likelihood criterion requires them to compare the various candidates so that some can be favored over others.[31] The trust that patients have in their physicians and health care institutions—so essential to effective health care—may be seriously undermined as a result. Patients will know that any information they supply which indicates that their recovery may be difficult will lessen their chances of receiving any treatment at all.[32]

Another form that a likelihood criterion might take would be to exclude from treatment any patient who does not have a high probability of benefiting medically if treated. In addition to the problems attending all likelihood criteria noted earlier, a special difficulty with this particular form is establishing precisely the cutoff point between high and low probability.[33] In fact, except at the ends of the spectrum—where there is extremely great or very little likelihood of medical benefit—the possibilities of distinguishing any groups of patients reasonably clearly may be slim.[34] Wherever a line is drawn, the distinction between those just above and those just below it would have little medical basis.[35] The difference between this form of likelihood criterion and an imminent-death criterion (chapter 11) is important at this point. Barely failing to meet the cutoff in the former case would result in death. In the latter case it would mean merely that one would have to wait a little longer before moving into the priority category.

A final questionable form of the likelihood-of-benefit criterion is one that would exclude groups of people who are less likely as a group than those in another group to benefit from treatment. The elderly have been denied treatment on this basis, as have manual laborers.[36] The difficulty with this approach is that it withholds resources from some individuals on grounds that do not apply to them. To classify some patients as old or handicapped in order to exclude them from treatments that such people often do not tolerate well seems unfair if those particular persons would likely tolerate treatment well.[37] Medicine arguably should always keep the needs of the individual patient clearly in view.[38]

Possible Common Ground

Although most versions of a likelihood-of-benefit criterion have met with serious objections, one form that appears to be more widely acceptable holds that any patient who is much more likely than others to benefit from treatment is to be given priority. Small differences in likelihood are not considered, and no fixed cutoff points are established. This form applies strictly to individuals; only if every person in a given group has a much greater likelihood of benefiting from treatment than others does that group receive priority.

Those who favor this form of the criterion generally justify it in terms of the way it greatly enhances the probability that scarce resources will be used in the most productive way. Although the ultimate reliance upon productivity will be opposed in chapter 19, there is evidence that this form of likelihood criterion can be broadly supported. Its appeal to those favoring productivity oriented arguments is evident.[39] To those more person oriented in their outlook, this form of likelihood criterion may constitute the least morally offensive way to grant some priority to productivity considerations. At least its goal—to save as many lives as possible—bears a close resemblance to a person oriented commitment to life.[40] Many of those who have indicated their support for a likelihood criterion may well have this particular form of the criterion in view.[41]

As noted previously, favoring those much more likely than others to benefit from treatment applies here to groups only when every member of the group necessarily merits priority. Age groups, for example, would not qualify, as explained in chapter 7. Certain age groups do better than others in relation to any treatment, statistically speaking. However, there generally are exceptional cases.

On the other hand, in blood typing (for ABO blood group compatibility and lymphocyte crossmatch) someone with an excellent blood match will consistently benefit much more from the transfusion of a given blood supply or a particular organ transplant than will one with a poor match.[42] A similar argument may be made regarding tissue typing for organ transplantation.[43] Antigen matching can markedly improve the prospects for a successful organ transplant in that antigens play an important role in immunity and can affect the body's reaction to an organ transplant. Only certain antigen matches (for example, a six-antigen HLA match in the case of kidneys) appear to be particularly advantageous, though, and caution is needed as long as the limited available supporting statistics remain controversial.[44] Moreover, the restricted survival time of certain organs limits the possibility of tissue typing in some cases.[45] The advent of effective immunosuppressive drugs like cyclosporin and monoclonal antibodies to combat organ rejection (see chapter 1) has also lessened the importance of tissue typing in forestalling rejection.[46] Whether organ transplants or other limited resources are being considered, the presence of multiple organ disease is one additional factor that can materially affect the likelihood that a patient will benefit from treatment (see the discussion of this factor in chapter 13).[47]

Two cautions, though, are in order. First, many of the instances just noted can be accounted for by a medical-benefit criterion. When there is a blood or tissue mismatch, for example, a patient may not meet even the basic requirements of this medical criterion (see chapter 10). Since a medical-benefit criterion is less controversial than a likelihood-of-benefit criterion, the former should probably be invoked as the primary justification wherever it is relevant. Second, owing to the uncertainties attending most estimations of likelihood, a likelihood-of-benefit criterion should probably not be employed if there is significant doubt as to whether or not one patient is much less likely than another to benefit from treatment.[48]

If a likelihood criterion is employed and it does turn out consistently to disadvantage certain social groups such as the poor and the handicapped, special treatment programs might be designed with criteria that would favor these groups. An additional case in point might be minority groups in whom HLA antigens are relatively less well defined, should antigen matching be accorded significant weight as discussed above.[49] The goal would be to learn if methods of care can be devised to compensate for the circumstances that have put these groups at a disadvantage in terms of the likelihood they will benefit from treatment. Should this effort prove successful, disadvantaged groups would no longer be ruled out by a likelihood criterion.[50]

An Illustrative Case

A four-day-old infant has been put on the last available respirator in the hospital because of severe respiratory deficiency. Partial Trisomy 18, a genetic disorder leading to mental retardation and various bodily abnormalities, has been diagnosed. While there have been numerous reports of patients with this anomaly living to adulthood, the infant is thought more likely than not to die before his first birthday.

At a conference being held to decide what to do with the infant, the chief of pediatrics reports several conversations with the parents. The mother, he notes, cannot bring herself to "abandon" her child under any circumstances. The father has insisted, "If you cannot guarantee my child will be normal, I don't want you to do anything for it." The chief says that he sympathizes with the father. The nurse, who has been most directly responsible for the care of the infant, responds with an obvious sense of outrage. She insists that the infant has every right to live and should not be allowed to die when this could be readily prevented. In fact, if necessary, she says she is willing to try to adopt the infant and care for him herself.

A pediatrics resident calls attention to a patient of her own who has a serious respiratory difficulty but cannot be put on a respirator because the infant under consideration is using the last available machine. All agree that to transfer either infant to the nearest hospital with an available respirator would be extremely risky. Without a respirator, the second infant will die soon. In fact, even with a respirator the resident's patient may die, but the odds are better than fifty-fifty that the infant will survive the first year. Which infant should be sustained by the hospital's respirator?[51]

The two infants are alike in many respects. A potentially major difference, at least from a medical perspective, is that one has a somewhat better likelihood of surviving with treatment than does the other. Is that a sufficient basis for deciding who should live and who should die?

As noted earlier, a likelihood-of-benefit criterion is not best used to rule out either patients who lack a high likelihood of benefiting from treatment or groups who generally but not always do poorly with treatment. If the criterion is not applied in either way here, then such considerations cannot be used to distinguish between the two infants. Instead, both infants should be viewed as having a significant possibility of receiving significant medical benefit from treatment.

The question then becomes whether or not there is a clear, major difference in the likelihood that the two will benefit. The case suggests that the difference is clear in that one appears to have more and one less than a 50 percent chance of benefiting. But the clarity of the difference would have to be explored with the physicians involved. Whether the difference is major is more doubtful. As stated, the difference in probabilities may be no more than a few percentage points—an insufficient basis for treating one and not the other. In fact, there may be no difference at all, if anything less than a year of life for the first infant is considered to be a reasonable medical benefit (see chapter 13 on length of benefit). When medical criteria other than medical benefit are employed, complicated tradeoffs among likelihood, length, and quality of benefit are not uncommon.

CHAPTER THIRTEEN

Length of Benefit

A length-of-benefit criterion may apply in various situations, though the central concern is always the length of additional life a treatment will give patients. Sometimes patients are relatively old and not expected to live as long as others. Sometimes patients have additional medical conditions that will either limit their ability to benefit from the scarce treatment in question or result in death earlier than would normally be expected for those undergoing the treatment.[1] The rate at which this early death approaches may even be hastened by the scarce treatment.[2] In order to calculate the expected length of benefit from a particular scarce treatment, only benefit above and beyond what patients could receive from other treatments that are not scarce should be considered.[3]

A length-of-benefit criterion in its various forms has been a source of great controversy in the past.[4] Nevertheless, it has often been employed in relation to treatments such as dialysis, where the presence of medical disabilities in addition to the illness of immediate concern can significantly limit the patient's ability to benefit a long time from treatment.[5] Although length-of-benefit considerations have not been as prominent in the selection of dialysis patients since the federal funding of dialysis in 1972, 71 percent of the dialysis directors in my U.S. study (see chapter 2) indicate that they still employ them to some degree. In the same study, 96 percent of the kidney transplantation directors indicate that they consider a length-of-benefit criterion in selecting patients, rating it on average as very important (mean score 3.6 out of 5). Other transplantable organs—for example, hearts—are also distributed on the basis of the recipient's expected length of benefit.[6] This consideration plays a role as well in decisions concerning which patients will receive scarce intensive care space.[7] One study indicates that the provision of even less intensive hospital care depends in part on how long patients are expected to live if treated.[8]

A length-of-benefit criterion is analogously employed in many countries around the world. The most common concern is simply to gain as many life-years as possible from each use of a scarce resource.[9] Sometimes this concern is explicitly identified, but it may be implicit in an expressed commitment to exclude patients with poor prognoses.[10] A poor prognosis is one with a grave outlook—an assessment that the patient's illness can at best be only temporarily controlled by treatment.[11]

A major instance in which the criterion is often employed is in the selection of patients to receive scarce dialysis resources in Great Britain.[12] Many anticipate that if decisions are made to limit the availability of dialysis in the United States, a length-of-benefit criterion similar to that employed in Great Britain will likely be observed.[13] This expectation is confirmed in my U.S. study: Whereas only 71 percent of the medical directors participating consider excluding patients from dialysis on this basis now, when resources are relatively abundant, 96 percent indicate that they would do so under conditions of scarcity.

Justifications

Some of the potential justifications for a length-of-benefit criterion hold for other criteria as well and are elaborated elsewhere. For instance, a concern to save as many life-years as possible with limited resources may also underlie an age criterion (see chapter 7). Similarly, the importance of producing a sufficiently sizable (including lengthy) benefit from treatment is often assumed by a progress-of-science criterion (see chapter 18).

When length-of-benefit considerations per se are defended, rationales are commonly stated in two ways. The intention is either to achieve some more-than-minimal length of benefit (see chapter 10 regarding "minimal length") or to prefer whichever patients will live the longest with treatment. The two rationales do have a common theme. In one way or another the length of additional time that a scarce treatment allows patients to live plays an important role in who should be treated. To be consistent, in fact, once this principle is acknowledged, the ability of one patient to survive longer than another should perhaps always entail some sort of special consideration for the longer-lived.[14]

The idea of preferring those who will live longer than others is essentially productivity oriented. Rather than seeing a person as a person, irrespective of what her or his future looks like, a length-of-benefit criterion considers such factors as expected life span to be crucial, often for utilitarian reasons.[15] Accordingly, those with a utilitarian bent have a natural affinity for this criterion.[16]

Among the possible productivity oriented justifications is the concern to achieve as much benefit as possible from the available resources.[17] Alternatively, the concern might be stated in terms of success. The longer a person is enabled by a treatment to live, the more successful that treatment might be considered. So in order to achieve maximum success according to this outlook, priority should be given to patients who have no additional illnesses that will limit the success of the scarce treatment.[18] In this way the patients who receive the treatment are truly being made well by it.[19] Reflecting this outlook, 38 percent of the respondents in a U.S. survey have indicated that a person suspected of having AIDS should be excluded from access to organ transplants.[20]

If the interest in success measured as length of survival is ruled out, various difficulties follow. Complications will develop in some patients who have multiple medical problems, with additional health care costs and suffering on the part of the patients resulting. These same patients will have a relatively hard time being sufficiently rehabilitated to become economically productive again.[21] The impact upon the morale of the medical staff is likely to be noticeable as well. Sicker patients are more demanding to work with, and it is frustrating constantly to see a patient's progress in one area undone by a relapse in another, or to see little progress at all.[22]

Interestingly, some of the most common person oriented justifications are also invoked on behalf of a length-of-benefit criterion—but in a way that evidences underlying productivity oriented concerns. For instance, the value of life is often appealed to, but the appeal is actually to the amount of life saved rather than to the persons per se who are involved.[23] Similarly, the concept of need is invoked on behalf of the criterion. However, need is not understood, as it usually is, to mean that all whose lives can be saved only by a given resource are equally in need of that resource (see chapter 10). Rather, those who can benefit the most (that is, the longest) are held to need the resource the most.[24]

Weaknesses

A number of largely person oriented responses to the rationales in favor of a length-of-benefit criterion are possible. One is that a life is a life, and that it is misguided to try to distinguish lives on the basis of quantifiable factors such as the length of time that patients are expected to live. Such considerations are arguably irrelevant when life itself is at stake.[25] This outlook has been voiced particularly strongly in Italy and Sweden. Italians have tended not to exclude from scarce dialysis even those patients who are suffering from terminal illnesses (beyond their kidney disease) that dialysis would not affect. Why, the Italians have reasoned, should those with a shorter life expectancy receive lower priority than those whose expectancy is longer through no merit of their own?[26] The sentiment in Sweden is similar regarding patients with multiple illnesses.[27]

Subjectively it is also difficult to hold that a longer life is more important to preserve than a shorter one. Each person's life is uniquely important to that person.[28] The objective counterpart to this argument is a concern for each person's equal right to life. Persons, it may be argued, are unique and worthy of special respect for a variety of reasons. Their right to life is not a right to a certain number of years of living, but an equal right of all to be kept alive if possible irrespective of one's circumstances. From this perspective age and multiple illness forms of the length-of-benefit criterion are open to question.[29]

Several related points might be emphasized with regard to cases in which patients have serious illnesses other than the one for which a scarce resource is being considered. Patients who will die soon from such illnesses with or without treatment would already be excluded from treatment by a medical-benefit criterion. When significant benefit is possible, the person's equal right to life arguably requires equal consideration, for this right does not diminish the sicker one gets. A length-of-benefit criterion, then, should not be conceived of as even an extension of a medical-benefit criterion, for such a conception confuses a successful treatment with a "successful" (that is, long) life.

The real reasons underlying the use of a length-of-benefit criterion (to exclude those with multiple illnesses) may be more personal or social than medical. For instance, the criterion has been invoked to exclude people with diabetes, tuberculosis, and even very poor eyesight from receiving dialysis.[30] However, none of these conditions has consistently prevented patients from doing well on dialysis.[31] Patients with these conditions are more difficult to care for, and this added burden on the medical facility staff may be the real reason that such patients are excluded. However, the idea of weighing the convenience of staff more heavily than the lives of those being denied lifesaving treatment is questionable.

Another underlying reason for rejecting patients who are not expected to live as long as others may be that they are not as valuable to society as others.[32] Such reasoning is open to all of the criticisms leveled at a social-value criterion (see chapter 3).[33] Those most hurt by this way of thinking are those who have already been most disadvantaged in society. Their access to health care is so limited that by the time they get treated their condition is generally worse than that of other people. Employing that worsened condition as a criterion for excluding them from treatment may provide a convenient excuse for the ultimate social disadvantage: no access to lifesaving resources.[34] Since the elderly as a group will not live as long as younger patients, a length-of-benefit criterion may also provide a medical cover for the same kind of unwarranted devaluing of the elderly as that described in chapter 7.[35]

Denying liver transplants to alcoholics is a case in point. Alcoholism per se should not be a basis for exclusion unless the decision makers simply want to be rid of alcoholics. As a state commission has advised, only in those cases in which alcoholism will prevent successful treatment (for example, because the patient cannot be enabled to follow the necessary immunosuppression regimen following transplantation) should this factor be considered.[36] If continued alcohol consumption is likely to be so excessive that a liver transplant will not last very long, then transplantation may already be ruled out on the basis of a medical-benefit criterion (see chapter 15 on alcoholism as a life style).

A final drawback of a length-of-benefit criterion is the uncertainty of the prognoses involved (see similar concerns in relation to a likelihood-of-benefit criterion in chapter 12). It is almost impossible to predict with precision how long a person will live.[37] With a patient who is suffering from multiple illnesses, predictions are especially problematic.[38] In one study of physicians who were given the same data on a particular patient, for example, a striking variability turned up in estimations of the length of benefit the patient would receive from treatment.[39] The high probability of the occurrence of major errors in prediction, coupled with the fact that human lives are at stake, may make it simply too risky to rely upon length of benefit as a basis for patient selection.

Possible Common Ground

The preceding discussion suggests that such disagreement exists over the moral and practical acceptability of a length-of-benefit criterion that a consensus in support of it is unlikely. The underlying reason for the lack of consensus may lie in the conflict of this criterion with other widely supported criteria. This criterion is devoted to saving as many life-years as possible, whereas other criteria are designed to save as many lives as possible. The two goals are not always compatible.

If one-time uses of resources are in view, as with organ transplants, the application of a length-of-benefit criterion results in the saving of the same number of lives as if no such criterion had been applied. More life-years, however, are saved. On the other hand, where reusable resources like dialysis and intensive care space are in view, employing the criterion ends up in the saving of the same number of life-years, but fewer lives. (In the latter instance, those who are given access to the limited resources remain on them longer, thereby preventing other lives from being saved.) The net effect of the criterion, all resources being considered, is that more life-years but fewer lives are saved.[40] If persons (and not merely life-years) matter, then this effect is an unattractive by-product of the length-of-benefit criterion.

The point is not that a focus on life-years—or even quality-adjusted life-years—has no place in medicine. Such a focus, for example, may provide a basis for deciding which of two treatments to fund for all in need or which of two possible treatments should be given to a particular patient.[41] It becomes inappropriate only when employed in the choosing between two candidates for the same scarce resource, in a way that recognizes the patients solely as different bundles of potential life-years rather than also as persons of like value in some fundamental sense.[42]

Length-of-benefit considerations, though, can play a role even in such choices between patients as long as it does not become an independent selection criterion. Some minimal standard of length of benefit is built into the medical-benefit criterion as explained in chapter 10. One way to ensure that length-of-benefit considerations do not exceed this role is to include for further consideration any patient who would be considered medically acceptable were resources not to be scarce.[43] Length-of-benefit considerations also have a place within a willingness criterion (see chapter 15). It may well be that only patients themselves can judge the value of even a limited extension of life and decide whether or not that value is so low that it should be sacrificed so that another may live.[44] A similar observation regarding quality of benefit is discussed at greater length in the next chapter.

An Illustrative Case

Valdez Regional Hospital is the main medical facility for the residents of Valdez County, Arizona. Its intensive care unit is the only one available in the entire county, and the closest comparable unit is eighty-five miles away in Somora County. Experience has shown that patients requiring intensive care cannot always survive the trip from Valdez to Somora.

One day sixty-eight-year-old Harry Aveni was brought to the emergency room of Valdez after he had collapsed on the patio of his house. Mr. Aveni responded well to emergency treatment. The fluid surrounding his heart was withdrawn, a glycoside medication was administered, and his condition seemed to stabilize. That evening there was a sudden onset of fibrillation— his heart started beating erratically. Again Mr. Aveni responded well to treatment, and after emergency defibrillation his condition stabilized.

"He needs to be put into the ICU," Dr. Ellen Gracian said. "We can't care for him sufficiently on the wards, because he's got to have constant monitoring."

"I don't think I can admit him," Dr. Franklin responded. "Here we have an elderly gentleman who has now gone through three episodes of congestive failure and also seems to have something wrong to cause the fibrillation. He didn't stick to his diet. In other words, his days are likely to be in the rather small numbers."

"But if he doesn't have intensive care, the numbers may well be even smaller," Dr. Gracian said.

"That's no doubt true," Dr. Franklin admitted. "However, the chances are real that somebody is going to need that bed, somebody we can do more for than we can do for your patient. Somebody who's got a better chance to live a longer life. It would be a lot harder to remove your patient from the ICU than never to put him there in the first place."

"But you don't know that somebody like you describe is going to come in," Dr. Gracian said. "And even if somebody did, should the prospect of a longer life really matter that much?"[45]

Although the two physicians are at odds over a number of issues in the case of Harry Aveni, the key sticking point seems to be the relatively few years that he has left to live. He is elderly and not in very good health overall. Monitoring in the ICU with immediate attention to any life-threatening developments will not give him nearly as many years of life as many other patients would receive as a result of intensive care. Primarily on this basis Dr. Franklin argues that Aveni should be denied the limited resources.

The ICU bed that Aveni needs, however, is available. Dr. Gracian rightly observes that there may be no other need for that bed. In fact, even if it were needed by another patient, that patient might have no better prognosis than Aveni. Meeting a real medical need is arguably more important than presupposing that a need could be met later with some added benefit (that is, more life-years preserved). If the medical team is committed to truthfulness as well as to Aveni, they could at least admit him provisionally to the ICU. He would have to agree first, though, to being transferred to the wards in the event that another patient arrives who has a prospect of living much longer if given intensive care.

Yet, the consideration of length of benefit at all in this case is troublesome, as the analysis in this chapter has explained. Aveni needs intensive care and would have been put in the ICU had space not been limited. Presumably Aveni would request intensive care if he had a choice, though this should not be taken for granted. Were he to want it, however (or were it determined, if he were incompetent, that it was in his best interests), the medical-benefit and willingness requirements would be met. The appeal to the length of time he is likely to live would then seem dubious.

CHAPTER FOURTEEN

Quality of Benefit

A quality-of-life selection criterion channels resources not only to patients who will live, but specifically to patients who will live a life worth living. As a comparative criterion, it does more than require that every recipient be expected to achieve a quality of life above some minimum level. Rather, it accords relative preference to whichever patients are expected to achieve qualitative benefits higher than those of others, even though they may be only indirectly related to the treatment in question. For example, the criterion has been used to favor dialysis candidates who can later receive kidney transplants and enjoy the better quality of life that accompanies them.[1] It may also favor those who have no medical complications (beyond the condition in question) that will limit their quality of life following treatment.[2]

Among the medical directors participating in my U.S. study (see chapter 2), a quality-of-benefit criterion is more broadly supported than any other criterion. Ninety-seven percent of the directors consider it relevant to patient selection. On the average, they rate it as very important (mean score 3.8 out of 5). This enthusiasm for qualitative consideration is shared by many medical professionals in countries throughout the world.[3] In the setting of neonatal intensive care, the debate is particularly animated over whether more than a minimal quality of benefit should be likely before expensive and limited resources are used.[4] Moreover, multiple studies have documented the use of a quality-of-benefit criterion in the provision of intensive care for adults.[5] Support for a high qualitative standard has been voiced in the organ transplant arena as well.[6] In fact, as suggested earlier, decisions to discontinue any expensive treatment in an era of limited health care dollars may be guided by this criterion.[7]

Justifications

Those who support this criterion are often concerned about the preoccupation that medicine seems to have with achieving patient survival at all costs.[8] Such preoccupation can produce some very unpleasant medical outcomes. Is mere survival the only appropriate concern of medicine, or is medicine responsible for producing lives with as high a quality as possible? Some go so far as to suggest that this latter responsibility is primary.[9]

A quality-of-benefit criterion may be supported for both productivity oriented and person oriented reasons, the former type being the more common. From the perspective of benefits generated, a quality-of-benefit criterion may make a lot of sense. Those who receive lifesaving resources often experience a higher quality of life than other patients would have.[10] Moreover, the recipients are more likely to be in sufficiently good condition to become productive members of society again.[11] The importance of this last consideration has been acknowledged by 72 percent of those participating in a survey of the U.S. public at large.[12] As supporters of a quality-of-benefit criterion admit, all such factors relevant to quality-of-life assessments need to be identified.[13]

According to a productivity oriented outlook, the value of life resides in its quality as experienced by everyone affected by that life, including the patient. The idea that life has intrinsic value is generally resisted. All lives, then, are not of equal value, and a person's value will vary depending upon age and other life circumstances. A patient's claim upon scarce lifesaving resources, from this perspective, will depend upon the value of that patient's life under the conditions most likely to be present subsequent to treatment.[14]

From a person oriented perspective, on the other hand, the reasoning behind a quality-of-benefit criterion can look quite different. The central concern may be for patients' autonomy, in the sense of their continuing ability to make the decisions that shape their future. As the quality of their lives deteriorates, patients lose more and more of the capacity to make genuinely free and informed choices, treatment-related or otherwise.[15] On the other hand, need may be the focal concern. According to this rather unconventional understanding of need (see chapter 3), one whose quality of life following a lifesaving treatment will be less than that of others is therefore in less need of the treatment.[16]

More limited justifications of a quality-of-benefit criterion are also possible. Some supporters of the criterion, worried about the practicality of applying it, favor distinguishing only between major differences in quality of benefit.[17] Further, if the treatment involved is experimental, qualitative considerations may become even more relevant, as will be explained in chapter 18.

Weaknesses

Since the justifications for a quality-of-benefit criterion spring from a fundamental conviction that quality of life lies at the heart of medicine's responsibility, it is not surprising that opponents of the criterion operate from a different understanding of medicine, one that is largely person oriented, though it could be argued on other grounds as well. According to this alternative understanding, medicine's task is solely to benefit the patient. Patients should be given every opportunity even though the treatment in view may not restore their quality of life completely.[18] To do less, according to this view, would be a matter of (mistaken) values, not medicine.

This theoretical objection can be reinforced by a number of practical difficulties. For example, quantifying qualitative considerations in order to compare patients, thereby placing a specific value upon life, probably is impossible. Even were it possible, it is unrealistic to think that one can predict the quality of life that will follow treatment sufficiently precisely to distinguish most patients.[19] Equally unrealistic is the notion that people will agree as to what factors characterize a good quality of life and how they should be ranked.[20] Physicians themselves differ radically in their assessment of the same patients, as studies have documented.[21] Also a problem is the identifying of precise tradeoffs between relative likelihood, length, and quality of benefit, if these considerations are given more than the minimal role ascribed to them by a medical-benefit criterion.[22]

One of the most commonly voiced objections to a quality-of-benefit criterion, though, focuses on the inappropriateness of people deciding what others' quality of life will be and whether that level is acceptable. People judge others' quality of life on the basis of various objective, observable indicators of quality of life. Unfortunately, much evidence suggests that such objective indicators do not correlate well with patients' subjective experience of their own lives.[23] Objectively it may appear to others that someone is experiencing a low quality of life, but the person living that life may not share that view.

The dilemma is partly a product of the objective–subjective difference. However, another part of the problem is that sick people (experiencing the quality) and well people (observing the quality) view issues of quality differently.[24] What is unacceptable to the well may be quite acceptable to the sick. In fact, studies document that physicians differ from patients (and from nursing assistants as well) in their assessment of the same patient's quality of life.[25] The validity of some people making qualitative judgments about others' lives, then, is open to serious question. In the eyes of many it involves some people illegitimately imposing their personal standards on others.[26]

It may be that one simply cannot make qualitative judgments without personally experiencing that which is being qualitatively evaluated. But in addition people have differing standards and contexts by which they subjectively judge quality of life.[27] The British debate over the discontinuing of dialysis for Derek Sage largely on the basis of a quality-of-benefit criterion graphically illustrates this point. Apparently because his quality of life was quite low, a British hospital decided to remove Sage from dialysis treatment. The warden at Simon House, a center for homeless men where Sage was living, responded that Sage had been doing well on dialysis and was eating and sleeping well. Yet hospital staff described Sage as a demented, intermittently violent, dirty, and doubly incontinent man with a tendency to expose himself and masturbate while being examined. The warden objected again, arguing that Sage's atypical behavior at the hospital was caused by his fear of the place.[28] It is admittedly difficult to be certain of all the factors that entered into this particular treatment decision. All too often, though, a judgment that a patient's quality of life is too low is really a statement that the person judging would rather not have to continue to deal with the patient in the patient's current condition.[29]

What may really be happening in such instances is that the person sitting in judgment is resorting to a veiled form of social-value assessment. Some are being excluded because their quality of life following treatment will be so low that they will provide little benefit to society in exchange for the precious resources they are receiving.[30] Empowering some to judge others in this way is dangerous, particularly for the very patients who have already been disadvantaged most by society and are the least productive as a result.[31] Certain social groups predictably bear the brunt of this discrimination—most notably the poor and the elderly.[32] They are reduced to their functional dimension as if there was nothing else in personhood worth respecting.[33] A preferable alternative, some would argue, would be to view successful treatment in terms of sustaining a quality of life that is significant in the eyes of the patient.[34]

In particular, the standard of vocational rehabilitation has been questioned in this regard. Even when patients are able to return to work while undergoing treatment for life-threatening conditions, they do not always choose to do so in light of the tenuousness of their lives.[35] If the good of society rather than the patient's own good is at issue, then the truly intended beneficiary should be openly acknowledged.

Considerations of justice that go beyond the mere utility of a quality-of-benefit criterion also come into play here.[36] If persons are fundamentally equal in some sense, this arguably must mean that they should have equal access to lifesaving resources. The relative quality of their lives becomes irrelevant when life itself is at stake.[37] There may be a price to pay for the protection of justice and life—but, then, things of great value are rarely obtained cheaply.[38] Sometimes the anticipated quality of life following treatment depends upon the efforts of persons other than the patient, such as family members. In these instances especially, the imposing of requirements of quality upon a patient's life seems unjustified (see chapter 9 on supportive environment).[39] According to many, a low quality of life is reason for providing special help wherever possible in addition to lifesaving treatment, not for withholding both.[40] These various objections to a quality-of-benefit criterion, it should be noted, apply for the most part whether the criterion in view requires the comparing of patients (even if only major differences in quality are in view) or it involves some fairly high qualitative levels that any recipient of scarce resources must be expected to reach.

Possible Common Ground

There are two affirmations that would appear to be widely supported, neither of which sanctions a quality-of-benefit criterion per se. One affirmation centers on the great importance of patients' quality of life. Medicine should rightly devote many of its resources to enabling people to live lives of the highest quality possible. These efforts, though, should try to make low-quality lives high quality, not low quality lives perish in order to preserve higher-quality lives.

The second affirmation focuses upon those situations in which patients themselves judge that their lives will be of insufficient quality to justify treatment deemed intolerable. In such cases the various problems besetting an externally imposed quality-of-benefit criterion do not apply for the most part. Rather, only the persons able to assess accurately both objective and subjective indicators of quality are making the decision (following a therapeutic trial if one is necessary to enable patients to make accurate assessments). When only the patients involved are allowed to make quality-of-life judgments, a form of willingness criterion, not an independent quality-of-life benefit criterion, is involved. As detailed in chapter 15 there are many strong reasons not to treat against the patient's wishes, including cases in which that unwillingness is based upon an assessment of quality of life during or following treatment.

However, if the patient's quality-of-benefit judgments are to be respected, then the caregiver must be confident that the patient is making informed judgments. Many of the challenges involved in ensuring that such judgments are truly informed are explained in chapter 15. A particularly significant challenge is making sure patients have sufficient accurate information to make their qualitative assessments. If data is available on how patients undergoing similar treatment have evaluated their own quality of life, providing such information to the patient can be most helpful.[41] In deferring to patients' choices, physicians, nurses, and others may also be overly reluctant to provide the assistance some patients need to evaluate their predicament and make a decision.[42] Recommendations from the physician are not inappropriate, but when they include qualitative considerations, these should be identified and their basis explained.[43] If physicians recommend against treatment because in their opinion the life that would result is not worth living, then this should be spelled out. Exactly what would seem so difficult to endure should be specified, so that patients can determine whether or not the difficulty is unacceptably great from the perspective of their own value systems.

Perhaps the best way for a patient to become informed as to what an extended treatment such as dialysis or intensive care will be like is to begin undergoing the treatment. Experience has shown that after a short time undergoing treatment, patients' errors in predicting quality of life with treatment become evident in a significant number of cases.[44] Patients have demonstrated a willingness to discontinue treatment at that point.[45] In fact, although statistics vary from study to study, it appears that dialysis is discontinued in one out of every eleven patients who begin it.[46] The real figure may be much higher. Patients and their families are becoming ever more aggressive in refusing treatment of dubious value (or perhaps physicians are becoming more circumspect in the face of malpractice lawsuits), and discontinuation of dialysis is underreported as a cause of death.[47] By some indications only a small percentage of dialysis patients' deaths are correctly classified in terms of the actual cause of death—a problem that is not unique to dialysis patients.[48] Ac-

cordingly, strong voices have been raised in such areas as dialysis, neonatal intensive care, and artificial heart therapy insisting that patients be
allowed to try treatment with the freedom to discontinue at any point.[49]

Allowing patients to make judgments about their own quality of life,
however, as noted previously, is really a form of willingness rather than
quality-of-benefit criterion. Recognizing the difficulties of comparatively
rating the subjective preferences of different people, willingness is concerned merely with whether or not treatment is desired by the patient.[50]
A genuine quality-of-benefit criterion would involve some people judging
others to have a relatively low quality of life and excluding them from
treatment on that basis, without reference to their consent. Broad support for this approach seems unlikely. Quality-of-life considerations,
then, have a legitimate place in medicine. However, what is appropriate
for the individual patient to consider (and perhaps appropriate for a
funding agency to consider—if considered correctly—when choosing
among treatments to fund) may be quite inappropriate when others
choose which individuals to treat.[51]

If there is an exception, it probably occurs with patients who are
incompetent and have not provided an indication of their wishes when
they were competent (see chapter 15 for a discussion of competence and
treatment directives). Under such circumstances, no procedure is truly
satisfactory. In a real sense, no one except the patient can truly determine whether or not an expected quality of life is acceptable to that
patient.[52] One suggestion is to follow the course elected by most competent patients under similar circumstances.[53] However, the disadvantage
is that every individual's decision is unique and may not be sufficiently
predictable from the "common situation" to warrant a decision to leave
that person to die without treatment. Perhaps the patient's family members are most often in the best position to evaluate qualitative considerations and make sound predictions. Their own values and interests,
however, occasionally will lead them to make decisions so manifestly
inappropriate that review by a hospital ethics committee or even a court
may be necessary.[54] Nevertheless, the case that follows illustrates the
more common situation.

An Illustrative Case

Karen was an eighteen-year-old girl, the second oldest of seven siblings.
She was first hospitalized in September 1968 with serious kidney problems.
She did not respond to medical treatment. By the spring of 1970 a rapid
decrease in renal function prompted the decision to plan for dialysis and

transplantation. Karen's kidneys were removed in August 1970, and she received a transplant of her father's kidney the following month. The transplant functioned well initially, but several months later problems developed. Suddenly in March 1971 the kidney completely ceased to function. Prior to surgery and following the transplant's failure, thrice-weekly hemodialysis was performed. Karen tolerated dialysis poorly, routinely experiencing chills, nausea, vomiting, severe headaches, and weakness.

In early April 1971, after it became clear that the kidney would never function, Karen and her parents expressed the wish to stop medical treatment and let "nature take its course." The medical staff was upset and could not agree on the proper course of action. The social worker and psychiatrist attempted to have the girl and her family explore their decision in the hope that with further understanding, they would reject it. Most other staff members conveyed to the family that such wishes were unheard of and unacceptable, and that a decision to stop treatment could never be an alternative. One person, though, suggested that Karen was benefiting so little that continued treatment was a poor use of limited medical resources. The family decided to continue dialysis, medication, and diet therapy. Karen's renal incapacity returned to its pretransplant levels, and she resumed a life of social isolation, diet restriction, chronic discomfort and fatigue.

On May 10 Karen was hospitalized following ten days of high fever. Three days later the transplanted kidney was removed. The pathological diagnosis resembled that of her own kidneys, and the possibility of a similar pathological reaction in subsequent transplants was acknowledged by the physicians involved.

On May 21 the arteriovenous shunt placed in Karen's arm for hemodialysis was found to be infected and had to be revised. During this phase of the hospitalization, Karen and her parents grudgingly went along with the medical recommendations, but they continued to ponder the possibility of stopping treatment. On May 24 the shunt clotted closed. Karen, with her parents' agreement, refused shunt revision and any further dialysis.[55]

Although these events took place in the United States prior to federal funding for the treatment of end-stage renal disease in 1972, their relevance today is great. As noted in chapter 1, access to kidney dialysis and transplantation alike is still limited in many countries. Moreover, apparent limitations upon health care dollars in the United States make any possible instance of overly aggressive treatment particularly troublesome.

Whether Karen's treatment is such an instance may not be immediately clear. She might have lived many more years; yet she would have endured serious discomfort and complications accompanying dialysis. So it is not surprising that voices are raised in support of both continuing and discontinuing treatment. Everyone involved seems to share a commitment to preserving life: yet what if that life is experienced more as torture than blessing?

Karen and her parents demonstrate a unified outlook even in the face of conflicting advice from others. Care must be taken to ascertain Karen's competency to make this decision, for someone in Karen's situation may reject treatment prematurely for various reasons, including depression or fear. Yet it is equally possible that Karen and her parents would reject lifesaving treatment because it offers an unacceptably low quality of life. Such a rejection would have legal as well as moral force in that treatment of patients against their will can by law be considered assault and battery.

In this light the reaction of most of the staff appears too negative. Trying to persuade patients to accept treatments that appear to be in their best interest is commendable, but to characterize the discontinuing of treatment as "unacceptable" and absolutely to rule it out as an alternative is excessive. When the transplant failed, there was good reason to suspect that a successful transplant would never be possible. Little reasonable hope of Karen's being able to avoid dialysis through transplantation was left by the time she agreed (under duress?) to have the shunt revised. Moreover, she had already experienced dialysis for some time as early as the point at which her transplant failed, and she had an accurate view of how low the quality of life was likely to be. The medical team's denying Karen even the possibility of refusing dialysis immediately following transplant failure, then, seems unwarranted, as does its overly aggressive opposition to discontinuing dialysis at the point when the shunt first needed revision.

On the other hand, should Karen have wanted dialysis following the failure of transplantation, the quality-of-benefit argument advanced by the one staff person to exclude her probably should not have been considered by the medical team. Too many problems arise when people other than the patient assess that patient's quality of life, especially if their conclusions conflict with the patient's own assessment.

PART FIVE

Personal Criteria

CHAPTER FIFTEEN

Willingness

Patients may make choices that affect their access to health care resources in two important ways. One involves their willingness to risk illness, the other their willingness to accept treatment. The first form of willingness criterion entails giving priority to those who are not responsible for causing their own medical problem. The latter form entails favoring those who genuinely want treatment. Although willingness to risk illness has rarely been considered in patient selection because of the difficulty of applying it in practice, it has begun to be considered in the realm of liver transplantation when liver disease is the result of alcohol or other drug use.[1] Indications are that it is being employed also to determine who receives scarce heart transplants and that its use to select patients for organ transplantation and intensive care will increase in the days ahead.[2]

Willingness to accept treatment, on the other hand, is commonly recognized in Western societies as a prerequisite to being treated. It is fundamental to relevant Anglo-American law, and some transplant centers explicitly acknowledge it as a requirement for acceptance into their programs.[3] It featured prominently as well in the selection of patients for dialysis in the United States before dialysis was federally funded.[4] Even today, 89 percent of the kidney transplantation and dialysis directors participating in my U.S. study consider this form of the criterion a necessary consideration in patient selection, with directors on average rating it very important (mean score 3.7 out of 5). The criterion is also widely supported in the context of intensive care.[5] At times, though, in the absence of clear protests from the patient, willingness is assumed rather than being more actively ascertained. The limited data available suggest that considering the will of the patient so seriously in making treatment decisions may not play nearly as prominent a role in non-Western cultures.[6]

Justifications

Although the two forms of a willingness criterion are fundamentally similar, I will address them separately, first the more commonly employed form. Willingness to accept treatment can be defended upon many grounds, most of them person oriented. However, a productivity oriented defense is possible as well since benefits to the patient, other people, and the overall health care system are at stake. Patients and their families are likely to be much happier with their medical care when their preferences are taken into account. Should they decide to forego a scarce treatment when physicians have recommended they be considered for it, other patients will benefit through increased chances of being selected for that treatment.[7] The efficiency of the health care system, meanwhile, is also enhanced, most notably if the decisions of patients to oppose treatment can be identified early in the patient selection process. Some of the expenses involved in ascertaining a patient's suitability for treatment, many struggles with uncooperative patients, and even much of the waste of particular scarce treatments can all be avoided.[8] Little medical benefit derives, for instance, from a patient committing suicide soon after being put on dialysis or receiving another person's organ.[9] In some cases a therapeutic trial may be appropriate. The patient is not committed to long-term use of a resource if the trial demonstrates to the patient that continued treatment would not be desirable.

More commonly a willingness-to-accept-treatment criterion is given a person oriented justification. For instance, it may be seen as respecting the dignity of persons.[10] Such respect requires giving people the freedom (autonomy) to accept or reject even lifesaving medical treatment.[11] Freedom of this sort is the right of every human being.[12] Some see this right primarily as a right to bodily integrity and self-determination.[13] Others add that a patient's right to the free exercise of religion may prevent physicians from instituting lifesaving therapy.[14] In one study, only 12 percent of patients responding are opposed to a so-called right to die. Of the 70 percent who agree with the concept, well over half agree strongly.[15]

Person oriented justifications also tend to take into account the uniqueness of individuals. Patients themselves can best assess whether or not the prognosis with treatment is sufficiently promising to warrant that treatment (see chapter 14 on quality of benefit).[16] People have their own unique life plans, and they differ in their attitudes toward dependence upon particular technologies.[17] Moreover, even the preferences of given individuals may change based upon such circumstances as upcoming family visits, marriages, and births.[18] For these reasons, only the patients involved can rightfully conclude that their lives are of insufficient worth to warrant receiving scarce life-saving resources.[19] Although some physicians may be tempted to think that they can always accurately assess their patients' best interests, many physicians and nonphysicians alike insist that the temptation must be resisted.[20]

To be sure, those advancing person oriented arguments are often committed to the value of every life and thus to the wrongness of suicide. A decision to forego lifesaving treatment, however, need not be characterized as a suicide. Such giving up of one's life arguably does not demean the value of life if it literally gives (a greater possibility of) life to others.[21] Unlike the case of suicide, the question here need not be whether life should be ended or not, but rather may be, Given the absolute unavoidability of death, who should die?[22] In this respect a decision to withdraw from treatment is no more suicide than a decision to forego treatment in the first place. At any point one may decide that another person's life would be better to save than one's own.[23] Moreover, the patient's action is not the medical cause of death, unlike the circumstances characteristic of a suicide. Rather, a disease is being allowed to take its course, for morally praiseworthy reasons.

As suggested earlier, the other form of willingness criterion has somewhat different justifications. When willingness to risk illness is at issue, the most common justification involves a person oriented focus on responsibility. If a person is the innocent victim of illness, some argue, that person should obtain access to scarce resources before another whose actions have caused that illness to occur. People must be responsible for their life styles.[24] Society need not subsidize personal choices, such as decisions to engage in drug abuse, that are medically irresponsible.[25] To do so would be unfair to those who have been responsible. Accordingly, 13 percent of those participating in a U.S. national survey favor excluding alcoholics from access to organ transplants.[26]

Another possible implication of recognizing responsibility in selecting patients to receive scarce treatments is that when society is responsible for a person's illness, society has corresponding responsibility to give that person first access to treatment. Such responsibility might be due to the destructive conditions in which one has been forced to live (for example, poverty) or work (for example, coal mines), or it may be the result of the past negligence of a specific health care institution.[27] For example, blacks in the United States have been disproportionately subjected to poverty and stress. If these factors are responsible for the high incidence of heart disease they experience, then they may have a greater claim than others to scarce heart transplants.[28] Compensating disadvantaged groups through health care, it could be argued, is more appropriate than even preferential access to jobs or higher education. The latter benefits are awarded on the basis of ability and are more likely to be given to those who have suffered the least from the effects of discrimination. Health care, on the other hand, is generally directed toward the most needy.[29] Many affirm that personal and social responsibility should at least theoretically be considered in selecting patients—though they admit that some of the practical difficulties to be noted shortly are problematic.[30]

At the same time, several productivity oriented considerations are relevant. For example, it is easier to obtain governmental funding if patients are perceived to be innocent victims than if they are thought to have caused their own problems.[31] The employing of a willingness-to-risk-illness criterion may also have a useful deterrent effect on unhealthy behavior.[32] The criterion almost certainly will screen out those who are least likely to benefit from treatment because their unhealthy behavior (for example, excessive alcohol consumption) either will cause the treatment (for example, a liver transplant) to fail or will interfere with essential follow-up care (for example, consistent taking of immunosuppressive drugs).[33]

Weaknesses

The weaknesses of the two forms of a willingness criterion are also best considered separately. Willingness to accept treatment, first of all, is open to question as a patient selection criterion on both pragmatic and theoretical grounds. One of the pragmatic difficulties is obtaining a truly informed decision from a potential resource recipient. There are a host of subtle pressures to accept whatever treatment is available.[34] Family and friends have expectations, and some resources such as donor organs have a way of suddenly forcing hesitant patients to make immediate decisions. Patients may perceive that by offering them an opportunity to give up their chance for treatment (so that others may live) the physician is subtly suggesting that they are not worthy patients.[35] On the other hand, adequate information may not have been made available to the patient. One study has found that over 20 percent of heart transplant recipients were not well informed by physicians and transplant center staff before the operation regarding the transplant procedure and the recovery. Nearly half of the patients were not adequately informed in advance about costs, with two-thirds of these given no cost information whatsoever.[36]

Two other pragmatic problems remain unresolved: (1) Ascertaining whether or not a patient is truly competent to reject treatment is quite difficult: for example, patients may refuse dialysis because their ability to think has been impaired by their uremic state.[37] (2) Distinguishing between degrees of willingness in order to help prioritize patients seeking scarce resources is virtually impossible, and rankings would be skewed by patients' abilities to sound convincing.[38]

Willingness to accept treatment as a criterion for patient selection is also dubious on theoretical grounds. There are two largely person oriented problems here. One involves the possibility that the decision not to accept treatment is a form of suicide. The issue is largely one of motivation. Although patients may be laying down their lives so that others might live, they may also be spurning life merely because it is not all that they want it to be. Respecting patients' decisions to forego treatment is problematic as well when others are hurt in the process. The U.S. legal system has acknowledged this by occasionally forcing dialysis (for example, when a prisoner has used treatment refusal to manipulate others), and ethicists have argued that treatment should not be foregone or discontinued until significant outstanding obligations to others have been fulfilled.[39]

Willingness to risk illness also has both pragmatic and theoretical shortcomings. Pragmatically, the concern about the cost to society of hazardous life style choices may be exaggerated. The increased cost of health care may be more than counterbalanced by other savings (for example, in social security and retirement funds) due to early deaths.[40] The use of a willingness-to-risk-illness criterion, if anything, may generate new costs in terms of privacy lost and funds required when a new policing agency is established to keep track of people's health-related (including sexual) behaviors.[41] Even attempts to prove after the fact that patients have freely chosen to act in ways that have caused their illness are terribly expensive because of the difficulty of the task.[42] The task, in fact, may be impossible. One obstacle is proving a causal link between patients' actions and their subsequent illnesses—for example, that severe breathing difficulties can only be due to excessive smoking. Generally there are many possible causes for an illness, few of which are within a person's control. Rarely is it possible to rule out all such external causes with the certainty necessary in effect to deny someone life itself.[43] Statistical likelihood is insufficient.[44] Even the link between cirrhosis of the liver and alcoholism is not well established in that some alcoholics appear more susceptible to liver damage than others, and many people develop cirrhosis for non-alcohol-related reasons.[45]

Other obstacles to proving a link between life style and illness involve the nature of the patient's past actions. If the patient did not engage in those actions with the understanding that they could lead to the illness that resulted, it is not clear that she or he should be held responsible for the illness. Even if it could be demonstrated that such understanding was present, responsibility cannot be established unless it can also be proven that the actions in question were freely carried out. However, advertising, peer pressure, cultural values, or dietary deficiencies may have significantly impaired the patient's ability to freely act or not act in certain ways.[46] Psychological instabilities or genetic predispositions may also be responsible.[47] The same imponderables attend the notion of proving that society (rather than personal or other uncontrollable influences) is responsible for a patient's illness.[48]

One final set of pragmatic hindrances besetting a willingness-to-risk-illness criterion revolves around the attempt to demonstrate a close link between unhealthy behaviors such as excessive alcohol consumption and unsatisfactory medical benefit from treatment. Even studies showing reduced survivability in alcoholic recipients of liver transplants demonstrate a survival rate higher than that of certain types of nonalcoholic patients who are considered medically suitable candidates for transplantation.[49] More recent studies have actually disputed the very notion that alcoholics necessarily fare less well medically than other liver transplant recipients.[50] It may be that it takes so long for alcohol consumption to produce cirrhosis that most transplant recipients die from other causes before alcohol becomes a fatal factor.[51]

On theoretical grounds, too, again largely person oriented, willingness to risk illness as a basis for patient selection is questionable. Injustice inheres in penalizing some patients for their behaviors if most other patients are not penalized for theirs.[52] In other words, the criterion arguably should not be employed on an illness-by-illness basis but withheld until it can be consistently applied. In light of the huge number of illnesses that are behavior related, consistent application would be a formidable task indeed.[53] It may also be unfair to exclude from treatment patients with objectionable life styles if the true (but perhaps unexpressed) justification for exclusion is their social value (see chapter 3).[54] Even if one disregards justice, compassion might well dictate that even victims of their own bad judgment should not be barred from the help of the community.[55] Medicine in particular has traditionally been a caring institution. If people are to be punished for bad behavior, presumably more appropriate institutions than medicine exist to serve this purpose.[56] Respect for persons and for their autonomy in a world of diverse values may also ultimately argue against a willingness-to-risk-illness criterion. Were the criterion to be employed, society's (health) care would be made contingent upon people affirming certain value-priorities (for example, health before the excitement of risk-taking).[57]

Possible Common Ground

Both forms of the willingness criterion have widely acknowledged justifications, with weaknesses that largely concern particular ways the criterion is put into practice. Accordingly, the widest consensus is likely to lie in identifying stringent conditions under which forms of the criterion may be employed. The practicality of satisfying these conditions will determine the viability of the criterion.

Consider, first, willingness to accept treatment. There is extensive support for the idea that patients should not be forced to undergo medical treatment. However, decisions to forego treatment that may well be medically beneficial must be made with patients' consent (or at least with their knowledge, if a society cannot make treatment available to them for economic reasons[58]—see chapter 10). For consent to be ethical, four conditions must be met. First, patients must be ethically (not merely legally) competent—that is, they must have decision-making capacity. In practice this means that patients must be able to understand the relevant information, to reflect on it in accordance with their values, and to communicate with caregivers. The capacity for making a particular treatment decision may be present without necessarily being there for all other purposes.[59] Second, consent must be voluntary. As explained earlier, patients must be freed as much as possible from the subtle pressures of others to decide for or against treatment. Third, consent must be informed. In order for patients to make responsible decisions for or against treatment they must be provided with all of the relevant information.[60] Because caregivers' and patients' values may differ, the caregiver needs a reasonable understanding of the patient's values in order to know what information about a treatment is relevant to that patient. The information provided should probably include the fact that a lifesaving resource under consideration is scarce, so that patients may elect to prefer others over themselves.[61] However, care must be taken not to encourage patients to forego treatment for this purpose if that truly does not reflect their wishes.[62]

The fourth condition of ethical consent is that it be based on genuine understanding. Patients must be helped by physicians, nurses, social workers, ministers, and others to appreciate the significance of all of the information provided within the unique context of their own lives.[63] If a trial use of the resource is possible, that should be encouraged (see chapter 14). With proper communication patients and physicians will generally be able to reach agreement as to whether or not to pursue treatment.[64] Physicians do need to listen carefully, though. In one study, physicians reflecting on the same case (and who were equally supportive of informed consent) split dramatically over whether or not the patient wanted treatment.[65]

Similar conditions apply to family members (though with less stringency) to the extent that they are involved in the decision-making process. However, although a family's and physician's agreement with the patient is to be sought as part of establishing willingness, their lack of agreement should not be allowed to override the patient's own wishes if at least a medical-benefit criterion (see chapter 10) has been satisfied.[66]

If a patient is incompetent to decide, then alternative ways of ascertaining the patient's wishes must be pursued. From a purely ethical perspective, past statements that patients have made are sufficient if it can be established that they were in fact ethically competent, truly voluntary, well informed, and based on genuine understanding. Legally, though, the ground for proceeding on the basis of past decisions is strongest if those wishes have been written down, signed, and witnessed—that is, incorporated into a living will.[67]

If neither written statements nor access to definitive statements that patients have made in the past exist, then somebody else needs to make the decision. The freedom and wishes of patients can still be respected if the decision can be made by persons designated in advance by patients. More and more frequently a durable power of attorney is being employed for this purpose.[68] In such cases, patients can identify persons who know best what their thinking is and what their values are—or at least those persons whose decisions they trust the most. Patients might, in fact, make both provisions: written statements as to what their wishes are plus the designation of particular persons who will be empowered to referee if the implications of these statements in the particular circumstances at hand are unclear.

In the absence of a person designated by a patient who cannot express his or her true wishes (or if the patient is a child), someone else has to make treatment decisions. The courts, among others, have differed as to who the best persons are to do that. Should it be the family, some group of medical personnel, a court, or others? The best ethical guideline here is still to find the person or persons in the best position to know or to ascertain the patient's wishes—or else best interests, if there is no way to determine the patient's wishes. Members of the patient's family are usually in the best position to employ these standards. Only if there is legitimate evidence that family members have disregarded these standards is there need, for example, for an institutional ethics committee (first) or court (last resort) to get involved.[69]

Several additional considerations will probably need to constrain a willingness (to accept treatment) criterion. Because of the complications noted above, degrees of willingness are probably best overlooked.[70] A patient should be identified as either willing or not willing (with the provisions for incompetence mentioned above). Unwillingness, then, becomes as valid a reason for discontinuing treatment already begun as for foregoing treatment in the first place.

The widest consensus seems to lie in allowing patients to refuse treatment for any reason. However, if patients have unfulfilled obligations to others that could be fulfilled if treatment were instituted, many would insist that patients be strongly urged to accept treatment. Even forcible imposition of treatment may be conceivable in the rare and unlikely case that the vital interests of others (for example, their lives) depend upon a patient being treated—though this matter is highly controversial.[71]

In light of earlier analysis, the other form of willingness criterion must be subjected to constraints as well. There is widespread sentiment that people should not be denied treatment on the basis that they are responsible for their medical disorder unless several conditions have been met. First, their disorder must have in fact been caused by their own actions and clearly not by other factors. Second, they must have been capable of freely engaging in these actions. Third, they must have been aware of the strong possibility that the disorder in question would result. Such awareness could not usually be verified by health care providers unless, prior to the institution of this form of willingness criterion, there were a suitable public education campaign to establish publicly the link between certain behaviors and particular medical disorders.[72] These conditions are so difficult to fulfill that a workable willingness-to-risk-illness criterion is not likely in the foreseeable future. If valid medical justifications for the criterion are evident, they should be evaluated on the basis of a medical rather than willingness criterion.[73]

Were a willingness-to-risk-illness criterion ever instituted, however, two further issues would become important. First, a suitable legal body would have to be established. Its central role would be to judge whether the conditions noted above have been met, for what is at stake here is no less than denying life(saving) to people. Second, the nature of the criterion would have to be explained clearly for it to meet with wide approval. It would need to be grounded in a respect for people's freedom to make choices and for the fairness of treating differently people who have made different choices—not in an intention to punish persons whose health habits do not meet with society's approval. Similarly, the purpose of a willingness-to-risk-illness criterion should not be to specially reward those with socially approved health habits. That intention stamps the criterion as more a form of the debatable social-value criterion (see chapter 3) than a willingness criterion.[74]

If fairness is to be central here, there are two further implications. One is that the search for all connections between personal behavior and medical disorders should at least be under way before personal responsibility is considered in any particular instances of patient selection. Alcoholics, for example, should not be singled out and required to pledge abstinence if there is no intention to require comparable abstinence on the part of those with other destructive behaviors (smoking, overeating, and so forth).[75] Particularly dubious is the requirement of a significant period of demonstrated abstinence before liver transplantation is approved. Such a requirement is tantamount to a death sentence.[76] Clinical evidence suggests that most alcoholics who are given liver transplants are highly motivated to refrain from alcohol, though an intention to do so at the time of transplantation is probably important.[77] The other implication of fairness is that compassion, although it perhaps cannot require that those clearly responsible for their disorder be treated the same as those who are not, may direct some of the latter to renounce voluntarily their own priority in order to improve the chances of the former to receive treatment. Moreover, compassion hopefully will move many to make available increased private and public funds so that more patients (including those responsible for their disorder) may be treated.

To sort out such considerations is important, but it remains the case that the establishing of personal or social responsibility for a particular medical disorder of a particular person is extraordinarily difficult. Extreme cases, such as choosing between a wounded bank robber and an innocent bystander wounded by the robber, may seem fairly straightforward.[78] However, the typical case is much closer to the one that follows.

An Illustrative Case

At the age of seventy, Mrs. Wilson has been admitted to the hospital for the fifth time in as many years for treatment of respiratory difficulty. The last time she was in the hospital she had nearly died. She has severe emphysema, and when she developed a cold (bronchopneumonia), her deterioration was so rapid that only artificial respiration in the emergency room saved her life. However, it proved very difficult to wean her from the respirator. She spent four weeks in the intensive care unit and required constant care from the medical staff, principally Paul Turner, an intern. After she was discharged, she remained short of breath even while sitting at rest.

Now, five months later, she has contracted another similar cold, apparently through her own carelessness, according to one of her sons, but this time Paul has managed to treat her without resorting to the ICU and the respirator. During her illnesses, Mrs. Wilson's two sons have been in constant contact with the medical staff. They have been anxious, agitated, and demanding.

It is now 2 A.M., and Paul is again called to see Mrs. Wilson, who is becoming increasingly lethargic. It is obvious that she is in respiratory failure and will probably die before morning if she is not placed on a respirator.

However, hospital policy requires that respirators be used only in the ICU, where the required supporting staff and facilities are available. There is only one bed open in the ICU. The residents like to save one bed for an emergency. As Paul approaches, Mrs. Wilson's sons are waiting. He knows their questions: What's wrong now? What needs to be done?[79]

Of the various issues raised by this case, one is fundamental: the ways that a patient's choices are relevant to treatment decisions. Here, for example, Mrs. Wilson appears to have chosen to act in ways that bring on her final life-threatening cold. The onset of illness creates the need for another important choice, one not explicitly recognized by any of the participants: the patient must decide—all things considered—whether or not to undergo a variety of possible treatments.

The first issue is the patient's willingness to risk illness. Mrs. Wilson has caught a cold, supposedly because she acted in a way that might have brought it on. However, it is not clear that she did not catch the cold because a thoughtless friend with a cold visited her. Her condition may have been so poor that no reasonable precautions would have protected her. It is also not clear that Mrs. Wilson's state of mind was such that she appreciated the risk entailed by her actions. In other words, the conditions outlined earlier for the ethical application of a willingness-to-risk-illness criterion have not been fulfilled.

Even if this form of willingness criterion does not apply in Mrs. Wilson's case, the other form arguably does. Mrs. Wilson herself—not just her sons—should have been consulted about ICU and respirator care once she had been stabilized upon returning to the hospital. Then at 2 A.M. the intern, Paul, might have had a publicly acceptable basis upon which to resist family demands and conserve scarce resources—that is, if Mrs. Wilson decided that further efforts at resuscitation would be more destructive of herself and others than helpful.

CHAPTER SIXTEEN

Ability to Pay

Many persons are not able to pay for the lifesaving treatments that they or their dependents need. The lack of such means is infrequently a basis for receiving special access to treatment, as was occasionally the case during the early days of dialysis. Sometimes this priority arose out of a concern for the special needs of the poor.[1] At other times it reflected a selection committee's preference to keep alive poor heads of households whose death would leave society with the burden of caring for their families.[2] A patient's history of struggling with great financial stresses has even been seen as an indicator that he or she is experienced in dealing with the stresses that accompany some lifesaving treatments such as heart transplants.[3]

However, for the most part an ability-to-pay criterion has functioned to exclude from treatment those who lack the means to pay for their treatment. This common form of the criterion, the focus of the present chapter, has a number of aspects.

The criterion is used to exclude from treatment those with insufficient funds or insurance to pay for scarce and expensive lifesaving treatment. In the United States, for example, health care has never been available to meet every need irrespective of one's ability to pay.[4] Many millions of people have inadequate private or government health care insurance, and many millions more have none at all. The consequences are predictable: the uninsured use health services only about half as much as the insured and die more frequently as a result.[5] When the poor (the underinsured as well as the uninsured) can afford certain treatments they are sometimes not told about them—a practice expected to become more frequent as health care becomes more expensive.[6]

Treatment for end-stage renal disease is one area in which ability to pay has figured prominently as a patient selection criterion. According to my recent U.S. study (see chapter 2), 43 percent of renal medical directors presently consider ability to pay a valid criterion, the average director rating it as slightly important (mean score 1.8 out of 5). This finding is consistent with the history of dialysis, for an ability-to-pay criterion was sometimes employed during the years of scarcity before dialysis was federally funded.[7] The provision of kidney transplants has also been guided by this criterion through the years.[8]

The distribution of other lifesaving resources in the United States is similarly affected by an ability-to-pay criterion.[9] Prominent examples include intensive care and non–kidney organ transplants.[10] Heart transplants (and, increasingly, temporarily implanted artificial hearts which may give recipients priority access to heart transplants) are perhaps the most common instances of the latter.[11] Liver transplants are also being done more frequently now that they have moved beyond the experimental stage.[12] Yet patients are being excluded when they cannot obtain the required finances.[13] Financial pressures have become so tight that some hospitals have withdrawn coronary bypass surgeons' operating privileges when they have admitted too many patients with inadequate insurance.[14]

Another way that an ability-to-pay criterion is employed even in relatively wealthy countries like the United States is through the denial of critical emergency health care to poor people.[15] Numerous instances of refusal to provide emergency care have been documented in such locations as Illinois, Texas, New York, Tennessee, and California.[16] In more than one case, legislation to prevent this patient "dumping" has been enacted as a result.[17] Sometimes dumping occurs when hospitals simply refuse to treat people who cannot pay, under circumstances in which delay of treatment may seriously jeopardize their health and even lives.[18] Those refused have included critically ill patients who have been transferred from smaller facilities that lack the specific resources required to treat them.[19] Hospitals often make at least some provision to transfer sick people who are already on their doorsteps to other hospitals. However, the delay can still prove hazardous—particularly if the transfer provisions include nothing more than handing sick people maps showing bus routes to other facilities.[20]

The international picture reflects an even greater reliance upon an ability-to-pay criterion. People who have financial resources often receive priority over those who do not.[21] Such prioritizing may even approach the level of national policy.[22] Although only blatant applications of the criterion in countries such as Great Britain get special media attention, they are indicative of a broad practice of favoring those who have access to the means to pay for their treatment.[23] If the needed treatment is not available in their own country, wealthy persons may travel to another country such as the United States, where willingness to pay several times the going rate for treatment has in the past gained patients priority even over local patients who have been waiting longer.[24]

An ability-to-pay criterion is usually employed to select patients who either have or can obtain the financial resources to pay for treatment, but it functions in several related ways as well. One is to select patients with the ability to pay for the support services that necessarily accompany certain treatments, for example, transportation to the medical center where treatment will occur. Accordingly, centers have sometimes favored dialysis and heart transplant candidates who live nearby, have the financial resources to relocate, or can afford transportation.[25] Transportation costs for an ongoing treatment like dialysis can easily be $2,000 a year—a cost unbearable for some.[26] When such hidden costs are borne by the patient, the stated 80 percent federal coverage for dialysis in the United States has amounted in some cases to little more than 50 percent of actual costs.[27] In addition to transportation, hidden costs may include living expenses away from home while staying near a medical center to receive an organ transplant, as well as whatever follow-up drugs, home care, and monitoring are needed.[28] Surveys conducted by the American Society of Transplant Surgeons and the American Society of Transplant Physicians indicate that many patients have been barred from transplantation because of their inability to afford follow-up immunosuppressive drugs.[29] Fortunately for such patients, federal resistance to financing drug coverage has largely faded.[30]

A related form of an ability-to-pay criterion involves the patient's ability to pay for a transplantable organ (as opposed to the surgery). At issue is whether or not it should be permissible to buy and sell organs. Evidence of people offering their organs (for example, kidneys) for sale has surfaced in the United States, West Germany, India, Brazil, and elsewhere.[31] The United States, among other countries, has forbidden the sale of organs for transplantation; but there is evidence that some wealthy persons, largely from other countries, have been able to obtain organs more quickly than usual by paying extra.[32]

Another way that ability-to-pay considerations have functioned recently is to favor those who can gain access to politicians or the media and thereby obtain federal funding, financial contributions from the community, or the donation of a needed organ. One's ability to gain such access is not much of a factor in some countries, such as Great Britain, and is far from definitive in others, such as the United States.[33] Nevertheless numerous U.S. examples, at least, have been documented.

Charles Fiske pleaded with the American Academy of Pediatrics—in the glare of extensive preplanned news coverage—for someone to donate a liver for his daughter Jamie.[34] Debbie Pinheiro needed a donated liver at the same time, and her parents looked on helplessly as their daughter went relatively unnoticed.[35] Hardie Clifton received a heart transplant and Ronnie DeSillers as well as an unidentified woman obtained a liver transplant because they were able to catch the attention of the White House.[36] Baby Jesse in California obtained a donated heart in direct response to the extensive news coverage arranged by his parents.[37] Meanwhile, Baby Calvin in Kentucky, though higher on the waiting list, was bypassed; and his publicity-shunning parents were furious.[38] When Kentuckian Leah Halsey needed a donated heart shortly thereafter, her parents understandably mounted a media campaign.[39]

This last form of an ability-to-pay criterion, then, functions in several ways. Those with the best access to the media are able to elicit sufficient financial contributions from the community to satisfy the traditional ability-to-pay criterion.[40] Alternatively, a community may be able to pressure a government or insurance company into funding treatment for a particular person.[41] In order to obtain major community support, though, a patient's family often must have the sizable amount of money necessary to finance a massive publicity effort.[42] If patients can get a famous personality or an influential politician to support their cases, they too have a particularly good chance of being treated.[43] The U.S. president has even had an aide on his staff who specializes in promoting the cases of certain individuals.[44] The aide's activities have purposely been kept quiet—meaning that only those with special media or political connections can obtain this special treatment.[45]

Some observers have suggested that the instances of special media and political appeals to date are indications of what may become a prerequisite for obtaining certain scarce medical resources.[46] Whether or not such is the case, even stronger indications are that growing financial restrictions in health care will increase the frequency with which an ability-to-pay criterion in its traditional form is employed.[47] According to my U.S. study, although only 4 percent of dialysis directors reject patients on this basis today, 45 percent would consider doing so under conditions of greater scarcity. It has similarly been projected that artificial hearts will be distributed largely on an ability-to-pay basis.[48]

Justifications

Some of the various reasons for supporting an ability-to-pay criterion involve the basic values that may be seen to undergird the criterion. One such (productivity oriented) value is social utility. By favoring the wealthy and those with social and political connections, an ability-to-pay criterion tends to favor persons who are likely to contribute most to society in the future.[49] A more person oriented value that may be seen as underlying this criterion is fairness. When people are viewed as being fundamentally equal, fairness calls for some sort of random basis upon which to allocate limited resources, and one's degree of wealth could conceivably be acknowledged as a sufficiently random basis to serve the purpose.[50]

The most widely cited (and largely person oriented) value buttressing an ability-to-pay criterion is that of freedom.[51] The primary way that the criterion operates is through a market system in which scarce resources are purchased by those with the greatest willingness and resources to pay.[52] Such a system leaves people free to devote their resources to whatever goods they prefer—medical or otherwise. Even if access to some basic level of health care is guaranteed by the government, freedom to purchase more care can operate above this level.[53] Freedom can be seen as essential to life—a value to which other moral considerations must generally conform.[54] Ultimately it is important that all persons, including noncitizens, be accorded this freedom and that it include leeway for all to make use of whatever political or media influence they can obtain.

Some other reasons for supporting an ability-to-pay criterion are more pragmatic in nature and for the most part may be either person oriented or productivity oriented. In the eyes of certain advocates the financial considerations involved in this criterion are simply obvious and unavoidable.[55] Health care has a cost and this must be paid if health care is to continue to remain available.[56] In this respect a 1980s national panel considering the distribution of the artificial heart found the rejection of an ability-to-pay criterion by a similar 1970s panel to be naive.[57]

Other, similarly pragmatic considerations apply. It arguably is also naive to provide a scarce treatment to someone who lacks the additional resources (for example, transportation) needed for treatment to achieve its medical objective.[58] Perhaps the greatest pragmatic advantage of an ability-to-pay criterion, though, is the fact that by leaving the distribution of scarce resources to the free market it requires less intervention and perplexing decision making by authorities than other approaches.[59]

The remaining type of justification has to do with the problems created if an ability-to-pay criterion is not employed. If people are not allowed to use their wealth to purchase scarce lifesaving resources, one might expect a black market in these items to emerge, with all of its attending problems.[60] Should the government be pressured into funding a particular treatment contrary to its overall priorities for the health care system, other more important health care priorities may go unachieved.[61]

Several specific forms of the criterion have their own justifications. For example, denying poor patients access to emergency treatment is understandable in that they are not only unable to pay for treatment but also likely to be sicker than average patients and more expensive to treat.[62] Other forms of the criterion such as permitting or requiring the purchase (and sale) of transplantable organs may be objectionable only if they are abused. If there is a danger of the poor being exploited, for instance, then legal protections could be tailored to meet this need. To assume that the poor cannot make autonomous decisions about their lives is to demean them and to exclude them from community decision making.[63] An opportunity to increase the organ supply may be lost in the process. Even allowing patient selection to depend upon media appeals has its virtues, for it respects the important values of personal initiative and communal charity.[64]

Weaknesses

Despite such a range of justifications, many countries have taken a dim view of an ability-to-pay criterion.[65] Popular polls in the United States consistently discover majority opposition to it.[66] In one multinational study nearly 90 percent of the countries indicated that their governments have assumed primary responsibility for financing the treatment of kidney disease (largely dialysis and kidney transplants).[67] The history of the literature on the subject also suggests an overwhelming consensus against the criterion when scarce lifesaving resources are at issue.[68] The reasons for this opposition are probably best explored first in general; comments on special forms of the criterion are reserved for later. The arguments against an ability-to-pay criterion are generally person oriented except when the workability of a market approach or an underlying justification such as social utility are questioned.

Three major values form the basis of an ability-to-pay criterion: social value (utility), fairness, and freedom. Each is open to question, notably the first. For example, the perception that by favoring the wealthy an ability-to-pay criterion necessarily favors those most valuable to society (presently or in the past) is factually untrue.[69] Also questionable is the assumption that those who lack most are least deserving of an opportunity to live. Some would argue that the socially disadvantaged are most deserving of whatever resources society is able to provide.[70]

One danger of employing social value justifications is that once they are allowed in defense of an ability-to-pay criterion, the door is wide open for a social-value criterion per se (see chapter 3).[71] Moreover, the spectacle of desperate patients bidding against each other in a free market system of distributing lifesaving resources tends to seriously erode whatever remains of a society's commitment to the incomparable and intrinsic value of human life.[72]

Similarly open to criticism is the fairness justification for an ability-to-pay criterion. If some form of random selection is called for, there are much more equitable forms than ability to pay. Using people's wealth as a random characteristic is inadequate according to at least two of the major tests of forms of random selection discussed near the end of chapter 17. For instance, wealth is not independent of human manipulation; rather, people may lack financial resources because of the individual or corporate injustice of others.[73]

Accordingly, an ability-to-pay criterion unfairly discriminates against a variety of people.[74] Those who are weak from illness are particularly vulnerable to exploitation under a free market system.[75] The elderly also are denied treatment disproportionately often because many are poor and less able to obtain long-term loans due to their age.[76] Whatever their age, in fact, the poor as a group are consistent losers when an ability-to-pay criterion is employed.[77] Such predictable discrimination for reasons sometimes beyond the victims' control is most odious when people's lives are at stake.[78] Denial of emergency care is a case in point.[79] The transferring of patients is not necessarily wrong,[80] even if they are in unstable condition (if they cannot be stabilized). However, doing so, at risk to their lives, is objectionable when done for economic rather than medical reasons. One proposed way to protect against unwarranted transfers is to require the informed consent of patients when they are competent.[81]

There are other senses as well in which an ability-to-pay criterion is unfair. If some lifesaving treatments are funded for all, then it would seem unfair not to fund other lifesaving treatments of comparable expense.[82] Furthermore, many scarce lifesaving treatments have been developed with public tax money paid in part by the current poor. Transplant technologies are one example.[83] Another is the artificial heart, whose development has been made possible by $200 million of public funds.[84] It seems unfair to deny people access to resources that they have helped pay to develop[85] and to deny the poor organ transplants when they as a group contribute to the supply of available organs.[86] For all of these reasons unbiased people hypothetically constructing a social contract probably would not agree to a social arrangement in which patients are denied lifesaving resources owing to their inability to pay. The contractors would realize that anyone can be born or fall into poverty and that there is no truly just compensation for denying a group of persons access to continued life.[87]

A third basic value underlying an ability-to-pay criterion is freedom, which as a justification for the criterion is vulnerable on a number of fronts. For example, an ability-to-pay criterion does not protect the freedom of all so much as it protects the freedom of those with resources to obtain treatment while insuring that those without resources will have no such freedom.[88] Because of the great expense of treating patients in high technology settings, only the freedom of the few is really protected.[89] In the eyes of some all that matters is that patients be free to trade what they rightly own for treatment rightly owned by the provider. However, as important as this freedom is, other moral considerations come into play to protect persons when this freedom removes whatever chance a person has to continue to live. Unbounded freedom can be very inhumane.[90]

A market system is ill-suited to the distribution of lifesaving treatment. Patients cannot always enter this market with similar knowledge and resources.[91] A free exchange is almost impossible when one party lacks something necessary for survival and the other party has the needed item without personally lacking anything necessary for survival.[92] This scenario generally leads to desperation bidding, in which nearly any price will be paid and the idea of just trade-offs seems out of place.[93] A person's level of desire for a lifesaving resource is often not accurately reflected. The poor lack what is minimally necessary to bargain for expensive items through the market, and the rich need devote no more than an insignificant portion of their resources to obtain continued life.[94] Granted that a market system is designed to respond to desires and demands, nevertheless a stronger moral claim, human need, is arguably involved here.[95] For this reason among others, a U.S. presidential commission in 1983 labeled a market approach inevitably unacceptable.[96]

In other words, market allocation may be fine if a variety of goods are in view. However, lifesaving medical care is different.[97] The primary difference is that life itself is at stake.[98] Life is the basic prerequisite without which all other goods and trades through the market are meaningless. Furthermore, to buy and sell life so explicitly may be to accelerate the dangerous cheapening of life that already appears to be occurring in many societies.[99] This cheapening, as well as most of the other problems previously noted, results from giving priority to those with full insurance as well as those with wealth.[100]

As discussed earlier in the chapter, inability to pay for a needed lifesaving resource is only one of the issues involved in an ability-to-pay criterion. Foreign citizenship, ability to pay for support services, the buying and selling of organs for transplant, and access to media and political influence are also important concerns. Each will be considered here individually.

Foreign citizenship per se is more properly examined in relation to a favored-group criterion (see chapter 4). The issue here is whether or not the ability of foreign nationals to pay for treatment (perhaps doubly or more) should be considered when recipients are selected. The same difficulties surrounding the favoring of any wealthy person apply in cases of foreign nationals.[101]

The entire range of difficulties is also relevant where the ability to pay for support services essential to successful treatment is in view.[102] Moreover, facilities can often provide such services inexpensively by giving patients special training or organizing volunteer services.[103] A good example is the "drivers for dialysis" program in the United States, which was developed in response to the inability of chronic hemodialysis patients to get to treatment facilities.

The buying and selling of organs, on the other hand, raises a number of special concerns—not surprising for a practice so widely opposed.[104] Several of these concerns are productivity oriented in that they have to do with efficiency. Allowing the commercialization of organs would increase the cost of transplantation and reduce the quality of the product by creating incentives to make use of medically unacceptable organs.[105] If living donors are involved, a tangle of moral and legal considerations would also arise (for example, the duty of the donor not to abuse the organ to be donated).[106]

Person oriented objections to commercialization include the following.

First, there are responses to key justifications. If increasing the supply
of organs were a satisfactory goal, then all sorts of immoral tactics (including force) could potentially be justified. Less objectionable means
of increasing the supply should be exhausted first. Banning commercialization is admittedly a mild restriction of liberty. However, restrictions of liberty are commonly justified when serious dangers are present
(see below).[107]

The commercialization of organs is also objectionable in its own right
and by its very nature undermines the present noncompetitive, altruistic
basis of organ donation, thereby weakening such virtues in society.[108] It
also brings the possibility of voluntary consent into question when poor
donors are involved. As has already been established with regard to
human experimentation, monetary inducement is unacceptable if it is so
great as to be potentially coercive.[109] Commercialization would almost
inevitably lead to exploitation of the poor, including the victimization of
people in less developed countries by people with access to transplantation technology in more developed countries.[110] The pricing of a priceless gift and the increased tendency to view human body parts as
commodities (and ultimately human beings as things) are also unsavory
implications of the commercializing of organs.[111]

As for distribution of scarce lifesaving resources according to one's
access to media or political influence (and resulting ability to pay), there
are again multiple problems. Several have to do with the inequity of this
arrangement. It is wonderful when special media coverage or political
efforts obtain lifesaving medical resources (for example, a scarce organ
or the necessary funds) for a person in need. The problem is that there
are many other people at the same time who are dying for lack of the
same resources.[112] When a person's opportunity to live depends upon
the publicity or political influence one has, there is a serious inequity.[113]
Ironically, the problem created here is the very one that politicians and
media programs themselves decry: people have unequal access to lifesaving care.[114]

Not all can obtain needed resources even if they energetically attempt
to mount a major media campaign. To counterbalance the Jamie Fiske
and Baby Jesse success stories are the stories like that of Zoann Brazie.
Zoann's parents mortgaged their small restaurant and made public appeals for funds but were able to raise only enough money to cover costs
to that point. None of the $125,000 required up front for their daughter's
needed heart transplant could be raised. She died after three months of
attempts.[115] In the case of one of Dr. Jack Copeland's heart transplant

patients, a twenty-two-year-old man, the fund-raising took too many weeks. By the time sufficient funds were accumulated there was not enough time to locate a donor organ, and the man died.[116]

All people simply are not sufficiently "cute and cuddly" or otherwise attractive to gain major media coverage.[117] All do not have the same connections with people in the publicity arena.[118] Are lives to depend on this? Some people have privileged relationships with key political figures or the kinds of skills to persuade insurance companies or others to provide needed funding.[119] It seems objectionable to many that such factors should sometimes become, in effect, prerequisites for receiving lifesaving medical treatment.

Other factors besides a patient's attractiveness and ability may affect media and political support. One is the extent to which one of the patient's physicians is willing to speak out publicly on the patient's behalf. Derrick Gordon's family was on welfare and had no way to raise the $125,000 needed for Derrick's heart transplant. So Dr. Linda Kocsis took the case to the media and sufficient funds were donated as a result.[120] Other physicians have sufficient political influence to accomplish the same end with public funds.[121]

In some cases the color of the patient's skin would seem to be a crucial factor. Black patients in the United States, for example, are not able to raise nearly the kind of money that white patients can. This predicament is attested to by statistics that show an overwhelming percentage of organ transplants going to white patients.[122] It is also confirmed by specific cases such as that of Mark Mitchell, a black twenty-three-year-old, who simply was not able to generate the same outpouring of public support as some of his white counterparts.[123]

Another reason for different media responses to different patients has to do with the timing of various patients' illnesses. If there have been a number of media stories and funding appeals in the recent past, there is likely to be less interest in another one.[124] In such a case—as when a physician's nonmedical efforts or the patient's skin color are at issue—the inequities loom large. It is dubious whether such considerations are legitimate reasons for allowing lifesaving resources to go to some and not to others.

In addition to the inequities involved, several other difficulties surround the selection of resource recipients based upon their access to media and political influence. One is its impracticality; another is its medical unsoundness. As one U.S. senator commented, it is just not practical to require every person who needs an organ transplant to gain special access to the president.[125] A government that encourages patients in their public and media appeals runs the risk of appearing to be inconsistent if it is unwilling to devote public money to support treating these patients.[126] The issue of medical soundness arises because of the way organs and recipients are matched. Organs may go to the media favorite rather than to the best medical candidate.[127]

A final drawback is the destructive impact of implicitly requiring media and political appeals in order to receive scarce lifesaving resources. This approach is demeaning to patients because it reduces them to begging for the privilege of remaining alive.[128] It also proves terribly disruptive to the lives of the families involved.[129] Ultimately society as a whole is the loser as patients are pitted against patients, physicians against physicians, and politicians against politicians—all clamoring for attention every time individuals need lifesaving resources. Decision by decibels brings discord.[130] The result is that people become desensitized to all appeals for financial help—perhaps even to the urgent need for organ donation.[131]

Possible Common Ground

A fairly broad agreement, signaled in the report of the U.S. Task Force on Organ Transplantation, seems to be emerging at least in the United States with regard to an ability-to-pay criterion. The criterion should be avoided whenever possible.[132] Needless to say, the importance of this criterion at the patient selection level depends in part upon decisions that are made at the budgetary macroallocation level. Although any society is free to budget according to whatever it sees as its priorities, these priorities, it is to be hoped, will be humane ones.[133] Lifesaving resources would seem to be prime candidates for priority.

One way to pursue this priority—without having to incur the inequities and dangers that accompany leaving the distribution of life itself to the marketplace—is for a society to develop only those lifesaving technologies that it is willing to fund for all.[134] Soon after a technology is invented, its ultimate costs would need to be projected and a decision made as to whether or not a nation could afford to develop it and provide it to all in need. That way, the awkward situation of denying treatment on financial grounds to people who have helped pay for its development through their taxes could be avoided. Alternatively, facilities that profit from the provision of scarce lifesaving treatments could perhaps be taxed to generate part of the funds required to make these treatments accessible to all. Such a tax would not in turn justify the profits (more on this later) but would be a way of ensuring that such profits, if earned, would at least in part be used for lifesaving purposes. Leaving this matter solely up to the charitable inclinations of profit-making facilities is not likely to prove sufficient, if past experience is a valid indicator (although there are admirable examples of generosity).[135]

Even if recipients of a scarce lifesaving resource are selected without regard for their ability to pay, it may not necessarily be unacceptable to allow patients to purchase treatment under certain conditions. Consider, for example, the situation in which a technology such as the artificial heart is available, but limited only by the funds publicly and privately allocated to purchase the equipment. There is nothing necessarily objectionable (in terms of the allocation of this resource) about people paying to have their own equipment built as long as the amount of resources available to others is not thereby affected.[136]

To be sure, such an arrangement does not make for a thoroughly egalitarian health care system.[137] It leaves unaddressed the possible injustice of the inequality of wealth that makes these special purchases possible only for some. However, even if some inequalities of wealth are unjust, a health policy cannot be held responsible for eradicating all social evils. Any health system would be more just if such prior injustice were eliminated. The health care system in Great Britain is one in which such special purchases are allowed alongside a general policy of resisting an ability-to-pay criterion.[138]

On the other hand, the scarcity involved may not be a matter of the money allocated, but of the very limited existence of the resource. The surgeons who have the skills to implant an artificial organ may be in short supply or a newly discovered drug may still be scarce relative to life-threatening medical need even though it is being produced by all capable facilities as rapidly as possible.[139] Under such circumstances, few would support allowing private parties to purchase the scarce resource. Others would thereby almost certainly be deprived of their lives because of this private action.

To this point the discussion of exceptions to the general position opposing an ability-to-pay criterion has assumed that the payment at issue involves money. Such may not be the case, however. When the scarce resource is a transplantable organ, for example, patients' ability to "pay" may entail their ability to provide their own organ. Similar considerations would apply here as in the case of money. The overall system is most equitable if treatment can be distributed without reference to patients' ability to provide or generate resources of any sort.[140] However, some people will donate their own or their child's organ, for example, only to a close relative, and if that relative is not allowed to have special access to the organ, then no one will receive it.

So it seems potentially acceptable to allow people to obtain their own organs, and this would include allowing people to designate their organs for specific recipients.[141] Some countries allow this practice particularly when living related donors are involved.[142] Examples can also be cited of organs probably not having been donated had it not been possible to designate a particular recipient.[143] Certain guidelines are necessary, though. Ultimately, to be acceptable this provision probably must not affect the supply of organs available for other patients. Donors might be required, for example, to sign affidavits testifying that they would not have donated the organ in question without the appeal from or information about a particular recipient, and that they are unwilling to make the organ available to anyone other than that recipient. A donor advocate could also be assigned to ensure that no pressures from the potential recipient or others have improperly influenced the donor's decision.[144] If such safeguards prove unworkable or insufficient, then it may be necessary to limit designated recipients to relatives of the donor—a limitation currently favored by the majority of people in the United States.[145]

Despite these conditions that allow the possibility of exceptions, the broadest consensus still seems to be against the implementation of an ability-to-pay criterion wherever possible. However, is this general opposition justified irrespective of the consequences? Here some distinctions must be made.

Something supremely important in most people's eyes—life itself—is at stake in the patient selection decisions being considered here. Hence only something equally significant can be expected to outweigh it, and few people consider financial profits to be as important as life. Accordingly, many oppose the idea that poor people should be excluded from treatment simply because profits would otherwise be threatened. They are troubled when economics eclipses ethics so decisively.[146]

If facilities will have to close (or never open in the first place), however, that is a different story. Such a case might well imply greater disregard for life than if ability to pay were considered.[147] Better to treat some (who can pay) than none at all—at least during the interim while the financial means to treat all are sought.[148] Note, however, that two conditions must be met if an ability-to-pay criterion is to be justified in this way. First, there must be no possibility that the facility can operate without employing the criterion. Some evidence does exist that many facilities are already at risk of failure.[149] Second, patients' lives must be jeopardized by such a failure—that is, there must be no other medical facilities in the area that could adequately treat the patients that the failed facility can no longer treat. The situation that fulfills both of these conditions is rare.

More than constricted profit is also at stake where the result of providing all a given resource without ability to pay is that other more important medical services must go unprovided. This outcome is relevant when evaluating both governmental funding of a particular treatment and an individual facility's provision of that treatment without regard to ability to pay.[150] Examples can be found in the United States and elsewhere illustrating the cutbacks in services that can result when an expensive lifesaving treatment is provided without reference to ability to pay.[151] Faced with such a predicament, a facility can only devote its available resources to the medical care it deems most important and leave other treatments unsubsidized. Whether or not unsubsidized treatments should even be provided to those who can pay will depend in part upon whether or not they (along with less financially able patients in need of these treatments) can be adequately handled by other facilities.

Whenever possible, then, an ability-to-pay criterion should probably be avoided—though avoidance may not always be possible, as explained above. In the instances where it is not, it is arguably best not to employ the criterion until the last minute. In other words, medical and any other legitimate criteria should be applied first, as in the case of any patient. Only after a patient has been identified as the best candidate for the next available resource on medical grounds should she or he be excluded on the basis of ability to pay.[152] The reasons for such a practice are twofold: first, it will enable those responsible for allocating limited resources among treatments to perceive more accurately the number of patients who are being left to die exclusively for lack of financial support; second, it will focus the kind of attention upon these patients that may well prompt the private donation of funds to pay for their treatment.[153]

An Illustrative Case

An unconscious man had been brought by the police to Oakbrook Hospital's emergency room.

"We started the IV, stopped his bleeding, patched him up, and evaluated his overall condition. But he still hasn't recovered consciousness. The police think it was a hit-and-run driver," explained Dr. Kathy McDowell.

"He didn't have any identification?" asked Dr. Paul Bridewell, director of the renal unit.

"That's right. They think that either the driver robbed him or somebody else who came along did. Anyway, he was wearing jeans and a sweatshirt and was carrying a small pack of belongings, but nothing that gives any clue as to his background. There is one thing we do know definitely."

"What's that?"

"His liver was hopelessly damaged, but his general physical condition is good. We think he's a good candidate for a transplant."

"Then you know we've got a guy whose brain waves we're waiting to flatten out?"

"Dr. Liebsbaum told me."

"You did a tissue check?"

"It's close enough."

"Too bad. What I mean is that I've got another candidate. Now we have to decide which of the two gets the liver."

"Who's the other candidate?"

"A Mrs. Benson. She's a woman in her early sixties who's active in local affairs. She was on the school board. Her husband's a rich lawyer, and both of them move in high social circles. She does a lot of work now with a foundation that's supposed to help minority children in school. She also happens to be a pretty good candidate physically for the transplant."

"So you'll choose her over my patient?"

"I didn't say that. How old is this guy?"

"I would estimate that he's in his early or middle thirties. He seems to be in good physical condition."

"But we don't know anything about him. He appears to be just a drifter passing through town."

"That's true," Dr. McDowell admitted.

"In that case," concluded Dr. Bridewell, "we really must favor Mrs. Benson. We simply can't go around giving away free care to anyone who wants it."[154]

The various considerations examined in this chapter can prove helpful in sorting out cases such as this. Apparently Mrs. Benson and the unidentified man are both good transplant candidates medically. For all we know the candidates arrived (or were referred, in Mrs. Benson's case) for treatment at about the same time; other factors are presumably equal. These assumptions as they have relevance to other legitimate patient selection criteria would of course need to be verified. Given this scenario, though, we are compelled to consider the relevance of the unidentified man's presumed inability to pay.

First of all, this inability should be verified if at all possible. If it turns out that the man is indeed unable to pay, then the reasons for excluding him on this basis need to be carefully scrutinized. What data, if any, underlie Dr. Bridewell's concern that the hospital "simply can't go around giving away free care to anyone who wants it"? Were "care" changed to "lifesaving treatment" and "wants" to "medically needs," what reasons for excluding the unidentified man could still be substantiated? Would the hospital close or other, more important services go unprovided? Such questions are best answered as a matter of policy with regard to the entire group of patients who need lifesaving care but cannot pay for it. If no such policy exists, then it is doubtful that treating this one man is likely to have sufficiently serious implications to warrant his exclusion.

Were he to be selected, the wealthy and well-connected Mrs. Benson would still be free to mount a public appeal to obtain an organ. In order for her to benefit from the organ, though, the donor probably should be required to certify that the obtained organ would not have been otherwise available to another patient. On the other hand, if the man must be excluded on the basis of a valid policy already in place, there is at least a chance that the acknowledgment of the reason for his exclusion may provoke donations to fund his treatment later—perhaps even a contribution from rich Mr. and Mrs. Benson, who know what it is like to wait helplessly for a lifesaving donation.

CHAPTER SEVENTEEN

Random Selection

When other selection criteria are judged to be unacceptable or indecisive, random selection is a possible alternative. Random selection generally takes one of two forms: a traditional lottery in which one name is randomly selected from among the names of all patients waiting for treatment; or a first-come, first-served approach. Since the time that one person as opposed to another is stricken with a medical condition and seeks treatment is more or less random, first-come, first-served functions as a sort of natural lottery.

Random selection may not seem to be a commonly employed form of decision making.[1] Yet it has been used many times throughout history to make especially important decisions. In earlier days a lottery was often used to discern God's will.[2] The Jewish and Christian Bibles affirm the use of a lottery and record numerous examples.[3] Lotteries were used to appoint the treasurers of Athena in classical Greece, to decide Germanic tribal procedures in the first century A.D., to identify murderers in ancient Frisian law, to make critical decisions (Oliver Cromwell, for example, used it), and to select Old Order Amish Church officials.[4] A U.S. judge recommended it to determine who should be tossed from an overcrowded lifeboat.[5] On other occasions the connection between a lottery and the divine will has been more implicit, as when Druid human sacrifices were selected and guilt versus innocence in ancient Irish culture was assessed.[6]

Alongside these instances are uses of the lottery that have no reference to God. Random selection in these cases is adopted to be sure that a decision does not reflect the value judgments or preferences of decision makers. The Jewish and Christian Bibles record numerous such examples.[7] Other ancient sages also recognized the potential of the lottery as a tool to insure fairness.[8] More recently, in the United States a lottery has been deemed the fairest way to award oil and gas rights to certain federally owned public land, determine who receives a special opportunity to immigrate, distribute certain types of broadcasting licenses, select people for military service, assign airport landing and departure spaces, and award lucrative vending contracts.[9] It has similarly been proposed to distribute government grants, determine who gets admitted to college, assign students to schools as part of desegregation plans, and allocate public housing and liquor licenses.[10] Its most familiar use, though, is probably as a means of identifying prizewinners in fund-raising schemes around the world.[11] First-come, first-served too has guided the distribution of scarce resources throughout history.[12]

The medical sphere in particular has not lacked instances in which random selection has been employed.[13] A first-come, first-served approach, for instance, has often guided decisions as to who receives lifesaving resources.[14] During the early years of dialysis in the United States, many centers employed this approach.[15] European countries have also favored it.[16] Selection of recipients for organ transplants is frequently done on a first-come basis as well.[17] Although less common, lotteries have been used instead in certain situations and locations. Again, selection for dialysis provides some of the best U.S. examples.[18] Distribution of scarce polio vaccine offers a good British parallel.[19] According to my U.S. study (see chapter 2), random selection is still a selection criterion with significant, albeit limited, support. Although the medical directors on average score it as slightly important (mean score 1.7 out of 5), nearly one-third (31 percent) of them accord it a place in patient selection.[20]

Justifications

The relatively low mean score given a random-selection criterion in the U.S. study just mentioned reflects an interesting feature of support for the criterion. It is often advocated only after another criterion such as likelihood of benefit, psychological ability, social value, favored group, or ability to pay has been met.[21] So the justifications noted here generally undergird the notion that some—not necessarily primary—place be given to random selection. The relative weight of this criterion will be examined later (chapter 19).

Some of the considerations in favor of this criterion are essentially productivity oriented. For instance, a random-selection criterion is easier to apply than some of the other criteria.[22] It is also less costly to administer.[23] By its very nature random selection provides the sort of randomized group of patients necessary for the gathering of certain useful medical data.[24] From the perspective of the decision makers, it circumvents the anguish and anxiety attending the process of comparing lives in order to save some and leave others to die.[25] Patients can be spared anguish as well—the anguish of being rejected because they are judged inferior.[26] Families, friends, and patients alike can better accept unfavorable results of random selection as bad luck or God's will and are less likely to take revenge on the system that has rejected them or those dear to them.[27]

Frequently a random-selection criterion is supported for person oriented reasons that are rooted in a conviction that the life of every person is of tremendous value.[28] Each person may be seen as irreducibly valuable, in that life is a value incommensurate with all others.[29] In particular, each life is so important that considerations of social value are irrelevant by comparison. Respect for life is common in creationist religions, where the created participate in some way with the divinity of God.[30] However, it is regularly invoked without religious reference as well.

One form that appeals to the value of human life take is the acknowledgment of people's right to life, that is, their right not to be deprived of life as far as this matter is under human control.[31] Such a right has been affirmed in numerous public declarations and analytical studies.[32] Although it is commonly observed that life is a prior requirement for receipt of any other goods, the ultimate basis of a right to life is not so commonly accepted.[33] Some, for instance, defend it by appealing to common intuitive notions of community or humanity, while others insist upon a theological basis in the form of natural law or revealed truth.[34] Whatever its basis, a right to life grounds the conviction that every person's life is worthy of protection, for the right to life is not subject to differences of degree.[35] For many this conviction leads to the conclusion that every person should have the kind of real opportunity to receive lifesaving resources that only random selection can ensure.[36]

A related person oriented justification for a random-selection criterion invokes the concept of justice. When a basic human right such as life is at stake, justice requires that people be treated equally. For a right to be called human entails all humans having it equally.[37] Equality is also a particularly appropriate element of justice in the context of health care distribution since all people are more or less randomly (even if not equally) susceptible to health crises. However, equality alone may sanction no medical treatment for anyone. Therefore a life-affirming concept of justice must also specify a standard according to which resources can be distributed equally.

The standard of need is especially appropriate in the context of health care.[38] Since the very reason that a distribution must take place is that some illness has placed certain people in a position of need, this need is rightfully the foundation of their claim to medical resources.[39] At the same time, a need standard accords well with the basic human right to life at issue here, for needs are essentially claims to that to which people are entitled simply as people.[40]

Random selection, one might assert, is a direct implication of the essential equality of persons.[41] Acknowledging that all alike cannot be treated, it preserves equality in the next best way by providing all with an equal opportunity to be selected for treatment.[42] Only those equally in need—that is, whose lives require the resource in question—are included.[43] In this light the arbitrariness of random selection can be seen as an asset rather than a liability. Differences among people are not recognized because they are irrelevant when life is at stake.[44]

Advocates of a random-selection criterion appeal also to its fairness, claiming that it is a criterion that all people theoretically would accept. That is, if self-interested persons were ignorant of their own circumstances (abilities, possessions, place in society, and so forth), they would want basic "goods" such as life itself available equally to all. They would want to be sure that they did not miss out on anything essential. Inequalities would be acceptable as long as everyone, especially the least advantaged, would benefit from them.[45] The only way to ensure the sort of equal opportunity envisioned here would arguably be through a random-selection criterion.[46] Whereas other criteria such as social value might be beneficial to society as a whole, they would not be likely to benefit everyone. In fact, the least advantaged in society not only would be disproportionately denied access to scarce lifesaving resources, but also would probably not benefit from the social benefits achieved by favoring others (especially if they die from lack of access to treatment).

In addition to the various concerns involving justice and life, two additional person oriented justifications of random selection should be noted. One involves the physician–patient relationship. Treatment of high quality so often depends upon patients' trust in their physicians and thus upon their willingness to provide all of the personal information the physicians need to make accurate diagnoses and prognoses. A random-selection approach is conducive to this trust because, unlike many other criteria, it refuses to consider nonmedical information in the selection of patients.[47] Patients need not worry that the information they share might jeopardize their receiving good care and even provide a basis for denying them access to lifesaving resources.[48] The important willingness criterion (chapter 15) depends upon patients enabling physicians to provide them with prognoses that are as accurate as possible so that they can make truly informed decisions about undergoing treatment. Otherwise, some patients will withhold information that might be used against them, mistakenly be selected for treatment, and end up wasting resources.

The final person oriented justification contends that random selection is the best way to avoid the subtle intrusion of social-value considerations.[49] A random-selection criterion would eliminate the need to attempt massive assessments of each patient's value to society—assessments that would inevitably be inaccurate and time-consuming.[50] The criterion accepts the fact that no one has the wisdom to judge and rank patients' lives.[51] Were random selection and its affirmation of the equality of persons to be rejected, the whole social climate in countries like the United States might well be affected. The stability and coherence of such societies, as many analyze them, rest upon the imperfectly realized ideal that people's lives (though perhaps not the things that make up those lives) are fundamentally equal.[52]

Defense of a random-selection criterion does not necessarily entail the claim that the criterion is perfect—merely that it is the best alternative available.[53] It may, for instance, give destructive people more consideration and past victims of social injustice less consideration than seems intuitively right to many people.[54] However, a patient selection procedure cannot take responsibility for rectifying every evil in society; and it is arguably better that a few scoundrels be selected than that scoundrels have the potential opportunity to assess people's value and thereby decide who is treated.[55] Similarly, random selection may mistakenly appear to be irresponsible, arbitrary, irrational, and inhuman.[56] Its detachment from human assessments and calculations, though, is really one of its greatest strengths, not a mere attempt to avoid playing God.[57] This detachment represents for many the best available way to affirm essential human values such as the equal worth of all persons.[58]

Weaknesses

Alongside the various justifications for random selection are a number of weaknesses, many of which are essentially productivity oriented. For instance, many of the social benefits that other criteria would generate would be lost if a random-selection criterion were adopted.[59] Sometimes socially destructive persons such as criminals would be selected rather than people who have contributed positively to society.[60] A world of random selection is no place for an Albert Schweitzer with bad kidneys and bad luck to match.[61] Similarly, survivability, rehabilitation potential, level of desire to live, and other beneficial considerations would not be given priority.[62] Those selected by chance might therefore feel less satisfied with being selected than if they had been chosen for some particular reason.[63]

Neglect of such considerations is justified by appeals to rights and equality; but these latter concepts may be understood in a variety of ways. All may be said to have a right to life; but that right arguably can be forfeited or diminished by destructive (for example, criminal) actions, which release society from its normal obligation to protect that right.[64] The right to life can also be interpreted as a right to a quality life—a perspective that would open the door to considerations beyond random selection.[65] On the other hand, the equal opportunity advocated by random-selection proponents may best be understood as requiring only that the merits of each candidate for treatment be completely and impartially taken into account.[66] The factors to be equally considered, according to this perspective, would have to be determined independently of an appeal to equality.

A final set of productivity oriented matters focuses upon the instability that random selection might engender. Rather than appeasing conflicting special interest groups it could upset them all.[67] Moreover, it could encourage the many not selected to reject the system by seeking treatments in other countries or through a black market.[68] By subjecting people's very lives to the workings of chance, a random-selection criterion, some fear, may also subtly encourage a gambling mentality.[69]

Several further questions about random selection can be raised that are more person oriented in nature. Random selection, for example, may not respect human dignity after all. Although the approach acknowledges a basic equality, it does so in a way that may not look at persons as the unique individuals they are. The most strident opponents state the problem this way: Random selection wipes away people's faces with this equality, reducing them to the level of mere things controlled by blind chance.[70] So arbitrary is random selection that it leaves its victims helpless and depersonalized.[71] It constitutes a kind of treason against human compassion.[72]

Related to this criticism is the worry that random selection may be irrational. In nonmedical arenas random selection has frequently met with this complaint.[73] The medical arena is no different.[74] It is unacceptable for random selection to be adopted just because other approaches are considered faulty. There need to be positive reasons for its adoption—reasons that can be given to those not selected in order to justify their rejection.[75] In other spheres of life decisions are made on the basis of generally accepted moral principles, so why not with regard to patient selection?[76] Random selection can be seen from this perspective as the ultimate display of irresponsibility.[77] Apparently out of cowardice or an inability to agree on other criteria, decision makers make no decisions.[78] They decide not to decide, leaving people to chance rather than to the thoughtful choices of people.[79]

Finally, a random-selection criterion cannot ensure objectivity and fairness, two of its primary justifications. Bias will likely continue to taint the selection of patients by influencing who is deemed medically suitable to enter the selection pool.[80] Equal opportunity for all will probably not be achieved because all afflicted with an illness do not have equal access to knowledge of what treatment resources are available.[81] If anything, random selection may even be seen as introducing additional unfairness. It does not take into account the matter of who deserves society's treatment resources the most, for example, on the basis of contributions to society in the past.[82]

Which Type?

As noted at the outset of the chapter, random selection can take a number of different forms, two of which have received significant support to date. Because first-come, first-served and a lottery raise such different considerations, they need to be examined individually.

A first-come, first-served (natural chance) approach has much to commend it, including all of the strengths of random selection already noted.[83] It has traditionally been a familiar part of medicine and continues to be so today.[84] A hospital's patients, for instance, do not all get ill at the same moment, but arrive over a period of time.[85] As they arrive they are considered for whatever resources they need and are available. If needed resources are already in use, then patients must wait (or go elsewhere). They can reasonably expect, though, if they wait, that they will be treated before others with the same level of need who arrive later. By waiting they have "paid their dues" and so deserve this priority.

Later arrivals regularly accept the fact that they are simply the victims of natural chance. They have gotten ill slightly later than others for no discernible reason. Similarly, if they contract a disease whose cure will not be developed until it is too late, they tend to accept their plight as unfortunate bad timing. Even beyond the sphere of medicine people are accustomed to waiting in lines, with those who have been waiting longest receiving the first opportunity to obtain the desired goods.

Several other factors commend a first-come, first-served approach. For instance, it is very easy to implement because the time at which a person was referred to receive a particular resource is a matter of record.[86] It also is beneficial to the patients because they can form realistic expectations. They know approximately how long they will have to wait and can seek treatment elsewhere if the wait is unacceptably long.[87] An added advantage of the first-come method is that it achieves the benefits of random selection in an appealing way. It does not publicly display equality to the exclusion of other important values in the way that a lottery does.[88]

A lottery may be faulted on other grounds as well. Unlike the first-come approach it can seem arbitrary and artificial.[89] It presumes that there is a pool of patients waiting rather than patients presenting themselves for treatment over time.[90] Although some claim that a lottery is the ultimate affirmation of equality, this is not necessarily the case. The burden of waiting for treatment, for instance, is not shared equally (as it is in a first-come system) and so may especially burden the elderly and the poor.[91] Moreover, not all patients are known at the time of a drawing, so not all have an equal opportunity. In any instance a drawing could have been scheduled a day later, thereby including additional patients.[92] This observation reveals an interesting fact. Who is included in the lottery is largely a result of the natural lottery of time. Those who became ill early enough have applied for treatment by the time treatment resources become available. If all have already participated in this natural lottery, then the instituting of a second lottery is unnecessary. The results of the first lottery can be considered determinative.[93] If it is acceptable for patients in effect to reject the results of the first lottery and call for a second, why is it not equally acceptable for patients (presumably the losers) to reject the results of the second lottery and call for a third, and so on?

A final problem with the lottery is its visibility. By its very existence a lottery advertises the fact that society is not willing to provide the resources necessary to protect the lives of all of its citizens. As a result, the notion that human life is priceless is undermined and tends to lose what guiding force it retains.[94] Publicizing the plight of those left to die without help from society, however, may create a very different problem if society cannot bear to see its commitment to human life so flagrantly violated. The resources necessary to save everyone in need may be made available—but at an unbearable cost, one that is out of line with actual public priorities.[95]

On the other hand, much can be said in favor of a lottery as compared with first-come, first-served. Some consider it to be the obvious way to institute a truly random selection.[96] While it has not traditionally played as big a part in medical care as has first-come, first-served, it has been employed periodically, as noted at the beginning of this chapter. Moreover, providing treatment only to certain patients who are selected by lot has become a standard part of research medicine.[97]

Two of the supposed strengths of a first-come, first-served approach may turn out to be greater advantages in the case of a lottery. First, by implementing equality so graphically, a lottery may well draw attention to the fact that society is not providing the resources necessary to save the lives of all of its citizens. However, such exposure is good rather than bad. People need to be aware of resource decisions that are not being made in accordance with their highest values, so that these decisions can be changed. If adopting a lottery for scarce resources leads to increased funding for those resources because society genuinely does place the highest value upon human life, then it would seem that a lottery is to be highly commended indeed.[98] Second, a lottery would allow some patients to be treated quickly rather than require that all wait a long (equal) time. This arrangement might be medically beneficial for those treated more quickly and not overly burdensome if those waiting longer are ultimately protected by an imminent-death criterion (see chapter 11).

Several other features also favor a lottery. A lottery form of a random-selection criterion works better together with other comparative selection criteria than does first-come, first-served. Unlike the latter, a lottery gathers a pool of candidates from whom selections are to be made. The pool is easily discernible, consisting of all whose need for treatment has been identified.[99] With such a pool at hand, it is relatively simple to give special priority to those in the pool who, for example, require disproportionately few resources or are especially likely to benefit from treatment.[100] Ultimately a lottery may be needed even if a first-come procedure is preferred, in that it may sometimes be difficult to establish which of two patients came first or that a minute difference in arrival time is significant ethically.[101] Since the remaining comparative strengths of a lottery merely reflect weaknesses inherent in a first-come, first-served approach, it is best at this point to examine these weaknesses directly.[102]

To fully appreciate these weaknesses we must place them in their larger context. A lottery and a first-come, first-served approach are only two of many forms that random selection could take. Limited resources could also be distributed according to other rather random factors, such as people's beauty or wealth or even their likelihood of benefiting from treatment.[103] In order to assess the relative merits of these alternatives, three tests may be applied. A first-come, first-served approach does not fare well on any of them.

The most important is the *manipulation test.* For an approach to be truly a form of random selection it must not be open to manipulation by patients (for example, to their benefit) or others (for example, to certain patients' detriment).[104] A first-come, first-served approach falls short on this test because the time at which a patient is referred for treatment with a scarce resource is far from purely random.[105] It depends on where one lives and the transportation available; medical resources are not distributed uniformly in any country, least of all in rural areas.[106] Transportation problems can be overcome by wealth, but disparities in wealth constitute an additional problem for a first-come approach. Those with greater wealth in any location have better access to health care generally and to referral networks in particular.[107] So do those with greater power, information, and confidence—attributes that tend to vary by socioeconomic class.[108]

Even physicians may undermine the randomness of the exact times that patients are referred for treatment (which is commonly the moment of "arrival" in a first-come approach).[109] Physicians may be unaware of the treatment, slow to refer patients in general, have personal biases that delay their referrals in certain cases, or overzealously put patients on waiting lists (for example, for organ transplantation) before their gradually deteriorating condition warrants it.[110] Lotteries are not immune to tampering, but they are not nearly so vulnerable.[111] Computer-generated random selections can do away with many problems, and other sources of tampering are more easily discovered than are the innumerable sources of manipulation that call into question a first-come, first-served approach.

A secondary test to be applied to forms of random selection is the *confusion test.* It should be clear what a selection procedure is trying to accomplish and exactly who should receive resources according to that procedure.[112] Although it is evident that a lottery is attempting to give each candidate an equal chance, the intent of first-come, first-served is not quite as clear. The latter is not obviously a random means of distribution but seems designed to reward those who have borne the burden of waiting the longest. Similarly, a specific person is drawn from the pool in a lottery, whereas there are various possible interpretations of who should receive treatment in a first-come system. Should it be, for example, the one who first consulted any physician for treatment of the illness in question, the one who was first referred for treatment involving the resource that is scarce, or the one who first deteriorates to the point of critically needing that resource?[113]

When the manipulation and confusion tests do not prove conclusive, a third test—the *implications test*—can be applied. Because this looks at the side benefits produced by a particular form of random selection, it is secondary to those tests designed to ensure that the approach is genuinely a form of random selection in the first place.[114] The implications test reveals two problematic features of a first-come, first-served approach that do not trouble a lottery. Because it always favors the patients who have been waiting longest for treatment, a first-come approach tends to select the sickest patients for treatment. As a result, resources more often produce limited results or are wasted entirely.[115] A first-come approach also creates legitimate expectations on the part of patients about the order in which they should be treated. Accordingly, it is difficult to give special priority to any of them, for example, because their deaths are imminent (see chapter 11) or the lives of others literally depend upon their survival (see chapter 6).[116] A lottery could be implemented without upsetting legitimate expectations, if a first-come, first-served system is already operating in the following way. All who are on the waiting list when the lottery is first instituted would simply be selected (first-come, first-served) before anyone who comes later is selected via the lottery.

As suggested earlier, these three tests could be used to compare the lottery with any possible form of random selection, not just first-come, first-served. A lottery consistently appears to be better. Some possible forms such as selecting patients according to their beauty fare especially poorly on the manipulation test because the ranking of patients reflects such nonrandom factors as personal grooming and the ever-changing tastes of society. (Distinguishing between fine degrees of beauty can also be confusing.) Other possible forms, such as selection according to likelihood of benefit, seem particularly dubious in light of the confusion test, since likelihoods cannot be distinguished in some cases and the actual outcomes being anticipated remain somewhat uncertain in every case. Social influences on either the exact severity of one's disease or one's ability to recuperate can also prove subtly manipulative. The primary weakness of "random" selection by level of wealth is that it, too, is open to manipulation. However, if economics is a factor, there would be serious implications as well. Saving only the wealthy might well mean that estate tax revenues would fall and less new spending would be generated by wealth changing hands—among other (difficult to anticipate) factors.

Possible Common Ground

To some degree a gulf may always remain between those who are person oriented in their thinking and favor random selection, and those who are productivity oriented and support social-value selection. Nevertheless in Western societies especially there does appear to be a general inclination in the public at large, reflecting religious and rationalistic perspectives alike, to favor the basic values that undergird a random-selection criterion.[117] Not surprisingly, then, this criterion appears to have widespread support.[118] Moreover, the prospect of eliminating or reducing the need for patient selection in the first place provides a powerful rationale for employing random selection when selection is unavoidable.

A society will restrict budgetary allocations to a particular area only if it can live with the resulting decisions to exclude certain people from benefits. Limited government allocations for dialysis are acceptable in Great Britain, for instance, because that society can live with the exclusion of the elderly that results.[119] Were random selection rather than social-value oriented criteria to be consistently employed, those with economic and political power would have great incentive to do everything in their power to make available resources to treat as many patients requiring scarce resources as possible. Their own lives and those of their families and friends might one day depend upon their having done so.[120] Absent the need to spend large amounts of money on social-value assessments, in fact, even more money would be available to reduce some resource shortages.[121]

Correspondingly, experience in the United States has shown that when funding for all in need is not realistically possible, the presence of social-value oriented criteria may lead to the withdrawal of whatever limited government funding is present.[122] The inequities involved are too great to be openly sanctioned by government. Moreover, calculated nonmedical assessments of patients give the appearance that a "solution" to resource shortages has been found. Such masking of the tragedy may lessen the urgency to find additional resources for treatment.[123]

Although it is reasonable to assume that a random-selection criterion has a broad base of support in society, the preferred form of random selection is less clear. The two obvious choices are first-come, first-served and a lottery. A few hospitals have tried to combine the two by gathering names of candidates for treatment over a period of time and then holding a lottery.[124] Because this approach results in lifesaving resources going unused for lengthy periods of time, though, it is not likely to be widely accepted. Other ways of combining the two, such as trying to weight the odds of winning the lottery in proportion to the number of lotteries one has already lost, generate the additional problems of administrative difficulties and conflicting justifications (as outlined earlier in the chapter).[125]

Of the two, a lottery is better justified according to the three tests explained earlier and other considerations to be summarized in chapter 19. Much of the current support for a first-come approach may be a product of custom rather than of conscious reflection.[126] However, it may well be that a lottery displays its egalitarianism and dependence upon chance too blatantly to be widely acceptable. First-come, first-served is more palatable in that neither its ethical base nor its random nature is conspicuous.[127] Moreover, an added appeal is that it has long been a standard feature in the practice of medicine. Under the exceptional conditions of disaster medicine, there is no time to institute a lottery without jeopardizing the lives of all. The relative merits of first-come, first-served in such a situation are especially likely to be widely acknowledged.[128]

This exception underscores the importance of taking the specifics of the particular resource problem involved into account when determining the best patient selection criteria. Sometimes the reasons that a criterion is justified in the first place require that the criterion take an unusual form. Organ transplantation is an example. Because antibodies, tissue types, and blood types vary among patients as well as among organ donors, the typical case of choosing among equals is not present here. There are two complications.

One is the fact that the distribution of organs according to good tissue and blood matches between recipients and donors may be conceived of as a particularly appealing form of random selection.[129] The practice is common in medicine and fares better than even the lottery on the three basic tests. Matching, like a lottery, scores well on the manipulation test since tissue and blood types cannot be altered. Matching proves superior to a lottery according to the implications test in that it results in less suffering from organ rejection and less waste of resources.

The outcome of the confusion test is less clear. The positive implications of matching prove definitive only when it is clear why tissue and blood typing are justified and how certain and significant the benefits of choosing some patients over others will be. New immunosuppressive therapies have had an impact in this latter regard by rendering the finest tuning of tissue typing unnecessary. However, matching is likely to be perceived more as a medical consideration (involving likelihood of benefit) than as a form of random selection. It may seem fairer to actual patients in need now to carry out a new random selection.[130] They may not realize that there has already been a sort of natural (or God-directed) lottery that has determined their blood and tissue types. If they are aware of this, they may be bothered by the fact that not all types are equally well represented in the population (and so not all people will have an equal likelihood of obtaining a good match).[131] However, unless there is reason to assume that the original distribution of types was unfair, types do in fact provide a good randomizing element if they pass the three tests explained here.

The confusion test, then, is the key. To the extent that confusion is unavoidable regarding the random-selection basis for considering type matching, matching cannot be sanctioned as a viable form of random selection. Matching must then rise or fall with the debatable (though perhaps acceptable) likelihood-of-benefit criterion (see chapter 12). Needless to say, as the problem of organ rejection is resolved and implantable artificial organs are used more frequently, the relevance of the tissue-and-blood-matching form of a random-selection criterion will diminish.[132] In the interim, this form of random selection may well meet with wide acceptance when the conditions specified can be met.

The second complication attending the distribution of organs for transplantation has to do with patients' antibodies. Some patients have so high a level of reactive antibodies that there are relatively few transplantable organs that will be of medical benefit to them. If they operate in the same random-selection process as other patients whenever any organ becomes available, they will not have an equal likelihood of receiving an organ transplant. They will be disqualified from receiving many organs by a medical-benefit criterion. In order to equalize the opportunity of those equally in need of a particular kind of transplantable organ, then, those with a high level of reactive antibodies must be given more than a random chance to receive one of the few specific organs with which they are compatible. The simplest way of accomplishing this may be to give such persons absolute priority when acceptable organs occasionally become available.[133] How high a level of antibodies warrants such priority, however, needs to be clearly established.[134] Should the result be that such patients end up receiving organs with a frequency disproportionately high in comparison with their numbers, then a more complicated relative priority system would need to be devised. Perhaps only those among them who have been waiting for more than a certain length of time could receive priority.

A clarification and extension of the exception involving antibody levels needs to be added: it is valid only if a lottery or first-come, first-served form of random selection is employed (though if the latter is used, patients with high antibody levels will already tend to receive priority because they will have been waiting the longest).[135] If tissue and blood matching is the randomizing device instead, then the difficulty of a particular group of patients obtaining suitable kidneys is no more a factor if antibody levels is the reason than if the problem is uncommon tissue types (see earlier discussion). Second, considerations analogous to those justifying the exception may support allowing blood-type-O kidneys to be transplanted only into blood-type-O recipients.[136] Without such a priority, type-O patients will not have as great an opportunity to receive a transplant as other patients (and type-A kidneys may be wasted if type-O and type-A kidneys have met the needs of all current type-A patients).[137]

An Illustrative Case

Paul and Don are two businessmen equally in need of a heart transplant. Their prognosis is quite similar without one. Moreover, they are both good matches for a particular heart which has just become available. The physicians involved can make no relevant medical distinction between the two. Both are in their late thirties, intelligent, otherwise in good health, and eager to cooperate in every way. An appeal is made to the hospital ethics committee for help in the selection.

The committee decides to select a candidate by flipping a coin. The two men are called in and told that the committee does not wish to choose between them on the basis of their worth to society, their importance to their families, or by any other value-dependent criteria. They wish to leave the matter to fate.

Paul protests. He argues that he would feel much more content, even if he were rejected for the program, if some reason could be given. Flipping a coin is much too cold and impersonal a way to decide to save or kill a man, he says, but adds that he would abide by such a decision if they will not change their minds.

The committee asks Don what he thinks. He says he is content to let the coin decide. "I'd rather not win just because I was thought to be a 'better citizen.' I'd never be able to live up to it. In fact, even if I was rejected, I'd rather it not be because I was judged not good enough."

The committee decides to proceed with the coin toss.[138]

Is the use of random selection to decide who will receive treatment a choice not to choose or is it choosing in a particular way? Both perspectives arise in the case above. Random selection affords the committee a way to avoid other irrelevant or dubious selection criteria, but is this shirking responsibility for the decision at hand?

The analysis in this chapter reveals why Don and Paul react as they do to the prospect of a lottery. Don is aware of the trauma that would accompany being selected according to social value rather than random selection. The proposed coin toss, however, so explicitly subjects Paul's life to the capricious workings of chance—fate, as the hospital ethics committee calls it—that Paul feels uneasy. What makes it much worse is the justification that the committee expresses for resorting to a lottery. Rather than explaining, for example, how a lottery is the best way to demonstrate the equal respect that the committee and hospital have for both patients, the committee indicates that it prefers to avoid taking responsibility for the decision that must be made.

Paul's willingness to abide by the committee's approach may suggest that he recognizes its ultimate fairness. Nevertheless, the committee could have helped him to embrace the approach more actively had they explained the positive values underlying a lottery. First-come, first-served might have seemed even less cold and impersonal. Everything would not have hinged upon one momentary toss of the coin, but the decision would have been the result of a familiar process of seeking medical care. Since an organ transplant is at issue, some special medical considerations might have arisen that would have taken priority over random selection. According to the narrative, though, no such considerations were relevant in this instance. In the end, random selection proved workable, but the case illustrates how helpful it is if acceptable criteria are acceptably justified.

PART SIX

An Overall Assessment

When Resources Are Experimental

A special set of considerations arises when the resource in view is experimental, that is, does not have proven therapeutic value. Under such circumstances more is at stake than deciding which patients among those whose lives could be saved should be selected. It is not even clear at this stage exactly whose lives can be saved. So there arguably is a need to evaluate the effectiveness of the treatment as efficiently as possible.[1] Complications and potentially harmful side effects need to be identified, as do the particular groups of patients who can (best) benefit from treatment.[2] For this reason experimental treatments are sometimes reserved for groups of patients thought most likely to benefit from treatment— based upon experience with other somewhat similar types of treatment.[3] (For example, random trials may be carried out only among these patient groups.)

There are other reasons for granting such priority to certain groups of patients. One is the need to prove the effectiveness of an experimental treatment as quickly as possible (using appropriate procedures) in order to obtain the attention and funding necessary to develop it further. A sufficiently high level of technical mastery must be developed in the process.[4] Second, the uncertainties (and thus possible harms) of an experimental procedure generally are significantly greater than with an accepted therapy. Accordingly, a relatively high likelihood of benefit may be necessary in order to justify the increased risk (at least when the possible harms are quite serious).

In light of these various considerations, some of the criticisms of selection procedures during the earliest days of dialysis may have been misguided. The criticisms evaluated the experimental procedure of dialysis as if it were an accepted form of therapy.[5] The distinction is important, though, and may highlight what is really an entire progression of substages through which any technology passes as it develops from the point of invention to that of mastery.[6] Other procedures that use scarce resources, such as heart transplantation, have followed a course

211

similar to dialysis. Quite stringent selection criteria have been applied during the experimental phase with the expectation that these would change somewhat when the therapeutic effectiveness of the treatment was demonstrated.[7] For example, possible contraindications such as age or other simultaneous illness have often been broadly defined with the intention of ruling out all but the best medically qualified candidates.

Serious problems, however, attend the notion that selection criteria during experimental and accepted-therapeutic stages should be quite different. One difficulty is pragmatic. The dividing line between the two so-called stages is far from clear—a point that has significant funding implications, as the history of organ transplantation will attest. Some heart transplants in the United States were funded by Medicare beginning in 1979. The change in policy was rather uncertain, however, funding being withdrawn in 1980 and then reinstated several years later. The underlying problem was a lack of clarity regarding the point at which a treatment becomes a legitimate therapy.[8] In fact, some have charged that the category "experimental treatment" is open to gross abuse by those involved in insuring against medical catastrophes.[9] Treatments such as liver transplantation, they argue, have been labeled as experimental long after they have become therapeutic (though even here the dividing line is not clear). The uncertainty over where to draw the dividing line between stages also impacts on selection committees, whose patient selection criteria may hinge in part on whether or not the treatment in view is still experimental.

More substantive difficulties are involved as well. The desirability of imposing stricter selection criteria during the experimental phase of a treatment may reflect more a recent trend in the West toward controversial utilitarian values (see chapter 19) than a broadly acceptable justification of stricter criteria. Some of the arguments for stricter criteria are telling in this regard. They may appeal, for example, to the concern of Swedish nephrologists to demonstrate the therapeutic effectiveness of dialysis by showing that patients undergoing dialysis could return to work. In order to demonstrate this, strict selection criteria had to be employed. However, this marked the first time that "effective treatment" was required to include social rehabilitation as well as medical benefit in Sweden.[10] The legitimacy of such restrictive selection criteria may thus depend more upon the legitimacy of the values underlying the minimum goals that medicine must achieve than upon the distinction between experiment and accepted therapy.

Accordingly, it seems excessive to suggest that the ethical concerns raised about U.S. dialysis patient selection criteria before federal funding in 1972 were mistaken because the resource was still experimental. For one thing, as early as 1967 a federal report had concluded that dialysis had moved beyond the experimental stage.[11]

Even before, the issue of greatest ethical controversy concerned not how to identify the medically "ideal" candidates, but how to select patients from among those who were ideally suited to benefit medically as much as possible from treatment. Some medical centers employed random selection.[12] Others gave preference to those considered likely to be most socially useful in the future—applying this criterion either subsequent to or together with medical considerations.[13] Social-value considerations are objectionable for the same reasons when treatment is experimental as when it is not (see chapter 3). Such considerations are viewed by many as irrelevant whenever medicine is engaged in the saving of lives.

Possible Common Ground

The experimental nature of a resource may not justify patient selection criteria that would not otherwise be legitimate, but it may well alter the way in which otherwise legitimate criteria are applied. A fresh look at many of the criteria examined in previous chapters—this time in the context of experimental treatments—is therefore needed.

There appears to be broad support, first of all, for the notion that standards of medical benefit (see chapter 10) must be higher when a resource is experimental as opposed to being a proven therapy. Strictly speaking, a medical-benefit criterion may not apply at all in that it has not been established, by definition, that anyone can benefit medically from a treatment that is experimental. In practice this means that it is impossible to apply the minimal likelihood-of-benefit, length-of-benefit, and quality-of-benefit standards that usually make up a medical-benefit criterion. Rather, these standards must be sufficiently high to ensure that the anticipated benefit–harm ratio is favorable and that treatment is thereby justified.

Identifying the exact dividing line between patients with favorable and unfavorable ratios is rarely easy.[14] Educated guesses based upon experience with analogous treatments is all that can be expected. If time shows that certain groups of selected patients do not do well, then restrictions on who may be considered for treatment may need to be further tightened (as has happened with heart transplants).[15] However, treatment may prove so successful—or gradually be so improved—that the restrictions can gradually be loosened. The development of dialysis followed such a pattern.[16]

If selecting patients with positive benefit-harm ratios is good, would it be even better to favor those patients with the highest benefit-harm ratios—those most likely to benefit the greatest from treatment? Many think so, though there is not unanimity on this point. The arguments in favor include those undergirding a likelihood-of-benefit criterion (see chapter 12, but see also the opposing view in chapter 19). Where those much more likely than others to benefit from treatment are favored, the limited resources available are bound to be more productive.[17] In the end more lives will probably be saved and the quality of more lives will probably be improved. Such advantages will most immediately accrue to patients being treated in the near term. However, many other patients will benefit in years to come from a treatment whose effectiveness was rapidly demonstrated because the candidates most likely to benefit were treated during the experimental phase.

Although such reliance upon likelihood considerations may well improve the results of experimental treatments, not as much will be learned about the relevance of various factors to the outcome of treatment. Eventually factors suspected of reducing the likelihood of benefiting from treatment will have to be examined, and some of these suspicions will be exposed as unfounded. In the meantime, certain types of patients will have been unfairly denied lifesaving resources and thus life itself for reasons that did not in fact apply to them.[18] With such considerations in mind, some researchers have decided not to prioritize according to likelihood of benefit the patients who satisfy the adjusted medical-benefit criterion.[19] Nevertheless, the importance of developing resources as quickly as possible, with all of the resulting benefits, overshadows such factors in the thinking of a majority of observers today.

As a result, most people probably would favor erring on the side of too high a standard of likelihood of benefit when selecting patients to receive scarce experimental resources. Sufficient support may exist even for a comparative ranking of the likelihood that each potential resource recipient will benefit, so that those with the highest ranking can be selected. Such support, however, would hinge upon the reliability of the data upon which the ranking is based, since exclusion means death for those excluded.[20]

On the other hand, comparative ranking of potential recipients by expected length and quality of benefit is not as widely acceptable. A certain minimum length of benefit following treatment, first of all, is necessary for there to be medical benefit even under nonexperimental conditions (see chapter 13). Under experimental conditions this would presumably include whatever period of time is required in order to establish the fact that a patient had indeed benefited medically from treatment.[22] In fact, under such circumstances the necessary length might well be longer than would otherwise be the case in order to counterbalance the risks that weigh against the treatment. Beyond that period of time, though, the same difficulties that surround a comparative length-of-benefit criterion under nonexperimental conditions apply.

The consideration of a quality-of-benefit criterion when a resource is experimental raises similar issues. Like likelihood and length considerations, it has a minimal relevance as part of a medical-benefit criterion even when the treatment involved is not experimental. Under experimental conditions, this relevance may somewhat expand, as does that of a length-of-benefit criterion. Comparative evaluations beyond this point, however, are seriously flawed, as explained in chapter 14. If anything, under experimental conditions qualitative assessments must be strictly the patient's own rather than the physician's. Otherwise the assessments may reflect only the physician's hope that an experimental treatment will work well rather than a realistic assessment of what the treatment will achieve and mean in the unique context of a particular patient's life.[23] The genuine consent of the patient (see chapter 15), facilitated by the physician and others, is vital.

In an experimental context an imminent-death criterion would not function much differently than it would in the context of an accepted therapy (see chapter 11). Those most gravely ill (in the sense that their death is imminent without treatment) would receive priority consideration, all else being equal. Such has often been the practice in the past— the thought sometimes being that this type of patient has nothing to lose. Because of the risks involved, though, sufficient medical benefit must be likely, as previously explained. That a patient will die otherwise is not sufficient justification for an experimental treatment. If the risk of added suffering from the treatment is sufficiently great and the hoped-for benefit sufficiently unlikely (or small), then the patient may be worse off with the treatment than without it (that is, the most likely outcome may be a worse death).

Overall, then, the experimental nature of a treatment has only a limited effect upon which medical selection criteria are most widely supportable. Essentially, the minimum likelihood, length, and quality standards of the medical-benefit criterion are somewhat raised. However, as in the case of nonexperimental resources, only comparative likelihood considerations have broad appeal beyond the standards dictated by medical benefit. In this light it is understandable why the investigators who implanted the first permanent artificial heart in Barney Clark concluded afterward that Clark may have been too sick to undergo the implantation. Although he survived for a limited period, it was perhaps not long enough or of sufficient quality to justify the risks to which he was exposed. In any case, they recognized, patients more likely to benefit should probably be chosen in the future.[24]

The three sociomedical criteria—age (see chapter 7), psychological ability (see chapter 8), and supportive environment (see chapter 9)—are similarly affected only moderately by the experimental nature of a scarce resource. In a nonexperimental context, as argued previously, these matters are best considered as factors to be included in assessments of medical benefit and likelihood of benefit, not as selection criteria in their own right. The same applies in an experimental context.

Since the minimum standards of the medical-benefit criterion are raised in an experimental context, however, considerations of age, psychological ability, and supportive environment will become more influential there. The importance of considering psychological ability in particular when determining whether or not a patient will benefit medically from an experimental treatment has frequently been affirmed.[25] The link between likelihood of benefit and both psychological ability and supportive environment has also been emphasized.[26] When problems of the last two varieties decrease the likelihood of benefit, though, most would agree that it is preferable to correct the problems if possible rather than exclude the patient from treatment because of them.[27]

As for a social-value criterion (see chapter 3), it is as problematic when treatment is experimental as when treatment is not. Public concern over it in the United States, for example, is evidenced by the government's expressed reluctance to fund experimental treatments in which a patient's social value is considered in the selection process.[28] Similarly, the experimental nature of a resource does not significantly affect the acceptability of the remaining criteria (see chapters 4–6, 15–17)—except that the relevance of otherwise acceptable criteria is generally limited by the tightening of medical-benefit standards. Apart from this consideration, acceptable criteria become even more vital, if anything, and questionable criteria even less important. For instance, willingness to accept treatment (see chapter 15) becomes especially critical when the outcome is less assured, while ability to pay becomes irrelevant when special funds are available to finance experimental treatment.

A Progress-of-Science Criterion

Some have suggested that the experimental nature of scientific progress actually creates a new criterion that should be applied in the selecting of patients to receive scarce lifesaving medical resources.[29] Because the medical conditions of patients vary considerably, their cases are not equally interesting from a scientific perspective. One patient's treatment may yield only limited knowledge about the effectiveness of the treatment—perhaps because of other complicating medical conditions—while another's reveals more useful information regarding the treatment's effectiveness in curing a particular disorder or perhaps a variety of disorders. A progress-of-science criterion would favor the latter patient on the grounds that treatment would then result in a greater contribution to the progress of science. The criterion has the same rationale regardless of who is being selected, recipients of an experimental resource or patients who will receive an accepted therapy.

Although a progress-of-science criterion has been advocated by various people, its use has gone virtually undocumented. Apparently it was employed in the United States during the days of dialysis scarcity before federal funding.[30] However, even then it was strongly resisted by many for reasons to be explained shortly.[31] According to my U.S. study (see chapter 2), support for it persists in the arcna of kidney transplantation and would resurface should dialysis resources again become scarce. Fifty-eight percent of the participating medical directors indicate their support for including this criterion in the process of patient selection. The criterion is rated on average as slightly important (mean score 2.0 out of 5) by the directors as a group.

That these figures are almost identical to those applicable to a social-value criterion confirms what might be suspected from the very nature of the criteria. The progress of science is fundamentally a form of social value, so the justifications and weaknesses of the latter criterion (see chapter 3) for the most part are applicable here. A few more particular observations, though, might be added.

A progress-of-science criterion is generally justified on productivity oriented grounds. It makes good pragmatic and utilitarian sense.[32] Research facilities, in particular, regularly select those patients who will most likely contribute to their investigations.[33] Since the same number of lives can be saved with or without the criterion, the scientific knowledge that can be gained through applying it simply provides a bonus.[34] Consider, for example, the possibility that a scarce resource might be able not only to save lives by limiting the damage of a life-threatening illness but also to combat another serious ailment. A hypothesis that surfaced during the days of major dialysis scarcity in the United States— that dialysis might alleviate schizophrenia as well as replace kidney function—has been cited as such an instance.[35] The knowledge to be gained may be particularly important when the treatment itself is experimental, as in the early phase of various transplantation techniques.[36]

The moral significance of the knowledge to be gained can be conceived of in more than one way. Various benefits to patients and well-being for others may be produced as a result.[37] Alternatively, the attraction of the criterion may lie in the expectation that additional lives may one day be saved—a consideration that may reflect an orientation toward either persons or productivity.

Nevertheless, the weaknesses of the criterion are formidable. As noted earlier, many serious weaknesses of a progress-of-science criterion are explained in the analysis of the more general social-value criterion. However, a few of the particularly relevant considerations are worth noting in this context. These objections may be characterized as either person oriented or productivity oriented, though they do tend to arise most commonly from the former orientation.

One such difficulty is the uncertainty involved in predicting which patients would yield the most useful information if given preferential treatment.[38] Because of the empiric nature of much of medical practice, it is rarely possible to anticipate accurately the relative likelihood and significance of information to be gained if one patient is selected for treatment rather than another. (Comparing the value of such information in a particular case with the other social values at stake is similarly problematic.)

The question of who benefits from the knowledge gained is also troublesome. People generally participate in a treatment experiment because they stand to benefit if the treatment proves effective. This scenario applies in the case of those selected according to a progress-of-science criterion. But more are involved in this experiment than those selected: those rejected are also involved in a big way, for they lose their only chance to live as a result of it. Moreover, since they will die they do not

have the same opportunity to benefit from the experiment as those selected.[39]

Within limits it may be ethically acceptable for patients to be subjected
to possible harm in excess of any likely gain, as in some forms of cancer
therapy (though certain and serious harm may be another matter). However, subjection to such harm arguably should be allowed only with the
consent of the patient, and no such consent is obtained (or likely could
be) from those rejected on the basis of a progress-of-science criterion.
There is a related problem associated with those who are selected as
well. One of the essential features of ethical consent is that it be truly
voluntary (see chapter 15). Coercion, though, is inherent in a progress-
of-science criterion by the very nature of the situation. Patients with
scientifically interesting disorders are basically told that they may either
consent to special gathering of information—and perhaps added tests
and procedures—or possibly be denied the treatment essential to save
their lives.

The rationale for a progress-of-science criterion would be strongest if
valuable medical knowledge could be gathered in no other way. Such is
not the case, however. Under a selection system without this criterion,
a sufficiently large group of the type of patients medical scientists are
interested in would eventually almost certainly be chosen; but they
would be spread all over the country rather than located in one place.
The information on these cases could still be centrally collected, and
sample cases could be examined at particular locations.[40] If a random-
selection criterion (see chapter 17) had been employed, this approach
would resemble a typical randomized clinical trial to some degree.[41]
Where a more controlled study is necessary, a large cooperative effort
with standardized procedures could be undertaken involving patients of
the required type who have been selected at various centers without
reference to a progress-of-science criterion; or such patients could all be
flown to the same medical center, assuming that the prospective value
of the research justified the expense. Both approaches have been employed in the past as part of experimental protocols. In other words, the
use of a progress-of-science criterion may truly be justified only by convenience—quite a weak rationale for denying some patients access to
lifesaving medical treatment.

A progress-of-science criterion, then, would seem to fare as poorly as
a social-value criterion, of which it is really a subtype. The difficulties,
especially with respect to pragmatic considerations, are so pervasive that
consensus in support of it seems unlikely. As with a social-value crite-

rion, exceptional cases may arise in which there is widespread agreement that the saving of additional lives warrants special consideration. But these cases are probably best provided for through the use of resources-required and special-responsibilities criteria (chapters 5 and 6).

CHAPTER NINETEEN

A Proposal

As the analysis in the previous chapters illustrates, the selection of patients who are to receive scarce lifesaving medical resources is as complex as it is essential. To render this complexity more manageable, the major conclusions of the book to this point are summarized here before an ethical assessment of these lifesaving decisions is undertaken. Following the ethical assessment, the larger context ultimately necessary in order to make sense of this or any other medical evaluation is examined.

Overview of Possible Common Ground

In the preceding chapters many conclusions have been reached through a careful consideration of the justifications and weaknesses of each criterion. The summary that follows indicates the thrust of these conclusions, although the chapters that address the various criteria should be consulted for the full range of specific recommendations concerning each criterion and the rationales underlying these recommendations. As in the previous analysis, the criteria are grouped here by type, starting with social and proceeding through sociomedical, medical, personal, and experimental criteria.

The social criteria vary in their acceptability. The least acceptable of them appears to be a social-value criterion (regardless of whether those who contributed most to society in the past or those with the greatest future potential are accorded priority). While opinion is sharply divided on this criterion, even supporters admit some doubts about the possibility of applying it accurately. Many of the patients who would be most strongly favored by this criterion can be granted priority on other, more widely acceptable grounds, such as medical benefit, willingness, and special responsibilities.

A favored-group criterion, allowing such considerations as place of residence and (military) veteran status, is for the most part also unacceptable—that is, when it is safe to assume that different groups do not have roughly similar access to a scarce lifesaving resource. If a patient's medical benefit or likelihood of benefit is at stake, then favored-group considerations are best accounted for by the appropriate medical crite-rion. Even then, favored-group considerations are so widely opposed in principle that they do not serve best as a basis for exclusion from treat-ment. Instead they identify a medically detrimental factor (for example, place of residence) that should be altered if possible so that treatment can be medically beneficial. Occasionally a group of people will produce new resources for the exclusive use of the group. This practice is not objectionable as long as other patients are not significantly harmed by the commitment of funds and effort to this end. Most health care, though, has been produced with the direct and indirect contributions of people from other groups. In such cases, a favored-group criterion is either invalidated or its application must be limited by some sort of compromise (for example, quota) arrangement.

The other two social criteria are much more broadly acceptable, at least in principle. One is a resources-required criterion. By prioritizing patients who require significantly fewer resources than others, this cri-terion represents a way of maximizing the effectiveness of resources without compromising the value of human life (since additional lives are saved each time it is applied). Several forms of the criterion, however, lack the widespread support of the general criterion. All long-term use of a resource should not be ruled out—short-term use need only be given relative priority. Patients, moreover, should not be limited to a fixed amount of resources irrespective of their need. Finally, neither patients who need a repeated treatment (for example, a second organ transplant) nor those who do not clearly need a disproportionately great amount of resources should be excluded from treatment.

The remaining social criterion, a special-responsibilities criterion, is likewise broadly acceptable within specific bounds. Most important, pa-tients with special responsibilities toward others may be preferred if three standards are met. First, the patient must be truly indispensable. Second, it must be reasonable to assume that, following treatment, the patient will be able to continue to fulfill the crucial role. Third, serious harms must be likely if the responsibilities are not carried out. Some-thing as morally serious as the loss of human life is in view here. Various procedural guidelines should be added to ensure that cases are consid-ered on their individual merits, preferably by a committee of diverse membership. The burden of proof is on those who would justify someone's treatment on the basis of this criterion, in part to ensure that the criterion remains genuinely exceptional.

The next set of standards includes the three sociomedical criteria: age, psychological ability, and supportive environment. These are relevant only as components of other criteria (medical benefit and likelihood of benefit) and are not widely acceptable as criteria in their own right. Even when they do raise questions of genuine medical significance, the burden of proof is on those who would exclude patients on the basis of any of these components. Questionable cases probably should not be excluded. One way of protecting against undue influence by these components is to employ them as if the resource in question were not scarce.

Some additional cautions apply to these components individually. Regarding age, it is easy to underestimate the ability of some elderly persons to endure treatment when their lives are at stake. Moreover, before excluding the elderly as a group, it may be necessary to treat them in large enough numbers to determine accurately how well different age groups can do, given proper care. As for psychological ability, it is very difficult to make predictions about the stability of a patient under a new stress. Owing to developments in treatment technology, frequent reevaluation of the relevance of various psychological characteristics of patients is necessary. If the medical significance of a patient's psychological limitations is unclear, the patient should have a trial period of treatment (or of conditions resembling treatment) in order to verify the medical significance. The medical implications of a patient's supportive environment, meanwhile, need to be carefully assessed case by case since cases vary radically. It must be established without doubt that medical criteria will necessarily be violated if a given patient is treated—with due attention to the fact that people may have differing ideas as to what constitutes a supportive environment.

The third set of criteria includes those that are most explicitly medical. Of the five medical criteria, three appear to have the potential for widespread support. Essential is a medical-benefit criterion, according to which only those who satisfy minimum standards regarding likelihood, length, and quality of benefit should receive treatment. Borderline cases should not be excluded, and no social considerations of any kind should be allowed to intrude. The criterion offers a rationale for discontinuing as well as starting treatment. Another attractive feature is the clear basis it provides for resisting a patient's or a family's demands for useless treatment.

The second widely acceptable medical criterion is an imminent-death criterion in a slightly modified form. Rather than strictly giving priority to those whose death is imminent (roughly within two weeks), the most acceptable form of the criterion selects those who are within roughly two weeks of being disqualified by the medical-benefit criterion. In practice the two versions of the criterion often yield similar results. Some imprecision in the criterion is necessary by the very nature of the dying process. However, to limit its impact, questionable cases probably should be grouped with those given higher priority. More precise subcategories of imminent death also should probably not be imposed. The imminent death of one patient may on rare occasion even warrant the temporary removal of another from treatment—but only under several narrow conditions designed to ensure the continuing health of the one removed.

The third acceptable medical criterion, likelihood of benefit, is more debatable. Yet it may well be that the criterion will continue to receive widespread support if its use is confined to preferring individuals (as opposed to categories of patients) who are much more likely than others to benefit medically from treatment. When such an anticipated disparity of benefit is unclear, the criterion is probably best not applied. Moreover, if certain social groups are consistently disadvantaged by the application of this criterion, special programs to alter the circumstances causing the disadvantage should probably be established.

On the other hand, two of the five medical criteria, length-of-benefit and quality-of-benefit, do not appear to be broadly supportable. Medicine should indeed be firmly committed to improving people's quality and length of life—but not at any price. Leaving to die those with less anticipated length and quality than others is too high a price in the eyes of many. The minimal length and quality of benefit that must be expected from treatment is already accounted for by a medical-benefit criterion. A willingness criterion already allows the only people who can accurately assess the value of their remaining length and quality of life—that is, patients themselves—to decide that the limited gain does not warrant using up a scarce resource. Such decisions, though, require a great deal of information and counsel from physicians and other caregivers—perhaps even a trial use of the resource if possible. When patients cannot make such decisions, surrogates (usually family members) must assume primary responsibility.

Like the social and medical criteria, the personal criteria also differ in terms of their acceptability. A willingness criterion in its most common form—favoring patients who are willing to accept treatment—is widely supported in both theory and practice. The major restrictions are that patients' decisions be based upon sufficient information and that willingness be considered as either present or absent. In other words, patients should not be ranked in terms of relative willingness. If the patient's wishes cannot be determined, the family is usually in the best position to ascertain the best interests of the patient. On the other hand, the willingness-to-risk-illness form of the criterion, while theoretically sound, is not likely to receive widespread support in the near future because of practical difficulties. It is extremely difficult to prove that a patient's actions caused a given medical disorder, that the patient knew of the causal link when engaging in the actions, and that the actions were freely entered into.

Of the three personal criteria, an ability-to-pay criterion is the least supported. Whenever possible it should probably be avoided. Suggestions for rendering it unnecessary have included prioritizing lifesaving treatments when budgetary decisions are made, developing resources only where there is a commitment to fund treatment for all in need, and taxing profits from lifesaving treatments to help provide for those who cannot pay. Nevertheless, under certain conditions it may not be possible to avoid an ability-to-pay criterion. Without the criterion a hospital may have to close, and no other facility will be able to care for all of its patients. Perhaps more important medical priorities will have to be disregarded if the criterion is not allowed in relation to a particular treatment. Such conditions cannot be casually assumed but must be responsibly demonstrated. Even then the criterion should probably not be applied until the last possible minute. That the criterion is generally undesirable does not mean that people must be barred from going outside of the health care system to produce their own resources, as long as others are not disadvantaged in the process.

A random-selection criterion is one of the more controversial selection criteria, although it appears in the end that there is broad support for the values that undergird it. The criterion is also attractive in that its widespread implementation would probably lead to increased funding and reduction of scarcity. Except for special cases (for example, organ transplantation, in which factors like tissue and blood type may provide a particularly appealing random basis for selection), there are two especially commendable forms that random selection can take. One, a lottery, appears to have less support than the other, a first-come, first-served approach. To be sure, a lottery is less susceptible to manipulation and confusion, and it has fewer negative implications. However, it so obviously displays its egalitarianism and dependence upon chance that it is distasteful to a large number of people. A first-come, first-served approach, moreover, is a more familiar practice in medicine. In some situations (for example, disasters), it is the only form of random selection possible.

When the scarce resources involved are experimental, the only major difference in terms of patient selection criteria is that the minimum standards that make up a medical-benefit criterion (likelihood, length, and quality of benefit) are significantly tightened. The influence of other criteria per se does not substantially change, although various factors that must be considered in applying the tightened standards of a medical-benefit criterion (age, psychological ability, supportive environment, and so on) become correspondingly more important. An explicit progress-of-science criterion is ruled out primarily on the same grounds as a social-value criterion, of which it is a form. Seemingly relevant cases in which lives would likely be saved if the criterion were applied are better accorded priority on another basis, such as a resources-required or special-responsibilities criterion.

Ultimately, then, seven different selection criteria, within specified limits, appear to be widely acceptable: medical benefit, imminent death, likelihood of benefit, resources required, special responsibilities, willingness (to accept treatment), and random selection (most often in the form of first-come, first-served). The other form of willingness criterion, involving willingness to risk illness, may be theoretically justifiable; however, it is realistically unworkable given current knowledge. Two further criteria, favored-group and ability-to-pay, are not broadly supported, though exceptional cases with widely acceptable justifications do exist. The remaining criteria are not likely to meet with extensive approval except as they are relevant as factors that should be considered in the application of other, legitimate criteria. This overall picture is not altered when scarce resources are experimental except that the minimum standards of the medical-benefit criterion are tightened.

Recommendations

To this point in the book the analysis has been more descriptive than normative. The concern has been to identify those selection criteria that appear to have the greatest potential to elicit social consensus. However, this potential does not necessarily make them right from an ethical perspective. Some evaluative comments are now in order. Recommendations here will address the basic ethical outlook to be adopted, its implications for various patient selection criteria, and the selection procedure that results.

Arguments for and against selection criteria have consistently been characterized throughout, wherever possible, as productivity oriented or person oriented. As explained in chapter 2, a productivity oriented argument is concerned with promoting the achievement of some good, such as efficiency or happiness. On the other hand, a person oriented argument is concerned with respecting people per se, irrespective of the goods they produce.

A key unanswered question is how the ethical weight of these two types of arguments should be compared. One could hold that only one type is valid. It is difficult to find examples of societies in which either extreme has been followed. Probably the closest to purely productivity oriented societies (or, at least, governments) are oppressive dictatorships under which almost any cruelty can be done to virtually anyone for the good of the society or government. The closest to purely person oriented societies may be extremely poor countries in which personal relationships are extensively cultivated but little attention is paid to opportunities for economic development.

The two countries in which empirical studies were conducted for this book, the United States and Kenya, fall between these extremes. In the United States the two types of argument appear to be given fairly even weight in public policy and individual treatment decisions, with each type of concern being periodically sacrificed for the other. In Kenya both types are present, but person oriented arguments vastly predominate.

The proper balance probably lies somewhere between the stances taken in these two countries. Persons should be the ultimate focus of social policies, with productivity a vital means of enhancing personal (that is, communal and individual) well-being. Productivity is therefore extremely important, but it undercuts its own justification if it demeans persons. Accordingly, as I have argued at length elsewhere, person oriented concerns should be given clear priority over productivity oriented concerns (contrary to priorities sometimes expressed in the United States and other Western nations)—yet without diminishing the fullest possible influence of productivity within the dictates of this priority (as sometimes occurs in Kenya and other less developed nations).[1]

The significance of pursuing this approach becomes more evident when the current drift toward utilitarian thinking in medicine is recognized. Increasingly, people are allowing considerations of productivity (efficiency, social well-being, and so on) to dominate medical decision making, without the healthy constraints provided by more person oriented concerns.[2] This drift appears to be widespread.[3] Western nations such as Great Britain and the United States are particularly marked by it.[4] Yet it is also spreading to other nations, such as Kenya, apparently through the values implicitly communicated through the educational system.[5] In chapter 2 the trend in Kenya is detailed by the documentation of the increasing propensity of the Akamba to view people in terms of their usefulness to society rather than their intrinsic worth.

Some of the problems with this drift are suggested in the analysis of the weaknesses of a social-value criterion (see chapter 3). Like a social-value criterion, a fundamentally productivity oriented approach to decision making is generally inadequately justified, unworkable, vulnerable to bias, and harmful.[6] The particularly serious harms of this approach—for example, the sacrifice of the few for the satisfaction of the many, or the sacrifice of the many for the satisfaction of the ruling few—will certainly not occur in every situation in which the approach is taken. However, there are no built-in safeguards, like those in the approach commended in this chapter, to ensure that productivity genuinely remains in the service of the common good, that is, the good of all people in common. Drawing upon cross-cultural sensitivities, the proposed approach does a much better job of fostering the regard for all so essential in today's increasingly international, culturally diverse world.[7]

To what extent does the proposed approach entail patient selection criteria different from those identified as most widely acceptable earlier in this chapter? The points of disagreement are not as extensive as one might at first expect. Criteria strongly justified by person oriented arguments tend to be affirmed by productivity oriented arguments as well and have therefore usually been identified as widely acceptable. Other criteria, those depending predominantly upon productivity oriented arguments with relatively little support from person oriented arguments, have generally not been so identified. As a result, the common ground identified in the book to this point is, with two major exceptions, ethically sound.

The first exception concerns the particular form of random selection to be adopted in most situations (that is, apart from the special cases noted near the end of chapter 17). As I explained earlier, first-come, first-served may well be easier than a lottery for people to accept because of its familiarity and its somewhat hidden dependence upon equality and chance. Nevertheless, it is a morally inferior form of random selection according to the manipulation, confusion, and implications tests. It is less fair, less clear, and less helpful.

By creating expectations in patients regarding the order in which they will be treated, moreover, it tends to conflict with other acceptable criteria. An imminent-death criterion is a case in point, for this criterion constantly upsets patients' expectations by moving extremely ill patients to the head of the line. A lottery eliminates this problem yet leaves patients confident that if their need becomes critical they will receive top priority (via an imminent-death criterion).

If the egalitarian and other person oriented arguments in behalf of random selection are to be taken seriously, then the most truly random form of random selection should be adopted and adopted openly. Resorting to chance is no abdication of responsibility if it is the best way of implementing the most important relevant ethical concerns. That first-come, first-served is the more familiar form of random selection need not dictate future practice once it is recognized that the lottery does what first-come is supposed to do and does it better.

Admittedly, there may be reasons beyond randomness to favor a first-come, first-served approach. In some cultures it is customary for the first arrival in any situation—including the first child born—to receive first priority. Sometimes this priority is rooted in the sense that those who have arrived first have waited longest and therefore deserve to be attended to first because they have "paid their dues." Although such a priority may well be justifiable in most situations, it must be disputed when life is at stake. No amount of waiting can make one person deserve life more than another. Such claims must give way when the person chosen will probably live and the one not chosen may well die. Some may have to wait longer than others because of "the luck of the draw"—but better that than some having to wait longer even to get on the waiting list because they are the victims of social inequities. Randomness is necessary for this and a host of other reasons explained in chapter 17; and a lottery is its truest form of implementation.

The second problem with the previously identified set of widely acceptable criteria involves the likelihood-of-benefit criterion. As noted near the end of chapters 12 and 17, many of the cases in which this criterion might be applied (for example, where blood or tissue typing is involved) can be handled by a medical-benefit or a random-selection criterion. The same would be true when resources are experimental—that is, the adjusted medical-benefit criterion can handle many of the relevant cases (see chapter 18).

Instances in which a medical-benefit criterion will not suffice typically involve two patients who both have a reasonable likelihood of benefiting medically from treatment. The difference between them is that, comparatively speaking, one has a much greater likelihood of benefiting than the other. Unfortunately, if the patient with the greater likelihood is preferred, that patient may end up dying anyway, while the other patient might have been saved. Such will not usually be the case, but the outcome is a matter of statistics: a certain percentage of the time this undesirable outcome will occur. Because it will not occur most of the time it is an acceptable cost from a productivity oriented perspective—outweighed by the more frequent occurrence that someone is saved when both might have died absent the criterion.

This gain, however, comes at the cost of denying some who meet the medical-benefit criterion any chance of obtaining lifesaving resources. In other words, a small number of patients are forced to give up their lives so that the limited resources available to society as a whole may be more productive. It is this priority of productivity over persons that is so objectionable according to the approach commended in this chapter. Under other criteria, for example, a special-responsibilities criterion, more lives are saved by every application of the criterion. Only when such is the case are productivity considerations legitimately being applied without overriding a moral commitment to persons. A likelihood-of-benefit criterion, then, is best avoided as a separate selection criterion that goes beyond a medical-benefit criterion.

The common ground identified throughout this book, as altered above, suggests the following basic approach to the selection of recipients of limited lifesaving medical resources:

> 1. Only patients who satisfy the medical-benefit and willingness-to-accept-treatment criteria are to be considered eligible.
> 2. Available resources are to be given first to eligible patients who satisfy the imminent-death, special-responsibilities, or resources-required criterion.[8]
> 3. If resources are still available, recipients are to be randomly selected, generally by lottery, from among the remaining eligible patients.

Two exceptional circumstances, also explained previously, should be kept in mind as well. On the occasions when a favored-group criterion is legitimate, it is a prerequisite criterion—alongside of medical benefit and willingness to accept treatment—that must be satisfied by any recipient of the resource involved. Legitimate applications of the ability-to-pay criterion, on the other hand, should not be made until a patient has actually been chosen according to the selection procedure outlined above.

The above proposal constitutes a set of ethical guidelines that will have various implications depending upon the medical setting. In particular, the considerations involved in establishing medical benefit (perhaps including age, environment, psychological ability, geographical location, and so on) will vary from resource to resource. For example, as indicated by the examples and cases presented throughout the book, medical-benefit considerations that are relevant in the context of organ transplants may differ markedly from those relevant in the context of intensive care. Despite the different forms that selection criteria necessarily take in different contexts, though, the set of criteria that is ethically legitimate to apply does not vary across contexts.

Most aspects of the proposal outlined above are likely to receive widespread approval. Only two provisions—a lottery as opposed to a first-come, first-served form of random selection and rejection of a likelihood-of-benefit criterion—will not easily garner broad support (see chapters 17 and 12, respectively). If necessary, first-come, first-served could replace the proposed lottery without structurally altering the selection procedure, and the likelihood-of-benefit criterion could be applied between steps two and three of the selection procedure. (Only when resources remain after it has been applied—not an unlikely prospect[9]—would random selection be necessary.) So the selection procedure recommended here can still be adopted, with simple alterations, even if neither of the provisions I have introduced in this chapter are accepted.

Despite the fact that my proposal represents a particular ethical approach, then, it also closely resembles an achievable consensus position. Its balance is reflected in its inclusion of two criteria from each of the social, medical, and personal realms. It incorporates all of the criteria that are truly undergirded by substantial person oriented as well as productivity oriented rationales. And it clarifies the real nature of many criteria that are properly relevant only as factors to be considered when other criteria (especially medical benefit) are being applied.

While this proposal, taken as a whole, is realistically achievable and yet moderately innovative, it is much more radical in the challenge it represents to many specific views held widely by those selecting patients today. (One prominent commentator has even labeled some of its provisions "breathtakingly radical.")[10] It conflicts in important ways, for example, with the computerized point system evolving in the United

States for the selection of organ transplant recipients.[11] Recall also the results of my U.S. study detailed in chapter 2. More than three-fourths of the medical directors in that study indicate some support for quality-of-benefit, psychological-ability, length-of-benefit, and age criteria, and more than half indicate some support for these same criteria plus supportive-environment, progress-of-science, and social-value criteria. Some of this support, however, may be unreflective in that it would disappear following careful consideration of the important distinctions made in this book (for example, between quality-of-benefit and willingness criteria and between age and medical-benefit criteria). Hopefully this book can facilitate such consideration. Some of the directors' support undoubtedly also represents more intentional support for the various criteria—support, though, that is not yet the result of careful consideration of all the implications of those criteria. Hopefully this book can also provoke such consideration.

The Larger Picture

The analysis in this book raises a broader, perhaps more challenging issue: the nature of ethical analysis itself. To this point in the discussion, a wide variety of ethical terms have been employed. Most, such as *responsibility* and *the human,* are commonly employed in discussions of medical ethics—so much so that their meaning is generally assumed without further thought. Yet such assumptions may be based upon a Judeo-Christian heritage that has lost much of its standing in the public arena. If a patient selection procedure or any medical policy is to be justified ethically, it must give its own account of common moral terms.[12]

Consider, for example, the notion of responsibility. Proponents of random selection have argued that other approaches, such as leaving all to die, are irresponsible, while opponents have responded that it is random selection that is really irresponsible.[13] What does *responsibility* mean in this context? The word itself suggests a story—that at some time in the past certain people have done certain things or in some other way have become "responsible" to someone or something for some sort of behavior. No such account is generally provided by those engaged in the patient selection debate.

The same difficulty surrounds the notion of *the human.* In the Holmes shipwreck legal case noted in chapter 1, the judge and Holmes's counsel argue, respectively, for and against random selection. The standard of acting in a human/humane way is invoked on both sides of the argument.[14] Random selection has also periodically been berated as inhuman in the context of selecting patients.[15] However, what is the basis for this intuitively recognized and commonly employed normative standard—the human? Again, there is an untold story here concerning what the human is and why it has normative significance. The same applies to the notions of justice and freedom that appear so frequently in discussions of patient selection criteria.

At first glance it may appear that the idea of a story is being used here to signify merely any sort of explanation—but perhaps more is required. The explanation that people intuitively know that all persons are fundamentally equal, for instance, may be too much at odds with common perceptions of the innumerable differences among people. Or, the explanation that acting responsibly toward others means acting on the basis of carefully considered moral principles does not touch the deeper issues of to whom and why people are responsible. Explanations can be given for justifications and then further justifications can be given for those explanations until some ultimate account—or story—must be given of the way things simply *are* in the world.

In Western culture people do not often tell the stories that ultimately lie behind their moral outlooks—much less tell stories to provide immediate justification for specific practices or actions. In this respect, Western ethics (and Westerners in general) may have something important to learn from other parts of the world, such as the Akamba people of Kenya.

The Akamba tend to think in terms of stories rather than mere explanations—at least more so than Westerners—because of their integrated view of life. Just as a story integrates a moral idea into an entire life context, so one sphere of life is almost invariably interconnected with another for them.[16] In particular, they are always alert to the relationship between medical problems and other aspects of a patient's life.[17] This alertness led Akamba healers to appreciate the interaction between the physiological and the psychological aspects of the human being much more readily than ever could have been expected in the case of Western medical practitioners.[18]

Today, Western medicine is more open to incorporating psychological and social considerations into its area of concern, but there is still a strong reluctance to incorporate the spiritual dimension, as do the

Akamba.[19] The Akamba share the so-called African view that "the natural is supernatural [and] the supernatural is quite natural."[20] Their stories make sense of the dilemmas of daily living by placing them in the larger context of life.[21] For example, one of the most basic and widely told stories among the Akamba is a story about the creation of people. From it can be gained insights into the Akamban perspective on life, justice, freedom, and the relation of God to all of these—as well as, in turn, insights into the outlook on access to health care that this perspective entails.[22]

Western ethics is impoverished and ultimately unconvincing to the extent that it lacks a story to explain and ground its concepts. In the past it has had such a story, the Judeo-Christian story, though with increasing secularization the story has suffered neglect. With the fading of this story has faded its wholistic, integrated perspective on people and life. The results have included the narrow, materialistic focus of much modern medicine noted earlier as well as a broad range of ethical views that often argue past one another, with few points of contact. The Akamba do not have these difficulties, for they have a nourishing story. It may not be the best story; in fact, it is being supplanted among many of the Akamba by the Christian and (to a lesser extent) the Muslim stories. However, it serves a purpose in its culture that is not being fulfilled in the West as it needs to be.

Without a larger frame of reference that can make sense of the many conflicting ethical arguments, there is no firm ground on which to argue for a particular patient selection procedure or any medical policy. The only appeal left is to people's preferences, with a utilitarian (essentially productivity oriented) approach representing a democratic way of allowing the preferences of the majority (or of those governing for the majority) to prevail. This approach may be fine to some degree, but most people recognize that people individually and collectively are not always what they should be and that their preferences are not always ethically legitimate.

To distinguish the legitimate from the illegitimate, some larger frame of reference, or story, is crucial. As the story that has nourished so much of modern medicine, the Judeo-Christian story merits much more attention than it has recently received in this regard. Its real merit, though, lies not in its history, but in its ability to provide a coherent way forward. It offers the kind of backdrop, for example, against which the approach to patient selection commended in this book makes sense.[23]

A Concluding Case

With all of the selection criteria now in view, the discussion of a somewhat complicated case may be a helpful way to illustrate how the approach to patient selection proposed here would look in practice.

Barbara's time was running out. She had just received "medical urgency" status on the national organ bank waiting list, and she was not expected to survive more than a week longer. Her life depended upon someone donating a liver for a transplantation procedure, which was just that year moving beyond the experimental stage.

At this point Barbara's parents decided they had waited long enough. Her father, a trustee of the hospital in which she was staying, decided to mount a media campaign to locate an organ for his five-year-old daughter. Through his many contacts in the community he was able to obtain major stories in several newspapers and an interview on a local TV news program.

Two responses to this publicity have occasioned the present meeting of the hospital Ethics Advisory Committee. Upon seeing the TV interview, the parents of another girl named Lisa (whose condition was equally urgent) have lodged a protest with the hospital. Lisa is the same age as Barbara but has been on the transplant waiting list longer, they argue—and they are paying customers! They are worried that any suitable organ will be given to Barbara because of her father's position with the hospital and media connections.

The second response to the publicity has come from a lawyer with the Legal Services Bureau. He had just finished successfully defending a poor, single mother of five in a child abuse case when he saw a newspaper article featuring a plea in behalf of Barbara. After discussing the matter with his client, whose son Tom was awaiting a liver transplant in the same hospital as Barbara, the lawyer decided to do some digging.

He has discovered that Tom is the same size as Barbara, and his situation is equally urgent. Tom is right behind her and Lisa in terms of time on the waiting list. However, because of other medical complications Lisa is reaching the point where a transplant will have virtually no likelihood of saving her. The lawyer expresses his concern that Tom will receive lower priority than Barbara and Lisa because he has not had speedy access to the health care system, he has had no media attention, and he alone of the three is black, poor, and has an unstable home environment in society's eyes. The lawyer adds that any organ donated to Barbara probably would have been

donated to the transplant program anyway without the special (and privileged) actions of Barbara's father, since the transplantation program's need
for organs has itself just recently been widely publicized.

However, Tom has some medical complications that will not be solved if
he receives a liver transplant. As Tom's physician summarizes his patient's
prognosis: Tom will have significant brain damage resulting in a relatively
low quality of life, there is a good chance that the complications will prove
fatal in five to ten years, and the transplant operation itself is a little less
likely to be successful than in Barbara's case (though the likelihood of a
successful transplant in both cases is reasonably high). Barbara's case is
also particularly interesting medically since, with parental consent, researchers could try a new immunosuppressive drug on her which might also
help treat another unrelated medical condition she has. Finally, Lisa's parents are insisting upon a transplant even in the face of Lisa's medical decline. A suitable liver may well be donated in the next few days. Perhaps
the donor's parents will refer to Barbara by name. Should that occur, how
should the hospital proceed?

So many considerations appear at first glance to be potentially relevant
in this case that it may be difficult intuitively to identify who should be
the first to receive an available liver transplant. Accordingly, potentially
relevant criteria are best examined individually. The justifications for the
various conclusions here are to be found in the appropriate chapters.

A willingness-to-accept-treatment criterion, first of all, appears to be
satisfied in relation to all three children. It is important to be sure that
the parents involved, though, have made treatment decisions that are
ethically competent, truly voluntary, well informed, and based upon genuine understanding. On the basis of a medical-benefit criterion, Lisa
would probably be ruled out as a transplant candidate, even if the treatment were not experimental. However, the adjusted medical standards
typically applied in an experimental situation would definitely rule her
out if the procedure were still considered experimental.

At the same time, even the more stringent likelihood, length, and
quality standards that make up a medical-benefit criterion under experimental circumstances do not seem helpful in ranking Barbara and Tom.
Barbara's likelihood of benefiting medically from treatment apparently
is not sufficiently greater than Tom's to warrant favoring her (though
either might ultimately be preferred if blood or tissue matching with the
organ donor is so definitive that one child is ruled out). Similarly, five
years is not too short a time to verify that Tom's transplant is a medical
success.

The only other evident medical bases for excluding Tom are his expected low quality of benefit and the medical implications of his unstable home environment. In order for Tom to remain on equal footing with Barbara in terms of possible selection, two conditions need to be met. The limited quality of life achievable through transplantation must be worth the risk to Tom, as determined by those deciding on his behalf in conversation with him. Also, it must be ascertained that the unstable home environment either will not prevent successful treatment or can be suitably altered so that it will not.

As is often the case, legitimate imminent-death, special-responsibilities, and resources-required criteria do not reveal any relevant differences between Tom and Barbara. So if the two remain on equal footing in light of all of the considerations noted above, then some form of random selection should be employed to choose between them and any other equally eligible candidates for treatment. The potential unfairness of a first-come, first-served form of random selection is particularly evident in this case. If tissue matching with the organ donor reveals a better antigen match with one of the two candidates, then this form of random selection might be adopted. Otherwise, a lottery is the best option. Other unacceptable considerations, such as Barbara's possibly greater value to society, the contribution that her case might make to the progress of science, and her parents' ability to obtain media coverage and to pay for surgery, should be rejected.[24]

This case represents but one of the countless cases of life and death patient selection taking place around the world today. The ethical dilemmas that such cases create will not go away, for new technologies will continue to engender the same dilemmas in new guises. These dilemmas will elude simple solution, for they are the product of conflicts between deeply held ethical convictions. However, just because a struggle cannot be avoided does not mean that people cannot prepare to engage in it. A number of factors—ethical criteria—appear again and again in patient selection dilemmas. Understanding their strengths and weaknesses in advance will make it possible to resist the tempting but dangerous lure of some criteria while heeding the wise counsel of others.

Indeed, careful ethical analysis is doubly warranted, for the stakes are high. At issue is not merely a transplantable organ, an intensive care bed, or a dose of antibiotic. Who lives and who dies are the decisions being made.

N O T E S

Full bibliographic information for each citation can be found in the References section that follows. Where a sentence in the text contains at least two ideas, each having groups of citations, these groups are listed here in the same order as the corresponding ideas in the text. A double slanted line indicates where citations corresponding to a different idea begin. Citations are listed in reverse chronological order except where particularly helpful sources have been moved ahead of others.

INTRODUCTION

1. Califano, 1986:178, 183; Rennie et al., 1985:332.
2. National Heart, 1984:Ch.45:56; Zawacki, 1985:57.
3. G. Richards, 1984:80; Somerville, 1981:1110.
4. Rosner, 1983a:355; Brent, 1983:57; Aaron and Schwartz, 1984:135; T. Cooper, 1987:24; Leenen, 1982:163; De Palma, 1983:830; "Ethics and the Neph.," 1981:596; Diamond, 1979:176; Rabinowitz and Van der Spuy, 1978:863; "Will," 1979:2. // National Heart, 1984:Ch.31:9, Ch.45:25,30,59. // Hewetson, 1982; Annas, 1977. // Ruchlin, 1984:8. // Hastings Center, 1986:cover; Caplan, 1986b:2; Bayer, 1986:18; Mechanic, 1979b:109. // Brand et al., 1968:8-I. // "The Life-and-Death," 1984:144. // Lyon, 1986:43; G. Richards, 1984:80; Gunby, 1983:1981. For literary works that portray the quandaries involved, see G. Shaw's *Doctor's Dilemma* (1950) and R. Cook's *Godplayer* (1983).
5. Pellegrino, 1988:267; Robertson, 1987:86; Lundberg, 1983a:2224; Toledo-Pereyra, 1983:830; Debakey and Debakey, 1983:9; R. Evans, 1983:2216; "Who Shall Be," 1984:717; White and Monagle, 1982:10; DePalma, 1983:904; Khoo, 1982:5; Smith, 1980:559; Leenen, 1979:175; Friedman and Richards, 1984:80. // Blank, 1988:246–47; Abram and Wolf, 1984:628; National Heart, 1984:Ch.45:63; Wehr, 1984:458; Minnesota, 1984:51. // Annas, 1985b:189; Shapiro and Spece, 1981:59. // Evans and Manninen, 1987:4; Hingson et al., 1981:98; Kunstadter, 1980:295; Rettig, 1976b:230. // Childress, 1985:19–20, 1978:1418; Winslow, 1987; Caplan, 1987a:10,18, 1985a, 1984:161; Leenen, 1982:36; Fromer, 1981:48; Beauchamp, 1978:251. // Gellman, 1984:113. // "Prolonging," 1985:11; T. Richards, 1986:86. // Fineberg, 1984:17ff.

6. Nichols, 1981:533; J. P. Smith, 1980:559. Even a presidential commission studying the field gave little attention to it. See Rosenblatt, 1983:398(n.21); Baily, 1984. In a letter of instruction to James F. Blumstein, dated June 4, 1981, the commission explicitly directed him to focus upon "items which are not of immediate, direct life and death significance." A noteworthy exception to the lack of detailed analysis is Gerald R. Winslow's helpful book *Triage and Justice* (1982).

7. Mechanic, 1979a:8; Feinberg, 1978:806; Basson, 1979:314–15; Thielicke, 1970:173; Morillo, 1976:86–87; Macklin, 1987:149–50.

8. National Heart, 1984:Ch.45:68; Gorney, 1968:314; Gustafson, 1977:156.

9. Bayer, 1986:18; Neuspiel, 1985:893; Mechanic, 1986:206–07.

10. Churchill, 1987:15; Caplan, 1986a:27; Leenen, 1982:33; Egdahl, 1983:1184. // President's Commission, 1983a:98–100; Knowles, 1977a:57; Leenen, 1979:163–65; United Nations, 1975:29; "A Policy," 1976:788. // F. Parsons, 1967:623; Leibel, 1977:512; President's Commission, 1983a:3–6; Del Guercio, 1977:168–69; Kolff, 1964:360.

11. Bayer, 1984:41–42; Cassel, 1985:557; Caplan, 1986a:26.

12. Avorn, 1984:1300; Gellman, 1984:113; National Heart, 1984:Ch.35:4; Austrian government in Winslow, 1982:91; Ogg, 1973:649.

13. Schwartz, 1987; Zawacki, 1985:57; Annas, 1985d:893–94; Lefebvre, 1980:185; Blustein, 1978:285; West, 1975:57.

14. Califano, 1986:184; Leenen, 1982:36; Winslow, 1982:167; Fromer, 1981:64; cf. Jane Hunt in Jonsen et al., 1975:763; Daniels, 1988a:142.

15. Winslow, 1987:206; Gorovitz, 1985a:185–86; Freund, 1971:281; M. Cooper, 1975:92; Schwartz, 1976:104; Morillo, 1976:88.

16. E.g., Winslow, 1982; "A Life," 1975:61; Hardin, 1980:59. // Baily, 1984; Mechanic, 1979a; R. Evans, 1983.

17. Rund and Rausch, 1981:11; Childress, 1983:551; Ramsey, 1978:244–45; Oden, 1976:55.

18. Hinds, 1975:8; G. Smith, 1985:144; Coulton, 1986:101–02; Jonsen et al., 1982:159–60; Childress, 1983:551; N. Bell, 1981:152; Manroe, 1979:1; Rund and Rausch, 1981:3–4; Engelhardt, 1976:82.

19. Macklin, 1985b:609; Baily, 1984.

20. See Caplan, 1989, for an analysis of these stages in the context of organ transplantation.

21. The reasons this issue is of particular concern in the United States (and also in Great Britain and Sweden, among others) are examined in Veatch, 1985c:192,199. Cf. A. Parsons, 1985:468, regarding Canada.

CHAPTER 1. LIMITED RESOURCES

1. Blank, 1988:246; Churchill, 1987:19; Hendee, 1986:9; Fuchs, 1985:1332; Mechanic, 1980:431; National Heart, 1984:Ch.35:2.

2. National Heart, 1984:Ch.35.1.

3. "Due Process," 1975:1735–36. // Mehlman, 1985:246. // Merriken and Overcast, 1985:17. // R. Hudson, 1975:20; Hinds, 1975:16. // Platt, 1966:151.

4. Mehlman, 1985:241; Sheehan, 1982; Hinds, 1975:10; Beecher, 1971:280–81.

5. Schreiner, 1968:463.

6. Sanders and Dukeminier, 1968:366; Basson, 1979:314; Hyatt, 1969:1; Caplan, 1981b:493; U.S. Bureau, 1967:2–4; Welt, 1968:623.

7. Davidson and Scribner, 1967:2.

8. Schreiner, 1968:463.

9. Waterfall, 1980:726.

10. De Wardener, 1966:107; Waterfall, 1980:726; "Scarce," 1969:638.

11. E.g., S. Alexander, 1962; Schmeck, 1962; "Who," 1962; Lawson, 1963; Haviland, 1965; Robbins and Robbins, 1967; Elkinton, 1964:310.

12. Section 2991 of the Social Security Act Amendments (Pub. L. No. 92–603, October 30, 1972). However, not until a further amendment in 1978 and related state legislation were passed were Medicare deductibles and copayments as well as home dialysis supplies significantly covered (cf. Ingman et al., 1987:259).

13. Iglehart, 1982:492; cf. Bermel, 1983:2. In a personal letter dated May 27, 1986, Robert A. Streimer, acting director of the H.C.F.A. Bureau of Eligibility, Reimbursement, and Coverage, estimates the figure at 7–10 percent.

14. The original research underlying this figure is described in chapter 2 ("The U.S. Study"). See also Munson, 1983:482.

15. Rettig, 1976a, 1979; Rettig and Marks, 1983; Caplan, 1984:158; Ingman et al., 1987:245.

16. Adams, 1978:42.

17. Abrams, 1987:53; Fleck, 1987:184; Childress, 1986b:144–45; Ashley and O'Rourke, 1986:114; Kutner, 1982:53; National Heart, 1984:Ch.32:95, Ch.35:2; Childress, 1981:89–90; Prottas et al., 1983:102; J. Beck, 1982:Sec. 1:18; Lomasky, 1981:84; Jensen, 1979:169; Wehr, 1984:458; Held et al., 1988; Evans et al., 1981. // Massachusetts, 1984:73; Annas, 1985:187; Childress, 1985:18; "The Life," 1984:145; Godshall, 1988:121.

18. U.S. Congress, 1972:33007.

19. This point is documented further when the current applications of an ability-to-pay criterion are discussed. // R. Evans, 1983:2048; Cassel, 1985:561; Em. Friedman, 1984:68; Stein, 1978:145. Cf. Mulley, 1983:302, regarding a similar avoidance problem in the area of intensive care resources.

20. Wilensky, 1985:36; White and Monagle, 1982:8; Winslow, 1982:ix; Klein, 1984:144; Veatch, 1975:6.

21. Zawacki, 1985:58; Bayer, 1984:37; Beauchamp, 1979:167; Beauchamp and Childress, 1979:192.

22. In some cases the committees are established for this purpose (cf.

N. Bell, 1981:155). In others, existing committees assume at least advisory responsibility for selection decisions. For example, during the summer of 1986 the Ethics Advisory Committee of Children's Hospital in Boston devoted time to developing expertise in this area. Cf. Page, 1977:7 on the trend here.

23. Merriken and Overcast, 1985:8; Novello and Sundwall, 1985; Wehr, 1984:454; D. Bryant, 1985:117.

24. National Heart, 1984:Ch.45:4; Caplan, 1987b:8, 1983b:24–25; Prottas, 1986:23; Childress, 1986b:134; Novello and Sundwall, 1985:1585. Organs for children in particular are "more priceless than gold" (Wallis, 1982:101).

25. The original research underlying a range of 100–3,000 is described in chapter 2. High figures or generalized statements without figures can also be found in Wallis, 1982:100; Harron et al., 1983:150; Lawton, 1979:266–67. Cf. figures in F. Rapaport, 1987a:169; Off. of Inspector Gen., 1986:1–2; Mark Siegler in Callaway et al., 1986.

26. Schroeder and Hunt, 1987:3143; Hiatt, 1987:216; Evans and Yagi, 1987:28; Evans et al., 1987:1896; Sullivan, 1987:B1; Casscells, 1986:1366; Mark Siegler in Callaway et al., 1986; Annas, 1985:187; Massachusetts, 1984:72; National Heart, 1984:Ch.3:24; Lubeck and Bunker, 1984:247; Thompson, 1983:67; Jn. Fletcher, 1983:1341.

27. National Heart, 1984:Ch.32:1–2; Minnesota, 1984:21.

28. National Heart, 1984:Ch.14:5; Wallis, 1982:100; Seligman et al., 1980: 39.

29. Working Group, 1985:16.

30. Evans and Yagi, 1987:28; Thompson, 1983:67.

31. Starzl et al., 1988a:133; Minnesota, 1984:49; Massachusetts, 1984:72; Annas, 1985b:187; Friedman and Richards, 1984:79; Kolata, 1983:139.

32. Straus et al., 1986:1143; King, 1986:170; Macklin, 1987:149–52, 1985b: 611; Pope John Ctr., 1984:80; Mulley, 1984:222; Diamond, 1979:173–74. For examples of particular facilities, see Kellerman and Hackman, 1988:1290; Reed et al., 1986:1429; Treaster, 1978:B1. R. Sullivan (1982:1) documents the analogous problem that can occur when emergency rooms are full.

33. D. Singer et al., 1983:1155ff.

34. Cullen and Schwartz, 1981:264; Mulley, 1983.

35. Jonsen and Lister, 1978:845; Childress et al., 1982; Pyeritz, 1978:50; Bishop, 1978:516. // Blank, 1988:130–31; Holzman, 1986:56; Teres, 1984:1059; Mulley, 1983:310; Cullen, 1981; Franklin et al., 1981:263.

36. Childress, 1983:547; cf. Massachusetts, 1984:75; Annas, 1985:187; A. Shaw, 1978; Thomasma and Griffin, 1983.

37. Zawacki, 1985:57; "Infant Sent," 1981:14A; Ismach, 1981:29. From mid-1985 to mid-1986 one hospital in the northeastern United States had to make 120 decisions regarding which of several acutely ill infants would be denied or removed from needed intensive care.

38. Kirklin, 1977:316. // Jonsen, 1979:169–70; Adams, 1978:49–50.

39. Himmelstein et al., 1984:495. Cf. Califano, 1986:166; Engel, 1984:B1. // Reinhold, 1988:A1,20; Kotulak, 1986a:1,4; Knox, 1984:1; Em. Friedman, 1982a:56, 1982b:77; Tessler and Kroll, 1982.

40. Several of the examples that follow are noted in Childress, 1981:90. Cf. Kirk, 1927:138–49.

41. Forty-four B.C.:365; cf. Donagan, 1977:174.

42. 311:152.

43. 392:71.

44. Gellman, 1984:114; Rosner, 1983a:357; Lieberman, 1963:124–27. Cf. Reines, 1978:170; L. Jacobs, 1978:176; Petuchowski, 1975:108.

45. Roach, 1980:154–56; Cahn, 1955:61–71; Cardozo, 1929:602–04. Cf. J. Hall, 1960:427–36; R. Perkins, 1957:847–51.

46. 1842. For a visual reenactment, see "The Right to Live," 1972.

47. 1884.

48. Tulpius, 1641.

49. E.g., regarding food, see Greene, 1975; regarding vital supplies for cave exploration, see Lon Fuller, 1949. Cf. Wilensky, 1985:36 concerning nonmedical resources in general.

50. Birch and Derr, 1979:64.

51. UNICEF, 1988:3; 1987:1.

52. Aslanian, 1981:1; Heymann, 1981; Rey, 1980:3; UNICEF, 1988:2; 1987:9,63.

53. UNICEF, 1988:2; 1987:27,29.

54. UNICEF, 1988:31–37.

55. World Bank, 1986.

56. J. Bryant, 1973:80–84, 1980:295; Khoo, 1982:6.

57. E.g., in South Africa (Rabinowitz and Van Der Spuy, 1978:861); Canada (A. Parsons, 1985:468); Singapore (Khoo, 1982:5); Japan (Winslow, 1982:29); West Germany (ibid.); Central Europe (Siebert and Waldrop, 1988:38). // Debakey and Debakey, 1983:11; cf. Friedrich, 1984:72.

58. Cummings, 1985:S133–34; "A Policy," 1976:787. See A. Kennedy (1981: 584–88) for examples from Ethiopia, Bangladesh, Egypt, India, Iraq, and Kuwait.

59. I. Kennedy, 1981:50. // Aaron and Schwartz, 1984:53. // Office of Health Economics, 1979; Weale, 1979:185; "Ethics and Priorities," 1976:105.

60. Jennett, 1984a:64–68; Aaron and Schwartz, 1984:28. Cf. F. Miller, 1985:31, and English et al., 1984:1889, regarding heart transplants (whose scarcity is largely due to the limited supply of hearts available for transplant).

61. Ingman et al., 1987:228; National Heart, 1984:Ch.44:30–31; Brahams, 1984:386; Challah et al., 1984:1121; Gabriel, 1983:36; Carter-Jones, 1983:100; Ferriman, 1980:4. Cf. Ward, 1986:61; Simmons and Marine, 1984:323.

62. Calne, 1983:124, 1982:998; "Renal Failure," 1982:1012. // Ferriman,

1980:4; Rennie et al., 1985:323; Wing, 1983:492; Aaron and Schwartz, 1984:28; "Renal Failure," 1982:1011–13; Hughes, 1985:3; "Some," 1977:4.

63. Evans and Yagi, 1987:28; Evans et al., 1986:1896–97; Robertson, 1987:77; Leaf, 1980:1087; Massachusetts, 1984:73; Annas, 1985:187.

64. Robertson, 1987:86. // Shapiro and Spece, 1981:767. Cultural barriers are even greater outside the United States. Cf. Suleiman et al., 1982:273. // F. Rapaport, 1987a:170. // Annas, 1985a:94; A. Parsons, 1985:469.

65. Edmunds, 1989:x–xi; Miles et al., 1988:410–11; T. Cooper, 1987:22; F. Rapaport, 1987a:169; Copeland et al., 1987; Minnesota, 1984:49; Rajakumar, 1984:4; Albert Gore in U.S. House, 1983:91.

66. U.S. Dept. of H.H.S., 1985; F. Rapaport, 1987b:3118; Kolata, 1983:32. // "FDA," 1986:B6; F. Rapaport, 1987a:169.

67. Evans and Yagi, 1987:28; Blank, 1988:131. Cf. Christopherson, 1982: 20.

68. Macklin, 1985b:611–12; Bermel, 1985:3–4; Off. of Tech. Assess., 1984: 73–74; Minnesota, 1984:43.

69. Oberdiek, 1976:85; Minnesota, 1984:29. Cf. Dukeminier and Sanders, 1971:1134; Lederberg, 1966:7. // Ashley and O'Rourke, 1982:240. // UNOS, 1989a:2. // Blank, 1988:131. // San Francisco, 1987; Winslow, 1982: 25–28; Morgan, 1976:18; Paule, 1975:24–29; Koughan, 1975:32. // Pledger, 1986:678.

70. National Heart, 1984:Ch.45:5–7; Minnesota, 1984:29; Aaron and Schwartz, 1984:113–14; Leenen, 1979:162.

71. Churchill, 1987:10; Coulton, 1986:104.

72. Caplan, 1986a:23; "The Life," 1984:144; National Heart, 1984:Ch.45:29; "A Policy," 1976:788.

73. Peel, 1973:107; Aaron and Schwartz, 1984:14; Caplan, 1984:158.

74. Hardwig, 1987:59; Thomasma, 1982:49.

75. U.S. Dept. of Commerce, 1988:86; "Health-Care," 1986:A2, summarizing the annual H.H.S. Dept. report. Cf. William L. Roper in U.S. Dept. of H.H.S., 1986.

76. Sheagren and Eiker, 1980:163. // El. Friedman, 1983:836; Caplan, 1986a: 24.

77. Blank, 1988:80; Hiatt, 1987:8; R. Evans, 1986:21; Hyman, 1986:41; Angell, 1985; Mulley, 1984:225; Morris Abram in Friedrich, 1984:73; Fineberg, 1984:18; Califano, 1986:178; "Rationing," 1985:6–7; "Will," 1979:2; Richards, 1984:86.

78. Chinard, 1985:121; Moskop, 1987a:178; National Kidney, 1986:Ch.1:37 and Ch.2:14; Colen, 1986:216; Susan Hansen in Kjellstrand et al., 1986:305; C. Levine, 1986:4; Chinard, 1985:121; Smirnow, 1984:237; Ruchlin, 1984:8; National Heart, 1984:Ch.45:41; Kolff, 1983:832; Robb, 1981:30; Kolata, 1980:476.

79. Rennie et al., 1985:332; Rosner, 1983a:354; Greifer, 1984:111; DePalma, 1983:829–30.

80. See survey results reported in Waldron, 1985 (confirmed by survey results described in ch. 2).

81. Prottas et al., 1983:102; Kolata, 1980:473. // Mailick and Ullmann, 1984:30; "Rationing," 1985:4.

82. Evans et al., 1984a:5–13.

83. Meyer, 1984:18; Clark et al., 1981:54; Altman, 1973:13.

84. G. Richards, 1984:81.

85. Schmidt et al., 1983; National Heart, 1984:Ch.44:41.

86. Institute of Medicine, 1973:8–9.

87. Jamieson, 1988:288; Macklin, 1987:160; Evans et al., 1986:1896; Graber et al., 1985:208; Clark, 1985:121; Smirnow, 1984:237; Oreopoulos, 1983:67; Lawrence, 1980:444. // Rennie et al., 1985:227; Minnesota, 1984:33; "Will," 1979:5.

88. Mechanic, 1986:216; Leaf, 1984:718; Clark, 1985:121. Cf. Barondess et al., 1988:934; Caplan, 1987b:5; Moskop, 1987b:13; Mehlman, 1985:241.

89. McCormick, 1988:122,125; Francis, 1986:120; Gorovitz, 1984:17; Waldholz, 1981:23.

90. Miles, 1988:409–10; Jamieson, 1988; Annas, 1977; Knox, 1978; Edelhart, 1981.

91. National Heart Institute, 1969:26–27.

92. See Caplan, 1985b; H. Green, 1984; National Heart Institute, 1969:26–35.

93. Working Group, 1985:19. See p. 17 for reasons why higher estimates are likely. // Smeeding, 1987:145; Colen, 1986:225–26; Preston, 1985:7. Cf. Lubeck and Bunker, 1982:372; Bernstein, 1984:63; Moskop, 1987b:13.

94. National Heart, 1984:Ch.43:17.

95. Greenberg, 1982:C5; "Artificial," 1983:4. // National Heart and Lung, 1973:141; Winslow, 1982:28–36; Debakey and Debakey, 1983:9.

96. Working Group, 1985:31; Lederberg, 1966:7; "Due Process," 1975:1735. // Caplan, 1982:23; Jonsen, 1973:4; American Heart Assn., 1976:824.

97. Leenen, 1979:162.

98. Callahan, 1987:123–26; Hunter et al., 1980; Jonsen, 1979:170; Scribner, 1964:209. // Reiser, 1977:55; Kass, 1985:26.

99. Altman, 1973:13. // Graber et al., 1985:207–08; cf. Oberdiek, 1976: 76,85. // Hamburger, 1981:12. // Stacey, 1983:7.

100. Bayer, 1984:50. Cf. R. Evans, 1983:2052; Rivin, 1978:44; Katz, 1973: 373; Ramsey, 1970a:268.

101. Levinsky, 1984:1575; Massachusetts, 1984:72; Lyon, 1983:8.

102. Altman, 1982.

103. "Rationing," 1985:6; Katz and Capron, 1975:5,135.

104. Moskop, 1987b:14; Anderson, 1977:785–86; "Prolonging," 1985:11; Felch, 1982:5.

105. Moskop, 1987a; Klein, 1984:144; "Ethics and Priorities," 1976:105; "Patient," 1969:1322.

106. Rothman, 1987:566–67; Mehlman, 1985:242; Bowen, 1984:453; "The Ethical Challenge," 1975; Rajakumar, 1984:4.

107. Ashley and O'Rourke, 1986:112; Lomasky, 1981:84; Attig et al., 1976; Feinberg, 1978:806; Abram and Wadlington, 1968:615.

108. Gorovitz, 1966:6; Hearn, 1977:321; Schreiner, 1968:464; Davidson and Scribner, 1967:2. // National Heart, 1984:Ch.43:17.

109. Ramsey, 1970a:243–44.

110. 1984:Ch.45:25.

CHAPTER 2. PLENTIFUL APPROACHES

1. Those who hold this view, including a few who participated in the study of medical directors explained later in the chapter, may simply not have had the opportunity to study the material footnoted in chapter 1.

2. Jonsen et al., 1982:160.

3. Margolis, 1985:178,184.

4. Kessel, 1985:208; Thielicke, 1970:173.

5. Caplan, 1981b:497, 1983a:114–15.

6. Westervelt, 1970; Cohen, 1977:224; Schreiner, 1966. Cf. the American College of Cardiology report cited in United Nations, 1975:70, and the analysis of it in Winslow, 1982:61.

7. Wilensky, 1985:37–38. Cf. Zawacki, 1985:58; Jn. Fletcher, 1983:1342.

8. Cahn, 1955; Cardozo, 1929.

9. "Scarce," 1969:622; Katz, 1973:385. Cf. Curran, 1973:147.

10. Young, 1975:445.

11. Thielicke, 1970:172.

12. Ramsey 1970a:254.

13. Winslow, 1982:80.

14. Childress, 1970:342.

15. Ramsey, 1970a:260, cf. 253.

16. Basson, 1979:315; cf. Winslow, 1982:90.

17. Mehlman, 1985:281; Roch. Green, 1984:69; "Scarce," 1969:653.

18. Kilner, 1984. Although this perspective emerges to some degree in the vast majority of the interviews, it is most eloquently expressed by Masika Musive (#117, Kisau Location), Mwau Muia (#141, Makueni Location), Nduku Mbithi (#147, Mbiuni Location), Kavuu Ndasya (#149, Mbiuni Location), and Wanza Kimolo (#154, Muvuti Location). Cf. esp. interview #65, 105, 125, 140, 146, 148, 156.

19. Significant inequalities do in fact exist among the Akamba. However, the Akamba have developed various cultural mechanisms to diminish their significance (Nida, 1962:147–49; Larby, 1944:13; Mbiti, 1970:229; Good, 1980:27; N. Miller, 1980:5; Dundas, 1913:532; Carothers, 1948:76; Penwill, 1951:29). At the same time, basic spheres of life such as the political (Oliver, 1965:426; Jacobs,

1961:113–14; Ndeti, 1972:108–09; Nida, 1962:147; Dundas, 1913:527) and the social (Ndeti, 1972:81; Nida, 1962:150; Muthiani, 1973:18ff; Lindblom, 1920: 553) are structured so as to preserve a fundamental equality.

20. Calabresi and Bobbitt, 1978:178.

21. Tempels, 1959:120–21; Good, 1980:29; Middleton and Kershaw, 1965: 83; Mbiti, 1970:216 (cf. 68, 244).

22. Mbiti, 1966:34; Middleton and Kershaw, 1965:83.

23. Ramsey, 1970a:260; Winslow, 1982:91.

24. Attig and Wasserstrom, 1976.

25. Ezorsky, 1972:158; Roach, 1980:154; Winslow, 1982:91.

26. Hinderling, 1968; Leenen, 1979:167; Winslow, 1982:52–59. Regarding the borderline case of overfilling an ICU unit, thereby exposing all to a risk of death, see chapter 11.

27. Ramsey, 1970a:265.

28. Katz, 1973:387.

29. Winslow, 1982:91.

30. Sanders and Dukeminier, 1968:376–77, coined the term.

31. If there are numerous ethical constraints, as in Gillon, 1985:268, then the approach is not genuinely ad hoc.

32. Blank, 1988:246–47; National Heart, 1984:Ch.35:1; Oberdiek, 1976:82.

33. Jane Hunt in Jonsen et al., 1975:763; various physicians in Childress et al., 1982.

34. Katz and Procter, 1969:25; Katz, 1970:676; Fox and Swazey, 1978b:269; "Due Process," 1975:1742–43.

35. S. Alexander, 1962:106; Robbins and Robbins, 1967; Sanders and Dukeminier, 1968:377.

36. Esp. Sanders and Dukeminier, 1968.

37. Katz, 1973:408.

38. Ramsey, 1970a:248.

39. Callahan, 1987:133; Haber, 1986:763; Veatch, 1985b:79.

40. Oglesby, 1975:713.

41. Calabresi, 1978:11; Dukeminier and Sanders, 1971:1134; Katz and Capron, 1975:192.

42. Haber, 1986:763; Hicks, 1985:105; Warmbrodt, 1985:4; "Who Shall Be," 1984:717; Grad, 1968:498; S. Alexander, 1962:106. Cf. Caplan, 1987b:12.

43. Fox and Swazey, 1978b:232.

44. Eisenberg, 1979; Roth, 1972:840–41; I. Kennedy, 1981:83–84.

45. Rabinowitz and Van der Spuy, 1978:862; Reidy, 1979:80; "Who Shall Be," 1984:717.

46. Parsons and Lock, 1980:174.

47. Lundberg, 1983a; Kass, 1985:26; Sanders and Dukeminier, 1968:378.

48. Kass, 1985:27; Winslow, 1982:62.

49. Veatch, 1985b:79.

50. Leenen, 1979:166.

51. Haber, 1986:763; Massachusetts, 1984:75–76; Annas, 1985b:188; Veatch, 1985b:79.

52. Katz and Capron, 1975:191.

53. Ibid.:192.

54. Fleck, 1987:185–87; Massachusetts, 1984:75; Annas, 1985b:188.

55. This study is reported in Kilner, 1988.

56. This study is reported in Kilner, 1984. See Kilner, 1983b, for a more detailed description of the methodology.

57. Mbiti, 1966. High correlations between responses to such cases and actual treatment decisions have been established: see Deber et al., 1985:97; Norman, 1984; Norman et al., 1982.

58. National Heart, 1984:Ch.36:3–4; Walters, 1987:2; Winslow, 1982:107–08; Aroskar, 1979:38–40; Curran, 1979:141–42; "Scarce," 1969:657; Thielicke, 1970:171.

59. Harron et al., 1983:150–51; Purtilo and Cassel, 1981:189–90; N. Bell, 1979b:86; Wojcik, 1978:119; Feinberg, 1978:809; Massachusetts, 1984:80; Annas, 1985b:189.

CHAPTER 3. SOCIAL VALUE

1. S. Alexander, 1962:106.

2. Tancredi, 1982:98; Katz, 1970:676–77; "Patient," 1969:1330. See chapter 14 for a more individual-oriented quality-of-life rationale, and Kolata, 1980:473–74, for a possible medical justification.

3. Davidson and Scribner, 1967:5. // Basson, 1979:317; Young, 1975:447.

4. Examples include Rosner, 1983a:356; Young, 1975:449. Most U.S. health care settings explicitly disavow favoring either sex. For the policies of other countries, such as Norway, see United Nations, 1975:32.

5. Caplan, 1987b; National Heart, 1984:Ch.9:4. // Randal, 1982:15. // Hiatt, 1987:215; Ferrans, 1987:109–10; Robbins, 1984:127; Wineman, 1982:291; Ramsey, 1970a:251. // Ogden, 1987:104; Suleiman et al., 1982:273. Data on the first three treatments is from the United States, that on the fourth from the United States and Malaysia.

6. National Heart, 1984:Ch.9:6, Ch.31:11, Ch.32:104; Mathieu, 1988:47. // Randal, 1982:14–15. // National Heart, 1984:Ch.32:104. // Callender, 1987:37; Ogden, 1987:104; End-Stage, 1985; Task Force, 1986:87; Held et al., 1988. (All U.S. data.)

7. E.g., regarding heart transplantation see Evans and Yagi, 1987:31,36; National Heart, 1984:Ch.9:4. See Kutner, 1987:31, for evidence that socioeconomic differences among races are also key influences. The farther one moves from explicit patient selection decisions, the more likely that prior medical or

social differences are central (e.g., with regard to the infant mortality rate, which for black babies is twice as high as for white babies—Hiatt, 1987:4).

8. National Heart, 1984:Ch.9:16; Royal, 1981:285; Verwilghen, 1981:556; Parsons and Lock, 1981:556; Large and Ahmad, 1981:556–57.

9. Evans et al., 1984:6.

10. United Nations, 1975:32. // Bergsten et al., 1977:7. // Ingman et al., 1987:239; Johnson et al., 1985; Carter-Jones, 1983; Parsons and Lock, 1980:174; V. Parsons, 1978:872. // Najman et al., 1982:1781–82.

11. "Scarce," 1969:654,658; Hiatt, 1987:7; National Heart, 1984:Ch.44:15, Ch.45:29–30; R. Evans, 1983:2209; Hingson et al., 1981:97; "Due Process," 1975:1743; "Patient," 1969:1326; Sanders and Dukeminier, 1968:367.

12. Katz and Procter, 1969; Ramsey, 1970a:250–51. Katz (1970:676–77) reports that the following related factors were considered important by numerous dialysis centers: future social contributions (thirty-six centers), social welfare burden (twenty centers), demonstrated social worth (twenty-eight centers), criminal record (twenty-two centers), and poor employment history (seventeen centers).

13. Waterfall, 1980:726; Bayer, 1984:37; Katz, 1967:56; Murray et al., 1962:316; "Doctor I Want," 1980; Wojcik, 1978:120–21.

14. Sanders and Dukeminier, 1968:373. // "Scarce," 1969:658; personal letters (dated March 27, 1986, and April 23, 1986) from Norman Levinsky, who served on the selection committee; Getze, 1965:3.

15. Blank, 1988:85; Loewy, 1987:438; Caplan, 1987b:7; Veatch, 1985b:73; Askham, 1982:2086; Lasagna, 1970:88; Shatin, 1966:98.

16. Crane, 1982:394; Uhlmann and McDonald, 1982:45A; Najman, 1982:1781–82.

17. Roth, 1972. // Coulton, 1986:97; Mulley, 1983:302–03; Veatch, 1975:6. Wetle and Levkoff (1984:224) report a study of one hundred physicians in which 31 percent consider "societal worth" to be very important in choosing between candidates for limited ICU space. An even higher percentage considered the criterion to have at least some relevance.

18. F. Miller, 1985:31; Dempsey, 1974:53; "Patient," 1969:1324–25. // National Heart, 1984:Ch.8:30–31, Ch.45:29–30; R. Evans, 1983:2209. // Lundberg, 1983b:2967; Consensus, 1983.

19. Elkowitz, 1986:127–28; Wetle and Levkoff, 1984:225.

20. Harron et al., 1983:151.

21. California Health, 1986:3. In a national survey (Evans and Manninen, 1987:4), 29 percent said that a person convicted of a major crime should be excluded from transplantation. Comparable figures regarding prostitutes and persons convicted of a minor crime were 9 percent and 3 percent respectively.

22. Nabarro, 1967:622; Beecher, 1971:288; Cummings, 1985:S134; Leenen, 1979:171; J. Bryant, 1973:95; Jonsen and Garland, 1976:152; Abram and Wadlington, 1968; Justices Clio and Euterpe in Annas, 1977:68,76. Cf. Hiatt, 1987:215,217.

23. McIntyre and Benfari, 1982:25; Kolata, 1980:473–74.

24. Loewy, 1987:440–41. // Attig and Wasserstrom, 1976.

25. Rescher, 1969:178; National Heart, 1984:Ch.36:13; Belliotti, 1980a:260; Rhodes, 1973:648; S. Alexander, 1962:123; Davidson and Scribner, 1967:7.

26. Leenen, 1979:171; Attig and Wasserstrom, 1976.

27. Basson, 1979:323–24, in this regard cites Shatin, 1966, Rescher, 1969, Katz and Procter, 1969, and S. Alexander, 1962.

28. Shatin, 1966:96–98.

29. Rescher, 1969:180; Young, 1975:444; Jos. Fletcher, 1968:1090; Davidson and Scribner, 1967:9; Sawyer, 1968:9; S. Alexander, 1962:106; Attig and Wasserstrom, 1976.

30. Basson, 1979:318–19.

31. Leach, 1972:260–61; Abram and Wadlington, 1968:618–19; Katz and Procter, 1969:26–27; Shackman, 1967:624; Wilson, 1967:624. // Nabarro, 1967: 622; F. Parsons, 1967:623. While these sources all support decision making by physicians, the role of social value considerations is not clear in every case.

32. Rescher, 1969:178; Basson, 1979:324.

33. Basson, 1979:323,327.

34. Belliotti, 1980a:255.

35. Basson, 1979:320; Belliotti, 1980a:260.

36. Shatin, 1966:97.

37. Jos. Fletcher, 1968:1090; Winslow, 1982:83.

38. Feinberg, 1978:809.

39. Brock, 1988a:91.

40. Shatin, 1966:99–100.

41. Belliotti, 1980a:256.

42. F. Parsons, 1967:623.

43. Rescher, 1966:197; Basson, 1979:317.

44. Soltan, 1982.

45. Loewy, 1987:440; Freedman, 1977a:33; Childress, 1981:95; Winslow, 1982:85. // O'Rourke and Brodeur, 1986:228–29.

46. Leenen, 1979:171; Rescher, 1969:179.

47. Belliotti, 1980a:260.

48. B. Brody, 1983:154; Belliotti, 1980a:260.

49. Childress, 1985:22; Leenen, 1979:170, 1982:35; National Heart, 1984: Ch.8:6.

50. National Heart, 1984:Ch.36:13–14.

51. Ibid.:17.

52. National Heart, 1984:Ch.35:2–3.

53. Working Group, 1985:31. // United Nations, 1975:32.

54. Fox, 1979:134. // Rettig, 1976c:13; Katz, 1973:408.

55. "Patient," 1969:1330.

56. Robertson, 1989; Leenen, 1979:170; Winslow, 1982:161–62; "Patient," 1969:1336; Ramsey, 1970a:256; Sanders and Dukeminier, 1968:376.

57. Bayer, 1984:39–40.

58. Winslow, 1982:97–98.

59. Katz, 1973:403.

60. National Heart, 1984:Ch.35:6–7. // Ramsey, 1978:232–33.

61. See also Sanders and Dukeminier, 1968:380, who oppose the kind of social-value ad hockery advocated by Davidson and Scribner, 1967:4,6.

62. Lefebvre, 1980:181; Outka, 1974:18–19; Leenen, 1979:171; National Heart and Lung, 1973:147; Childress, 1981:94; Sanders and Dukeminier, 1968: 376–78.

63. Rescher, 1969:179; Basson, 1979:330.

64. Dukeminier and Sanders, 1968:1136; Broome, 1984:50; Boyd and Potter, 1986:199; Macklin, 1987:157, 1985b:616; Fromer, 1981:58; Leenen, 1982:35; Katz and Capron, 1975:189; Ramsey, 1970a:275; Sanders and Dukeminier, 1968:373.

65. Young, 1975:451; Rescher, 1969:179.

66. Weckman and Willy, 1987:16; Robbins, 1984:124; L. Schwartz, 1976: 104; Bertrand, 1976:26; Childress, 1970:344; "Patient," 1969:1330; "Scarce," 1969:662.

67. Ingman et al., 1987:231; Wauters et al., 1983; Parsons and Lock, 1980.

68. Childress, 1970:345; Gorovitz, 1966:7; National Heart and Lung, 1973: 241.

69. Sanders and Dukeminier, 1968:376; "Patient," 1969:1326, 1338.

70. Childress, 1981:94. // Ferrans, 1987:117; Coulton, 1986:102. // Kluge, 1979:104; Ramsey, 1970a:258–59.

71. Leenen, 1982:35.

72. Ferrans, 1987:117; Mehlman, 1985:258; Roach, 1980:158; Childress, 1970:345–46.

73. Katz, 1973:407–08; Davidson and Scribner, 1967:8; Sawyer, 1968:10,17; "Patient," 1969:1338.

74. Katz and Capron, 1975:189.

75. "Patient," 1969:1331.

76. Ibid.:1331,1336,1340.

77. Bayer, 1986:16, 1984:39; Boyd and Potter, 1986:199; Mehlman, 1985:257; Macklin, 1987:158, 1985b:617; Leenen, 1982:34. // Glover, 1977:225; Belliotti, 1980a:260. // Gorovitz, 1977:192.

78. Winslow, 1982:159.

79. R. Potter, 1971:628; Kolff, 1964:360; Young, 1975:451–52.

80. Basson, 1979:319–20; Gorney, 1968:314.

81. Leach, 1972:260; Ramsey, 1970a:247; S. Alexander, 1962:124.

82. Ramsey, 1970a:248. // Loewy, 1987:438; Broome, 1984:50; N. Bell, 1979a:14; "Scarce," 1969:658–62; "Patient," 1969:1331.

83. Ferrans, 1987:113; Em. Friedman, 1984:68; Fox and Swazey, 1978b:232; Childress, 1970:345; Sanders and Dukeminier, 1968:377.

84. Fox and Swazey, 1978b:230–31; Leenen, 1982:35; Shatin, 1966:98.

85. Caplan, 1987b:11; Sawyer, 1968:11.

86. Mehlman, 1985:258; Veatch, 1977b:238; Jonsen and Garland, 1976:152; Levinsky (personal letter March 27, 1986); Westervelt, 1970:360; "Scarce," 1969:662. Cf. Ferrans, 1987:110.

87. Munson, 1983:485; Leach, 1972:260; "Scarce," 1969:660.

88. Hyman, 1980:265.

89. Rawls, 1978:32; Robbins, 1984:124–25.

90. B. Williams, 1973:145.

91. Ramsey, 1970a:255–58; Thomasma, 1986a:7; Feinberg, 1978:809; Katz, 1973:408; Katz and Capron, 1975:190; "Patient," 1969:1331. Cf. Kamm, 1987: 256.

92. Veatch, 1976:139; Ferrans, 1987:116; Macklin, 1987:158, 1985b:617; N. Bell, 1979b:94.

93. C. Lyons, 1970:89–90; Caplan, 1987a:15; N. Bell, 1979b:88; Outka, 1974:17–18; "Scarce," 1969:658.

94. Basson, 1979:327–28.

95. Henikoff, 1986; Varga, 1984:226; American Medical, 1982:2; Veatch, 1977:232; National Heart and Lung, 1973:147; Katz and Capron, 1975:190; Sanders and Dukeminier, 1968:374.

96. Massachusetts, 1984:77; Annas, 1985b:188; "Scarce," 1969:670; "Patient," 1969:1329.

97. Jones, 1985:391; Macklin, 1985a:376.

98. Parsons and Lock, 1983:44–45.

99. Campbell, 1978:81; Bayer, 1986:16, 1984:40; Jones, 1985:391; Veatch, 1976:139.

100. Oberdiek, 1976:85–86. // Leenen, 1982:35; "Patient," 1969:1329–30.

101. Jonsen and Garland, 1976:152–53.

102. Winslow, 1982:137.

103. Macklin, 1987:157, 1985b:616; Robbins, 1984:125; National Heart, 1984: Ch.31:6; Campbell, 1978:34.

104. Weckman and Willy, 1987:17; Mehlman, 1985:258; National Heart, 1984:Ch.31:12–13, Ch.32:41–42. // Leenen, 1982:35, 1979:171. // Task Force, 1986:89. Regarding all three types of persons, see also references in notes 4–8 above.

105. Leenen, 1982:35, 1979:171.

106. Leenen, 1982:35, 1979:170; Childress, 1970:345; "Scarce," 1969:659; Sanders and Dukeminier, 1968:378; Gorovitz, 1966:7.

107. Hiatt, 1987:215; Macklin, 1987:157, 1985b:616; Bayer, 1986:16; Arras, 1984:34–35; Robbins, 1984:125; Campbell, 1978:34.

108. Bayer, 1986:16; Young, 1975:451.

109. Lefebvre, 1980:185.

110. Thielicke, 1970:183–84; Gorovitz, 1966:6–7; Nelson and Rohricht, 1984: 196; Outka, 1974:19–20; Winslow, 1982:84; "Patient," 1969:1329.

111. Roach, 1980:158; Veatch, 1976:139; Thielicke, 1970:170–71.

112. Ramsey, 1970a:256. // Fried, 1975:241–42; Thielicke, 1970:171.

113. Hughes, 1985:3; S. Alexander, 1962:124.

114. Gillon, 1985:267.

115. Kamm, 1987:261.

116. Loewy, 1987:437; Sanders and Dukeminier, 1968:379.

117. Pellegrino, 1980:176; Macklin, 1987:164, 1985b:621; Caplan, 1986a:24; Mehlman, 1985:250; Palmer, 1980:267; Beauchamp and Childress, 1979:195; Harron et al., 1983:151.

118. Held et al., 1988; Comptroller General, 1975:16–17; "Due Process," 1975:1735; Lyon, 1986:59; Fox and Swazey, 1978b:249. Cf. Kilner, 1988.

119. Katz and Capron, 1975:190.

120. Hastings Group, 1979:52; Rickham, 1976:746.

121. Broad, 1934:252; Broome, 1984:41.

122. Palmer, 1980:267; Ellington, 1978:132.

123. Glover, 1977:225.

124. Attig and Wasserstrom, 1976; "Scarce," 1969:663.

125. Thielicke, 1970:171.

126. Ellington, 1978:131; Thielicke, 1970:171,193.

127. Basson, 1979:319.

128. Glover, 1977:218,222.

129. Munson, 1983:484–85; Glover, 1977:223; "Utilitarianism," 1984:116.

130. Jonsen et al., 1982:163.

131. Parsons and Lock, 1983:45–46.

132. Adapted from S. Alexander, 1962:110.

133. E.g., see chapter 1, note 11. Also: Davidson and Scribner, 1967; Sawyer, 1968; Fox and Swazey, 1978; Winslade and Ross, 1986.

CHAPTER 4. FAVORED GROUP

1. Beauchamp and Childress, 1979:194; "Scarce," 1969:640–43.

2. Task Force, 1986:86. Accordingly, over 75 percent of the people in a national survey indicated that local distribution of donated organs is not essential (Evans and Manninen, 1987:4).

3. Minnesota, 1984:50; Kanoti, 1985; Katz, 1970:676–77; S. Alexander, 1962:108. // Warmbrodt, 1985:3–4.

4. Off. of Inspector Gen., 1986:4; Robertson, 1987:82; Em. Friedman, 1984:68,72. See Gruson (1985:5) for the positions of the American Council of Transplant Physicians and the American Society of Transplant Surgeons.

5. Midwest, 1986:2; Mandel, 1986:48–49.

6. Evans et al., 1984a:6,12; Off. of Inspector Gen., 1986:16; John McDonald, Paul Terasaki, and Henry Krakauer in U.S. House, 1983:88,92,108.

7. Minnesota, 1984:50; Levinsky, 1986:11; Sommers, 1986:16.

8. Coulton, 1986:99; "Rationing," 1985:4; DePalma, 1983:829; Em. Friedman, 1984:72; Bermel, 1983:2.

9. Bermel, 1983:2.

10. Rescher, 1969:176; Starzl et al., 1988a:136; Off. of Inspector Gen., 1986:15–16.

11. Childress, 1985:24.

12. Young, 1975:442; Rescher, 1969:177; Silva, 1986.

13. Levinsky, 1986:13.

14. Jonasson, 1986:24; Off. of Inspector Gen., 1986:10–17.

15. Off. of Inspector Gen., 1986:17.

16. Leenen, 1979:168.

17. UNOS, 1988:32; Starzl et al., 1988a:133; Mathieu, 1988:47; F. Rapaport, 1987b:3118; Childress, 1985:23–24.

18. Off. of Inspector Gen., 1986:11.

19. Off. of Inspector Gen., 1986:10,15; Gruson, 1985:5. // UNOS, 1988:32; Starzl et al., 1988a:132–33; Robertson, 1987:82.

20. Sommers, 1986:16–17.

21. Levinsky, 1986:11.

22. Sommers, 1986:17.

23. Graber et al., 1985:211.

24. Stiller, 1985:135. See also sources in note 6 above.

25. Prottas, 1986:23. // John McDonald in U.S. House, 1983:88.

26. Jonasson, 1986:24; Prottas, 1986:23.

27. Prottas, 1986:23.

28. Task Force, 1986:93,97; Jonasson, 1986:24; Colen, 1986:221; Transpl. Society, 1985:715; Gruson, 1985:5; Warren Reich in U.S. House, 1983:44.

29. Nickel, 1986:21; Kleinig, 1986:25.

30. Jonasson, 1986:24.

31. Off. of Inspector Gen., 1986:9,13.

32. Schneider and Flaherty, 1985; Off. of Inspector Gen., 1986:14.

33. Barbara Lindsay in U.S. House, 1983:25.

34. Off. of Inspector Gen., 1986:7.

35. Lyon, 1986:58; Schneider and Flaherty, 1985. // Sch. and Fl., 1985; Bermel, 1986:3. On the scope of the overall problem, see Ogden, 1987:105; Transpl. Society, 1985:715.

36. Prottas, 1986:23–24.

37. Childress, 1978:1415; "Scarce," 1969:642; Ramsey, 1970a:246.

38. Murray, 1962:316; Ramsey, 1970a:252; Childress, 1985:23.

39. Massachusetts, 1984:77; Annas, 1985b:188; Winslow, 1982:130; Beauchamp and Childress, 1979:194.

40. Young, 1975:442.

41. Task Force, 1986:91; Rescher, 1969:176; "Scarce," 1969:642.

42. Rescher, 1969:178.

43. Hunsicker et al., 1987:1329; Mathieu, 1988:47.

44. Katz, 1973:412–13.

45. Jonasson, 1986:24.

46. George Shreiner (U.S. House, 1983:199) reports an increase in organ donation among the 65,000 ethnic Greeks in Washington, D.C., when Georgetown University opened their kidney transplantation program to Greek nationals.

47. Robertson, 1987:83.

48. Gore, 1987:4.

49. Sommers, 1986:17.

50. Levinsky, 1986:12; "Scarce," 1969:641.

51. Kleinig, 1986:25; Winslow, 1982:132.

52. Task Force, 1986:86.

53. Jonasson, 1986:24.

54. Nickel, 1986:21.

55. Childress, 1985:1; Evans and Manninen, 1987:3,4; Mandel, 1986:48–49; Williams et al., 1984.

56. Kleinig, 1989; Jonasson, 1986:24; Task Force, 1986:93–94; Ashley and O'Rourke, 1986:112; Peter Ivanovich and John McDonald in U.S. House, 1983:13,88.

57. Nickel, 1986:22; Warren Reich in U.S. House, 1983:53–54. The story is recorded in the Christian Bible (Luke 10:30–37).

58. Task Force, 1986:94.

59. F. Rapaport, 1987b:3119; Jonasson, 1986:24; cf. Rescher, 1969:176, on medical tradition in general.

60. Task Force, 1986:93–94; Peter Ivanovich in U.S. House, 1983:13.

61. Paul Terasaki in U.S. House, 1983:92. // Peter Ivanovich in U.S. House, 1983:5.

62. B. Brody, 1983:154; Langtry, 1977:377–78.

63. Christopherson, 1982:20; Rescher, 1969:176; S. Alexander, 1962:108. Cf. Munson, 1983:476 on the county level.

64. Mathieu, 1988:47.

65. "Scarce," 1969:641.

66. Bell, 1979b:59; "Scarce," 1969:642; Ramsey, 1970a:242–43.

67. Off. of Inspector Gen., 1986:16.

68. Ibid.:2.

69. Mandel, 1986:48–49; Task Force, 1986:93–94.

70. Task Force, 1986:94.

71. American Society, 1986:1; Task Force, 1986:93; Transpl. Society, 1985:715; Warren Reich in U.S. House, 1983:45.

72. Kleinig, 1986:25.

73. Nickel, 1986:22.

74. Childress, 1985:25–26; Warren Reich in U.S. House, 1983:54.

75. Task Force, 1986:95; Nickel, 1986:22.

76. American Society, 1986:1; Off. of Inspector Gen., 1986:5; Jonasson, 1986:24. Cf. Paul Terasaki in U.S. House, 1983:100, and the University of Pittsburgh approach explained in Starzl et al., 1987b:3074. // Task Force, 1986:94.

77. Task Force, 1986:137–38. // Off. of Inspector Gen., 1986:15–16.

78. E.g., Childress, 1985:25–26.

79. Off. of Inspector Gen., 1986:5. Cf. Ogden, 1987:105.

80. Schneider and Flaherty, 1985; Off. of Inspector Gen., 1986:7; Albert Gore in U.S. House, 1983:79.

81. Prottas, 1986:24; Off. of Inspector Gen., 1986:11.

82. Jonasson, 1986:24.

83. Nickel, 1986:22–23.

84. Off. of Inspector Gen., 1986:5.

85. Kleinig, 1986:25.

86. Winslow, 1982:132; Task Force, 1986:94; Kleinig, 1986:25.

87. United Nations, 1975:30; Kleinig, 1986:25; Task Force, 1986:94.

88. Jonasson, 1986:24.

89. Adapted from "In Organ Transplants," 1986:23.

CHAPTER 5. RESOURCES REQUIRED

1. Winslow, 1982:74.

2. Roe, 1981:93.

3. Roper, 1975:73. Also see note 32 below. // Evans et al., 1984:6,12; A. Kennedy, 1981:586. Cf. Khoo, 1982:6,10, where quality of life considerations also seem to be in view.

4. A. Kennedy, 1981:585.

5. N. Bell, 1981:152, in opposition; Glover, 1977, in support. Childress, 1983:559, also in support, uses the term *medical utility*.

6. Basson, 1979:325.

7. Hardin, 1980:59.

8. Woodward, 1981:531–40; Leiman, 1978:9; Zawacki, 1985:59; Hewetson, 1982:304; Freedman, 1977a:38; Katz, 1973:417.

9. King, 1986:170; Foot, 1967:9; "Scarce," 1969:652.

10. Dubos, 1967:57ff.

11. Parfit, 1978:301; Sanders and Dukeminier, 1968:385.

12. Ezorsky, 1972:160–62.

13. Jn. Harris, 1975. // Sanders and Dukeminier, 1968:385.

14. Kamm, 1985:189; Winslow, 1982:142.

15. Kamm, 1985:181.

16. Morrillo, 1976:87.

17. Hardin, 1980:70.

18. Menzel, 1983:212. Cf. Taurek, 1977.

19. Anscombe, 1967:16–17; N. Bell, 1981:153–54.

20. Weale, 1979:189; N. Bell, 1981:152.

21. Ramsey, 1970a:262.

22. N. Bell, 1981:153.

23. Leiman, 1983:258.

24. N. Bell, 1979b:53.

25. Mavrodes, 1984:110.

26. Block, 1985:7, provides a poignant case of such a denial. The frequency of repeat transplants is documented, for example, in Off. of Organ Transpl., 1985; Task Force, 1986:90. Cf. Matt Armany in "Transplant Groups," 1987:90.

27. Brock, 1988:99.

28. Task Force, 1986:90–91; Childress, 1985:22.

29. Caplan, 1987a:17; Robertson, 1987:82.

30. Winslow, 1982:74.

31. Steven E. Rhoads in Hunter et al., 1980; Rhoads, 1980:304–05; Trachtman, 1985:14. On the influence of identifiable lives at times even in broad budgetary decisions such as the U.S. govt. decision to fund dialysis, see Rettig, 1976c:34–35, 1976b:219–20; U.S. House, 1971: pt. 7:1524–46 and pt. 10:2226–29; Perkoff et al., 1976:12; Blumstein, 1983:356.

32. Constructed from information in Hyatt, 1969:25, and "Scarce," 1969:651–52.

33. Rescher, 1969:177–78, examines it within the context of a likelihood-of-benefit criterion. Cf. Young, 1975:448.

CHAPTER 6. SPECIAL RESPONSIBILITIES

1. A. Russell, 1980:5. // United Nations, 1975:32.

2. Em. Friedman, 1984:68; Murray et al., 1962:316; National Heart, 1984:Ch.45:29–30; R. Evans, 1983:2209; "Scarce," 1969:658–59; Katz, 1967:56.

3. Robert Eckel in Attig et al., 1976.

4. National Heart, 1984:Ch.45:29–30; R. Evans, 1983:2209.

5. E.g., Hayes and Gunnells, 1969:528, where the criteria to be employed are identified in purely medical terms, but the decision is described as a choice between a "man" and a "25-year-old mother of three children."

6. Wetle and Levkoff, 1984:224.

7. Winslow, 1982:77.

8. Sawyer, 1968:9–10; Davidson and Scribner, 1967:7.

9. Beecher, 1971:280–81; Bok, 1981:26. // Pledger, 1986:678; Robbins, 1984:125–26.

10. Winslow, 1982:27–28.

11. Basson, 1979:330; Purtilo and Cassel, 1981:190.

12. Winslow, 1982:78.

13. Manroe, 1979:9; "Patient," 1969:1335.

14. Leenen, 1979:170, 1982:35. // Rescher, 1969:178. // Colen, 1977:A21. // Belliotti, 1980a:260; Glover, 1977:222; Rosner, 1983b:22–23; Winslow, 1982:78; Ruth Macklin in Attig et al., 1976.

15. S. Alexander, 1962:123; Winslow, 1982:78.

16. Thiroux, 1977:33; Rosner, 1983b:22–23; Winslow, 1982:77,153; Beauchamp and Childress, 1979:197–98; Childress, 1981:96.

17. Winslow, 1982:70.

18. Rosner, 1983a:354; Leenen, 1982:35, 1979:171; Glover, 1977:223.

19. Young, 1975:448.

20. Ramsey, 1970a:256–57,275; Childress, 1981:95–96; Beauchamp and Childress, 1979:197. // Basson, 1979:326.

21. Roe, 1981:93; Jonsen et al., 1982:160,164.

22. Winslow, 1982:77; B. Brody, 1983:154; O'Rourke and Brodeur, 1986: 228–29.

23. Leach, 1972:261. Cf. Bok, 1981:26.

24. "Scarce," 1969:663; Annas, 1977:68. Cf. Bok, 1981:26. // Childress, 1970:354, 1981:97.

25. Veatch, 1976:136,142.

26. Ron. Green, 1976:118; Winslow, 1982:152,204; Lefebvre, 1980:185. All three draw upon Rawls, 1971.

27. Freedman, 1977a:33; Winslow, 1982:71–73,157–58.

28. Cf. Rawls, 1971:284–93.

29. Aranow, 1980:304; "Scarce," 1969:664; Winslow, 1982:79.

30. Winslow, 1982:140.

31. Lefebvre, 1980:181; S. Alexander, 1962:125; Ramsey, 1970a:247.

32. Beauchamp and Childress, 1979:196; Childress, 1981:92.

33. Robbins, 1984:124. Cf. Leenen, 1979:175.

34. Ramsey, 1970a:245. // Robbins, 1984:124; Katz, 1973:408–09.

35. Kolff, 1983:832.

36. Roberts, 1974:186–87; Dundas, 1913:488; Mbiti, 1971:6.

37. Ndeti, 1972:114–15.

38. Kabwegyere, 1979:9; Mbiti, 1969:107.

39. While this perspective was expressed to varying degrees by many of the medical people interviewed, it was articulated most forcefully in the interviews with Makumbi Mbithi (#166, Iveti Location), Mbindyo Solo (#142, Kisau Location), Muia Kilile (#130, Muvuti Location), Wambua Mutweia (#115, Mwala Location), and Agnes Mueni (#56, Machakos Nursing Home). Cf. esp. interviews #165, 135, 44, 23.

40. Young, 1975:446; Freedman, 1983:100–01; N. Bell, 1979b:105–15.

41. Winslow, 1982:152.

42. Ibid.:71–73.

43. Shackman, 1967:623; Childress, 1981:353; Beauchamp and Childress, 1979:197–98; Young, 1975:449; "Scarce," 1969:662–63. Cf. Robbins, 1984:124.

44. Leach, 1972:261; "Scarce," 1969:664.

45. Young, 1975:448; Childress, 1970:353; cf. Frankena, 1973:47. This distinction is more blurred than opposed in, e.g., Rescher, 1969:178–79,185; Ramsey, 1970a:247; Beauchamp and Childress, 1979:197–98; and Childress, 1981:96.

46. "Scarce," 1969:664. Cf. Kamm, 1987:270.

47. Childress, 1970:353, 1978:1418, 1981:96; Beauchamp and Childress, 1979:197–98.

48. Freedman, 1983:110.

49. Sidgwick, 1907:248; "Scarce," 1969:659; cf. Rescher, 1969:178.

50. Thielicke, 1970:174; Beauchamp and Childress, 1979:197–98; Childress, 1970:353–54; "Scarce," 1969:665. Cf. La Puma et al., 1988:1810–11; Caplan, 1987b:11.

51. Beauchamp and Childress, 1979:197–98; Childress, 1981:96, 1970:353.

52. Fried, 1975:245; Childress, 1981:96, 1970:354.

53. "Scarce," 1969:666.

54. Boyd and Potter, 1986:197–99; Ramsey, 1970a:257; Freund, 1969:xiii; Beecher, 1969; "Patient," 1969:1334–35; T. O'Donnell, 1960:70.

55. Freedman, 1982:88–90.

56. Weckman and Willy, 1987:15; Kirklin, 1977:317; N. Bell, 1979b:90; John W. Hoyt in Childress et al., 1982.

57. Mehlman, 1985:272–74; Beauchamp and Childress, 1979:198; "Scarce," 1969:664; Basson, 1979:316–17.

58. N. Bell, 1979b:90; Basson, 1979:317; Rescher, 1969:178; "Scarce," 1969:664.

59. Boyd and Potter, 1986:197; Ramsey, 1970a:258; Beauchamp and Childress, 1979:197. // Kamm, 1985:192; Freedman, 1983:100–01, 1982:89.

60. Adapted from Levine and Veatch, 1984:96.

CHAPTER 7. AGE

1. Hendee, 1986:8; Meissner, 1986:6; Uddo, 1986:40.

2. Figures in parentheses indicate support vs. opposition to age criteria. National surveys: Pacific, 1987:1 (35 percent vs. 58 percent); Evans and Manninen, 1987:4 (57 percent support). State surveys: California Health, 1986:3 (19 percent vs. 57 percent); Washington, 1986:5 (40 percent vs. 43 percent); Oregon, 1984 (12 percent vs. 71 percent).

3. Regarding treatment of breast cancer, see Greenfield et al., 1987. Cf. Samet et al., 1986; Wetle, 1987:516. Regarding treatment of acute illnesses, see Kayser-Jones, 1986. Cf. sources in note 93 below.

4. R. Evans, 1983:2209; "Scarce," 1969:643–45; Katz, 1970:676, 1967:56;

Katz and Procter, 1969; Ramsey, 1970a:250; Sanders and Dukeminier, 1968:368. // "Patient," 1969:1324–25; Sawyer, 1968:8.

5. Gruson, 1985:5; Howard and Najarian, 1978:1161. On age criteria in organ transplantation generally, see Ogden, 1987:104; F. Miller, 1985:31.

6. Kayser-Jones, 1986:1282.

7. Debakey and Debakey, 1983:9; National Heart, 1984:Ch.8:30, Ch.10:25; U.S.H.C.F.A., 1981:7073. // Thompson, 1983:66; National Heart, 1984:Ch.8: 18,50,58,66; Evans and Yagi, 1987:27,29.

8. National Heart, 1984:Ch.9:2,4.

9. DeVries et al., 1984:278; Friedrich, 1984:73; Smeeding, 1987:144.

10. Gunby, 1982:1946. A national panel (National Heart and Lung, 1973:45) had earlier recommended seventy-four as the age cutoff.

11. Barondess et al., 1988:920; McClish, 1987:983; Saqueton, 1982:70.

12. Wetle and Levkoff, 1984:224.

13. Charlson et al., 1986:1319. Cf. Scitovsky, 1986; Barondess et al., 1988:921.

14. Evans et al., 1984a:6,12.

15. Khoo, 1982:5. // Suleiman, 1982:263. // Prottas et al., 1983:98.

16. Wing et al., 1978:13–14.

17. Bermel, 1983:2; Felch, 1982:11; "Will," 1979:5. // United Nations, 1975:32. // Steven Schroeder in "European Hospitals," 1984:24; Caplan, 1981b: 502. // Sage et al., 1987:316; Challah et al., 1984:1122. Cf. Knaus et al., 1982:643–45. // United Nations, 1975:32; Winslow, 1982:188.

18. Haber, 1986:762; Childress, 1986a:318; Lasagna, 1970:87–88; Calabresi and Bobbitt, 1978:184–85; Kerr, 1967:1,195–96; Veatch, 1985b:76.

19. Berlyne, 1982:189; Haber, 1986:762. Cf. many in following note. // Schwartz and Grubb, 1985; J. Evans, 1988:119; Wing, 1983b; Aaron and Schwartz, 1984:34,37; Prottas et al., 1983:97.

20. F. Parsons, 1983:9; Cameron, 1981:555; Challah et al., 1984:1120; Francis and Francis, 1987:129; Deitch, 1984:53; Halper, 1985:55. // Chinard, 1985: 121; Royal, 1981. // Ingman et al., 1987:227; Gabriel, 1983:35; Debakey and Debakey, 1983:9. // Sanders, 1986:26–27; Simmons and Marine, 1984:323; Parsons and Lock, 1980:175.

21. Johnson et al., 1985; Schwartz and Grubb, 1985:24; National Heart, 1984:Ch.45:28; Francis, 1986:120; Caplan, 1987b:13, 1984:158, 1983a:118, 1981a:727; Stacey, 1983:8; Bermel, 1983:2.

22. Hiatt, 1987:105; Califano, 1986:180; "Selection," 1978:1449; Jennett, 1984a:98; Wing et al., 1978:13.

23. Annas, 1985b:188; Deitch, 1984:53. // Iglehart, 1984; National Heart, 1984:Ch.44:30.

24. National Kidney, 1986:Ch.2:17; Haber, 1986:762; National Heart, 1984: Ch.44:25–26,32; Aaron and Schwartz, 1984:110; Schwartz and Aaron, 1984:53.

25. Norman Levinsky in Kotulak, 1986b:12; White and Monagle, 1982:8; Schwartz, 1976:104; Clark, 1985:119–20; Stacey, 1983:7.

26. Daniels, 1986:1; Francis, 1986:118; Levinsky, 1984:1574.

27. Caplan, 1984:161; Ralph Crawshaw in Kotulak, 1986b:12. // Papper, 1983:51–52; Levinsky, 1984:1574; "Rationing," 1985:9.

28. Barondess et al., 1988:920; Leach, 1972:257; David Thomasma in Lyon, 1986:59; Moody, 1978:199–200; Rescher, 1969:183; Young, 1975:444.

29. Aday and Andersen, 1981:9; Katz, 1973:413; Annas, 1977:72.

30. Blank, 1988:85; Abrams, 1987:54; Evans and Yagi, 1987:37–38; Robertson, 1987:81; Smeeding, 1987:143; Childress, 1986a:318; John Najarian in Kjellstrand et al., 1986:305; Fineberg, 1984:79; C. Lyons, 1970:94; Young, 1975:447.

31. Barondess et al., 1988:920; Kraus et al., 1983:574; Task Force, 1986:90; Childress, 1985:22, 1986a:318; Carl Kjellstrand in Kjellstrand et al., 1986:348; "Scarce," 1969:644–45. Cf. Battin, 1987:338.

32. G. Richards, 1984:84; Thomasma, 1984b:913; C. Lyons, 1970:94; Winslow, 1982:67. // Barondess et al., 1988:920; Wetle, 1987:516.

33. Off. of Technology, 1987:157; Wetle, 1987:516; Thomasma, 1986b:23; F. Miller, 1985:31; Arras, 1984:34–35; Robbins, 1984:126; Pearlman and Speer, 1983:115; Basson, 1979:324–25.

34. Rescher, 1969:178–79; Young, 1975:447; Piettre, 1977:254; Lachs, 1976:8; David, 1972:584.

35. Stiller, 1985:135; Rescher, 1969:182; Young, 1975:448.

36. Taube et al., 1983:2020; Jonsen et al., 1982:31; Ramsey, 1970a:257; Freund, 1969:xiii.

37. Waldholz, 1981:32.

38. Hyman, 1986:41; Geelhoed, 1985:11; Harry Schwartz in G. Richards, 1984:81.

39. Callahan, 1987:65ff.; Becker, 1979:550.

40. Daniels, 1985:96–97; David Thomasma in Lyon, 1986:59.

41. Veatch, 1979:218, 1977c:232; Hastings Group, 1979:54–56,82; Gunby, 1983:1982.

42. Menzel, 1983:191.

43. Glover, 1977:220; Menzel, 1983:191.

44. Callahan, 1987:137ff., 1988:128–29. Cf. Barondess et al., 1988:935; Ingman et al., 1987:246. In support of the idea that there is a fixed human life span that humanity has nearly reached, see Fries, 1980.

45. Daniels, 1983a, 1986:16–18, 1988a:Ch.5; Veatch, 1985a:17–18, 1985b:77.

46. National Heart, 1984:Ch.38:26; Daniels, 1988a:8–9; cf. Callahan, 1987:148ff.

47. Battin, 1987:324ff.

48. Daniels, 1986:19–20, 1985:96–97.

49. "Scarce," 1969:665.

50. De Wardener, 1966:107; Sanders and Dukeminier, 1968:368; Thielicke,

1970:174; "Scarce," 1969:664; Young, 1975:444–45. Cf. Davidson and Scribner, 1967:3; Royal, 1981:285.

51. National Heart, 1984:Ch.44:30; Childress, 1970:343.

52. Caplan, 1987b:13–14; Childress, 1984a:29; Schwartz and Aaron, 1984: 54; Aaron and Schwartz, 1984:101.

53. Swales, 1982:117–18; Schwartz and Aaron, 1984:54.

54. Aaron and Schwartz, 1984:35. // Anthony Wing in Ferriman, 1978:4.

55. Kirby, 1986:20–21. See also sources in previous three notes.

56. Caplan, 1987b:6–7.

57. Calabresi and Bobbitt, 1978:185.

58. Siegler, 1984:27.

59. Stacey, 1983:7.

60. Off. of Technology, 1987:159; Uddo, 1986:40. Cf. Cole, 1983:34. // Hastings, 1987:135.

61. N. Bell, 1979b:69.

62. Thielicke, 1970:172; Off. of Technology, 1987:158–59.

63. N. Bell, 1979b:71.

64. "Scarce," 1969:665.

65. Veatch, 1985b:43, 1986:146.

66. Francis, 1986:121.

67. Daniels, 1986:17; Francis, 1986:127.

68. Schneider and Brody, 1983. Even Callahan (1988:128) admits, "the average life expectancy continues to increase, with no end in sight."

69. Callahan, 1987:197–98.

70. E.g., Callahan, 1987:66,172. Accordingly, Callahan (1988:128) does not consider the elderly to be as worthy of attention as younger generations: the elderly's "primary orientation should be to the young."

71. Wikler, 1988:67; Daniels, 1988a:59ff.

72. Callahan, 1987:184–85.

73. J. Evans, 1988:120; Francis, 1986:121; Sage et al., 1986:782.

74. Daniels, 1985:111, 1988a:96; Battin, 1987:340.

75. Daniels, 1988a:97; cf. Wikler, 1987a:98.

76. Daniels, 1983a:289–91, 1985:113, 1988a:96; Battin, 1987:340.

77. Battin, 1987:340.

78. Francis, 1986:124.

79. Daniels, 1985:99, admits the possibility of this problem. Cf. Off. of Technology, 1987:159; Veatch, 1985b:21,48.

80. Veatch, 1985b:56.

81. Daniels, 1988a:129.

82. Childress, 1984a:29; contra generalization in Daniels, 1988a:129–30.

83. Barondess et al., 1988:924.

84. Callahan, 1987:194.

85. Battin, 1987:337.

86. Wikler, 1987:96–97.

87. "Scarce," 1969:665.

88. Calabresi and Bobbitt, 1978:230.

89. Ramsey, 1970a:244–45.

90. Katz, 1973:415.

91. Working Group, 1985:26; Swales, 1982:117–18; Clark, 1985:121; Katz and Capron, 1975:192. In the early days of hemodialysis in Seattle, age was considered at the second stage by the social committee rather than at the first stage by the medical committee: S. Alexander, 1962:106.

92. Lasagna, 1970:83; Clark, 1985:122. Cf. Aday and Andersen, 1981:9.

93. Scitovsky and Capron, 1986:72–73; Spector and Mor, 1984:332–34; Lubitz and Prihoda, 1984; Hilfiker, 1983:717; Crane, 1977:58–61, 1982:392. Cf. Wetle, 1985:263. See also sources in note 3 above.

94. Robb, 1981:29; John Sadler in Kolata, 1980:473.

95. Avorn, 1984; Daniels, 1986:19–20; Roger Evans in Canale et al., 1986:49–50.

96. J. G. Harris, 1987:110; Clark, 1985:122; Foner, 1985:27–31. See Cole (1983) for an analysis of the history of U.S. culture in this regard. // Palmore, 1982; Barondess et al., 1988:920,923; Eglit, 1987:1–1; Wetle, 1987:516; Maitland, 1987:2ff; Winslade and Ross, 1986:190; Cole, 1983:34.

97. Wetle, 1985:263; Crane, 1977:60; cf. Cassel, 1985:9.

98. Francis and Francis, 1987:129; Aday and Andersen, 1981:9; National Heart, 1984:Ch.36:33; United Nations 1975:32; "Patient," 1969:1330; "Scarce," 1969:658–59.

99. Greiffer, 1984:111.

100. Ndeti, 1972:104.

101. The important place ascribed to the elderly among the Akamba is attested by the roles the elderly play in Akamba families and society. Each member of an Akamba family contributes to its welfare according to her or his experience, age, wisdom, skill, and vitality. While the young are generally strong and are best suited to raise the crops, tend the animals, and engage in various other business activities, the elderly are better equipped by long experience to impart to others the knowledge and (especially) wisdom necessary for day-to-day living. One important aspect of this role is the instruction of children; another is maintaining the spiritual and communal vitality of the entire family (Ndeti, 1972:68–69). The consistent commitment among the Akamba to this view of the family has drawn special comment even from those who otherwise tend to emphasize the diversity of these people (Oliver, 1965:427).

The second place where the elderly play a particularly important role among the Akamba is in the governing of society. Rather than the Akamba being ruled overall by an individual or group of individuals, localized sections of their land are governed by councils of elderly men who are called *atumia* (elders)—a term of great respect. The power and responsibility of any given elder increases according to seniority. When disputes arise between localities, they are settled by a joint council of elders from the localities involved (Mbiti, 1971:7; Larby, 1944:4). Any man of wealth or outstanding personality may attract followers and be called *muneme* ("big man"), but if he is young he can have no place of social leadership (Middleton and Kershaw, 1965:75).

Although only men can become elders in the particular sense just explained, older women also have a special place among the Akamba due to their age. Like the men, they have much wisdom to impart to the children and are responsible for safeguarding the spiritual and communal vitality of the family. Consequently, old age is a time much looked forward to by Akamba women—a time of security and relief from the physical exhaustion of manual labor (Edgerton, 1965a:4, 1965b:443). In fact, one of the most common verbal blessings bestowed by the Akamba upon men and women alike is that God may grant them the privilege of being old (Mbiti, 1970:207).

102. Morgan, 1967:65; Edgerton, 1965a:4–5. // Muthiani, 1973:74; Ndeti, 1969:1186; Middleton and Kershaw, 1965:72.

103. The expressions here are taken from the interviews with Kiua Mulela (Muvuti Location) and Esther Nthenya (Mbiuni Location).

104. Brody, 1981:225; Hallan and Harris, 1970:212; Katz, 1973:418; Velez, 1981:356. For a cross-cultural study documenting the great variety in the ways that elderly people are treated, see Foner, 1984.

105. Barondess et al., 1988:920; Perkoff et al., 1976b:918.

106. Horn, 1987:62–67; Mehlman, 1985:258; Berlyne, 1982:189.

107. Off. of Technology, 1987:157; Maitland, 1987:Ch.3; J. G. Harris, 1987; Veatch, 1985b:40; Cassell, 1985:8; Porter, 1985:406. // May, 1986:51–61; Califano, 1986:175. // Fox and Swazey, 1978b:238.

108. Gillund, 1987; Horn, 1987.

109. Ramsey, 1978:xii–xiii, 1970a:258–59; Beauchamp and Childress, 1979: 196.

110. E.g., by Battin, 1987:335.

111. Leenen, 1982:34; Somerville, 1981:1110; Robin, 1964:624.

112. Parsons and Lock, 1983:43; Berlyne, 1982:189; Roxe, 1983:832.

113. Battin, 1987:336.

114. Calabresi and Bobbitt, 1978:184–85; "Scarce," 1969.

115. J. Evans, 1988:120; Levinsky, 1984:1574; Wetle, 1987:516; Hastings, 1987:136; Caplan, 1987a:16; Thomasma, 1984b:910; Parsons and Lock, 1983:43; Leenen, 1982:34, 1979:169; N. Bell, 1981:155.

116. McKevitt et al., 1986:135; C. Lyons, 1970:96.

117. Wetle, 1987:516; Thomasma, 1986b:22; Goldman, 1981:242.

118. Collette and Windt, 1987; Sage et al., 1986.

119. In one study (Wetle and Levkoff, 1984) more than half the physicians and nurses choosing whether to treat a thirty-five- or a seventy-five-year-old patient attributed preexisting dementia to the older patient even though "clear cognitive function" was emphasized in the case description. Cf. Wetle, 1987:516.

120. Norman Levinsky in Johnson et al., 1985.

121. Murray, 1962:316; Hayes and Gunnells, 1969:522; Ramsey, 1970a:244. // Beauchamp and Childress, 1979:193–94; Young, 1975:445; Ramsey, 1970a: 252.

122. Massachusetts, 1984:78; Annas, 1985b:188. // Horn, 1987:63–66; Caplan, 1987a:16; Veatch, 1985b:50–51; Childress, 1984a:28; Levinsky, 1984:1574; Binstock, 1983; Austin and Loeb, 1982:264–65; N. Bell, 1981:155.

123. Calabresi and Bobbitt, 1978:39; Childress, 1984a:29, 1986:318; Task Force, 1986:90. Cf. Maitland, 1987, on the importance of symbols in shaping the way the elderly are treated in society.

124. Longman, 1987:237.

125. Lubeck and Bunker, 1984:248; De Wardener, 1966:108.

126. McKevitt et al., 1986:137; Katz, 1973:415. // Thomasma, 1984b:907.

127. Sutherland et al., 1982:24–25.

128. Wetle, 1987:516; Hiatt, 1987:50–51; Somerville, 1986:160; Adami et al., 1986; Perkoff, 1976b:917; Annas, 1977:72–73.

129. Leenen, 1982:34, 1979:169; National Heart, 1984:Ch.9:2,4; Childress, 1981:92.

130. Starzl et al., 1987:484; Evans and Yagi, 1987:29; Ogden, 1987:105; National Heart, 1984:Ch.36:34. // Callahan, 1987:126; Mulley, 1983:304; Thibault et al., 1980:301A. Cf. Goldman, 1981:242.

131. Westlie et al., 1984; European Dialysis, 1981; Chester et al., 1979; Hutchinson et al., 1982; Weller et al., 1982; Taube et al., 1983. Cf. Swales, 1982:117–18; Knapp, 1982:847; Caplan, 1984:158; Deitch, 1984:53; Richard M. Freeman in Waldholz, 1981:23.

132. Brock, 1988:90. Cf. J. Evans, 1988:122; Task Force, 1986:90; Childress, 1985:22.

133. Bergsten et al., 1977:8; V. Parsons, 1978:873; Hayes and Gunnells, 1969.

134. Cf. Wetle, 1987:516. // Calabresi and Bobbitt, 1978:230. Cf. D'Amico, 1983:96.

135. Adapted from Munson, 1983:473–76.

136. Even supporters of a nonmedical age criterion such as Callahan (1987: 139) admit that a consensus seems to be emerging against it.

CHAPTER 8. PSYCHOLOGICAL STABILITY

1. Leenen, 1979:169; "Patient," 1969:1338–39; Sanders and Dukeminier, 1968:368–69.

2. Katz, 1970:676–77, 1967:56; Katz and Proctor, 1969:26; Fox and Swazey, 1978b:244; Ramsey, 1970a:250; "Patient," 1969:1324–25; Sanders and Dukeminier, 1968:367.

3. Winslade and Ross, 1986:190; Rodgers, 1984:61. // National Heart, 1984:Ch.10:25; Krauthammer, 1986:A19. // Howard and Najarian, 1978:1161.

4. Kayser-Jones, 1986:1280–81. // Wetle and Levkoff, 1984:224.

5. Evans et al., 1984a:6,12; United Nations, 1975:31.

6. E.g., in Singapore: Khoo, 1982:5. In Great Britain: Aaron and Schwartz, 1984:34; Calabresi and Bobbitt, 1978:185; Kerr, 1967:1,198.

7. Gould, 1981:826; Gorovitz, 1966:7; Nabarro, 1967:622.

8. Davidson and Scribner, 1967:3; Leenen, 1982:34. This is not to suggest that loss of motivation to live is necessarily psychological instability.

9. Lefebvre, 1980:182; Young, 1975:443; Ramsey, 1970a:249.

10. Evans and Yagi, 1987:29; Massachusetts, 1984:85; Thompson, 1983:66; Leenen, 1979:169; Davidson and Scribner, 1967:3; Sanders and Dukeminier, 1968:368; Katz, 1967:61.

11. Rodgers, 1984:62.

12. Childress, 1981:91–92, 1970:343–44; Abram et al., 1971; Goldstein and Reznikoff, 1971.

13. Rescher, 1969:185; Thielicke, 1970:174.

14. Schroeder and Hunt, 1987:3143; Stiller, 1985:135; Rescher, 1969:179.

15. Working Group, 1985:26; Knapp, 1982:848; Sanders and Dukeminier, 1968:369,379–80; Abram, 1972:56; Fox and Swazey, 1978b:256.

16. Simmons and Simmons, 1972:369 (Minnesota); Sanders and Dukeminier, 1968:369 (California); Davidson and Scribner, 1967:8; Sawyer, 1968:10 (the last two, Washington).

17. *Pushkin* v. *University of Colorado*, 658 F.2d 1372, 1381 (10th Cir. 1981).

18. National Heart, 1984:Ch.32:22.

19. Sanders and Dukeminier, 1968:369.

20. Rodgers, 1984:64; Rabinowitz and Van der Spuy, 1978:861.

21. Parsons, 1978:873; Rabinowitz and Van der Spuy, 1978:861; "Scarce," 1969:656.

22. N. Bell, 1981:155; Ramsey, 1970a:249.

23. Merriken and Overcast, 1985:17; Beecher, 1969.

24. Abram, 1972:53.

25. Katz, 1973:411; Abram, 1972:52–53; Crammond, 1971. Cf. Rodgers, 1984:67.

26. Parsons and Lock, 1983:44; Howard and Najarian, 1978:1164; Parsons, 1978:874; Katz, 1973:412; Sanders and Dukeminier, 1968:369.

27. Auer, 1983:207. // Rodgers, 1984:62.

28. Calland, 1972:334.

29. N. Bell, 1979a:18.

30. National Heart, 1984:Ch.10:24; Knox, 1980.

31. Merriken and Overcast, 1985:19–20.

32. Christopherson, 1971:37; Sanders and Dukeminier, 1968:379.

33. Caplan, 1984:161.

34. Brock, 1988.

35. N. Bell, 1979b:41. // Merriken and Overcast, 1985:17.

36. Katz, 1973:410–11.

37. Caplan, 1984:155; Katz, 1973:409.

38. Royal, 1981:285.

39. Verwilghen, 1981:556; Large and Ahmad, 1981:556–57.

40. Leenen, 1982:34; Beauchamp and Childress, 1979:194; "Patient," 1969: 1326; Ramsey, 1970a:251.

41. Attig and Wasserstrom, 1976.

42. N. Bell, 1979a:17–18; Goldhaber et al., 1985:405. // Krauthammer, 1986:A19.

43. "Scarce," 1969:655; Sanders and Dukeminier, 1968:380. // Robbins, 1984:124; Leenen, 1979:169; "Patient," 1969:1338.

44. Winslade and Ross, 1986:190; Rodgers, 1984:64–65; Winslow, 1982:65; N. Bell, 1979a:18; Ramsey, 1970a:249.

45. Abram, 1972:52. // National Heart, 1984:Ch.31:6.

46. Fox, 1979:133. // Fox, 1981:741; Ramsey, 1970a:244.

47. Sawyer, 1968:17.

48. Affleck, 1977:52; Tizes and Tizes, 1977:8CC; Sanders and Dukeminier, 1968:379.

49. E.g., R. Levine, 1984:1459.

50. Katz, 1973:412; R. Levine, 1984:1459; Carter-Jones, 1983:105; Sanders and Dukeminier, 1968:380.

51. "Scarce," 1969:647; also sources in notes 13–21 above.

52. Katz, 1973:410; also sources addressing this issue in chapter 5.

53. Abram, 1972:52.

54. Macklin, 1984:18–19; National Heart, 1984:Ch.36:35; N. Bell, 1979a:19.

55. Perkoff et al., 1976a:10; Katz, 1973:411.

56. Bergsten, 1977:9; Merriken and Overcast, 1985:16; Parsons and Lock, 1983:44; Ramsey, 1970a:249; Sanders and Dukeminier, 1968:379; "Scarce," 1969:647–48.

57. Moore, 1971:1208; "Scarce," 1969:648; National Heart, 1984:Ch.8.

58. Copeland et al., 1987:6; Rodgers, 1984:62; Greenberg, 1973:276.

59. Katz, 1973:412; "Patient," 1969:1339.

60. Childress, 1981:92; Beauchamp and Childress, 1979:194; "Scarce," 1969:656.

61. National Heart, 1984:Ch.10:24.

62. Leach, 1972:261–62.

63. Parsons and Lock, 1983:44; Knapp, 1982:848.

64. Weckman and Willy, 1987:16.

65. Adapted from Veatch, 1977b:233–34.

CHAPTER 9. SUPPORTIVE ENVIRONMENT

1. Sanders and Dukeminier, 1968:370.

2. "Patient," 1969:1325; Katz, 1967:56.

3. Abram and Wadlington, 1968:618. For another study confirming wide-spread use of the criterion, see Katz, 1970:676–77.

4. National Heart, 1984:Ch.45:29–30; R. Evans, 1983:2209.

5. Pennock et al., 1982:170; National Heart, 1984:Ch.8:6,58–59,66, Ch.10:22,24.

6. Haber, 1986:763; F. Miller, 1985:31. // Paulus, 1986:323.

7. Evans et al., 1984a:6,12.

8. Khoo, 1982:5,10.

9. Parsons and Lock, 1980:174. Cf. Ward, 1984:1712, for more explicit evidence of the criterion's use.

10. U.S.H.C.F.A., 1981:7074; National Heart, 1984:10:25–26; Thompson, 1983:66; Katz, 1967:61.

11. McKevitt et al., 1986:135.

12. Krauthammer, 1986:A19.

13. Watts et al., 1984; Evans and Yagi, 1987:29.

14. Leenen, 1979:170, 1982; Abram and Wadlington, 1968.

15. Fineberg, 1984:79; Task Force, 1986:90.

16. Khoo, 1982:10.

17. Stiller, 1985:135.

18. Chambers, 1986:16.

19. Ackerman, 1980:297–300 (in a related context).

20. "Scarce," 1969:649.

21. Working Group, 1985:26.

22. Rodgers, 1984:62–63.

23. E.g., U.S.H.C.F.A., 1981:7074; National Heart, 1984:Ch.10:25–26.

24. N. Bell, 1979b:80.

25. N. Bell, 1979a:18.

26. N. Bell, 1981:155.

27. Christopherson, 1971:37.

28. Royal, 1981:285; Parsons and Lock, 1981:556; Verwilghen, 1981:556.

29. Working Group, 1985:26; F. Miller, 1985:31; Ramsey, 1978:232–33.

30. Childress, 1985:21; R. Levine, 1984:1459.

31. Meissner, 1986:7ff.

32. "Scarce," 1969:655.

33. Working Group, 1985:26. // Paulus, 1986:323.

34. National Heart, 1984:Ch.32:41.

35. Knox, 1980:572; Katz, 1973:409.

36. Weckman and Willy, 1987:16; Haber, 1986:763; Massachusetts, 1984:77; Annas, 1985b:188.

37. National Heart, 1984:Ch.36:35; F. Miller, 1985:31; Carter-Jones, 1983:105.

38. K. Smith, 1980:310; Aranow, 1980:307.

39. Katz, 1973:408–09.

40. N. Bell, 1979a:17.

41. Knox, 1980:575.

42. Copeland et al., 1987:7; Rodgers, 1984:63.

43. National Heart, 1984:Ch.9:37.

44. Brock, 1988a:90; Childress, 1970:343–44. // Robertson, 1987:81.

45. Constructed from accounts in Chambers, 1986; Wallis, 1986; Caplan, 1986b; Torriero, 1986; "Young," 1986; "Hospital," 1986.

46. Schroeder and Hunt, 1987:3143.

47. Krauthammer, 1986:A19. Cf. brief discussion of this case in the opening section of chapter 16.

48. Caplan, 1986b:1–2.

49. Chambers, 1986:16.

CHAPTER 10. MEDICAL BENEFIT

1. Leenen, 1982:34 // Schiffer, 1977:21–22; Childress, 1970:343.

2. For example, Starzl et al., 1988a:134–35, 1987b:3073; Gordon et al., 1986b:705ff. Cf. Henry Krakauer in U.S. House, 1983:106–09.

3. National Heart, 1984:Ch.8; Working Group, 1985:26; Sanders and Dukeminier, 1968:367 // Brock, 1988a:88; Belliotti, 1980a:261; Hyman, 1980:265; Zawacki, 1985:59; Ramsey, 1970a:242; "Patient," 1969:1330.

4. The other 5 percent are probably those who always follow a patient's (or a parent's) wishes even when, strictly speaking, there is no medical warrant for doing so. Accordingly, it is not surprising to find a lower percentage (83 percent) of the public at large in a national survey (Evans and Manninen, 1987:3) supporting a medical-benefit criterion.

5. Winslow, 1982:64; Childress, 1981:91; Weckman and Willy, 1987:15.

6. Childress, 1970:343, 1981:91.

7. Katz, 1973:399.

8. Jos. Fletcher, 1968:1090.

9. Barber, 1987:662–63; Reidy, 1979:74–75; J. Bryant, 1973:94.

10. Thomasma, 1986a:7; Daniels, 1983b; B. Williams, 1973; J. Bryant, 1977:711.

11. D. Miller, 1976:149; Winslow, 1982:92; McCormick, 1978:35.

12. Winslow, 1982:135.

13. Graber et al., 1985:209; Gillon, 1985:267.

14. Thompson, 1983:65.

15. Linzer, 1984:470; Campbell, 1978:35; National Heart, 1984:Ch.43:9,11. Cf. Seymour Perry in U.S. House, 1984:11ff., regarding the importance of improved technology assessment.

16. Winslow, 1982:191; Mathieu, 1988:48. // Mehlman, 1985:299–300.

17. National Heart, 1984:Ch.9:14,15.

18. Caplan, 1984:158; Graber et al., 1985:210; F. Parsons, 1967:623; Leach, 1972:259–60; Oreopoulos, 1982:750.

19. Francis and Francis, 1987:132; Aaron and Schwartz, 1984:101; "Rationing," 1985:7–8.

20. "Ethics and the Neph.," 1981:595.

21. Aaron and Schwartz, 1984:35.

22. Michael, 1981:556; "Selection," 1978:1449.

23. Challah et al., 1984:1119; Rennie et al., 1985:328.

24. Aaron and Schwartz, 1984:101.

25. Ibid.:36.

26. Schwartz and Aaron, 1984:54; Aaron and Schwartz, 1984:102. Cf. Ward, 1986:62, 1984:1712.

27. Caplan, 1984:161.

28. Aaron and Schwartz, 1984:101–02.

29. Somerville, 1986:160; Brahams, 1984:386; National Heart, 1984:Ch.44: 29.

30. Douglas, 1985:1320; Brahams, 1984:386.

31. "Audit," 1981:262. // Oreopoulos, 1983:68.

32. Evans et al., 1984:9. For more examples, see U.N., 1975:32. // National Heart, 1984:Ch.44:33.

33. Greifer, 1984:110–12.

34. Kellerman and Hackman, 1988:1290; Strauss et al., 1986; Graber et al., 1985:210. // Rosner, 1983a:354.

35. Levinsky, 1984:1574; Aaron and Schwartz, 1984:127–28.

36. Abrams, 1987:64; Ward, 1984:1712; Shapiro and Spece, 1981:847; Childress, 1981:92; Ramsey, 1970a:249; Sanders and Dukeminier, 1968:379.

37. Caplan, 1981a:727; Royal, 1981; Hunter et al., 1980; Massachusetts, 1984:78; Annas, 1985b:188. // Annas, 1977:62.

38. Engelhardt, 1986:347; Henikoff, 1986; Roe, 1981.

39. Basson, 1979:316.

40. Working Group, 1985:35.

41. N. Bell, 1981:155. Cf. Loewy, 1987:439.

42. G. Smith, 1985:148.

43. "Scarce," 1969:649.

44. N. Bell, 1979b:39.

45. Rajakumar, 1984:4; N. Bell, 1981:155, 1979b:130.

46. Leenen, 1979:168.

47. Massachusetts, 1984:79; Annas, 1985b:188; Beauchamp and Childress, 1979:194; Sanders and Dukeminier, 1968:379.

48. Young, 1975:444; "Patient," 1969:1339. // "Scarce," 1969:656.

49. Taylor et al., 1975:380–81.

50. "Scarce," 1969:665; C. Lyons, 1970:91–92. // Minnesota, 1984:50. See D. Bell, 1985, for a general critique of the Minnesota proposal.

51. National Heart, 1984:Ch.10:21–22; Massachusetts, 1984:78; Boyd, 1979: 76. // Leaf, 1984:719; Leenen, 1979:168; Graber et al., 1985:210; Katz and Capron, 1975:194.

52. Larson, 1986:7.

53. Starzl et al., 1987b:3075.

54. Kraus et al., 1983:572, for example, suggest a cutoff point well below a 10 percent likelihood of survival.

55. Challah et al., 1984:1122. // Annas, 1985b:188; "Ethics and the Neph.," 1981:596. Because of this diversity, the U.S. federal Task Force on Organ Transplantation (1986:86) simply affirmed the need to identify "acceptable" minimal levels of benefit.

56. Glover, 1977:224. // Massachusetts, 1984:79; Annas, 1985b:188.

57. Childress, 1985:20; Young, 1975:443.

58. Katz and Capron, 1975:194; Katz, 1973:400; "Scarce," 1969:656.

59. Civetta, 1976:504–05; Towers et al., 1974.

60. Beauchamp and Childress, 1979:194; Childress, 1981:92; Gellman, 1984: 114; "Scarce," 1969:654. The argument here assumes that there is not an abundance of resources available to meet every life-threatening human need. If there were, then the faintest hope of benefit could justify the use of a particular medical resource. See Freedman, 1982:91.

61. Rickham, 1976:746; Leb, 1980:432; Fox and Swazey, 1978b:370, 1978a: 815; Fox, 1981:774, 1979:139–40.

62. Jennett, 1984a:64, 1984b:1709; Engelhardt and Rie, 1986:1164.

63. Adapted from Reiser et al., 1977:663–64.

64. Even in the face of such discomfort, most ICU medical directors will favor Peter over John. See Childress et al., 1982.

CHAPTER 11. IMMINENT DEATH

1. Meyers, 1977:328; Jackson and Annas, 1986:119; Jonsen et al., 1982:32.

2. Jackson and Annas, 1986:119; Jonsen et al., 1982:31–32.

3. "Patient," 1969:1326–27.

4. Starzl et al., 1988a:132,138; Warmbrodt, 1985:4; Midwest, 1986:2.

5. Hinds, 1975:16.

6. Beecher, 1971:279.

7. Robertson, 1987:82; Matt Armany in "Transplant Groups," 1987:90; Henry Krakauer in U.S. House, 1983:106–09; Denny, 1983:27. // Hume et al., 1966:352; Warmbrodt, 1985:3; George Schreiner and Amy Peele in U.S. House, 1983:19,80. // F. Miller, 1985:32; National Heart Institute, 1969:5ff.; Shapiro, 1969:6ff.; Katz and Capron, 1975:14,51; National Heart, 1984:Ch.9:17.

8. Kirklin, 1977:316–17.

9. Coulton, 1986:97.

10. Leenen, 1982:36; Childress, 1985:21.

11. Hinds, 1976:33; Roe, 1981:93; Beauchamp and Childress, 1979:197; Childress, 1981:96.

12. S. Bell et al., 1985.

13. Campbell, 1977:820; J. Bryant, 1977:711.

14. Thomas Peter in Kjellstrand et al., 1986:305; Westervelt, 1970:359.

15. Robertson, 1987:82; O'Rourke and Brodeur, 1986:228; Katz, 1973:402; "The Sale," 1974:1206.

16. "Patient," 1969:1341; S. Alexander, 1962:117.

17. Brock, 1988a:91–92.

18. Meyers, 1977:328.

19. California National Death Act, 1976:665.

20. Garland, 1976:6. // Ramsey, 1978:319.

21. Vincent, 1977. // Novak, 1984:72. G. Smith (1987:53) documents the relevant legislation in thirty-six states.

22. Ramsey, 1978:327; cf. Veatch, 1977a:6–8.

23. Shannon, 1977:28; Rabkin et al., 1976; Levenson et al., 1981:564. // Byrn, 1975:13–16; Tizes and Tizes, 1977.

24. Beauchamp, 1979:168 // National Academy, 1968:806.

25. Evans and Manninen, 1987:4.

26. "Patient," 1969:1341.

27. Annas, 1985b:189; Massachusetts, 1984:81.

28. Massachusetts, 1984:81.

29. Caplan, 1987a:17.

30. Coulton, 1986:103; C. Lyons, 1970:92; Wooley, 1984:295. Mathieu (1988: 43–50) presents cases in which this has occurred.

31. Brock, 1988:92; Robertson, 1987:82; Task Force, 1986:88; Olga Jonasson in Callaway et al., 1986; Childress, 1985:21; Winslow, 1982:33,94–95.

32. Caplan, 1985b:166.

33. Young, 1975:445. Cf. Brock, 1988a:91–92.

34. Friedrich, 1984:73.

35. Lebacqz, 1977:14 (though in the context of the California Natural Death Act).

36. Wooley, 1984:295; Eichwald et al., 1981:4.

37. E.g., see Starzl et al., 1988a:132.

38. Beecher, 1971:281.

39. Civetta, 1976:502. Also see cases at end of chapter.

40. Skillman, 1974:636.

41. Engelhardt and Rie, 1986:1164; Mulley, 1984:222; Childress, 1983:561.

42. Glover, 1977:209–10.

43. Jonsen and Garland, 1976:193. // Jonsen et al., 1982:160–61.

44. Young, 1975:451–52.

45. Childress, 1983:560.

46. Leach, 1972:259; Leenen, 1982:36; F. Parsons, 1967:623.

47. Rescher, 1969:185.

48. Beauchamp and Childress, 1979:38, suggest that commitment may be respected on more productivity oriented terms as well, but others find that unlikely. See Schreiner, 1966:127–28; Ramsey 1970a:247; Childress, 1970:346.

49. Matt Armany and Ruth Purtilo in "Transplant Groups," 1987:90,91; Beauchamp and Childress, 1979:37; Rescher, 1969:186; Basson, 1979:329.

50. Graber et al., 1985:218; Sanders and Dukeminier, 1968:382–83; Beecher, 1971:288.

51. Fried, 1975:244; Winslow, 1982:75–76.

52. Cohen, 1977:225.

53. Sanders and Dukeminier, 1968:383.

54. Leenen, 1979:172; Civetta, 1976:505.

55. Jennett, 1984a:595.

56. Beauchamp, 1979:167–68.

57. P. Singer et al., 1988:540–41. // Jonasson, 1989.

58. Thompson, 1983:67. // Malatack, 1988.

59. Sanders, 1986:29.

60. Annas, 1985b:189; Massachusetts, 1984:1981.

61. Cohen, 1977:225.

62. Donagan, 1977:178–80. Cf. Pope John Ctr., 1984:82.

63. Beauchamp and McCullough, 1984:147; Johnson et al., 1985.

64. E.g., as in the case of Susan Von Stetina, who suffered serious brain damage in an overcrowded ICU unit. See Von Stetina, 1982; Engelhardt and Rie, 1986:1161; Knaus, 1986:1176–77.

65. Constructed from information in Treaster, 1978:131.

CHAPTER 12. LIKELIHOOD OF BENEFIT

1. "Scarce," 1969:655; Basson, 1979:323.

2. Blank, 1988:84; Coulton, 1986:97; Mulley, 1984:222; Wetle and Levkoff, 1984:224.

3. Jackson and Annas, 1986:119. // Robertson, 1987:81; Thompson, 1983. // John Najarian in Kjellstrand et al., 1986:305; Amy Peele in U.S. House, 1983:81.

4. Califano, 1986:179.

5. United Nations, 1975:31; Peterson, 1985:1331; "European Hospitals," 1984:24.

6. Evans and Yagi, 1987:39; Cummings, 1985:S-134; Peterson, 1985:1331; Jennett, 1984a:595; Frederick Westervelt in Jos. Fletcher, 1979:50.

7. Ramsey, 1970a:253.

8. Working Group, 1985:26; Leenen, 1979:168.

9. R. Evans, 1987:15; Engelhardt and Rie, 1986:1161,1164; Gillon, 1985: 267; Shatin, 1966:99; Rescher, 1969:177.

10. Childress, 1983:559; Moskop, 1987b:15. // Katz, 1973:404. // Rescher, 1969:177.

11. National Heart, 1984:Ch.36:31. // Evans et al., 1984:1357. // Mathieu, 1988:45.

12. C. Lyons, 1970:94; Young, 1975:443; cf. Robb, 1981:29.

13. Krakauer et al., 1983.

14. Glover, 1977:206.

15. Childress, 1983:558.

16. Winslow, 1982:141.

17. E.g., Basson, 1979:316.

18. Ebersole, 1988:110; Broome, 1984:48.

19. National Heart, 1984:Ch.36:30–31; Christopherson, 1982:19.

20. J. Evans, 1988:120; Fried, 1975; Winslow, 1982:68–69; James F. Childress in Hunter et al., 1980.

21. Campbell, 1978:88.

22. E.g., Weale, 1979:193.

23. Moskop, 1987b:15; National Heart, 1984:Ch.36:30, Ch.45:65–66.

24. Mehlman, 1985:267–68.

25. Callender and Dunstan, 1988:25; Callender, 1987:37; Krakauer et al., 1983. // C. Levine, 1985:3.

26. National Heart, 1984:Ch.31:6.

27. Winslow, 1982:115; Rawls, 1971:76–78; cf. Ron. Green, 1976. A variation of this concern is raised by Benjamin (1989) and Caplan (1989), who suggest that truly ethical criteria should be acceptable not just to society in general but especially to those patients rejected by them.

28. Weckman and Willy, 1987:16; Brock, 1988a:94; Spicker and Raye, 1981; Brett, 1981:1150–52; "Who Shall Die?" 1980:172; Felch, 1982:13; "Scarce," 1969:656.

29. In medicine generally: Macklin, 1987:155, 1985b:613; King, 1986:174; Coulton, 1986:101; Levinsky, 1984:1574; President's Commission, 1983b:300–01; Caplan, 1986a:26. In intensive care: Mulley, 1983:302; Knaus et al., 1985:827. In treatment of renal disease: National Kidney, 1986:Ch.1:37.

30. Winslow, 1982:166; Fromer, 1981:60; Rescher, 1969:181; Ramsey, 1970a:249.

31. Zawacki, 1985:59; Katz and Capron, 1975:194. Cf. Weale, 1979:192.

32. Lefebvre, 1980:183.

33. Katz, 1973:404.

34. Skillman, 1974:636.

35. Katz, 1973:404–05.

36. Rescher, 1969:177; Young, 1975:443–44. // Calabresi and Bobbitt, 1978:230.

37. On the elderly, see chapter 7. Cf. chapter 3 on the handicapped (and see esp. Merriken and Overcast, 1985:18–19).

38. National Heart, 1984:Ch.45:38–39; R. Evans, 1983:2211.

39. Rescher, 1969:177.

40. Macklin, 1987:157, 1985:616. Cf. Childress, 1983:558, whose view represents a change from his earliest, opposing position in 1970:343 and more neutral comments in 1981:91.

41. Belliotti, 1980a:261; Hyman, 1980:265; Leenen, 1979:168; Jonsen et al., 1982:163.

42. Starzl et al., 1988a:135–36; Gordon et al., 1986a:342ff.; Gillon, 1985: 267; "Who Shall Die?" 1980:171.

43. UNOS, 1988; Starzl et al., 1987b:3073; Hunsicker, 1987:1329; D. Cook, 1987; Gilks et al., 1987; Hors et al., 1987; Opelz, 1987; Van Rood, 1987; Olga Jonasson in Callaway et al., 1986; Sanfilippo et al., 1984; D. Lyons, 1976:106–07; National Heart, 1984; Massachusetts, 1984; Minnesota, 1984; Paul Terasaki in U.S. House, 1983:94; "Patients," 1969:1342.

44. Matas and Tellis, 1987:1328; Task Force, 1986:88. // Kaufman et al., 1988; Matas and Tellis, 1987:1328; Harris et al., 1985; National Heart, 1984: Ch.9:28,32; Henry Krakauer in U.S. House, 1983:106–10; Oyer et al., 1981.

45. Warmbrodt, 1985:4; Matas and Tellis, 1987:1328; Midwest, 1986:2.

46. National Kidney, 1986:Ch.1:13; Childress, 1985:21; Midwest, 1986:1; Macek, 1983.

47. Stiller, 1985:135; Evans et al., 1984a:6,12.

48. Childress, 1983:559; Winslow, 1982:143.

49. Matas and Tellis, 1987:1328; Dillard and Callender, 1984:1157.

50. National Heart, 1984:Ch.36:35; Task Force, 1986:92.

51. Adapted from Veatch, 1977b:36–37.

CHAPTER 13. LENGTH OF BENEFIT

1. Hayes and Gunnells, 1969:522.

2. Perkoff et al., 1976a:9.

3. Sutherland et al., 1982:26.

4. Childress, 1970:343.

5. Abram and Wadlington, 1968:618; "Patient," 1969:1324–25; Katz and Proctor, 1969; Ramsey, 1970a:250; Katz, 1970:676.

6. Task Force, 1986:87. // Robertson, 1987:81; Thompson, 1983:65–66.

7. Coulton, 1986:97.

8. Charlson et al., 1986:1319.

9. United Nations, 1975:31.

10. Evans et al., 1984:6,12.

11. Rosner, 1983a:357.

12. Jennett, 1984a:96–97; Aaron and Schwartz, 1984:34.

13. National Kidney, 1986:Ch.2:17; National Heart, 1984:Ch.44:32.

14. Freedman, 1977a:33.

15. Thielicke, 1970:172. At other times the rationale is not stated, as in Barondess et al., 1988:935.

16. Rescher, 1969:178; Young, 1975:447.

17. Brock, 1988a:90; Ashley and O'Rourke, 1986:112.

18. Davidson and Scribner, 1967:3; Evans and Yagi, 1987:37–38.

19. Sanders and Dukeminier, 1968:367.

20. Evans and Manninen, 1987:4.

21. Rettig, 1976c:21. Cf. Coulton, 1986:104.

22. Fox and Swazey, 1978b:371; Rettig, 1976c:21.

23. O'Rourke and Brodeur, 1986:228; Task Force, 1986:87.

24. Barber, 1987:663.

25. Thielicke, 1970:172.

26. Calabresi and Bobbitt, 1978:182.

27. Hallan and Harris, 1970:212; Katz, 1973:418.

28. Jn. Harris, 1987:118; M. O'Donnell, 1986:59; Roxe, 1983:832.

29. Robin, 1964:624. See chapter 7 regarding this argument against an age criterion.

30. Royal, 1981:285.

31. N. Bell, 1979a:15; Parsons and Lock, 1981:556; Bilous et al., 1981:726–27; Michael, 1981:556; Verwilghen, 1981.

32. Annas, 1977:72.

33. Leenen, 1982:34.

34. Attig and Wasserstrom, 1976.

35. Grimes, 1987:616; A. Smith, 1987:1135; Somerville, 1986:161.

36. Massachusetts, 1984:85.

37. Detsky et al., 1981:668. Cf. Macklin, 1987:157, 1985b:616.

38. Working Group, 1985:26.

39. Pearlman et al., 1982:425.

40. Cf. Jn. Harris, 1987:118.

41. A. Williams, 1986: 338.

42. Grimes, 1987; M. O'Donnell, 1986; G. Thomas, 1986; Jn. Harris, 1987.

43. "Scarce," 1969:656. In other words, the minimal standard should not be raised due to severity. Cf. Engelhardt and Rie, 1986:1162–63.

44. Winslow, 1982:67–68.

45. Adapted from Munson, 1983:513–14.

CHAPTER 14. QUALITY OF BENEFIT

1. Khoo, 1982:6.

2. Schroeder and Hunt, 1987:3143; Khoo, 1982:6.

3. United Nations, 1975:31. For example, regarding the provision of dialysis in Great Britain, see Ward, 1986:61, 1984:1712; Schwartz and Grubb, 1985:24.

4. Weir, 1984, 1985; Frader, 1985; Kohrman, 1985; Churchill, 1985; Murray, 1985.

5. Scitovsky, 1986; Charlson et al., 1986:1319; Wetle and Levkoff, 1984: 224. Cf. Barondess et al., 1988:921; Piettre, 1977:254.

6. Task Force, 1986:87; Jackson and Annas, 1986:119; Minnesota, 1984:50. For example, with regard to kidney transplantation, see my U.S. study and Thomas Peter in Kjellstrand et al., 1986:305; with regard to heart transplantation, see Robertson, 1987:81; Schroeder and Hunt, 1987:3142; Thompson, 1983:65–66.

7. A study documenting this is reported in Kayser-Jones, 1986:1280–81. For a standard case involving ICU resources and the elderly, see Munson, 1983:513.

8. Irvine, 1973:649; Rhodes, 1973:648.

9. E.g., Aiken, 1976.

10. Brock, 1988a:91; Manroe, 1979:9.

11. Evans, 1985:558; Edlund and Tancredi, 1985:598; Thomas Peter in Kjellstrand et al., 1986:305. Cf. Schroeder and Hunt, 1987:3142 (the goal is a "functional life style").

12. Evans and Manninen, 1987:3.

13. Singer, 1985:99. Spitzer et al., 1981, represents one attempt to do so.

14. Ferrans, 1987:115; Belliotti, 1980a:257.

15. Campbell, 1978:87.

16. Barber, 1987:663.

17. Macklin, 1987:157, 1985b:616; Engelhardt and Rie, 1986:1163.

18. Kayser-Jones, 1986:1283–85; Katz, 1973:415.

19. Grimes, 1987:616; Boyd and Potter, 1986:199; Pearlman and Jonsen, 1985:344.

20. Lo, 1988:142; A. Smith, 1987:1135; Ferrans, 1987:112–13; Boyd and Potter, 1986:199; Somerville, 1986:161; Kayser-Jones, 1986:1285; Edlund and Tancredi, 1985:598; Pearlman and Speer, 1983:117.

21. Pearlman et al., 1982:424–25; Wetle, 1987:516. Cf. Pearlman and Jonsen, 1985:347.

22. Winslow, 1982:67.

23. Off. of Tech. Assess., 1987:261–62; Sage et al., 1987:316, 1986:782; Ferrans, 1987:120; National Kidney, 1986:Ch.6:25–27; J. Evans, 1988:119; Campbell et al., 1976; Evans, et al., 1985:557–58; Neu and Kjellstrand, 1986:18; Knapp, 1982:848; "Selection of Patients," 1978:1449–50.

24. Lo, 1988:141; M. O'Donnell, 1986:59; Uddo, 1986:43.

25. Starr et al., 1986; Pearlman and Jonsen, 1985:349. // Kayser-Jones, 1986:1280–85.

26. Lo, 1988:141; A. Smith, 1987:1135; M. O'Donnell, 1986:59; Thomasma, 1986b:22, 1984b:910; Pearlman and Speer, 1983:115.

27. Ferrans, 1987:113–14; Shragg and Albertson, 1984:66; Bertrand, 1976:

26. // As Harris (1987:120–21) notes, a particular patient may desperately want to live longer to attend to some personal or familial matters and so will be happy to endure conditions unacceptable to most.

28. C. Levine, 1985:2; Hughes, 1985a:3; "Prolonging," 1985:11; Brahams, 1985.

29. Gillon, 1985:267; Fox and Swazey, 1978b:373. Cf. Kirby, 1986:20.

30. National Kidney, 1986:Ch.6:25–27; Pearlman and Jonsen, 1985:349; Massachusetts, 1984:79; Annas, 1985b:188.

31. Oreopoulos, 1983:69. // Jn. Harris, 1987:119–20.

32. Meissner, 1986:7ff.; Uddo, 1986:43. // Lo, 1988:141; Jn. Harris, 1987: 119; Ferrans, 1987:112–13; Uddo, 1986:43.

33. Destro, 1986; Thomasma, 1986b:22.

34. Brock, 1988a:91; Lockwood, 1987; Ferrans, 1987:120; Ward, 1986:63; Pearlman and Jonsen, 1985:349; Working Group, 1985:26; Pearlman and Speer, 1983:115; Becker, 1979:550.

35. E. Rapaport, 1982:4; Gutmann et al., 1982:33; Ferrans, 1987:113.

36. A. Smith, 1987:1135; Ferrans, 1987:113; Boyd and Potter, 1986:198.

37. Ferrans, 1987:117; Jn. Harris, 1987:121; Uddo, 1986:42; Ward, 1986: 61,63; Hentoff, 1984:A21; Childress, 1983:556–57; Pearlman and Speer, 1983: 117; Ramsey, 1978:243:45.

38. Jn. Harris, 1987:121; Sanders, 1986:28.

39. Childress, 1983:559.

40. Working Group, 1985:27.

41. E.g., regarding heart transplants, see National Heart, 1984:Ch.9:42.

42. Thomasma, 1984b:911–12; Gadow, 1980.

43. Hentoff, 1984:A21; Gross et al., 1983.

44. Kaye, 1981:111. Cf. Elaine Crowner in Kjellstrand et al., 1986:348.

45. D. Brahams, 1985:177; Leach, 1972:252; Sanders and Dukeminier, 1968:381–82.

46. Rodin, 1981; Neu and Kjellstrand, 1986.

47. Neu and Kjellstrand, 1986:16–18.

48. Ibid. As the study of Plough and Salem (1982) suggests, the reason for this may be that causes of death perceived as reflecting badly on the dialysis team are regularly reported under a heading acceptable to the team.

49. Carl Kjellstrand in Kjellstrand et al., 1986:348; Knapp, 1982:848. // Ismach, 1981:32. // Working Group, 1985:30.

50. Ferrans, 1987:114.

51. Grimes, 1987:615; G. Thomas, 1986:338.

52. Fox, 1981:747.

53. Thomasma, 1986b:23, 1984a:526.

54. Lo, 1988:141.

55. Adapted from Veatch, 1977b:230–31.

CHAPTER 15. WILLINGNESS

1. Winslade and Ross, 1986:196; Em. Friedman, 1984:72.
2. Robertson, 1987:81; cf. Task Force, 1986:90. // Blank, 1988:199.
3. Lebacqz, 1977:14. // National Heart, 1984:Ch.8:30–31.
4. Katz, 1967:56.
5. Wetle and Levkoff, 1984:224; Coulton, 1986:97.
6. H. Perkins, 1986.
7. Cohen, 1977:219.
8. Massachusetts, 1984:83; Annas, 1985b:189.
9. Freedman, 1977a:33.
10. Freedman, 1977b:22.
11. Schreiner and Maher, 1965:554; Purtilo and Cassel, 1981:189; Winslow, 1982:135; Annas, 1985b:189; Massachusetts, 1984:83.
12. Veatch, 1977b:231; Lebacqz, 1977:14; Gorney, 1968:313; Gotthard Booth in "M.D.'s," 1966:9.
13. Khoo, 1982:10; Cantor, 1973:263–64. Cf. Kamm, 1985:181.
14. Byrn, 1975:36; Cohen, 1977:219.
15. National Heart, 1984:Ch.9:41–42.
16. Caplan, 1987b:14; Oreopoulos, 1982:745; Carl Malchoff in Childress et al., 1982.
17. Winslow, 1982:67–68. // President's Commission, 1983a:97.
18. President's Commission, 1983a:97.
19. Ramsey, 1970a:265.
20. Freedman, 1977b:22; National Heart and Lung, 1973:66; Winslow, 1982:42.
21. Cantor, 1973:263–64; Thielicke, 1970:169.
22. When resources are not scarce this rationale, of course, would not apply. Even then, though, the idea that foregoing lifesaving treatment demeans life may be disputed. See Hastings Group, 1979:63.
23. Hardwig, 1987:54; Schreiner, 1966:129–30; Schreiner and Maher, 1965:554; Oreopoulos, 1982:745.
24. Caplan, 1987a:16; Childress, 1984b:60–61; Knowles, 1977b:1103; Orient, 1983:415.
25. Engelhardt, 1984:70; Sher, 1983:11; Veatch, 1976:140; Hanink, 1976:225.
26. Evans and Manninen, 1987:4; cf. Manes, 1986.
27. Childress, 1984b:62; Winslow, 1982:145; Sidel, 1978:347.
28. Jones, 1985:388.
29. Ibid.
30. Regarding personal responsibility for health-related actions: Nagelbach, 1978:100; P. Singer, 1977:221; National Heart, 1984:Ch.36:17–18; Wikler, 1982.

Regarding social responsibility for people's health: Jones, 1985:389–90; Winslow, 1982:145.

31. Caplan, 1987b:7.

32. Wikler, 1978b:338; Blank, 1988:233.

33. Macklin, 1987:152; Robertson, 1987:81; Task Force, 1986:90; O'Rourke and Brodeur, 1986:228. Scharschmidt (1984) documents lower survival probability in liver transplant recipients who are alcoholics. // Manes, 1986.

34. National Heart, 1984:Ch.37:11–12; Robb, 1981:30.

35. Boyd and Potter, 1986:199–200; Neuspiel, 1985:893.

36. National Heart, 1984:Ch.9:41,57,60.

37. Fox and Swazey, 1978b:261; Gustafson, 1975:50.

38. Winslow, 1982:135–36.

39. Harvey, 1980:16. // Gustafson, 1975:50.

40. Childress, 1984b:62–63.

41. Wikler, 1987b:337; Childress, 1984b:62.

42. Nagelbach, 1978:100.

43. Brock, 1988a:93; Childress, 1985:22; Curran, 1979:165–66; Nagelbach, 1978:100; Winslow, 1982:162; P. Singer, 1977:221; Outka, 1974; Jn. Harris, 1975:87; Smurl, 1980.

44. National Heart, 1984:Ch.36:17–18; Callahan, 1977:32.

45. Flavin, 1988:1546–47; Sorensen et al., 1984; "Liver Transplantation," 1983:2963.

46. Blank, 1988:198,233; Brock, 1988a:93; Castro et al., 1987; Wikler, 1987b:338,341; Macklin, 1987:153; Task Force, 1986:90; Daniels, 1985:159; Childress, 1985:22, 1984b:61–62; Callahan, 1977:31–32; National Heart, 1984:Ch.36:17–18; Allegrante and Green, 1981:1528–29.

47. Blank, 1988:232–33; Lewin, 1987; Price, 1987; Schukit, 1985; Childress, 1984b:62; Callahan, 1977:32.

48. Winslow, 1982:145.

49. Atterbury, 1986:2 (commenting upon Scharschmidt, 1984).

50. Starzl et al., 1988b:2544. Cf. Iwatsuki et al., 1988.

51. Atterbury, 1986:2.

52. Godshall, 1988:122–23; Wikler, 1987b:340; Macklin, 1987:153; Curran, 1979:165–66.

53. Blank, 1988:198; Wikler, 1987b:342; Winslade and Ross, 1986:196.

54. Atterbury, 1986:3; Pearlman and Speer, 1983:115; Starzl et al., 1988b:2544; Macklin, 1987:152.

55. Godshall, 1988:122–23; Wikler, 1987b:337; Task Force, 1986:90; Childress, 1985:22, 1984:62.

56. "The Heart," 1982:398; Reidy, 1979:80–81.

57. Macklin, 1987:154.

58. Regarding why some countries cannot afford informed consent, see Schwartz and Grubb, 1985.

59. Hastings, 1987:23; Chell, 1988; Brock, 1987:110–17; Drane, 1985.

60. Office of Technology, 1987:93–97; Joesten, 1987; Engelhardt, 1986:269–79; Faden and Beauchamp, 1986.

61. President's Commission, 1983a:99.

62. Neuspiel, 1985:893; Annas, 1985d:893–94.

63. Reemtsma, 1964:358; Gadow, 1981:135–36; National Heart, 1984:Ch.37:11; Khoo, 1982:10.

64. Leenen, 1982:36, 1979:176.

65. Pearlman et al., 1982:424.

66. The example in National Heart, 1984:Ch.8:30–31, is perhaps worded a little too strongly in this regard.

67. Lederer and Brock, 1987; Society, 1986; President's Commission, 1983a:121–70.

68. Abrams, 1988:206–08; Hastings, 1987:78–80; Steinbrook and Lo, 1984.

69. Carl Kjellstrand in Kjellstrand et al., 1986:301; Thomasma and Griffin, 1983:66; Cantor, 1973:263–64; Reemtsma, 1964:358; President's Commission, 1983a. Regarding informed consent when children are involved, see Moskop, 1987a:176–77; Kanoti, 1986:44–45.

70. Winslow, 1982:135–36.

71. Gustafson, 1975:50; Pizzulli, 1975:50–51; Cantor, 1973:263–64.

72. Veatch, 1977:235.

73. Atterbury, 1986:2.

74. Winslow, 1982:162.

75. Atterbury, 1986:2.

76. Flavin, 1988:1547; Starzl et al., 1988b:2542.

77. Starzl et al., 1988b:2544; cf. Flavin, 1988:1547. // Starzl et al., 1988b.

78. Glover, 1977:225.

79. Adapted from Levine and Veatch, 1984:92.

CHAPTER 16. ABILITY TO PAY

1. Winslow, 1982:96; "Scarce," 1969:652.

2. S. Alexander, 1962:110; N. Bell, 1979b:45; Ramsey, 1970a:246.

3. Lois Christopherson in Knox, 1980:572.

4. Barondess et al., 1988:934; E. R. Brown, 1987:70–71; Macklin, 1987:162, 1985b:617–18; Kotulak, 1986a:4; Aday et al., 1984:94–95.

5. Copeland et al., 1989; R. Evans, 1989; Hiatt, 1987:4; Churchill, 1987:10–11.

6. R. Evans, 1989; Task Force, 1986:87; Winslade and Ross, 1986:190. // Hardwig, 1987:53.

7. Hyatt, 1969:1; R. Evans, 1983:2209; National Heart, 1984:Ch.45:29–30; Katz, 1970:676–77; Sanders and Dukeminier, 1968:367; "Patient," 1969:1325–26; "Scarce," 1969:652; Davidson and Scribner, 1967:2; Winslow, 1982:155–56.

8. Held et al., 1988; Howard and Najarian, 1978:1161.

9. Data from the American Hospital Association and the National Center for Health Statistics, cited in "Unfunded," 1984:22.

10. Coulton, 1986:97. // Smeeding, 1987:155; Caplan, 1987b:6; Colen, 1986:219; Veatch, 1985b:74.

11. Evans and Yagi, 1987:28; Robertson, 1987:82–83; Task Force, 1986: 86,100; National Heart, 1984:Ch.9:51–54, Ch.45:29–30; R. Evans, 1983:2209; "Dying for," 1983:49. // Miles, 1988:411.

12. Task Force, 1986:18.

13. Task Force, 1986:86,100; Minnesota, 1984:59.

14. Friedrich, 1984:1977.

15. Kellerman and Hackman, 1988:1289–90; National Council, 1986:3–10; Dallek and Waxman, 1986:1413; Relman, 1986:579. See chapter 1 for additional sources on this point.

16. Schiff et al., 1986:554–56; Bernard, 1985:A19; Godshall, 1988:127. // Ansell and Schiff, 1987:1501; Reed et al., 1986:1431. // Annas, 1986:74. // Kellerman and Hackman, 1988:1289. // Annas, 1986:75.

17. Reinhold, 1986:4E; Kotulak, 1986a:4; Annas, 1986:74.

18. Annas, 1985c:16–18; Lefton, 1984:1; Relman, 1985:372. As Jonasson and Barrett (1987:1519) point out, patients who benefit from transfer to a public hospital (e.g., because of its twenty-four-hour-a-day surgical staffing) are not victims of "dumping."

19. Wrenn, 1985:373–74.

20. Gentleman and Jennett, 1981:853; Meltzer, 1981:232; Relman, 1985:372–73; Em. Friedman, 1982a:55. // Bernard, 1985:A19; Engel, 1984:B4.

21. Rajakumar, 1984:4; Fuchs, 1984:1572; A. Kennedy, 1981:586.

22. Evans et al., 1984a:6,12.

23. Johnson et al., 1985.

24. Schneider and Flaherty, 1985; Bermel, 1986:3; Childress, 1985:19.

25. "Scarce," 1969:645–46; "Patient," 1969:1325–26. // National Heart, 1984:Ch.9:16, Ch.45:29–30; R. Evans, 1983:2209. // Thompson, 1983:66; Katz, 1970:677.

26. National Kidney, 1986:Ch.16:13.

27. Rennie et al., 1985:327; Campbell and Campbell, 1978.

28. Christopherson, 1982:20. // Katz, 1973:409; "Scarce," 1969:645–46.

29. U.S. Dept. of H.H.S., 1985:18.

30. R. Evans, 1989; Moskop, 1987b:14; Gore, 1987:5.

31. Varga, 1984:226. // Seibert and Waldrop, 1988:38. // Transpl. Society, 1985:716. // O'Rourke and Brodeur, 1986:57; Transpl. Society, 1985:716. // Transpl. Society, 1985:716.

32. Blank, 1988:49–50. // Task Force, 1986:86,96; Johnson, 1986; Manne, 1985; see also sources in note 18 here and note 28 of chapter 4.

33. Aaron and Schwartz, 1984:98. // Sullivan, 1987:B5; Warmbrodt, 1985:3.

34. O'Rourke and Brodeur, 1986:57; Gunby, 1983:1973.

35. Wallis, 1982:100.

36. Meyer, 1984:C1,8. // "Donations," 1987:A2. // Iglehart, 1983:127.

37. Torriero, 1986; "Baby with," 1986:A2; Chambers, 1986:16.

38. Fain, 1986:A19; Chambers, 1986:16; Hackett, 1986:B1.

39. T. Richards, 1986:C2.

40. Blank, 1988:97; Colen, 1986:219; Dyer, 1986:5–6; Chambers, 1986:16; Gunby, 1983:1980.

41. Fineberg, 1984:18.

42. Wallis, 1982:100.

43. "Free," 1987:A2. // Blank, 1988:48; Gore, 1987:3; Winslade and Ross, 1986:195–96; Fain, 1986:A19; Wehr, 1984:453.

44. Iglehart, 1983:127; Meyer, 1984:C1.

45. Wehr, 1984:455–56.

46. Aaron and Schwartz, 1984:133–34. Cf. the scenario introducing one of the three major components of the 1986 national teleconference "Who Lives, Who Dies, Who Decides?" (Koppel et al., 1986). In this scenario, the most appealing patients (and families) are selected for media promotion to obtain the lifesaving resource(s) needed.

47. Relman, 1985:372; Annas, 1985c:16–18; DePalma, 1983:829–30; cf. sources on this matter cited in chapter 1.

48. Strauss, 1984:336.

49. Shatin, 1966:99; Aday and Andersen, 1981:9; Annas, 1977:76.

50. Mavrodes, 1984:111–13.

51. Aday and Andersen, 1981:9.

52. Ferrans, 1987:110; Bayer, 1986:17; Coulton, 1986:103; John Najarian in Wallis, 1982:101; Leiman, 1978:9.

53. Engelhardt and Rie, 1986:1162; Bayer, 1986:17.

54. National Heart, 1984:Ch.36:22, and Hastings Group, 1979:56, drawing upon the work of Robert Nozick (e.g., 1974); National Heart and Lung, 1973:243–47; Engelhardt, 1986:343,365–66.

55. Thielicke, 1970:174; Sanders and Dukeminier, 1968:380.

56. Jack Copeland in "Dying for," 1983:49.

57. Working Group, 1985:31, reflecting on National Heart and Lung, 1973; cf. Jonsen, 1986:10.

58. Leenen, 1982:34.

59. Leake, 1967:47; Fried, 1976; Winslow, 1982:156.

60. Engelhardt, 1986:343. For evidence that money is already clandestinely buying special access to lifesaving resources, see sources in note 14 above.

61. Baily, 1988:208–09; Daniels, 1988b:213–14; Jonsen, 1985:38; "Patient," 1969:1334.

62. National Council, 1986:5.

63. Humber, 1985:19,24–25.

64. Weckman and Willy, 1987:20.

65. United Nations, 1975:31.

66. California Health, 1986:3; Washington, 1986:5. Cf. Brock, 1988a:87; Caplan, 1987a:11; Atterbury, 1986:3.

67. Evans et al., 1984a:13.

68. National Heart, 1984:Ch.35:2–3, Ch.36:22.

69. Mehlman, 1985:263; Katz and Capron, 1975:187–88.

70. Thomasma, 1982:52.

71. Loewy, 1980:697; Tobin, 1980:288.

72. Katz and Capron, 1975:186.

73. Massachusetts, 1984:74–75; Annas, 1985b:187. See also sources in note 27 of chapter 15.

74. Loewy, 1987:440; Mechanic, 1976:36.

75. Teuber, 1981:526.

76. Working Group, 1985:32.

77. Mathieu, 1988:145; Jamieson, 1988:288; Caplan, 1987b:9; Walters, 1987:2; Thomasma, 1986a:7; Leake, 1967:47; Preston, 1985:7; White and Monagle, 1982:10; Fox, 1979:134; Calabresi and Bobbitt, 1978:32,144; Mechanic, 1978:78.

78. Winslow, 1986:16; Paulus, 1986:323; Kass, 1985:26; National Heart, 1984:Ch.36:22–23; Menzel, 1983.

79. Kellerman and Hackman, 1988; Ansell and Schiff, 1987; Henry et al., 1986; Reed et al., 1986; Relman, 1986; Annas, 1986.

80. Barrett and Jonasson, 1986:1421.

81. Kellerman and Ackerman, 1988.

82. Task Force, 1986:103–04.

83. Caplan, 1987a:11; Haber, 1986:762; Annas, 1985b:187; Massachusetts, 1984:74.

84. Jamieson, 1988:288; DeVries et al., 1984:273; Strauss, 1984:336; Caplan, 1985b:169; Willard Gaylin in "Dying for," 1983:50; Working Group, 1985:9.

85. Caplan, 1986a:24; Varga, 1984:239.

86. Robertson, 1987:84; Walters, 1987:2; Caplan, 1987a:11; Task Force, 1986:104; Childress, 1985:23.

87. Winslow, 1982:157; Wilensky, 1985:37.

88. Loewy, 1987:440; Campbell, 1978:12–15.

89. Mathieu, 1988:145–46; Childress, 1970:344.

90. Parsons and Lock, 1980:175; Boyd, 1983:27; Reidy, 1979:77–78.

91. Off. of Tech. Assess., 1984:154; Coulton, 1986:98; Mathieu, 1988:145.

92. Ozar, 1981:138; Thomasma, 1982:51.

93. Elkowitz, 1986:126; Calabresi and Bobbitt, 1978:235; Outka, 1974:19–21.

94. Em. Friedman, 1984:68. // Katz and Capron, 1975:187.

95. F. Rapaport, 1987:3119; Jonasson, 1986:24; Thomasma, 1986a:7; Veatch, 1979:219; H. Smith, 1979:67.

96. President's Commission, 1983b:26.

97. Daniels, 1988a:141–43; Mathieu, 1988:145; Bayer, 1984:40.

98. F. Miller, 1985:32; Hyman, 1980:264; Nagelbach, 1978:47; Massachusetts, 1984:74; Annas, 1985b:187; National Heart and Lung, 1973:148.

99. Willard Gaylin in "Dying for," 1983:50; Friedrich, 1984:77.

100. Katz and Capron, 1975:186–87.

101. Childress, 1985:25.

102. Katz, 1973:409.

103. N. Bell, 1979a:16. // N. Bell, 1979b:76.

104. Transpl. Society, 1985:716; Pryor, 1983:22.

105. Transpl. Society, 1985:716; Annas, 1984:23.

106. Casscells, 1986:1366.

107. Annas, 1984:22.

108. Gorovitz, 1985b:30–32; Warren Reich in U.S. House, 1983:43.

109. Annas, 1984:23.

110. Winslade and Ross, 1986:194–95; Casscells, 1986:1366; Humber, 1985:23; Varga, 1984:226; Warren Reich in U.S. House, 1983:42.

111. Annas, 1984:23.

112. Clark, 1983:39; Iglehart, 1983:127.

113. Blank, 1988:80; Caplan, 1987b:7; Daniel Callahan and Robert Veatch in Gunby, 1983:1982.

114. Blank, 1988:97–98; Childress, 1986b:145–46.

115. Johnson et al., 1985.

116. "Dying for," 1983:50.

117. Bloch, 1985:4; Wehr, 1984:456.

118. Senator Albert Gore, Jr. in Chambers, 1986:16; Kathryn Pratt in Callaway et al., 1986; Wallis, 1982:101; Minnesota, 1984:50.

119. Fain, 1986:A19. // Blank, 1988:98; Mechanic, 1979b:110–11; Fineberg, 1984:18.

120. "Dying for," 1983:49.

121. Comaish, 1976:512; Leenen, 1979:165.

122. Kolata, 1983b:139.

123. D. Bryant, 1985:116.

124. Wallis, 1982:101.

125. Wehr, 1984:454.

126. Iglehart, 1983:127.

127. Blank, 1988:49,98.

128. Massachusetts, 1984:74; Annas, 1985b:187; Blank, 1988:99; Haber, 1986:762.

129. Fain, 1986:A19.

130. Blank, 1988:99; Haber, 1986:762; Comaish, 1976:512; Thurow, 1984:1571.

131. Winslade and Ross, 1986:178; Blank, 1988:98–99.

132. Task Force, 1986:105.

133. Engelhardt, 1984.

134. Nelson and Rohricht, 1984:196.

135. Kopelman, 1985:94. Cf. Daniels, 1987:77–78. // One such U.S. example is an Ohio consortium of transplant surgeons and institutions who agreed to devote 25 percent of transplant-related fees and gifts to transplants for the poor—see Jackson and Annas, 1986:118.

136. Working Group, 1985:55; Camenisch, 1979:304–05; Sanders and Duke-minier, 1968:1136.

137. Lomasky, 1981:82.

138. Aaron and Schwartz, 1984:55.

139. Annas, 1977:63.

140. Roger Evans in Chambers, 1986:16.

141. James Walters in Chambers, 1986:16.

142. Evans et al., 1984a:6,12.

143. "Dying Friend," 1988:A10; Gore, 1987:3.

144. Transpl. Society, 1985:716; F. Rapaport, 1987a:170–72.

145. O'Rourke and Brodeur, 1986:229. // Evans and Manninen, 1987:4.

146. Kilner, 1986a:191.

147. Robb, 1981:30; Caplan, 1987b:8; Engel, 1984:B4.

148. "Scarce," 1969:653.

149. R. Evans, 1989. Of the hospitals responding to a survey by Touche Ross (1986:3), 43 percent have indicated that they are at risk of failure.

150. Baily, 1988:208–09; Daniels, 1988b:213–14; Jonsen, 1985:38; Bayer, 1984:40; Working Group, 1985:55. // Elkinton, 1973:129; Gilson, 1983:22.

151. Debakey and Debakey, 1983:9; Michael and Adu, 1982:990.

152. Fineberg, 1984:79.

153. Katz, 1973:412–13.

154. Adapted from Munson, 1983:510–11.

CHAPTER 17. RANDOM SELECTION

1. Katz, 1973:402–03.

2. Weckman and Willy, 1987:18.

3. Proverbs 16:33. // Joshua 18:6–10; I Samuel 10:20–21, 14:42; I Chronicles 26:13; Nehemiah 10:34; Esther 3:7; Proverbs 18:18; Jonah 1:7–8; Acts 1:24–26. Many of the examples of lotteries cited in notes 2–5 and 8–9 are discussed in Olshan, 1983:3–12.

4. Staveley, 1972:46. // Kendall, 1968:336. // Vinogradoff, 1917:519. // Pic-ton, 1882:281; Gillingham, 1976:98. // Luthy, 1975; McGrath, 1977:7.

5. *United States* v. *Holmes.* On this case as a precedent for selecting patients to receive lifesaving medical resources, see Bell, 1979b:124; "Patient," 1969:1329; Ramsey, 1970a:253; Childress, 1970:340–43.

6. Rutherford, 1978:121; C. Potter, 1949:340. // O'Curry, 1873:cclxxix.

7. Numbers 26:55; Judges 20:9–10; Job 6:27; Joel 3:3; Obadiah 1:11; Nahum 3:10; Matthew 27:35.

8. Hasoter, 1967; Rabinovitch, 1973; Winslow, 1982:203.

9. "Wanna Win," 1981:25; Berry, 1981:82. // "10,000 Win," 1987:A4. // U.S. House, 1982. // Broome, 1984:38–39; Stoddard, 1969. // "U.S. Puts," 1982:26. // "Remember," 1982:42.

10. Abert, 1972:65. // Wolff, 1969:142; Hellegers, 1977:20. // "Judge Asks," 1981:A13. // Mehlman, 1985:269.

11. E.g., in Italy, England, Canada, Australia, and the United States—see Mackenzie, 1986.

12. Beecher, 1971:276.

13. "Patient," 1969:1326; Rosner, 1983a:357.

14. Harron et al., 1983:151.

15. David, 1972:584; Winslow, 1982:100; Ramsey, 1970a:252. Cf. Katz, 1967:58.

16. Regarding Great Britain, see Wilensky, 1985:37; F. Miller, 1985:32; Henry Krakauer in U.S. House, 1983:108. Regarding Italy, see Calabresi and Bobbitt, 1978:182.

17. UNOS, 1988:24; Warmbrodt, 1985:4; Jackson and Annas, 1986:119; Elaine Crowner in Kjellstrand et al., 1986:348; Olga Jonasson in Callaway et al., 1986; Midwest, 1986:2; Hume et al., 1966:352.

18. "Scarce," 1969:660; Winslow, 1982:102; Ramsey, 1970a:252.

19. Hinds, 1975:16–17; Winslow, 1982:147.

20. Kilner, 1986a.

21. Zawacki, 1985:59. // Gorovitz, 1966:7. // Belliotti, 1980a:261; Leenen, 1982:36, 1979:174; Rescher, 1969:183–84. // Minnesota, 1984:51. // Working Group, 1985:31.

22. Conrad and Fotion, 1985:15; Battin, 1982:25.

23. Broome, 1984:41; Katz and Capron, 1975:193; "Patient," 1969:1331.

24. Winslow, 1982:103–04.

25. Broome, 1984:41; Glover, 1977:219; David, 1972:584; Katz and Capron, 1975:193; Rescher, 1969:184.

26. Weckman and Willy, 1987:18–19; Broome, 1984:41; Lefebvre, 1980:184; Nelson and Rohricht, 1984:197; Glover, 1977:219; Childress, 1970:351; "Scarce," 1969:663.

27. Rescher, 1969:184. // Fromer, 1981:59.

28. Childress, 1983:561, 1981:94, 1970:347–49; Winslow, 1982:102.

29. M. O'Donnell, 1986:59; J. Bryant, 1977:711. // Ramsey, 1970a:256.

30. Thomasma, 1982:50–51. See Gellman, 1984:114–15, for a Jewish perspective and Kilner, 1986b, for a Christian perspective. Cf. Browning, 1986:73.

31. Blustein, 1978.

32. United States "Declaration," 1776; France "Declaration," 1791; Insti-

288

Notes to Pages 194–96

tute, 1929; United Nations, "Universal," 1948. // Engelhardt, 1986; Veatch, 1981; Rogers, 1975; Callahan, 1969; Bernardin, 1977.

33. Schambeck, 1974, surveys possible justifications.

34. Dyck, 1977; Hostler, 1977. // Veatch, 1976. // Maritain, 1944. // Brunner, 1945.

35. Feinberg, 1978:809.

36. Mehlman, 1985:268; Lefebvre, 1980:184; Boyd, 1979:76; Winslow, 1982: 102; Childress, 1970:342–43; Ramsey, 1970a:253–58.

37. Fried, 1976:30.

38. Hinds, 1976:33; Campbell, 1977:820.

39. Outka, 1974:586; B. Williams, 1971; Telfer, 1976:111.

40. Benn, 1967:301.

41. Brock, 1988a:93; Weckman and Willy, 1987:18; O'Rourke and Brodeur, 1986:229; F. Miller, 1985:32; Rosner, 1983b:28; B. Potter, 1981:162; Ramsey 1970a:255–66; "Patient," 1969:1329.

42. Kamm, 1987:261; Grimes, 1987:616; Broome, 1984:45; Varga, 1984:226; Connery, 1983:61; Hyman, 1986:42–43, 1980:265; Lefebvre, 1980:184; Winslow, 1982:100,148; Reidy, 1979:76; Ramsey, 1962:245, 1970a:252–61.

43. Task Force, 1986:89; Coulton, 1986:103; Varga, 1984:226; Ashley and O'Rourke, 1982:240; Calabresi and Bobbitt, 1978:42; J. Bryant, 1977:711; Ramsey, 1970a:259.

44. Gellman, 1984:115; Lavelle, 1977:102.

45. Rawls, 1971:12–14,83,302–03. According to Rawls, 1971:251–57, this conception of justice as fairness is rooted in Kant's moral philosophy (e.g., Kant, 1964).

46. Winslow, 1982:147; Childress, 1970:350; J. Bryant, 1977:709–11. Rawls himself (1971:64, 1968:53) indicates that he is not addressing the kinds of specific selection decisions in view here, though at one point his support for random selection in such an instance is apparent (1971:374). For a more direct connection between Kant and random selection, see Munson, 1983:484.

47. Childress, 1981:94–95, 1970:349; Nelson and Rohricht, 1984:197.

48. Bell, 1979b:127.

49. Macklin, 1987:158, 1985b:617; Bridgers, 1980:113; Sanders and Duke-minier, 1968:380; "Scarce," 1969:662.

50. Rescher, 1969:183–84; Ramsey, 1970a:256. // Lefebvre, 1980:183.

51. Grimes, 1987:616; Oberdiek, 1976:85; Freund, 1969:xiii; U.S. Congress, 1972:33007; Katz and Capron, 1975:193.

52. National Heart, 1984:Ch.36:2; Glover, 1977:218; Annas, 1977:73; Nelson and Rohricht, 1984:197. Cf. Caplan, 1987b:14–15.

53. Connery, 1983:61; Childress, 1970:349; Katz, 1973:402; Thielicke, 1970: 174.

54. Childress, 1970:351; N. Bell, 1979b:121. // Winslow, 1982:98.

55. Hyman, 1986:43; Broome, 1984:40.

56. Palmer, 1980:268; Childress, 1981:94. // Childress, 1970:347–48. // Feinberg, 1978:809.

57. Broome, 1984:52.

58. Hyman, 1980:265; Shapiro and Spece, 1981:848.

59. Bayer, 1986:15; B. Brody, 1983:154–55; Young, 1975:446; Rescher, 1969:186.

60. Hiatt, 1987:217; Lyon, 1986:59; Winslow, 1982:104; Shatin, 1966:100; Davidson and Scribner, 1967:5; Sawyer, 1968:8.

61. Belliotti, 1980b:271.

62. Hiatt, 1987:217; Bayer, 1986:15; Conrad and Fotion, 1985:17. // Fromer, 1981:60. // Katz and Capron, 1975:193. // Evans and Yagi, 1987:28; B. Brody, 1983:154–55; Bayer, 1984:38; Leenen, 1979:166.

63. Basson, 1979:322–23; Glover, 1977:219.

64. Belliotti, 1980a:258.

65. Aiken, 1976; Belliotti, 1980a:257.

66. L. Brown, 1978:512; Belliotti, 1980a:256–57; Boyd, 1983:27. Cf. Mill, 1863:468; Rashdall, 1948:227; Broome, 1984:44–45.

67. Lomasky, 1981:82.

68. Fried, 1976:31; Winslow, 1982:105. // Fromer, 1981:60.

69. Weckman and Willy, 1987:19; Munson, 1983:477.

70. Jos. Fletcher, 1979:50–51; Broome, 1984:52; Hewetson, 1982:314; Belliotti, 1980a:255–56; Lomasky, 1981:82.

71. G. Smith, 1985:148; Leiman, 1978:9; Fox, 1979:133; Calabresi and Bobbitt, 1978:134; Belliotti, 1980a:262; Basson, 1979:330.

72. Leach, 1972:260. Cf. Thomasma, 1986a:6–7.

73. Regarding induction into U.S. selective service: Gerhardt, 1971:322; Stoddard, 1969:274; Hays, 1967:18; Erikson, 1967:281. Regarding saving lives at sea: Cahn, 1955:71; Leiman, 1978:9. Regarding U.S. government licensing: Kahaner and Durniak, 1982:54. Regarding length of prison sentencing: "A Flap," 1982:E7.

74. Loewy, 1987:440; Em. Friedman, 1984:74; Bayer, 1984:39; Cohen, 1977:224; Calabresi and Bobbitt, 1978:134; Leiman, 1978:9; Jos. Fletcher, 1979:50–51.

75. Wasserstrom in Attig and Wasserstrom, 1976.

76. Belliotti, 1980a:255.

77. Weckman and Willy, 1987:17; Loewy, 1987:440; Leach, 1972:260; Fox and Swazey, 1978b:256; Winslow, 1982:104.

78. Munson, 1983:477; Basson, 1979:324. // "Who Shall Die?" 1980:171.

79. Leenen, 1979:167; Jos. Fletcher, 1979:50–51.

80. Fox and Swazey, 1978b:255–56.

81. Hewetson, 1982:314.

82. Loewy, 1987:438–40; B. Brody, 1983:154–55; Leach, 1972:260; Boyd, 1979:27; Belliotti, 1980a:260; Winslow, 1982:104.

83. On the characterization of first-come, first-served as a form of random selection, see Brock, 1988a:93; Atterbury, 1986:3; Conrad and Fotion, 1985:15.

84. "Patient,"1969:1341–42. // Mehlman, 1985:270; F. Parsons, 1967:623; Rescher, 1969:184; Childress, 1970:351.

85. Birch and Derr, 1979:63; Childress, 1981:134, 1970:352.

86. Winslow, 1982:99.

87. Mehlman, 1985: 270; Winslow, 1982:99.

88. Annas, 1985b:189; Massachusetts, 1984:81.

89. Mechanic, 1986:217; Bayer, 1986:16; Robbins, 1984:127; C. Lyons, 1970:95.

90. Jonsen et al., 1982:163; Wilensky, 1985:37; Conrad and Fotion, 1985:17; National Heart, 1984:Ch.36:19; Leenen, 1982:33.

91. Conrad and Fotion, 1985:16.

92. Leenen, 1979:166; Winslow, 1982:148–49.

93. Trammell and Wren, 1977:333; O'Neil, 1978:125; M. Green, 1979:400–01.

94. Annas, 1987:29; Haber, 1986:763; Boyd, 1983:27; Calabresi and Bobbitt, 1978:42.

95. Winslow, 1982:148.

96. J. Evans, 1988:123; Hudson, 1975:58; Katz and Capron, 1975:192–93.

97. Winslow, 1982:103.

98. Katz and Capron, 1975:195.

99. Mehlman, 1985:270.

100. Bayer, 1984:39.

101. O'Rourke and Brodeur, 1986:229.

102. Wasserstrom in Attig and Wasserstrom, 1976; N. Bell, 1979b:130–31.

103. Mavrodes, 1984:115; Shevory, 1986:758. // National Heart, 1984:Ch.36:32–33.

104. Gore, 1987:4; Weckman and Willy, 1987:18.

105. Graber et al., 1985:210; Mavrodes, 1984:115; Katz, 1973:402.

106. Kilner, 1986a:166; Bayer, 1986:15; Conrad and Fotion, 1985:15; National Heart, 1984:Ch.35:3; Glover, 1977:206; N. Bell, 1979b; Leenen, 1979:166.

107. Mehlman, 1985:271; Haber, 1986:763; Massachusetts, 1984:76; Annas, 1985b:188; Conrad and Fotion, 1985:16–17; Robbins, 1984:126.

108. Boyd, 1979:76–77; Bayer, 1986:15, 1984:38; Conrad and Fotion, 1985:15; Jonsen et al., 1982:163; Winslow, 1982:146.

109. Starzl et al., 1988a:135, 1987b:3073.

110. Kilner, 1986a:166. // Mehlman, 1985:271; Leenen, 1982:33, 1979:166. // Conrad and Fotion, 1985:15; Childress, 1981:134. // Jonasson, 1989.

111. On the possibility of tampering, see Willard, 1980; Jn. Harris, 1975; Mehlman, 1985:270–71; National Heart, 1984:Ch.36:19.

112. Task Force, 1986:85–86.

113. Westervelt, 1970:359.

114. It is relevant, "other things being equal" (Mavrodes, 1984:106–07). Cf. Kamm, 1987:257,262.

115. Veatch, 1977b:238; Winslow, 1982:101; Leach, 1972:259.

116. Cf. Winslow, 1982:106.

117. Palmer, 1980:266–67; Veatch, 1985b:74. Cf. chapter 19 regarding the present gradual shifting of values.

118. Weckman and Willy, 1987:21; Broome, 1984:41; Rosner, 1983b:22.

119. Engelhardt, 1986:348.

120. Mehlman, 1985:269; Ingman et al., 1987:239; Fromer, 1981:59; Gorovitz, 1966:7; Oberdiek, 1976:84; Wasserstrom in Attig and Wasserstrom, 1976; Childress, 1970:352.

121. Hewetson, 1982:312.

122. Childress, 1985:18–19.

123. Boyd, 1979:76; Bayer, 1984:39.

124. John Monagle in Attig et al., 1976.

125. Cf. N. Bell, 1979b:123–24.

126. Conrad and Fotion, 1985:16.

127. Masachusetts, 1984:81; Annas, 1985b:189.

128. Winslow, 1982:154.

129. Brock, 1988a:95; Annas, 1985b:189; Massachusetts, 1984:80.

130. Brock, 1988a:95.

131. Starzl et al., 1987b:3075.

132. Massachusetts, 1984:86.

133. Task Force, 1986:83; Warmbrodt, 1985:3; Midwest, 1986:1; Childress, 1985:21; Amy Peele, Paul Terasaki, and Henry Krakauer in U.S. House, 1983:80, 94, 106–09. As Brock (1988a:92–93) notes, the person oriented concern for equal opportunity is key to the justification in that the resulting transplants may not be as successful since tissue matching is deemphasized.

134. Matas and Tellis, 1987:1328.

135. Matas and Tellis, 1987:1328; Starzl et al., 1987b:3075.

136. UNOS, 1988:13.

137. Task Force, 1986:74.

138. Adapted from Wojcik, 1978:116–17.

CHAPTER 18. WHEN RESOURCES ARE EXPERIMENTAL

1. Working Group, 1985:23; De Wardener, 1966:108.

2. Merriken and Overcast, 1985:8.

3. Stickel et al., 1967:731.

4. Caplan, 1981b:495, 1983a:114–15; V. Parsons, 1978:872.

5. Caplan, 1980:28, 1981b:489–90.

6. Fox and Swazey, 1978b:Ch.3; Caplan, 1981b:491.

7. Reiss et al., 1982:412; National Heart, 1984:Ch.35:7.

8. Felch, 1982:11.
9. E.g., William Schwartz in Wehr, 1984:454.
10. Bergsten et al., 1977:7; Caplan, 1981b:497.
11. U.S. Bureau, 1967:2–4; Rettig, 1976a:16; Caplan, 1981b:493.
12. Schupak, 1967; Retan and Lewis, 1966; Hume, 1966.
13. Abram and Wadlington, 1968; Murray et al., 1962; Rubini, 1966.
14. Fox, 1979:133.
15. National Heart, 1984:Ch.9:14.
16. "Ethics and the Neph.," 1981:595; Davidson and Scribner, 1967:6–8; Sawyer, 1968:9.
17. Leenen, 1979:168; National Heart, 1984:Ch.36:34–35.
18. Christopherson, 1982:19.
19. Hume et al., 1966:352–53.
20. Christopherson, 1982:19.
21. Howard and Najarian, 1978:1161; U.S.H.C.F.A., 1981:7073–74.
22. Working Group, 1985:23; R. Levine, 1984:1459.
23. Gorovitz, 1984:16.
24. Berenson and Grosser, 1984:916.
25. Working Group, 1985:23; U.S.H.C.F.A., 1981:7074; National Heart, 1984:Ch.45:29–30; R. Evans, 1983:2209.
26. Gunby, 1982:1946; Working Group, 1985:26.
27. Christopherson, 1982:19.
28. Childress, 1985:18–19.
29. Nelson and Rohricht, 1984:196.
30. "Scarce," 1969:643.
31. Graber et al., 1985:209.
32. Caplan, 1987a:16.
33. Rescher, 1969:177.
34. Belliotti, 1980a:260.
35. Graber et al., 1985:209.
36. C. Lyons, 1970:94–95.
37. Rescher, 1969:176.
38. Young, 1975:442.
39. C. Lyons, 1970:96–97; Leenen, 1979:168.
40. Young, 1975:442.
41. E.g., see Platt, 1966:151.

CHAPTER 19. A PROPOSAL

1. For an ethically more sophisticated defense of this approach (and its implications for patient selection), see Kilner, 1983b. There this approach is evaluated in relation to major alternatives, using the standards of comprehensiveness, consistency, and counterproductivity. See esp. pp. 34–47, 114–34, 198–

211, and 289–304 for a critical examination of the views of normative reasoning, the person, and society underlying these various approaches.

2. Siegler, 1984:25; Browning, 1986:73; Fein, 1982:863; Cooper and Cohen, 1982:958; Barker, 1976:viii; Brandt, 1983; Mooney, 1984:183–85. // Palmer, 1980:266.

3. McKinlay, 1981:401; Belliotti, 1980a:254–55; Winslow, 1982:22.

4. Brooks, 1984:148; Swales, 1982:118. // G. Smith, 1987:50–51; D. Smith, 1981:52; Purtilo, 1982:48; Curran, 1979:141; Brandt, 1983:37; L. Alexander, 1949:46.

5. Kilner, 1984:19–21.

6. For a detailed analysis of utilitarian thinking as it applies to patient selection, see Kilner, 1983b (esp. pp. 27–190).

7. Cf. Barber, 1987:661.

8. If all eligible candidates who satisfy at least one of these criteria cannot be treated with available resources, the selection that saves the greatest number of lives is to be preferred. Ties are to be broken (and ambiguous situations resolved) by means of a lottery.

9. Task Force, 1986:89.

10. A. Williams, 1986:338.

11. Some conflicts may be apparent only. For example, Mathieu (1988:48) argues that the point system may not exclude patients who deteriorate to the point that they will no longer benefit significantly from treatment. The medical-benefit criterion proposed in this book does exclude such patients, but there is no reason in principle why the point system could not also. Other conflicts are more serious. For instance, since organs remain viable only for a limited period, there comes a time (earlier for hearts and livers, later for kidneys) when only certain patients are located close enough to the organ to benefit from receiving it. The point system (e.g., Starzl et al., 1987b:3074) tends to address this issue by giving extra points to suitably located patients. As a result, patients living too far away to benefit may end up receiving higher priority than those who could benefit, because they have received many points for such factors as waiting time and antigen matches. The approach proposed in this book seeks to avoid that problem by incorporating such favored-group considerations into the medical-benefit criterion (which must be satisfied before a patient can be selected). A similar problem arises in the handling of patients whose death is imminent. The point system (e.g., UNOS, 1988:17,26; Starzl et al., 1988a:136, 1987b:3075) merely gives such patients extra points. As a result, patients who have waited longer or have better antigen matches may take priority over patients whose death is imminent. This outcome is problematic for the various reasons explained in chapter 11. The proposal in this book assures the priority of the imminent-death criterion by making it definitive among candidates who satisfy the medical-

benefit and willingness criteria. Responses of the point system's proponents to criticisms of the type above are telling. When Matas and Tellis (1987) offered an example of a poor selection that the point system would recommend, proponents responded by saying that various factors tend to be reinforcing, and that as a result the example cited usually would not occur (Starzl, 1987:1329; cf. Starzl et al., 1987b:3075, where a similar argument is also offered with regard to the imminent-death issue). They could not claim that it would never occur, because the relevant data indicate otherwise. Why not construct a patient selection procedure that will ensure that poor selections of this sort will not take place? Furthermore, if antigen matching is to be central, as it is in the point system, its ethical foundation would be stronger if it was justified as a form of random selection rather than on the basis of the likelihood of benefit (cf. chapters 12 and 17). Revisions to the UNOS point system for allocating kidneys, adopted February 28, 1989 (UNOS, 1989b), eliminate points for recipient location and imminent death because these considerations are so rarely relevant regarding kidneys (as opposed to other transplantable organs). How exceptional cases are to be handled is difficult to specify in a point system and is not fleshed out in the governing document. Cases of medical urgency, for example, are to be "flagged in the computer" and "dealt with on an individual basis" (p. 40). The weight to be accorded the criterion is unclear.

12. For a critique of justifying arguments on the basis of rational intuitions and cultural assumptions, see Kilner, 1983a.

13. Childress, 1970:342. // Belliotti, 1980a:255–56; Leach, 1972:260; Jos. Fletcher, 1979:50–51.

14. *United States* v. *Holmes,* 1842.

15. Hewetson, 1982:314; Calabresi and Bobbitt, 1978:134.

16. Carothers, 1948:73–74; U.S.A.I.D., 1980:60.

17. Nida, 1962:147; Mutungi, 1977:18; Mburu, 1977:164.

18. Ndeti, 1978:186–89, 1972:138.

19. Mburu, 1977:163ff.; Ndeti, 1972:172–73; Tempels, 1959:120. This reluctance is also manifested in the antisupernaturalist bias in critical assessments of the Akamban outlook (e.g., N. Miller, 1980:3–7; A. Thomas, 1975:278.)

20. A. Beck, 1981:64; Achernecht, 1971:122; Middleton and Kershaw, 1965:83–84; Carothers, 1948:74.

21. Tempels, 1959:117.

22. Lindblom, 1935:96–99; Mbiti, 1970:99,148,163; Muthiani, 1973:12–13; Hobley, 1910:51.

23. E.g., see Kilner, 1986b, 1983b:280–358,380–85. Cf. Ramsey, 1970a:xi–xiii,240–66; 1970b:22–32. For a demonstration of the significant common ground between the implications of this story and positions argued from other perspectives, see Kilner, 1981.

24. Before the possibility should be considered that Barbara be given priority access to an organ obtained through media coverage, two demanding conditions

must be met. Barbara's parents must prove conclusively both that the organ has been donated only because of their publicity efforts and that the donor's parents are not willing to make it available to anyone except Barbara. Rarely can the first condition be satisfied, particularly when (as here) the general need for organs has been publicized by the medical center involved. Ability to pay for the surgery should also not come into play unless one of two sets of conditions is met. Either (1) the hospital will have to close if the ability to pay for liver transplants is not a requirement, and no other facility will be able to care for all of its patients, or (2) more important medical priorities will be disregarded if liver transplants are provided for all in need without regard to their ability to pay. However, if either or both of these sets of conditions applies, then the government should probably fund liver transplants for all in need, or else greater emphasis in health care should be accorded to other lifesaving interventions that can be made available to all.

REFERENCES CITED

"A Flap Over A Flip." 1982. *New York Times* (February 7): E7.

"A Life in the Balance." 1975. *Time* 106 (November 3): 52–61.

Aaron, Henry J., and William B. Schwartz. 1984. *The Painful Prescription: Rationing Hospital Care.* Washington, D.C.: Brookings Institution.

Abert, James. 1972. "Since Grantsmanship Doesn't Work, Why Not Roulette?" *Saturday Review* (October 21): 65–66.

Abram, Harry S. 1972. "Psychological Dilemmas of Medical Progress." *Psychiatry in Medicine* 3 (January): 51–58.

Abram, Harry S., and Walter Wadlington. 1968. "Selection of Patients for Artificial and Transplanted Organs." *Annals of Internal Medicine* 69 (September): 615–20.

Abram, Harry S., et al. 1971. "Suicidal Behavior in Chronic Dialysis Patients." *American Journal of Psychiatry* 127 (March): 1199–1203.

Abram, Morris B., and S. M. Wolf. 1984. "Public Involvement in Medical Ethics: A Model for Government Action." *New England Journal of Medicine* 310 (March 8): 627–32.

Abrams, Fredrick R. 1987. "Access to Health Care." In Gary Anderson and Valerie Glesnes-Anderson (eds.), *Health Care Ethics.* Rockville, MD: Aspen: 49–68.

———. 1988. "Advance Directives: When the Patient Cannot Communicate." In John F. Monagle and David C. Thomasma (eds.), *Medical Ethics.* Rockville, MD: Aspen: 205–08.

Achernecht, Erwin H. 1971. *Medicine and Ethnology.* Baltimore: Johns Hopkins University Press.

Ackerman, Terrence F. 1980. "Meningomyelocele and Parental Commitment: A Policy Proposal Regarding Selection for Treatment." *Man and Medicine* 5: 291–303.

Adami, Hans-Olov, et al. 1986. "The Relation between Survival and Age at Diagnosis in Breast Cancer." *New England Journal of Medicine* 315 (August 28): 559–63.

Adams, Lorraine R. 1978. "Medical Coverage for Chronic Renal Disease: Policy Implications." *Health and Social Work* 3: 40–53.

Aday, Lu Ann, and Ronald M. Andersen. 1981. "Equity of Access to Medical

Care: A Conceptual and Empirical Overview." *Medical Care* 19 (December Suppl.): 4–27.

Aday, Lu Ann, et al. 1984. *Access to Medical Care in the U.S.: Who Has It, Who Doesn't.* Chicago: Pluribus.

Affleck, Glenn. 1977. "The Right to Survive." *Mental Retardation* 15 (February): 52.

Aiken, Henry D. 1976. "Life and the Right to Life." In J. M. Humber and R. F. Almeder (eds.), *Biomedical Ethics and the Law.* New York: Plenum Press: 465–75.

Alexander, Leo. 1949. "Medical Science Under Dictatorship." *New England Journal of Medicine* 141 (July 14): 39–47.

Alexander, Shana. 1962. "They Decide Who Lives, Who Dies." *Life* 53 (November 9): 102–25.

Allegrante, John P., and Lawrence W. Green. 1981. "When Health Policy Becomes Victim Blaming." *New England Journal of Medicine* 305 (December 17): 1528–29.

Altman, Lawrance K. 1973. "Costs of Kidney Therapy: Two Fundamental Questions Raised." *New York Times* (January 23): 13.

———. 1982. "Health Quality and Costs: A Delicate Balance." *New York Times* (March 30): A1, C2.

Ambrose. 392. *Duties of the Clergy,* trans. H. de Romestin et al. In Philip Schaff et al. (eds.), *Nicene and Post-Nicene Fathers of the Christian Church,* 2d ser., vol. 10. Grand Rapids, MI: Wm. B. Eerdmans, 1978: 1–89.

American Heart Association, Committee on Ethics. 1976. "Ethical Considerations of the Left Ventricular Assist Device." *Journal of the American Medical Association* 235 (February 23): 823–24.

American Medical Association. 1982. "Allocation of Health Resources, Op. 2.02." Current Opinions of the Judicial Council.

American Society of Transplant Surgeons. 1986. "Guidelines for Organ Donation and Transplantation." Des Plaines, IL: A.S.T.S., May.

Anderson, C. A. 1977. "Who Shall Live?" *Minnesota Medicine* 60 (November): 785–86.

Angell, Marcia. 1985. "Cost Containment and the Physician." *Journal of the American Medical Association* 254 (September 6): 1203–07.

Annas, George J. 1977. "Allocation of Artificial Hearts in the Year 2002: Minerva v. National Health Agency." *American Journal of Law and Medicine* 3 (Spring): 59–76.

———. 1984. "Life, Liberty, and the Pursuit of Organ Sales." *Hastings Center Report* 14 (February): 22–23.

———. 1985a. "Regulating the Introduction of Heart and Liver Transplantation." *American Journal of Public Health* 75 (January): 93–95.

———. 1985b. "The Prostitute, the Playboy, and the Poet: Rationing Schemes for Organ Transplantation." *American Journal of Public Health* 75 (February): 187–89.

———. 1985c. "Adam Smith in the Emergency Room." *Hastings Center Report* 15 (August): 16–18.

———. 1985d. "Response [to Neuspiel's 'On Rational Organ Transplantation.']." *American Journal of Public Health* 75 (August): 893–94.

———. 1986. "Your Money or Your Life: 'Dumping' Uninsured Patients from Hospital Emergency Wards." *American Journal of Public Health* 76 (January): 74–77.

———. 1987. "Siamese Twins: Killing One to Save the Other." *Hastings Center Report* 17 (April): 27–29.

Anscombe, G. E. M. 1967. "Who Is Wronged?" *The Oxford Review* 5: 16–17.

Ansell, David A., and Robert L. Schiff. 1987. "Patient Dumping: Status, Implications, and Policy Recommendations." *Journal of the American Medical Association* 257 (March 20): 1500–02.

Aranow, Henry, Jr. 1980. "Commentary on Ackerman's Meningomyelocele and Parental Commitment." *Man and Medicine* 5: 304–07.

Aroskar, Mila A. 1979. "Ethical Issues in Community Health Nursing." *Nursing Clinics of North America* 14 (March): 35–44.

Arras, John D. 1984. "Utility, Natural Rights, and the Right to Health Care." In James Humbers and Robert Almeder (eds.), *Biomedical Ethics Reviews*. Clifton, NJ: Humana: 23–45.

"Artificial Hearts and Real Questions." 1983. *America* 148 (January 8): 4.

Ashley, Benedict M., and Kevin D. O'Rourke. 1982. *Health Care Ethics: A Theological Analysis,* 2d ed. St. Louis: Catholic Health Association of the United States.

———. 1986. *Ethics of Health Care.* St. Louis: Catholic Health Association of the United States.

Askham, Janet. 1982. "Professionals' Criteria for Accepting People as Patients." *Social Science and Medicine* 16: 2083–89.

Aslanian, R. 1981. "Expanded Program on Immunization: Survey to Determine the Public Health Importance of Measles in the Rural Areas of Nepal." Report to the World Health Organization, South-East Asia Region, on WHO Project NEP EPI 001. August 26.

Atterbury, Colin E. 1986. "The Alcoholic in the Lifeboat: Should Drinkers Be Candidates for Liver Transplantation?" *Journal of Clinical Gastroenterology* 8 (February): 1–4.

Attig, Tom, and Richard Wasserstrom. 1976. "Biomedical Ethics: Problems of the Allocation of Scarce Lifesaving Therapy" (video). Bowling Green, OH: WBGU-TV, Bowling Green State University.

Attig, Tom, et al. 1976. "Biomedical Ethics: The Right to Live and the Right to Die" (video). Bowling Green, OH: WBGU-TV, Bowling Green State University.

"Audit in Renal Failure: The Wrong Target?" 1981. *British Medical Journal* 283 (July): 261–62.

Auer, J. 1983. "Social and Psychological Issues of End-Stage Renal Failure." In F. M. Parsons and C. S. Ogg (eds.), *Renal Failure—Who Cares?* Lancaster, England: MTP: 205–14.

Austin, Carol D., and Martin B. Loeb. 1982. "Why Age Is Relevant in Social Policy and Practice." In Bernice L. Neugarten (ed.), *Age or Need?* Beverly Hills: Sage: 263–88.

Avorn, Jerry. 1984. "Benefit and Cost Analysis in Geriatric Care: Turning Age Discrimination into Health Policy." *New England Journal of Medicine* 310 (May 17): 1294–1301.

"Baby With New Heart Undergoing Dialysis." 1986. Associated Press News Service (e.g., in *Lexington [KY] Herald-Leader,* June 16, B2).

Baily, Mary A. 1984. " 'Rationing' and American Health Policy." *Journal of Health Politics, Policy and Law* 9 (Fall): 489–501.

———. 1988. "Economic Issues in Organ Substitution Technology." In Deborah Mathieu (ed.), *Organ Substitution Technology.* Boulder, CO: Westview: 198–210.

Barber, Richard L. 1987. "Public Policy and the Allocation of Scarce Medical Resources." *Journal of Philosophy* 84 (November): 655–65.

Barker, Stephen F. 1976. "Preface." In Owsei Temkin et al. (eds.), *Respect for Life.* Baltimore: Johns Hopkins University Press.

Barondess, Jeremiah A., et al. 1988. "Clinical Decision-Making in Catastrophic Situations: The Relevance of Age." *Journal of American Geriatrics Society* 36 (October): 919–37.

Barrett, John, and Olga Jonassen. 1986. "Transfers to a Public Hospital." *New England Journal of Medicine* 315 (November 27): 1421.

Basson, Marc D. 1979. "Choosing among Candidates for Scarce Medical Resources." *The Journal of Medicine and Philosophy* 4 (September): 313–33.

Battin, Margaret P. 1982. "Two Cardiac Arrests, One Medical Team: Commentary." *Hastings Center Report* 12 (April): 25.

———. 1987. "Age Rationing and the Just Distribution of Health Care: Is There a Duty to Die?" *Ethics* 97 (January): 317–40.

Bayer, Ronald. 1984. "Justice and Health Care in an Era of Cost Containment." *Social Responsibility* 9: 37–52.

———. 1986. "Ethical Considerations in Rationing Health Care." In James Hamner III and Barbara Jacobs (eds.), *Life and Death Issues.* Memphis: University of Tennessee Press: 13–20.

Beauchamp, Tom L. 1978. "The Regulation of Hazards and Hazardous Behavior." *Health Education Monographs* 6 (Summer): 242–57.

———. 1979. "Can We Stop or Withhold Dialysis?" In George E. Schreiner (ed.), *Controversies in Nephrology.* Washington, D.C.: Georgetown University, Nephrology Division: 163–70.

Beauchamp, Tom L., and James F. Childress. 1979. *Principles of Biomedical Ethics.* Oxford: Oxford University Press.

Beauchamp, Tom L., and Laurence B. McCullough. 1984. *Medical Ethics: The Moral Responsibilities of Physicians.* Englewood Cliffs, NJ: Prentice-Hall.

Beck, Ann. 1981. *Medicine, Tradition, and Development in Kenya and Tanzania, 1920–1970.* Waltham, MA: Crossroads Press.

Beck, Joan. 1982. "Who Can Afford a New Heart?" *Chicago Tribune* (December 6): 1:18.

Becker, E. Lovell. "Finite Resources and Medical Triage." *American Journal of Medicine* 66 (April): 549–50.

Beecher, Henry K. 1969. "Scarce Resources and Medical Advancement." *Daedalus* 98 (Spring): 275–313.

———. 1971. *Research and the Individual.* Boston: Little, Brown.

Bell, Donald C. 1985. "The Price of Life: Ethics and Economics." *Minnesota Medicine* 68 (February): 145–50.

Bell, Nora K. 1979a. "Why Medical Criteria Won't Work in the Allocation of Scarce Medical Resources." *Georgia Journal of Science* 37 (January): 13–20.

———. 1979b. "Ethical Considerations in the Allocation of Scarce Medical Resources." Ann Arbor: University Microfilms. (Ph.D. dissertation, University of North Carolina at Chapel Hill, 1978.)

———. 1981. "Triage in Medical Practices: An Unacceptable Model?" *Social Science and Medicine* 15F (December): 151–56.

Bell, Stacey J., et al. 1985. "Allocations of Feeding Pumps: An Ethical Question." *Journal of the American Dietetic Association* 85 (June): 697–99.

Belliotti, Raymond A. 1980a. "Moral Assessment and the Allocation of Scarce Medical Resources." *Values and Ethics in Health Care* 5: 251–62.

———. 1980b. "Reply to Commentaries on 'Allocation of Resources.'" *Values and Ethics in Health Care* 5: 270–72.

Benjamin, Martin. 1989. "Value Conflicts in Organ Allocation." Paper presented at conference on patient selection criteria in organ transplantation, Transplant Policy Center, University of Michigan (March 14). Forthcoming in *Transplantation Proceedings.*

Benn, S. I. 1967. "Justice." In Paul Edwards (ed.), *The Encyclopedia of Philosophy,* vol. 4. New York: Macmillan and Free Press: 298–302.

Berenson, Claudia K., and Bernard I. Grosser. 1984. "Total Artificial Heart Implantation." *Archives of General Psychiatry* 41 (September): 910–16.

Beresford-Stooke, George. 1928. "Akamba Ceremonies Connected with Dreams." *Man* 28 (October): 176–77.

Bergsten, E., et al. 1977. "A Study of Patients on Haemodialysis." *Scandinavian Journal of Social Medicine* 11, Suppl.: 7–31.

Berlyne, G. M. 1982. "Over 50 and Uremic = Death." *Nephron* 31: 189–90.

Bermel, Joyce. 1983. "The Phoenix Memo: Rationing Dialysis for Indian Patients." *Hastings Center Report* 13 (April): 2.

———. 1985. "Very Sick Patients: A Danger to Hospitals' Financial Health." *Hastings Center Report* 15 (August): 3–4.

————. 1986. "Organs for Sale: From Marketplace to Jungle." *Hastings Center Report* 16 (February): 3–4.

Bernard, Bruce P. 1985. "Private Hospitals' Dumping of Patients." *New York Times* (October 28):A19.

Bernardin, Joseph L. 1977. "The Right to Life—A Gauge of U.S. Values." *Hospital Progress* 58 (October): 88–90.

Bernstein, Barton J. 1984. "The Misguided Quest for the Artificial Heart." *Technology Review* 87 (November/December): 13–19 + .

Berry, Ted. 1981. "Great Onshore Oil Lottery." *New York Times Magazine* (October 11): 76 + .

Bertrand, Marie-Andree. 1976. "What Does the Quality of Life Mean to You?" *The Canadian Nurse* 72 (May): 26.

Bilous, R. W., et al. "Audit in Renal Failure." *British Journal of Medicine* 283 (September 12): 726–27.

Binstock, Robert H. 1983. "The Aged as Scapegoat." *The Gerontologist* 23 (April): 136–43.

Birch, Charles, and Thomas S. Derr. 1979. "Ethical Dilemmas in the Biological Manipulation of Human Life." In Paul Abrecht (ed.), *Faith, Science and the Future.* Philadelphia: Fortress: 52–65.

Bishop, Veronica A. 1978. "A Nurse's View of Ethical Problems in Intensive Care and Clinical Research." *British Journal of Anesthesia* 50 (May): 515–18.

Blank, Robert H. 1988. *Rationing Medicine.* New York: Columbia University.

Bloch, Susan. 1985. "Confronting the 'New Medicine.' " *Duke* 71 (July–August): 2–7.

Blumstein, James F. 1983. "Rationing Medical Resources: A Constitutional, Legal, and Policy Analysis." In President's Commission for the Study of Ethical Problems in Medicine and Biomedical and Behavioral Research, *Securing Access to Health Care,* vol. 3. Washington, D.C.: U.S. Government Printing Office (March): 349–94.

Blustein, Jeffrey. 1978. "Allocation of Scarce Lifesaving Resources and the Right Not to be Killed." In Elsie L. Bandman and Bertram Bandman (eds.), *Bioethics and Human Rights.* Boston: Little, Brown: 285–89.

Bok, Sissela. 1981. "The Relevance of Moral Philosophy to Medicine." In Herbert Gleason (ed.), *Getting Bigger.* Cambridge, MA: Oelgeschlager, Gunn and Hain: 23–31.

Bowen, Otis R. 1984. "Experimental Medical Devices, Drugs and Techniques: Their Future Social, Medical and Political Implications," Parts 1–4. *Indiana Medicine* 77 (June–September): 450–53 + .

Boyd, Kenneth M. 1983. "The Ethics of Resource Allocation." *Journal of Medical Ethics* 9 (March): 25–27.

Boyd, Kenneth M. (ed.). 1979. *The Ethics of Resource Allocation in Health Care.* Edinburgh: Edinburgh University Press.

Boyd, Kenneth M., and Brian T. Potter. 1986. "Priorities in the Allocation of Scarce Resources." *Journal of Medical Ethics* 12 (December): 197–200.

Brahams, Diana. 1984. "End-stage Renal Failure: The Doctor's Duty and the Patient's Right." *Lancet* 1 (February 18): 386–87.

———. 1985. "When Is Discontinuation of Dialysis Justified?" *Lancet* 1 (January 19): 176–77.

Brand, Paul, et al. 1986. "Biomedical Decision Making: The Blessings and Curses of Modern Technology." *Christianity Today* 30 (March 21): 1I–16I.

Brandt, Richard B. 1983. "The Real and Alleged Problem of Utilitarianism." *Hastings Center Report* 13 (April): 37–43.

Brent, Leslie. 1983. "Deciding Who Gets What." *Lancet* 1 (January 1/8): 57.

Brett, Allan S. 1981. "Hidden Ethical Issues in Clinical Decision Analysis." *New England Journal of Medicine* 305 (November 5): 1150–52.

Bridgers, William F. 1980. "Ethical and Policy Implications [of Coronary Artery Disease]." In Edgar D. Charles and Jennie J. Kronenfeld (eds.), *Social and Economic Impacts of Coronary Artery Disease*. Lexington, MA: Lexington Books: 105–29.

Broad, C. D. 1934. *Five Types of Ethical Theory*. New York: Harcourt, Brace: 246–53.

Brock, Dan W. 1987. "Informed Consent." In Donald VanDeVeer and Tom Regan (eds.), *Health Care Ethics*. Philadelphia: Temple University Press: 98–126.

———. 1988a. "Ethical Issues in Recipient Selection for Organ Transplantation." In Deborah Mathieu (ed.), *Organ Substitution Technology*. Boulder, CO: Westview: 86–99.

———. 1988b. "Justice and the Severely Demented Elderly." *Journal of Medicine and Philosophy* 13 (February): 73–99.

Brody, Baruch. 1983. *Ethics and Its Applications*. New York: Harcourt Brace Jovanovich.

Brody, Howard. 1981. *Ethical Decisions in Medicine,* 2d ed. Boston: Little, Brown.

Brooks, Simon A. 1984. "Dignity and Cost-Effectiveness: A Rejection of a Utilitarian Approach to Death." *Journal of Medical Ethics* 10 (September): 148–51.

Broome, John. 1984. "Selecting People Randomly." *Ethics* 95 (October): 38–55.

Brown, E. Richard. 1987. "DRGs and the Rationing of Hospital Care." In Gary Anderson and Valerie Glesnes-Anderson (eds.), *Health Care Ethics*. Rockville, MD: Aspen: 69–90.

Brown, Laurence D. 1978. "The Scope and Limits of Equality as a Normative Guide to Federal Health Care Policy." *Public Policy* 26 (Fall): 481–532.

Browning, Don S. 1986. "Hospital Chaplaincy as Public Ministry." *Second Opinion* 1: 66–75.

Brunner, Emil. 1945. *Justice and the Social Order,* trans. Mary Hottinger. New York: Harper & Brothers.

Bryant, D'Orsay D., III. 1985. "Spare Part Surgery: The Ethics of Organ Transplantation." *Journal of the National Medical Association* 77 (February): 113–17.

Bryant, John H. 1973. "Human Criteria in Health Care." *Ecumenical Review* 25 (January): 80–86 and 91–98.

———. 1977. "Principles of Justice as a Basis for Conceptualizing a Health Care System." *International Journal of Health Services* 7: 707–19.

———. 1980. "Health for All by the Year 2000: Can We Afford Such a Future?" *Journal of the Medical Association of Georgia* 69 (April): 293–97.

Byrn, Robert M. 1975. "Compulsory Lifesaving Treatment for the Competent Adult." *Fordham Law Review* 44 (October): 1–36.

Cahn, Edmond. 1955. *The Moral Decision.* Bloomington: Indiana University Press.

Calabresi, Guido, and Philip Bobbitt. 1978. *Tragic Choices.* New York: W. W. Norton.

Califano, Joseph A., Jr. 1986. *America's Health Care Revolution: Who Lives? Who Dies? Who Pays?* New York: Random House.

California Health Decisions. 1986. "Preliminary Analysis—Small Group Meetings." Tustin, CA: C.H.D.

"California Natural Death Act." 1976. California Health and Safety Code, div. 7, pt. 1, chap. 3, 9, secs. 7185–95, October (signed into law). In Stanley Reiser et al. (eds.), *Ethics in Medicine.* Cambridge: MIT Press, 1977: 665–67.

Callahan, Daniel. 1969. "The Sanctity of Life." In Donald Cutler (ed.), *The Religious Situation: 1969.* Boston: Beacon Press: 297–339.

———. 1977. "Health and Society: Some Ethical Imperatives." *Daedalus* 106 (Winter): 23–33.

———. 1987. *Setting Limits: Medical Goals in an Aging Society.* New York: Simon and Schuster.

———. 1988. "Aging and the Ends of Medicine." *Annals of the New York Academy of Sciences* 530: 125–32.

Calland, Chad H. 1972. "Iatrogenic Problems in End-Stage Renal Failure." *New England Journal of Medicine* 287: 334–36.

Callaway, John, et al. 1986. "Diagnosis Critical: Health Care in the 80's" (video). Broadcast on WTTW (Chicago), October 29.

Callender, Clive O. 1987. "Organ Donation in the Black Population: Where Do We Go from Here?" *Transplantation Proceedings* 19 (April): 36–40.

Callender, Clive O., and George M. Dunston. 1988. "Organ Donation in Blacks: Once a Dilemma, Now a National Commitment." *Black Health* 1 (Summer): 22–25.

Calne, R. Y. 1982. "What Has Happened to Charity?" *British Medical Journal* 284 (April 3): 998–99.

———. 1983. "The Current United Kingdom Transplant Situation." In F. M. Parsons and C. S. Ogg (eds.), *Renal Failure—Who Cares?* Lancaster, England: MTP: 121–26.

Camenisch, Paul F. 1979. "The Right to Health Care: A Contractual Approach." *Soundings* 62 (Fall): 293–310.

Cameron, Stewart, et al. 1981. "Audit in Renal Failure." *British Medical Journal* 283 (August 22): 555–56.

Campbell, Alastair V. 1977. "Establishing Ethical Priorities in Medicine." *British Medical Journal* 1 (March 26): 818–21.

———. 1978. *Medicine, Health and Justice: The Problem of Priorities.* Edinburgh: Churchill Livingstone.

Campbell, Angus, et al. 1976. *The Quality of American Life.* New York: Russell Sage Foundation.

Campbell, J. D., and A. R. Campbell. 1978. "The Social and Economic Costs of End-Stage Renal Disease." *New England Journal of Medicine* 299: 386–92.

Canale, Dee J., et al. 1986. "Panel Discussion." In James Hamner III and Barbara Jacobs (eds.), *Life and Death Issues.* Memphis: University of Tennessee Press: 41–54.

Cantor, Norman L. 1973. "A Patient's Decision to Decline Life-Saving Medical Treatment: Bodily Integrity Versus the Preservation of Life." *Rutgers Law Review* 26: 228–64.

Caplan, Arthur L. 1980. "Ethical Engineers Need Not Apply: The State of Applied Ethics Today." *Science, Technology and Human Values* 6 (Fall): 24–32.

———. 1981a. "Audit in Renal Failure." *British Medical Journal* 283 (September 12): 727.

———. 1981b. "Kidneys, Ethics and Politics: Policy Lessons of the ESRD Experience." *Journal of Health Politics, Policy and Law* 6 (Fall): 488–503.

———. 1982. "The Artificial Heart." *Hastings Center Report* 12 (February): 22–24.

———. 1983a. "How Should Values Count in the Allocation of New Technologies in Health Care?" In Ronald Bayer et al. (eds.), *In Search of Equity.* New York: Plenum Press: 95–124.

———. 1983b. "Organ Transplants: The Costs of Success." *Hastings Center Report* 13 (December): 23–32.

———. 1984. "The Selection of Patients for Dialytic Therapy—Should Treatment Be Left to Chance?" *Dialysis and Transplantation* 13 (March): 155–61.

———. 1985a. "If There's A Will, Is There a Way?" *Law, Medicine & Health Care* 13 (February): 32–34.

———. 1985b. "Des Affairs de Coeur: Problèmes ethiques et politiques lies au developpement du coeur artificiel aux Etats-Unis." *Culture Technique* 15 (November): 165–69.

———. 1986a. "A New Dilemma: Quality, Ethics and Expensive Medical Technologies." *New York Medical Quarterly* 6 (No. 1): 23–27.

———. 1986b. "Baby Jessie and Beyond." *Update* 2 (July): 1–2.

———. 1987a. "Equity in the Selection of Recipients for Cardiac Transplants." *Circulation* 75 (January): 10–19.

————. 1987b. "Obtaining and Allocating Organs for Transplantation." In Dale H. Cowan et al. (eds.), *Human Organ Transplantation*. Ann Arbor, MI: Health Administration Press: 5–17.

————. 1989. "Getting on the List: Are 'Medical' Criteria Purely Medical? Can They Be?" Paper presented at conference on patient selection in organ transplantation, Transplant Policy Center, University of Michigan (March 14). Forthcoming in *Transplantation Proceedings*.

Cardozo, Benjamin N. 1929. "What Medicine Can Do for Law." *Bulletin of the New York Academy of Medicine*, 2d ser. 5 (July): 581–607.

Carothers, J. C. 1948. "A Study of Mental Derangement in Africans, and an Attempt to Explain its Peculiarities, More Especially in Relation to the African Attitude to Life." *Psychiatry* 11 (February): 47–86.

Carter-Jones, L. 1983. "Politics, Mortality and Economics—Are There Choices?" In F. M. Parsons and C. S. Ogg (eds.), *Renal Failure—Who Cares?* Lancaster, England: MTP: 99–106.

Casscells, Ward. 1986. "Heart Transplantation: Recent Policy Developments." *New England Journal of Medicine* 315 (November 20): 1365–68.

Cassel, Christine K. 1985a. "Doctors and Allocation Decisions: A New Role in the New Medicare." *Journal of Health Politics, Policy, and Law* 10 (Fall): 549–64.

————. 1985b. "Health Care for the Elderly: Meeting the Challenges." In Marshall B. Kapp et al. (eds.), *Legal and Ethical Aspects of Health Care for the Elderly.* Ann Arbor, MI: Health Administration Press: 3–14.

Castro, Felipe G., et al. 1987. "A Multivariate Model of the Determinants of Cigarette Smoking among Adolescents." *Journal of Health and Social Behavior* 28 (September): 273–89.

Challah, S., et al. 1984. "Negative Selection of Patients for Dialysis and Transplantation in the United Kingdom." *British Medical Journal* 288 (April 14): 1119–22.

Chambers, Marcia. 1986. "Tough Transplant Questions Raised by 'Baby Jesse' Case." *New York Times* (June 15): 1+.

Charlson, Mary E., et al. 1986. "Resuscitation: How Do We Decide?" *Journal of the American Medical Association* 255 (March 14): 1316–22.

Chell, Byron. 1988. "Competency: What It Is, What It Isn't, and Why It Matters." In John Monagle and David Thomasma (eds.), *Medical Ethics.* Rockville, MD: Aspen: 99–110.

Chester, Alexander C., et al. 1979. "Hemodialysis in the 8th and 9th Decades of Life." *Archives of Internal Medicine* 139 (September): 1001–05.

Childress, James F. 1970. "Who Shall Live When Not All Can Live?" *Soundings* 53 (Winter): 339–55.

————. 1978. "Rationing Medical Treatment." In Warren T. Reich (ed.), *Encyclopedia of Bioethics.* New York: Free Press: 1414–19.

————. 1981. "Allocating Health Care Resources." *Priorities in Medical Ethics.* Philadelphia: Westminster Press: 74–97, 129–35.

———. 1983. "Triage in Neonatal Intensive Care: The Limits of Metaphor." *Virginia Law Review* 69 (April): 547–61.

———. 1984a. "Ensuring Care, Respect, and Fairness for the Elderly." *Hastings Center Report* 14 (October): 27–31.

———. 1984b. "Rights to Health Care in a Democratic Society." In James Humber and Robert Almeder (eds.), *Biomedical Ethics Reviews*. Clifton, NJ: Humana: 47–70.

———. 1985. "The Scarcity of Human Organs for Transplantation: Charity, Justice, and Public Policy." Paper presented at a colloquium at The Wilson Center (July 9).

———. 1986a. "Artificial and Transplanted Organs." In James F. Childress et al. (eds.), *Biolaw,* vol. I. Frederick, MD: University Publications of America: 303–31.

———. 1986b. "The Gift of Life: Ethical Problems and Policies in Obtaining and Distributing Organs for Transplantation." *Critical Care Clinics* 2 (January): 133–47.

Childress, James F., et al. 1982. "Triage: Who Will Get the Last Bed in the ICU?" (video). Charlottesville, VA: University of Virginia Medical Center, Health Sciences Library.

Chinard, Francis P. 1985. "Ethics and Technology." *Journal of the Medical Society of New Jersey* 82 (February): 119–23.

Christopherson, Lois K., and Donald T. Lunde. "Selection of Cardiac Transplant Recipients and Their Subsequent Psychosocial Adjustment." *Seminars in Psychiatry* 3 (1971): 36–45.

———. 1982. "Heart Transplants." *Hastings Center Report* 12 (February): 18–21.

Churchill, Larry R. 1985. "Which Infants Should Live? On the Usefulness and Limitations of Robert Weir's Selective Nontreatment of Handicapped Newborns." *Social Science and Medicine* 20 (No. 11): 1097–1102.

———. 1987. *Rationing Health Care in America: Perceptions and Principles of Justice.* South Bend, IN: University of Notre Dame Press.

Cicero, Marcus T. 44 B.C. *De Officiis,* trans. Walter Miller. New York: Macmillan, 1913.

Civetta, Joseph M. 1976. "The ICU Milieu: An Evaluation of the Allocation of a Limited Resource." *Respiratory Care* 21 (June): 498–506.

Clark, Matt. 1983. "The New Era of Transplants." *Newsweek* (August 29): 38–44.

Clark, Matt, et al. 1981. "When Doctors Play God." *Newsweek* (August 31): 48–54.

Clark, Phillip G. 1985. "The Social Allocation of Health Care Resources: Ethical Dilemmas in Age-Group Competition." *Gerontologist* 25 (April): 119–25.

Cohen, Cynthia B. 1977. "Ethical Problems of Intensive Care." *Anesthesiology* 47 (August): 217–27.

Cole, Thomas R. 1983. "The 'Enlightened' View of Aging: Victorian Morality in a New Key." *Hastings Center Report* 13 (June): 34–40.

Colen, B. D. 1977. "A Health Care Concern." *The Washington Post* (October 31): A1,21.

———. 1986. *Hard Choices*. New York: G. P. Putnam's Sons.

Collette, John, and Peter Y. Windt. 1987. "Medical Decision-Making, Dying, and Quality of Life among the Elderly." In Timothy M. Smeeding (ed.), *Should Medical Care Be Rationed by Age?* Totowa, NJ: Rowman & Littlefield: 99–112.

Comaish, J. S. 1976. "How to Set Priorities in Medicine." *Lancet* 2 (September 4): 512–14.

Comptroller General of the United States. 1975. "Report to the Congress: Treatment of Chronic Kidney Failure: Dialysis, Transplant, Costs, and the Need for More Vigorous Efforts." Washington, D.C.: U.S. Dept. of Health, Education, and Welfare.

Connery, John R. 1983. "Implanting Artificial Heart Raises Allocation-of-Resources Issue." *Hospital Progress* 64 (April): 60–61.

Conrad, Constance C., and Nicholas G. Fotion. 1985. "'First-Come First-Served': Analysis of an Allocation Principle." *Pharos* 48 (Summer): 15–17.

Cook, D. 1987. "Long-Term Survival of Kidney Allografts." In P. I. Terasaki (ed.), *Clinical Transplants 1987*. Los Angeles: UCLA Tissue Typing Laboratory.

Cook, Robin, 1983. *Godplayer.* New York: Putnam.

Cooper, Michael H. 1975. *Rationing Health Care*. London: Croom Helm.

Cooper, Richard, and Robert Cohen. 1982. "The Language of Medicine." *New England Journal of Medicine* 307 (October 7): 958.

Cooper, Theodore. 1987. "Survey of Development, Current Status, and Future Prospects for Organ Transplantation." In Dale Cowan et al. (eds.), *Human Organ Transplantation*. Ann Arbor, MI: Health Administration: 18–26.

Copeland, Jack G., et al. 1987. "Selection of Patients for Cardiac Transplantation." *Circulation* 75 (January): 1–9.

Coulton, Claudia J. 1986. "Resource Limits and Allocation in Critical Care." In Stuart J. Youngner (ed.), *Human Values in Critical Care Medicine*. New York: Praeger: 87–108.

Crammond, W. A. 1971. "Renal Transplantation: Experiences with Recipients and Donors." *Seminars in Psychiatry* 3: 116–32.

Crane, Diana. 1977. *The Sanctity of Social Life: Physicians' Treatment of Critically Ill Patients*. New Brunswick, NJ: Transaction Books.

———. 1982. "Decisions to Treat Critically Ill Patients: A Comparison of Social Versus Medical Considerations." In John B. McKinlay (ed.), *Law and Ethics in Health Care*. Cambridge, MA: MIT Press: 372–404.

Cullen, David J. 1981. "Surgical Intensive Care: Current Perceptions and Problems." *Critical Care Medicine* 9 (April): 295–97.

Cullen, David J., and Stephanie Schwartz. 1981. "How Many Intensive Care Beds Does Your Hospital Need?" *Critical Care Medicine* 9 (March): 264.

Cummings, Nancy B. 1985. "Uremia Therapy: The Resource Allocation Dilemma from a Global Perspective." *Kidney International* 28, Suppl. 17: S133–35.

Curran, Charles E. 1973. *Politics, Medicine, and Christian Ethics.* Philadelphia: Fortress Press.

Dallek, Geraldine, and Judith Waxman. 1986. " 'Patient Dumping': A Crisis in Emergency Medical Care for the Indigent." *Clearinghouse Review* 19 (April): 1413–17.

D'Amico, G. 1983. "Treating End-Stage Renal Failure in Italy." In F. M. Parsons and C. S. Ogg (eds.), *Renal Failure—Who Cares?* Lancaster, England: MTP: 89–98.

Daniels, Norman. 1983a. "Am I My Parents' Keeper?" In President's Commission for the Study of Ethical Problems in Medicine and Biomedical and Behavioral Research, *Securing Access to Health Care,* vol. 2. Washington, D.C.: Government Printing Office (March): 265–91.

———. 1983b. "Health Care Needs and Distributive Justice." In Ronald Bayer et al. (eds.), *In Search of Equity.* New York: Plenum Press: 1–41.

———. 1985. *Just Health Care.* London: Cambridge University Press.

———. 1986. "Is Age-Rationing Just?" Paper delivered at the Pacific Section of the American Philosophical Association, San Francisco (March).

———. 1987. "The Ideal Advocate and Limited Resources." *Theoretical Medicine* 8 (February): 69–80.

———. 1988a. *Am I My Parents' Keeper? An Essay on Justice between the Young and Old.* New York: Oxford University Press.

———. 1988b. "Justice and the Dissemination of 'Big-Ticket' Technologies." In Deborah Mathieu (ed.), *Organ Substitution Technology.* Boulder, CO: Westview, 1988: 211–20.

David, David S. 1972. "The Agony and the Ecstasy of the Nephrologist." *Journal of the American Medical Association* 222: 584–85.

Davidson, Robert C., and Belding H. Scribner. 1967. "Patient Selection for Maintenance Dialysis." In R. C. Davidson and B. H. Scribner (eds.), *A Physician's Syllabus for the Treatment of Chronic Uremia.* Seattle: University of Washington and Seattle Artificial Kidney Center: 2–10.

Debakey, Michael E., and Lois Debakey. 1983. "The Ethics and Economics of High-Technology Medicine." *Comprehensive Therapy* 9 (December): 6–16.

Deber, Raisa B., et al. 1985. "The Impact of Selected Patient Characteristics on Practitioners' Treatment Recommendations for End-Stage Renal Disease." *Medical Care* 23 (February): 95–109.

Deitch, Rodney. 1984. "UK's Poor Record in Treatment of Renal Failure." *Lancet* (July 7): 53.

Del Guercio, Louis R. M. 1977. "Triage in Cold Blood." *Critical Care Medicine* 5 (July–August): 165–69.

Dempsey, David. 1974. "Transplants are Common; Now It's the Organs That Have Become Rare." *New York Times Magazine* (October 13): 40–41+.

Denny, Donald. 1983. "How Organs Are Distributed." *Hastings Center Report* 13 (December): 26–27.

DePalma, John R. 1983. "Patient Rationing or: Who Shall Live? 1984." *Dialysis and Transplantation* 12 (December): 829–30+.

Destro, Robert A. 1986. "Quality-of-Life Ethics and Constitutional Jurisprudence: The Demise of Natural Rights and Equal Protection for the Disabled and Incompetent." *Journal of Contemporary Health Law and Policy* 2 (Spring): 71–130.

Detsky, Allan S., et al. 1981. "Prognosis, Survival, and the Expenditure of Hospital Resources for Patients in an Intensive-Care Unit." *New England Journal of Medicine* 305 (September 17): 667–72.

DeVries, William C., et al. 1984. "Clinical Use of the Total Artificial Heart." *New England Journal of Medicine* 310 (February 2): 273–78.

De Wardener, H. E. 1966. "Some Ethical and Economic Problems Associated with Intermittent Haemodialysis." In G. F. W. Wolstenholme (ed.), *Ethics in Medical Progress: With Special Reference to Transplantation.* Boston: Little, Brown: 104–18.

Diamond, Louis H. 1979. "Can We Stop or Withhold Dialysis?" In George E. Schreiner (ed.), *Controversies in Nephrology—1979.* Washington, D.C.: Georgetown University, Nephrology Division: 171–80.

Dillard, Martin G., and Clive O. Callender. 1984. "End-Stage Renal Disease in Blacks: A National or International Problem?" *Journal of the National Medical Association* 76 (December): 1157–58.

"Doctor, I Want. . . ." 1980. Hard Choices Video Series. Seattle, WA: Station KCTS.

Donagan, Alan. 1977. *The Theory of Morality.* Chicago: University of Chicago Press.

"Donations Pouring in for Young Liver Patient." 1987. Associated Press News Service (e.g., in *Lexington [KY] Herald-Leader,* February 14:A2).

Douglas, James F. 1985. "Renal Failure and the Law." *Lancet* (June 8): 1319–21.

Drane, James. 1985. "The Many Faces of Competency." *Hastings Center Report* 15 (April): 17–21.

Dubos, Rene. 1967. "Individual Morality and Statistical Morality." *Annals of Internal Medicine* 67 Supplement 7 (September): 57–60.

"Due Process in the Allocation of Scarce Lifesaving Medical Resources." 1975. *Yale Law Journal* 84 (July): 1734–49.

Dukeminier, Jesse, Jr., and David Sanders. 1971. "Legal Problems in Allocation of Scarce Medical Resources: The Artificial Kidney." *Archives of Internal Medicine* 127 (June): 1133–37.

Dundas, Charles. 1913. "History of Kitui." *Journal of the Royal Anthropological Institute* 43: 480–549.

Dyck, Arthur J. 1977. *On Human Care*. Nashville: Abingdon.

Dyer, Allen R. 1986. "Patients, Not Costs, Come First." *Hastings Center Report* 16 (February): 5–7.

"Dying for Want of a Transplant: One Man's Plight; Society's Burden." 1983. *Medical World News* 24 (November 14): 49–50.

"Dying Friend Extends Life Through Heart Transplant." 1988. Associated Press News Service (e.g., in *Lexington [KY] Herald-Leader,* November 17: A10).

Ebersole, Myron. 1988. "Organ Transplants." In John Rogers (ed.), *Medical Ethics, Human Choices: A Christian Perspective*. Scottdale, PA: Herald: 103–12.

Edelhart, Mike. 1981. "Spare Body Parts." *Ambassador* (December): 60–67.

Edgerton, Robert B. 1965a. "An Ecological View of Witchcraft in Four East African Societies." Paper prepared for the Neuropsychiatric Institute, University of California, Los Angeles.

———. 1965b. "'Cultural' vs. 'Ecological' Factors in the Expression of Values, Attitudes, and Personality Characteristics." *American Anthropologist* 67 (April): 443–47.

Edlund, Matthew, and Laurence R. Tancredi. 1985. "Quality of Life: An Ideological Critique." *Perspectives in Biology and Medicine* 28 (Summer): 591–607.

Edmunds, Lavinia. 1989. "The Long Wait for a New Life." *Johns Hopkins Magazine* 41 (February): IX–XVI.

Egdahl, Richard H. 1978. "Ways for Surgeons to Increase the Efficiency of the Use of Hospitals." *New England Journal of Medicine* 309 (November 10): 1184–87.

Eglit, Howard C. 1987. *Age Discrimination*. Colorado Springs, CO: Shepard's/McGraw-Hill.

Eisenberg, John M. 1979. "Sociologic Influences on Decision-Making by Clinicians." *Annals of Internal Medicine* 90 (June): 957–64.

Elkinton, J. Russell. 1964. "Moral Problems in the Use of Borrowed Organs, Artificial and Transplanted." *Annals of Internal Medicine* 60 (February): 309–13.

———. 1973. "Ethical and Moral Problems in the Use of Artificial and Transplanted Organs." In Robert H. Williams (ed.), *To Live and to Die: When, Why, and How.* New York: Springer-Verlag: 123–33.

Elkowitz, Andrew. 1986. "Physicians at the Bedside: Practitioners' Thoughts and Actions Regarding Bedside Allocation of Resources." *Journal of Medical Humanities and Bioethics* 7 (Fall/Winter): 122–32.

Ellington, Preston D. 1978. "Right to Life, An Ethical Dilemma: A Physician's Viewpoint." *Journal of the Medical Association of Georgia* 67 (February): 131–32.

End-Stage Renal Disease Network of the Greater Capital Area. 1985. *Outcomes of Renal Transplantation in the Washington, D.C. Area 1983–1984*. Chevy Chase, MD: E.S.R.D.N.G.C.A.

Engel, Margaret. 1984. "Hospitals Refusing to Admit Poor." *Washington Post* (October 15): B1+.

Engelhardt, H. Tristram, Jr. 1976. "Individuals and Communities, Present and Future: Towards a Morality in a Time of Famine." In George R. Lucas, Jr., and Thomas W. Ogletree (eds.), *Lifeboat Ethics*. New York: Harper and Row: 70–83.

———. 1984. "Shattuck Lecture—Allocating Scarce Medical Resources and the Availability of Organ Transplantation." *New England Journal of Medicine* 311 (July 5): 66–77.

———. 1986. *The Foundations of Bioethics*. New York: Oxford University.

Engelhardt, H. Tristram, Jr., and Michael A. Rie. 1986. "Intensive Care Units, Scarce Resources, and Conflicting Principles of Justice." *Journal of the American Medical Association* 255 (March 7): 1159–64.

English, T. A., et al. 1984. "Selection and Procurement of Hearts for Transplantation." *British Medical Journal* 288 (June 23): 1889–91.

Erikson, Erik H. 1967. "Memorandum for the Conference on the Draft." In Sol Tax (ed.), *The Draft: A Handbook of Facts and Alternatives*. Chicago: University of Chicago Press: 280–83.

"Ethics and Priorities." 1976. *Journal of Medical Ethics* 2 (September): 105–06.

"Ethics and the Nephrologist." 1981. *The Lancet* (March 14): 594–96.

European Dialysis Transplantation Association. 1981. *Annual Report*. London: Pitman Medical.

"European Hospitals Less Technology-Intensive, Less Expensive than U.S.'" 1984. *Medical World News* 25 (March 12): 23–24.

Evans, J. Grimley. 1988. "Age and Equality." *Annals of the New York Academy of Sciences* 530: 118–24.

Evans, Roger W. 1983. "Health Care Technology and the Inevitability of Resource Allocation and Rationing Decisions" (2 parts). *Journal of the American Medical Association* 249 (April 15 and 22/29): 2047–53 and 2208–19.

———. 1986. "Economic Issues in Health Care Rationing." In James Hamner III and Barbara Jacobs (eds.), *Life and Death Issues*. Memphis: University of Tennessee Press: 21–40.

———. 1987. "Public Perception and the Realities of Organ Transplantation." *Michigan Hospitals* 23 (December): 13–18.

———. 1989. "Money Matters: Should Ability to Pay Ever Be a Consideration?" Paper presented at conference on patient selection criteria in organ transplantation, Transplant Policy Center, University of Michigan (March 15). Forthcoming in *Transplantation Proceedings*.

Evans, Roger W., and Diane L. Manninen. 1987. "Public Opinion Concerning Organ Donation, Procurement, and Distribution." Results of a survey conducted for UNOS by Battelle Human Affairs Research Centers, Seattle, WA. Partially published in *Transplantation Proceedings* 20 (October 1988): 781–85.

Evans, Roger W., and Junichi Yagi. 1987. "Social and Medical Considerations

Affecting Selection of Transplant Recipients: The Case of Heart Transplantation. Ann Arbor, MI: Health Administration Press: 27–41.

Evans, Roger W., et al. 1981. "Implications for Health Care Policy: A Social and Demographic Profile of Hemodialysis Patients in the United States." *Journal of the American Medical Association* 245 (February 6): 487–91.

———. 1984a. "National Policies for the Treatment of End-Stage Renal Disease." Seattle: Battelle Human Affairs Research Centers.

———. 1984b. "A Comparative Assessment of the Quality of Life of Successful Kidney Transplant Patients According to Source of Graft." *Transplantation Proceedings* 16 (October): 1353–58.

———. 1985. "The Quality of Life of Patients With End-Stage Renal Disease." *New England Journal of Medicine* 312 (February 28): 553–59.

———. 1986. "Donor Availability as the Primary Determinant of the Future of Heart Transplantation." *Journal of the American Medical Association* 255 (April 11): 1892–1898.

Ezorsky, Gertrude. 1972. "How Many Lives Shall We Save?" *Metaphilosophy* 3 (April): 156–62.

Faden, Ruth R., and Tom L. Beauchamp. 1986. *A History and Theory of Informed Consent*. New York: Oxford University Press.

Fain, Jim. 1986. "Organ Transplants: Game of Chance." Cox News Service (e.g., in *Lexington [KY] Herald-Leader*, July 24: A19).

"FDA Approves Kidney Transplant Drug." 1986. Associated Press News Service (e.g., in *Lexington [KY] Herald-Leader*, June 20: B6).

Fein, Rashi. 1982. "What Is Wrong with the Language of Medicine?" *New England Journal of Medicine* 306 (April 8): 863–64.

Feinberg, Joel. 1978. "Justice." In Warren T. Reich (ed.), *Encyclopedia of Bioethics*, vol. 2. New York: Free Press: 802–11.

Felch, William C., et al. 1982. "Should Services Be Rationed?" *The Internist* 23 (October): 4–13.

Ferrans, Carol E. 1987. "Quality of Life as a Criterion for Allocation of Life-Sustaining Treatment: The Case of Hemodialysis." In Gary Anderson and Valerie Glesnes-Anderson (eds.), *Health Care Ethics*. Rockville, MD: Aspen: 109–24.

Ferriman, Annabel. 1980. "1000 Kidney Patients Die Because Treatment Unavailable!" London *Times* (March 20): 4.

Fineberg, Harvey V. 1984. "Irresistible Medical Technologies: Weighing the Costs and Benefits." *Technology Review* 87 (November/December): 17–18+.

Flavin, Daniel K., et al. 1988. "Alcoholism and Orthotopic Liver Transplantation." *Journal of the American Medical Association* 259 (March 11): 1546–47.

Fleck, Leonard M. 1987. "DRGs: Justice and the Invisible Rationing of Health Care Resources." *Journal of Medicine and Philosophy* 12 (May): 165–96.

Fletcher, John C. 1983. "Cardiac Transplantation and the Artificial Heart: Ethical Considerations." *Circulation* 68 (December): 1339–43.

Fletcher, Joseph. 1968. "Donor Nephrectomies and Moral Responsibility." *Journal of the American Medical Women's Association* 23 (December): 1085–92.

———. 1979. *Humanhood: Essays in Biomedical Ethics.* Buffalo, NY: Prometheus Books.

Foner, Nancy. 1984. *Ages in Conflict: A Cross-Cultural Perspective on Inequality between Old and Young.* New York: Columbia University Press.

———. 1985. "Old and Frail and Everywhere Unequal." *Hastings Center Report* 15 (April): 27–31.

Foot, Philippa. 1967. "The Problem of Abortion and the Doctrine of Double Effect." *The Oxford Review* 5: 5–15.

Fox, Renée C. 1979. "The Medical Profession's Changing Outlook on Hemodialysis (1950–1976)." *Essays in Medical Sociology: Journeys into the Field.* New York: Wiley: 122–45.

———. 1981. "Exclusion from Dialysis: A Sociologic and Legal Perspective. *Kidney International* 19 (May): 739–51.

Fox, Renée C., and Judith P. Swazey. 1978a. "Kidney Dialysis and Transplantation." In Warren T. Reich (ed.), *Encyclopedia of Bioethics,* vol. 2. New York: Free Press: 811–16.

———. 1978b. *The Courage to Fail,* 2d ed. Chicago: University of Chicago Press.

Frader, Joel E. 1985. "Selecting Neonatal Ethics." *Social Science and Medicine* 20 (No. 11): 1085–90.

France. 1971. "Declaration of Rights."

Francis, John G., and Leslie P. Francis. 1987. "Rationing of Health Care in Britain: An Ethical Critique of Public Policy-making." In Timothy M. Smeeding (ed.), *Should Medical Care Be Rationed by Age?* Totowa, NJ: Rowman & Littlefield: 119–34.

Francis, Leslie P. 1986. "Poverty, Age Discrimination, and Health Care." In George R. Lucas (ed.), *Poverty, Justice, and the Law.* Lanham, MD: University Press of America: 117–29.

Frankena, William K. 1973. *Ethics,* 2d ed. Englewood Cliffs, NJ: Prentice-Hall.

Franklin, Cory M., et al. 1981. "Retrospective Analysis of Medical Intensive Care Unit Readmissions." *Critical Care Medicine* 9:263.

"Free Concert to Help Fund Liver Patients' Transplants." 1987. Associated Press News Service (e.g., in *Lexington [KY] Herald-Leader,* March 16: A2).

Freedman, Benjamin. 1977a. "The Case for Medical Care, Inefficient or Not." *Hastings Center Report* 7 (April): 31–39.

———. 1977b. "The Last Bed in the ICU: Commentary." *Hastings Center Report* 7 (December): 22.

———. 1982. "Approaches to Justice in Allocation and Distribution of Health Resources." In Harold Coward and Donald Larsen (eds.), *Ethical Issues in the Allocation of Health Care Resources.* Calgary, Alberta, Canada: Calgary Institute for the Humanities: 74–105.

———. 1983. "The Eyes of Beholders: Roles and the Distribution of Scarce Medical Resources." *Theoretical Medicine* 4 (February): 93–111.

Freund, Paul. 1969. "Introduction." *Daedalus* 98 (Spring): viii–xiv.

———. 1971. "Organ Transplants: Ethical and Legal Problems." *Proceedings of the American Philosophical Society* 115 (August): 276–81.

Fried, Charles. 1975. "Rights and Health Care—Beyond Equity and Efficiency." *New England Journal of Medicine* 293 (July 31): 241–45.

———. 1976. "Equality and Rights in Medical Care." *Hastings Center Report* 6 (February): 29–34.

Friedman, Eli A. 1983. "Is Patient Rationing in Our Future? Limit Dollars, Not Patients." *Dialysis and Transplantation* 12 (December): 836.

Friedman, Emily. 1982a. "The 'Dumping' Dilemma: The Poor Are Always with Some of Us." *Hospitals* 56 (September 1): 51–56.

———. 1982b. "The 'Dumping' Dilemma: Finding What's Fair." *Hospitals* 56 (September 16): 75–84.

———. 1984. "Rationing and the Identified Life." *Hospitals* 58 (May): 65–66+.

Friedman, Emily, and Glenn Richards. 1984. "Life and Death in a Policy Vacuum." *Hospitals* 58 (May 16): 79–80.

Friedrich, Otto. 1984. "One Miracle, Many Doubts." *Time* 124 (December 10): 70–77.

Fries, James F. 1980. "Aging, Natural Death, and the Compression of Morbidity." *New England Journal of Medicine* 303 (July 17): 130–35.

Fromer, Margot J. 1981. *Ethical Issues in Health Care.* St. Louis, MO: C. V. Mosby.

Fuchs, Victor R. 1984. "The 'Rationing' of Medical Care." *New England Journal of Medicine* 311 (December 13): 1572–73.

———. 1985. "The Rationing of Medical Care." *New England Journal of Medicine* 312 (May 16): 1332–33.

Fuller, Lon L. 1949. "The Case of the Speluncean Explorers." *Harvard Law Review* 62: 616–45.

Gabriel, Roger. 1983. "Chronic Renal Failure in the United Kingdom: Referral, Funding and Staffing." In F. M. Parsons and C. S. Ogg (eds.), *Renal Failure—Who Cares?* Lancaster, England: MTP: 34–40.

Gadow, Sally. 1980. "Existential Advocacy: Philosophical Foundation of Nursing." In Stuart Spicker and Sally Gadow (eds.), *Nursing: Images and Ideals.* New York: Springer: 79–101.

———. 1981. "Advocacy: An Ethical Model for Assisting Patients with Treatment Decisions." In Cynthia B. Wong and Judith P. Swazey (eds.), *Dilemmas of Dying.* Boston: G. K. Hall: 135–42.

Garland, Michael. 1976. "Politics, Legislation, and Natural Death: The Right to Die in California." *Hastings Center Report* 6 (October): 5–6.

Geelhoed, Glenn W. 1985. "Access to Care in a Changing Practice Environment." *Bulletin of the American College of Surgeons* 70 (June): 11–15.

Gellman, Marc A. 1984. "Triage of Resources to Patients." *Mount Sinai Journal of Medicine* 51 (January–February): 113–15.

Gentleman, Douglas, and Bryan Jennett. 1981. "Hazards of Inter-Hospital Transfer of Comatose Head-Injured Patients." *Lancet* 2 (October 17): 853–55.

Gerhardt, James M. 1971. *The Draft and Public Policy: Issues in Military Manpower Procurement 1945–1970.* Columbus: Ohio State University Press.

Getze, George. 1965. "Kidney Machines Force Doctors to Choose Patients Who Will Live." *Los Angeles Times* (July 5): 1–3 +.

Gilks, W. R., et al. 1987. "Beneficial HLA Matching: Its Phase of Impact on Graft Survival." *Transplantation Proceedings* 19 (February): 664–65.

Gillund, Gary. 1987. "Memory Processes in the Aged." In Timothy M. Smeeding (ed.), *Should Medical Care Be Rationed by Age?* Totowa, NJ: Rowman & Littlefield: 48–60.

Gillingham, John. 1976. *Cromwell: Portrait of a Soldier.* London: Weidenfeld and Nicolson.

Gillon, Raanan. 1985. "Justice and Allocation of Medical Resources." *British Medical Journal* 291 (July 27): 266–68.

Gilson, Estelle. 1983. "Who Shall Live? Who Shall Die? No Easy Answers." *Present Tense* 10 (Spring): 21–25.

Glover, Jonathan. 1977. *Causing Death and Saving Lives.* New York: Penguin Books.

Godshall, Stan. 1988. "Allocating Limited Medical Resources." In John Rogers (ed.), *Medical Ethics, Human Choices: A Christian Perspective.* Scottdale, PA: Herald: 121–31.

Goldhaber, Samuel Z., et al. 1985. "Cardiac Surgery for Adults with Mental Retardation: Dilemmas in Management." *American Journal of Medicine* (October): 403–06.

Goldman, Ralph. 1981. "Ethical Confrontations in the Incapacitated Aged." *Journal of the American Geriatrics Society* 29 (June): 241–45.

Goldstein, A. M., and M. Reznikoff. 1971. "Suicide in Chronic Hemodialysis Patients from an External Law of Control Framework." *American Journal of Psychiatry* 127 (March): 1204–07.

Good, Charles M. 1980. "A Comparison of Rural and Urban Ethnomedicine among the Kamba of Kenya." In Priscilla R. Ulin and Marshall H. Segall (eds.), *Traditional Health Care Delivery in Contemporary Africa.* Syracuse: Maxwell School of Citizenship and Public Affairs, Syracuse University: 13–56.

Gordon, Robert D., et al. 1986a. "Liver Transplantation Across ABC Blood Groups." *Surgery* 100 (August): 342–48.

———. 1986b. "The Antibody Crossmatch in Liver Transplantation." *Surgery* 100 (October): 705–15.

Gore, Albert, Jr. 1987. "National Transplantation Network: UNOS or NBC." *Update* (Loma Linda U. Ethics Ctr.) 3 (January): 3–5.

Gorney, Roderic. 1968. "The New Biology and the Future of Man." *U.C.L.A. Law Review* 15: 273–356.

Gorovitz, Samuel. 1966. "Ethics and the Allocation of Medical Resources." *Medical Research Engineering* 5 (Fourth Quarter): 5–7.

———. 1977. "Theories of Justice and Life-extending Technologies." In The Futures Group, *A Technology Assessment of Life-extending Technologies* (Supplementary Report, vol. 6). Glastonbury, CT: The Futures Group: 169–95.

———. 1984. "The Artificial Heart: Questions to Ask, and Not to Ask." *Hastings Center Report* 14 (October): 15–17.

———. 1985a. *Doctors' Dilemmas*. New York: Oxford University Press.

———. 1985b. "Global Objections to Kidney Sales: A Response to Professor Humber." In James M. Humber and Robert F. Almeder (eds.), *Biomedical Ethics Reviews*. Clifton, NJ: Humana: 27–33.

Gould, Donald. 1981. "Condemned to Live." *New Scientist* 92 (December 17): 826.

Graber, Glenn C., et al. 1985. *Ethical Analysis of Clinical Medicine*. Baltimore: Urban & Schwarzenberg.

Grad, Frank P. 1968. "Legislative Responses to the New Biology: Limits and Possibilities." *U.C.L.A. Law Review* 15: 480–509.

Green, Harold P. 1984. "An NIH Panel's Early Warnings." *Hastings Center Report* 14 (October): 13–15.

Green, Michael B. 1979. "Harris's Modest Proposal." *Philosophy* 54: 400–06.

Green, Rochelle. 1984. "Health Care Rationing: Can It Happen Here?" *Medical World News* 25 (November 12): 50–74.

Green, Ronald M. 1976. "Health Care and Justice in Contract Theory Perspective." In Robert M. Veatch and Roy Branson (eds.), *Ethics and Health Policy*. Cambridge, MA: Ballinger: 111–26.

Greenberg, Daniel S. 1982. "We Gotta Have Heart—But Not This One." *Washington Post* (December 12): C5.

Greenberg, Roger P., et al. 1973. "The Psychological Evaluation of Patients for a Kidney Transplant and Hemodialysis Program." *American Journal of Psychiatry* 130 (March): 274–77.

Greene, Wade. 1975. "Triage." *The New York Times Magazine*. (January 5): 9–11+.

Greenfield, Sheldon, et al. 1987. "Patterns of Care Related to Age of Breast Cancer Patients." *Journal of the American Medical Association* 257 (May 22/29): 2766–70.

Greifer, Ira. 1984. "Triage: From Departments to Patients." *Mount Sinai Journal of Medicine* 51 (January–February): 110–12.

Grimes, David S. 1987. "Rationing Health Care." *Lancet* 1 (March 14): 615–16.

Gross, Richard H., et al. 1983. "Early Management and Decision Making for the Treatment of Myclomeningocele." *Pediatrics* 72 (October): 450–58.

Gruson, Lindsey. 1985. "Some Doctors Move to Bar Transplants to Foreign Patients." *New York Times* (August 10): 1, 5.

Gunby, Phil. 1982. "Utah Group to Implant 'Jarvik 7' Heart Soon." *Journal of the American Medical Association* 248 (October 22/29): 1944–46.

———. 1983. "Media-Abetted Liver Transplants Raise Questions of 'Equity and Decency.'" *Journal of the American Medical Association* 249 (April 15): 1973:74 +.

Gustafson, James M. 1975. "Ain't Nobody Gonna Cut on My Head!'" *Hastings Center Report* 5 (February): 49–50.

———. 1977. "Interdependence, Finitude, and Sin: Reflections on Scarcity." *Journal of Religion* 57 (April): 156–68.

Gutmann, Mary C., et al. 1982. "Coronary Artery Bypass Patients and Work Status." *Circulation* 66, Supplement 3 (November): 32–42.

Haber, Paul A. 1986. "Rationing is a Reality." *Journal of the American Geriatrics Society* 14 (October): 761–63.

Hackett, George W. 1986. "Louisville's Baby Calvin Gets New Heart." Associated Press News Service (e.g., in *Lexington [KY] Herald-Leader,* June 14: B1).

Hall, Jerome. 1960. *General Principles of Criminal Law,* 2d ed. Indianapolis: Bobbs-Merrill.

Hallan, Jerome B., and Benjamin S. H. Harris. 1970. "Estimation of a Potential Hemodialysis Population." *Medical Care* 8 (May–June): 209–20.

Halper, Thomas. 1985. "Life and Death in a Welfare State: End-stage Renal Disease in the United Kingdom." *Milbank Memorial Fund Quarterly* 63 (Winter): 52–93.

Hamburger, Jean. 1981. "The Future of Transplantation." *Transplantation Proceedings* 13 (March): 10–12.

Hanink, J. G. 1976. "On the Survival Lottery." *Philosophy* 51 (April): 223–25.

Hardin, Garrett. 1980. *Promethean Ethics: Living with Death, Competition, and Triage.* Seattle: University of Washington Press.

Hardwig, John. 1987. "Robin Hoods and Good Samaritans: The Role of Patients in Health Care Distribution." *Theoretical Medicine* 8 (February): 47–59.

Harris, John. 1975. "The Survival Lottery." *Philosophy* 50 (January): 81–87.

———. 1987. "QALYfying the Value of Life." *Journal of Medical Ethics* 13 (September): 117–23.

Harris, J. Gordon. 1987. *God and the Elderly.* Philadelphia: Fortress.

Harris, K. R., et al. 1985. "Azathioprine and Cyclosporine: Different Tissue-Matching Criteria Needed?" *Lancet* 2 (October 12) 802–04.

Harron, Frank, et al. 1983. *Health and Human Values.* New Haven: Yale University Press.

Harvey, Joseph H. 1980. "The Unanswered Questions." *Boston Globe* (April 7): 16.

Hasofer, A. M. 1976. "Studies in the History of Probability and Statistics: Random Mechanisms in Talmudic Literature." *Biometrika* 54: 316–21.

Hastings Center. 1986. "At the Center." *Hastings Center Report* 16 (June): cover.

————. 1987. *Guidelines on the Termination of Life-Sustaining Treatment and the Care of the Dying*. Briarcliff Manor, NY: Hastings Center.

Hastings Center Research Group. 1979. "Values and Life-Extending Technologies." In Robert M. Veatch (ed.), *Life Span*. San Francisco: Harper and Row: 29–79.

Haviland, James W. 1965. "Experiences in Establishing a Community Artificial Kidney Center." *Transactions of the American Clinical and Climatological Association* 77 (October): 125–36.

Hayes, Charles P., Jr., and J. Caulie Gunnells, Jr. 1969. "Selection of Recipients and Donors for Renal Transplantation." *Archives of Internal Medicine* 123 (May): 521–30.

Hays, Samuel H. 1967. "A Military View of Selective Service." In Sol Tax (ed.), *The Draft: A Handbook of Facts and Alternatives*. Chicago: University of Chicago Press: 7–22.

"Health-Care Costs Rise to Record Level." 1986. Associated Press News Service (e.g., in *Lexington [KY] Herald-Leader,* July 30: A2).

Hearn, Thomas K. 1977. "The Allocation of Medical Resources—Who Should Decide and How." *Alabama Journal of Medical Sciences* 14 (July): 319–21.

Held, Philip J., et al. 1988. "Access to Kidney Transplantation: Has the U.S. Eliminated Income and Racial Differences?" *Archives of Internal Medicine* 148 (December): 2594–2600.

Hellegers, Andre F. 1977. "A Lottery for Lives?" *O. B. Gyn. News* 12: 20–21.

Hendee, William R. 1986. "Rationing Health Care." In James Hamner III and Barbara Jacobs (eds.), *Life and Death Issues*. Memphis: University of Tennessee Press: 1–10.

Henikoff, Leo M. 1986. "Rationing and Allocation of Health Care Services and Technologies." Address given at the joint A.M.A.–Hastings Center conference "A New Ethic for the New Medicine?" New Orleans (March 14–16).

Henry, Mark C., et al. 1986. "Economic Triage: Emergency Physicians Should Say 'No.'" *Annals of Emergency Medicine* 15 (August): 983–84.

Hentoff, Nat. 1984. "Life-and-Death Lottery in the Nursery." *Washington Post* (April 19): A21.

Hewetson, Debra S. 1982. "Scarce Medical Resource Allocation—The Case of First Impression: A Hypothetical Opinion of the Twelfth Circuit United States Court of Appeals." *Journal of Legal Medicine* 3 (June): 295–315.

Heymann, David L. 1981. "Expanded Programme on Immunization (Childhood Mortality in Thailand)." Report to the World Health Organization, South-East Asia Region, on WHO Project THA EPI 001. July 13.

Hilfiker, David. 1983. "Allowing the Debilitated to Die: Facing Our Ethical Choices." *New England Journal of Medicine* 308 (March 24): 716–19.

Himmelstein, David U., et al. 1984. "Patient Transfers: Medical Practice as Social Triage." *American Journal of Public Health* 74 (May): 494–97.

Hiatt, Howard H. 1987. *America's Health in the Balance: Choice or Chance?* New York: Harper and Row.

Hicks, Neville. 1985. "Public Health, Public Policy and 'Neon' Issues in Ethics." *Medical Journal of Australia* 143 (August 5): 104–07.

Hinds, Stuart W. 1975. "Triage in Medicine." In George R. Lucas (ed.), *Triage in Medicine and Society*. Houston: Texas Medical Center, Institute of Religion and Human Development.

———. 1976. "On the Relations of Medical Triage to World Famine: An Historical Survey." *Soundings* 59 (Spring): 29–51.

Hingson, Ralph, et al. 1981. *In Sickness and in Health*. St. Louis, MO: C. V. Mosby.

Hobley, C. W. 1910. *Ethnology of A-Kamba and Other East African Tribes*. Cambridge: Frank Cass.

Holzman, David. 1986. "Intensive Care Nurses: A Vital Sign." *Insight* (December 1): 56.

Horn, John L. 1987. "Comments on Gillund's 'Memory Processes in the Aged.'" In Timothy M. Smeeding (ed.), *Should Medical Care Be Rationed by Age?* Totowa, NJ: Rowman & Littlefield: 61–68.

Hors, J., et al. 1987. "Dissection of the Respective Importance of HLA-A,B,DR Matching in 3,789 Prospective Kidney Transplants." *Transplantation Proceedings* 19 (February): 687–88.

"Hospital to Consider Baby for Transplant." 1986. Associated Press News Service (e.g., in *Lexington [KY] Herald-Leader,* June 6: A3).

Hostler, John. 1977. "The Right to Life." *Journal of Medical Ethics* 3 (September): 143–45.

Howard, Richard J., and John S. Najarian. 1978. "Organ Transplantation: Medical Perspective." In Warren T. Reich (ed.), *Encyclopedia of Bioethics,* vol. 3. New York: Free Press: 1160–66.

Hudson, Robert P. 1975. "How Real Is Our Reverence for Life?" *Prism* 3 (June): 18–21 + .

Hughes, Colin. 1985a. "Call for Inquiry on Kidney Patient." London *Times* (January 8): 3.

———. 1985b. "Decision to Stop Treating Kidney Patient Taken 'On Medical Grounds.'" London *Times* (January 9): 3.

Humber, James M. 1985. "Coercion, Paternalism, and the Buying and Selling of Human Organs." In James Humber and Robert Almeder (eds.), *Biomedical Ethics Reviews*. Clifton, NJ: Humana Press: 13–26.

Hume, David M., et al. 1966. "Comparative Results of Cadaver and Related Donor Renal Homographs in Man, and Immunologic Implications of the Outcome of Second and Paired Transplants." *Annals of Surgery* 164 (September): 352–97.

Hunsicker, L. G., et al. 1987. "Selection of Kidney Recipients." *Journal of the American Medical Association* 258 (September 11): 1329.

Hunter, Thomas H., et al. 1980. "Heart Transplants: Pros and Cons" (video). Charlottesville, VA: University of Virginia Medical Center, Health Sciences Library.

Hutchinson, Tom A., et al. 1982. "Predicting Survival in Adults with End-Stage Renal Disease: An Age Equivalence Index." *Annals of Internal Medicine* 96 (April): 417–23.

Hyatt, Jim. 1969. "The Cost of Living: Some Kidney Patients Die for Lack of Funds for Machine Treatment." *Wall Street Journal* (March 10): 1, 25.

Hyman, Allen I. 1980. "Commentary on Belliotti's 'Allocation of Resources.' " *Values and Ethics in Health Care* 5: 263–65.

———. 1986. "Ethical Considerations in Intensive Care." In Frederic Herter et al. (eds.), *Human and Ethical Issues in the Surgical Care of Patients with Life-Threatening Disease.* Springfield, IL: Charles C. Thomas: 39–43.

Iglehart, John K. 1982. "Funding the End-Stage-Renal-Disease Program." *New England Journal of Medicine* 306 (February 25): 492–96.

———. 1983. "Transplantation: The Problem of Limited Resources." *New England Journal of Medicine* 309 (July 14): 123–28.

———. 1984. "The British National Health Service under the Conservatives—Part II." *New England Journal of Medicine* 310 (January 5): 63–67.

"Infant Sent Away by Hospital, Dies." 1981. *St. Louis Post-Dispatch* (July 5): 14A.

Ingman, Stanley R., et al. 1987. "ESRD and the Elderly: Cross-National Perspective on Distributive Justice." In Stuart Spicker et al. (eds.), *Ethical Dimensions of Geriatric Care.* Boston: D. Reidel: 223–62.

"In Organ Transplants, Americans First?" 1986. *Hastings Center Report* 16 (October): 23.

Institute of International Law. 1929. "International Declaration of the Rights of Man."

Institute of Medicine. 1973. "Disease by Disease Toward National Health Insurance? Implications of a Categorical Catastrophic Disease Approach to National Health Insurance." Washington, D.C.: National Academy of Sciences.

Irvine, Donald. 1973. "Doctors and Society." In "Priorities in Medicine." *British Medical Journal* 2, No. 5867 (June 16): 649–50.

Ismach, Judy M. 1981. "The Smallest Patients." *Medical World News* 22 (September 14): 28–36.

Iwatsuki, Shunzaburo, et al. 1988. "Experience in 1000 Liver Transplants under Cyclosporine-Steroid Therapy: A Survival Report." *Transplantation Proceedings* 20 (February): 498–504.

Jackson, David L., and George J. Annas. 1986. "The Introduction of Major Organ Transplantation on the State Level: Ethical and Practical Considerations in the Development of Public Policy." In Stuart Youngner (ed.), *Human Values in Critical Care Medicine.* New York: Praeger: 109–22.

Jacobs, Donald R. 1961. "The Culture Themes and Puberty Rites of the Akamba." Ph.D. dissertation. New York: New York University.

Jacobs, Louis. 1978. "Greater Love Hath No Man . . . The Jewish Point of View of Self-Sacrifice." In Menachem Kellner (ed.), *Contemporary Jewish Ethics.* New York: Sanhedrin Press Book, Hebrew Publishing Co.: 175–83.

Jamieson, Dale. 1988. "The Artificial Heart: Reevaluating the Investment." In Deborah Mathieu (ed.), *Organ Substitution Technology*. Boulder, CO: Westview: 277–93.

Jennett, Bryan. 1984a. *High Technology Medicine*. London: Nuffield Provincial Hospitals Trust.

———. 1984b. "Inappropriate Use of Intensive Care." *British Medical Journal* 289 (December 22/29): 1709–11.

Joesten, Leroy B. 1987. "What's at Stake in Informed Consent?" *Second Opinion* 6 (November): 128–34.

Johnson, Roger S. 1986. "Restrictive Policies Voted on by U.S. Task Force on Organ Transplantation." *Contemporary Dialysis and Nephrology* 7: 18, 20.

Johnson, Timothy, et al. 1985. "Medical Miracles: Can We Afford the Bill?" ABC News Nightline (August 29).

Jonasson, Olga, 1986. "In Organ Transplants, Americans First?" *Hastings Center Report* 16 (October): 24–25.

———. 1989. "Waiting in Line: Should Selected Patients Ever Be Moved Up?" Paper presented at conference on patient selection criteria in organ transplantation, Transplant Policy Center, University of Michigan (March 14). Forthcoming in *Transplantation Proceedings*.

Jonasson, Olga, and John A. Barrett. 1987. "Transfer of Unstable Patients: Dumping or Duty?" *Journal of the American Medical Association* 257 (March 20): 1519.

Jones, Gary E. 1985. "Preferential Treatment and the Allocation of Scarce Medical Resources." *Philosophical Quarterly* 35 (October): 382–93.

Jonsen, Albert R. 1973. "The Totally Implantable Artificial Heart." *Hastings Center Report* 3 (November): 1–4.

———. 1979. "Ethical Problems in Home Total Parenteral Nutrition," *Journal of Parenteral and Enteral Nutrition* 3 (May–June): 169–70.

———. 1985. "Organ Transplants and the Principle of Fairness." *Law, Medicine and Health Care* 13 (February): 37–39, 44.

———. 1986. "The Artificial Heart's Threat to Others." *Hastings Center Report* 16 (February): 9–11.

Jonsen, Albert R., and George Lister. 1978. "Life-Support Systems." In Warren T. Reich (ed.), *Encyclopedia of Bioethics,* vol. 2. New York: Free Press: 840–48.

Jonsen, Albert R., and Michael J. Garland. 1976. "A Moral Policy for Life/Death Decisions in the Intensive Care Nursery." In A. R. Jonsen and M. J. Garland (eds.), *Ethics of Newborn Intensive Care*. San Francisco: University of California Health Policy Program: 142–55.

Jonsen, Albert R., et al. 1975. "Critical Issues in Newborn Intensive Care: A Conference Report and Policy Proposal." *Pediatrics* 55 (June): 756–68.

———. 1982. *Clinical Ethics*. New York: Macmillan.

"Judge Asks a Busing Lottery." *New York Times* (August 7): A13.

Kabwegyere, T., and J. Mbula. 1979. *A Case of the Akamba of Eastern Kenya.* The Changing African Family Project Series, Monograph No. 5. Canberra: Australian National University.

Kahaner, Larry, and Anthony Durniak. "The Dangers of Letting Lady Luck Award Fee Licences." *Business Week* (July 26): 54.

Kamm, Frances M. 1985. "Equal Treatment and Equal Chances." *Philosophy and Public Affairs* 14 (Spring): 177–94.

———. 1987. "The Choice between People: 'Common Sense' Morality, and Doctors." *Bioethics* 1 (July): 255–71.

Kanoti, George A. 1985. "Informed Consent in the Transplant Patient: A Year's Activity Screening Cardiac, Liver, and Pancreas/Renal Patients." Paper presented at the Annual Meeting of the Society for Health and Human Values, Washington, D.C., October 26.

———. 1986. "Ethical Considerations in Solid Organ Pediatric Transplants." *Transplantation Proceedings* 18 (June, Suppl. 2): 43–46.

Kant, Immanuel. 1964. *Groundwork of the Metaphysics of Morals,* trans. H. J. Paton. New York: Harper and Row.

Kass, Leon. 1985. "The New Biology: What Price Relieving Man's Estate?" *Toward a More Natural Science.* New York: Free Press: 17–42.

Katz, Alfred H. 1967. "Who Shall Survive?" *Medical Opinion and Review* 3 (March): 52–61.

———. 1970. "Patients in Chronic Hemodialysis in the United States: A Preliminary Survey." *Social Science and Medicine* 3: 669–77.

———. 1973. "Process Design for Selection of Hemodialysis and Organ Transplant Recipients." *Buffalo Law Review* 22 (Winter): 373–418.

Katz, A. H., and D. M. Procter. 1969. "Social-Psychological Characteristics of Patients Receiving Hemodialysis Treatment for Chronic Renal Failure." U.S. Department of Health, Education, and Welfare, Kidney Disease Control Program. Washington, D.C.: Government Printing Office.

Katz, Jay, and Alexander M. Capron. 1975. *Catastrophic Diseases: Who Decides What?* New York: Russell Sage Foundation.

Kaufman, D., ct al. 1988. "Rcnal Allograft Functional Survival Rates for Kidneys from Zero Halotype Matched Sibling Donors." XII International Congress of the Transplantation Society.

Kaye, Michael. 1981. "Triage and the Patient with Renal Failure." *Journal of Medical Ethics* 7 (June): 111.

Kayser-Jones, Jeanie S. 1986. "Distributive Justice and the Treatment of Acute Illness in Nursing Homes." *Social Science and Medicine* 23 (No. 12): 1279–86.

Kellermann, Arthur L., and Bela B. Hackman. 1988. "Emergency Department Patient 'Dumping': An Analysis of Interhospital Transfers to the Regional Medical Center at Memphis, Tennessee." *American Journal of Public Health* 78 (October): 1287–92.

Kellermann, Arthur L., and Terrence F. Ackerman. 1988. "Interhospital Patient Transfer: The Case for Informed Consent." *New England Journal of Medicine* 319 (September 8): 643–47.

Kendall, Maurice. 1968. "Chance." In Philip P. Wiener (ed.), *Dictionary of the History of Ideas,* vol. I. New York: Charles Scribners Sons: 335–40.

Kennedy, Arthur C. 1981. "The Problem of ESRD in Developing Countries." In *Proceedings of the 8th International Congress of Nephrology.* Athens: 584–89.

Kennedy, Ian M. 1981. *The Unmasking of Medicine.* Boston: Allen and Unwin.

Kerr, D. N. S. 1967. "Regular Hemodialysis." *Royal Society of Medicine Proceedings* 60: 1, 195–99.

Kessel, Ross. 1985. "Triage: Philosophical and Cross-Cultural Perspectives." In John C. Moskop and Loretta Kopelman (eds.), *Ethics and Critical Care Medicine.* Boston: D. Reidel: 207–14.

Khoo, Oon T. 1982. "The Social Issues and Ethics of End Stage Renal Disease (ESRD) Management." *Singapore Medical Journal* 23 (February): 4–11.

Kilner, John F. 1981. "A Moral Allocation of Scarce Lifesaving Medical Resources." *Journal of Religious Ethics* 9 (Fall): 245–85.

———. 1983a. "Hurdles for Natural Law Ethics: Lessons from Grotius." *American Journal of Jurisprudence* 28: 149–68.

———. 1983b. "Who Shall Be Saved? An Ethical Analysis of Major Approaches to the Allocation of Scarce Lifesaving Medical Resources." Ann Arbor, MI: University Microfilms (Ph.D. dissertation, Harvard University).

———. 1984. "Who Shall Be Saved? An African Answer." *Hastings Center Report* 14 (June): 18–22.

———. 1986a. "Who Receives Scarce Medical Resources? An Empirical and Ethical Study." In Alan B. Anderson (ed.), *The Annual of the Society of Christian Ethics.* Washington, D.C.: Georgetown University Press: 157–201.

———. 1986b. "A Needy World—A Needed Word: Scarce Medical Resources and the Christian Story." *Asbury Theological Journal* 41 (Fall): 23–58.

———. 1988. "Selecting Patients When Resources Are Limited: A Study of U.S. Medical Directors of Kidney Dialysis and Transplantation Facilities." *American Journal of Public Health* 78 (February): 144–47.

King, Thomas C. 1986. "Ethical Dilemmas of Restricted Resources." In Frederic Herter et al. (eds.), *Human and Ethical Issues in the Surgical Care of Patients with Life-Threatening Disease.* Springfield, IL: Charles C. Thomas: 169–75.

Kirby, Michael D. 1986. "Bioethical Decisions and Opportunity Costs." *Journal of Contemporary Health Law and Policy* 2 (Spring): 7–21.

Kirk, Kenneth E. 1927. *Conscience and Its Problems.* London: Longmans.

Kirklin, John W. 1977. "The Allocation of Medical Resources—Who Should Decide and How." *Alabama Journal of Medical Sciences* 14 (July): 316–18.

Kjellstrand, Carl, et al. 1986. "Ethical Controversies in Nephrology." *Dialysis and Transplantation* 15 (June): 300–05+.

Klein, Rudolf. 1984. "Rationing Health Care." *British Medical Journal* 289 (July 21): 143–44.

Kleinig, John I. 1986. "In Organ Transplants, Americans First?" *Hastings Center Report* 16 (October): 25.

———. 1989. "Non-Immigrant Aliens." Paper presented at conference on patient selection criteria in organ transplantation, Transplant Policy Center, University of Michigan (March 15). Forthcoming in *Transplantation Proceedings*.

Kluge, Eike-Henner W. 1979. "The Allocation of Limited Medical Resources in Crisis Contexts and the Principle of Double Effect." In James B. Wilbur (ed.), *The Life Sciences and Human Values: Proceedings of the Thirteenth Conference on Value Inquiry, SUNY-Genesco*. Genesco, NY: State University, College of Art & Sciences: 94–106.

Knapp, Martin S. 1982. "Renal Failure—Dilemmas and Developments." *British Medical Journal* 284 (March 20): 847–50.

Knaus, William A. 1986. "Rationing, Justice, and the American Physician." *Journal of the American Medical Association* 255 (March 7): 1176–77.

Knaus, William A., et al. 1982. "A Comparison of Intensive Care in the U.S.A. and France." *Lancet* 2 (September 18): 642–46.

———. 1983. "The Use of Intensive Care: New Research Initiatives and Their Implications for National Health Policy." *Milbank Memorial Fund Quarterly/Health and Society* 61 (Fall): 561–83.

———. 1985. "APACHE II: A Severity of Disease Classification System." *Critical Care Medicine* 13 (October): 818–29.

Knowles, John H. 1977a. "The Responsibility of the Individual." *Daedalus* 106 (Winter): 57–80.

———. 1977b. "Responsibility for Health." *Science* 198 (December 16): 1103.

Knox, Richard A. 1978. "Vision of 1998: Artificial Hearts Allotted by Lottery." *Boston Globe* (May 1): 1+.

———. 1980. "Heart Transplants: To Pay or Not to Pay." *Science* 209 (August 1): 570–72+.

———. 1984. "Fund Cuts Are Linked to Infant Death Rise." *Boston Globe* (May 24): 1+.

Kohrman, Arthur F. 1985. "Selection Nontreatment of Handicapped Newborns: A Critical Essay." *Social Science and Medicine* 20 (No. 11): 1091–95.

Kolata, Gina B. 1980. "Dialysis after Nearly a Decade." *Science* 208 (May 2): 473–76.

———. 1983a. "Organ Shortage Clouds New Transplant Era." *Science* 221 (July 1): 32–33.

———. 1983b. "Liver Transplants Endorsed." *Science* 221 (July 8): 139.

Kolff, Willem J. 1964. "Letters and Comments." *Annals of Internal Medicine* 61 (August): 359–61.

———. 1983. "Is Patient Rationing in Our Future? Are We Returning to Life and Death Committees?" *Dialysis and Transplantation* 12 (December): 832–36.

Kopelman, Loretta M. 1985. "Justice and the Hippocratic Tradition of Acting for the Good of the Sick." In John C. Moskop and Loretta Kopelman (eds.), *Ethics and Critical Care Medicine.* Boston: D. Reidel: 79–103.

Koppel, Ted, et al. 1986. "Who Lives, Who Dies, Who Decides?" (video of national teleconference). San Francisco: Pacific Presbyterian Medical Center.

Kotulak, Ronald. 1986a. "Poor Patients Given the Silent Treatment." *Chicago Tribune* (July 14): 1, 4.

———. 1986b. "Never-Say-Die Policy Prompts Rationing Call." *Chicago Tribune* (July 15): 1+.

Koughan, Martin. 1975. "Goodbye, San Francisco: Measuring the Effect of the Inevitable Earthquake." *Harper's Magazine* (September): 30–36.

Krakauer, Henry, et al. 1983. "Assessment of Prognostic Factors and Projection of Outcomes in Renal Transplantation." *Transplantation* 36 (October): 372–78.

Krauthammer, Charles. 1986. "Lifeboat Ethics: The Case of Baby Jesse." *Washington Post* 109 (June 13): A19.

Kunstadter, Peter. 1980. "Medical Ethics in Cross-Cultural and Multi-Cultural Perspectives." *Social Science and Medicine* 14B (November): 289–96.

Kutner, Nancy G. 1982. "Cost-Benefit Issues in U.S. National Health Legislation: The Case of the End-Stage Renal Disease Program." *Social Problems* 30 (October): 51–64.

———. 1987. "Issues in the Application of High Cost Medical Technology: The Case of Organ Transplantation." *Journal of Health and Social Behavior* 28 (March): 23–36.

Lachs, John. 1976. "Questions of Life and Death." *Wall Street Journal* (March 31): 8.

Lactantius, Lucius C. F. 311. *The Divine Institutes,* trans. William Fletcher. In A. Cleveland Coxe (rev. ed.), *The Ante-Nicene Fathers,* vol. 7. Grand Rapids, MI: Wm. B. Eerdmans, 1951: 9–223.

Langtry, Bruce. 1977. "Young on Decisions Concerning Medical Aid." *Theory and Decision* 8 (October): 377–79.

La Puma, John, et al. 1988. "Ethics, Economics, and Endocarditis: The Physician's Role in Resource Allocation." *Archives of Internal Medicine* 48 (August): 1809–11.

Larby, N. 1944. *The Kamba.* Nairobi: W. Boyd.

Large, B., and Rasheed Ahmad. 1981. "Audit in Renal Failure." *British Medical Journal* 283 (August 22): 556–57.

Larson, David R. 1986. "What Should Transplant Committees Consider?" *Update* 2 (July): 7.

Lasagna, Louis. 1970. "Physicians' Behavior Toward the Dying Patient." In Orville B. Brim, Jr., et al. (eds.), *The Dying Patient.* New York: Russell Sage Foundation: 83–101.

Lavell, Michael J. 1977. "An Economic Analysis of Resource Allocation for Care of the Aged." *Hospital Progress* 57 (September): 99–103.

Lawrence, Susan V. 1980. "Heart Transplants: Blessing or Boondoggle?" *Forum on Medicine* 3 (July): 441–45.

Lawson, Herbert. 1963. "Kidney Machines Saved 'Doomed' Lives but Raise Ethical Issues." *Wall Street Journal* (August 22): 1, 12.

Lawton, Richard L. 1979. "Living Non-related Donor." In George E. Schreiner (ed.), *Controversies in Nephrology—1979.* Washington, D.C.: Georgetown University, Nephrology Division: 226–37.

Leach, Gerald. 1972. *The Biocrats: Ethics and the New Medicine.* Baltimore: Penguin Books.

Leaf, Alexander. 1980. "The MGH Trustees Say No to Heart Transplants." *New England Journal of Medicine* 302 (May 8): 1087–88.

———. 1984. "The Doctor's Dilemma—and Society's Too." *New England Journal of Medicine* 310 (March 15): 718–21.

Leake, Chauncey D. 1967. "Technical Triumphs and Moral Muddles." *Annals of Internal Medicine* 67 (Suppl., September): 43–50.

Leb, Daniel E. 1980. "Moral Issues in End Stage Renal Disease." *Dialysis and Transplantation* 9 (May): 432–33.

Lebacqz, Karen. 1977. "On 'Natural Death.'" *Hastings Center Report* 7 (April): 14.

Lederberg, Joshua. 1966. "The 'Heart Gap' Will Cause Soul-Ache." *Washington Post* (July 24): E7.

Lederer, Daniel H., and Dan W. Brock. 1987. "Surgical Risks and Advance Directives." *Hastings Center Report* 17 (August): 18–19.

Leenen, H. J. J. 1979. "The Selection of Patients in the Event of a Scarcity of Medical Facilities—An Unavoidable Dilemma." *International Journal of Medicine and Law* 12 (Fall): 161–80.

———. 1982. "Selection of Patients." *Journal of Medical Ethics* 8 (March): 33–36.

Lefebvre, Diane. 1980. "Allocations of Scarce Medical Resources." In Sanford A. Lakoff (ed.), *Science and Ethical Responsibility.* Reading, MA: Addison-Wesley: 179–86.

Lefton, Doug. 1984. "Public Hospital Limits Care to Tampa's Poor." *American Medical News* 27 (April 20): 1+.

Leibel, Rudolph L. 1977. "Thanatology and Medical Economics." *New England Journal of Medicine* 296 (March): 511–13.

Leiman, Sid Z. 1978. "The Ethics of Lottery." *Kennedy Institute Quarterly Report* 4 (Summer): 8–11.

———. 1983. "Therapeutic Homicide: A Philosophic and Halakkic Critique of Harris' 'Survival Lottery.'" *Journal of Medicine and Philosophy* 8 (August): 257–67.

Levenson, S. A., et al. 1981. "Ethical Considerations in Critical and Terminal Illness in the Elderly." *Journal of the American Geriatrics Society* 29: 563–67.

Levine, Carol. 1985. "Stopping Dialysis for 'Low Quality' of Life: A Case from Britain." *Hastings Center Report* 15 (February): 2–3.

———. 1986. "Killing the Messenger: The Bad News about Ending Dialysis." *Hastings Center Report* 16 (August): 3–4.

Levine, Carol, and Robert M. Veatch (eds.). 1984. *Cases in Bioethics,* rev. ed. Hastings-on-Hudson, NY: Hastings Center.

Levine, Robert J. 1984. "Total Artificial Heart Transplantation—Eligibility Criteria." *Journal of the American Medical Association* 252 (September 21): 1458–59.

Levinsky, Norman G. 1984. "The Doctor's Master." *New England Journal of Medicine* 311 (December 13): 1573–75.

———. 1986. "Health Care for Veterans: The Limits of Obligation." *Hastings Center Report* 16 (August): 10–15.

Lewin, Roger. 1987. "National Academy Looks at Human Genome Project, Sees Progress." *Science* 235 (February 13): 747–48.

Lieberman, Saul. 1963. "How Much Greek in Jewish Palestine?" In Alexander Altmann (ed.), *Biblical and Other Studies.* Cambridge: Harvard University Press: 123–41.

Lindblom, Gerhard. 1920. *The Akamba in British East Africa.* 2d ed. Uppsala: J. A. Lundell.

———. 1935. "Kamba Tales of Supernatural Beings and Adventures." *Archives d'Etudes Orientales* 20:2.

Linzer, Mark. 1984. "Doing What 'Needs' to be Done." *New England Journal of Medicine* 310 (February 16): 469–70.

"Liver Transplantation—Consensus Conference." 1983. *Journal of the American Medical Association* 250 (December 2): 2961–64.

Lo, Bernard. 1988. "Quality of Life Judgments in the Care of the Elderly." In John Monagle and David Thomasma (eds.), *Medical Ethics.* Rockville, MD: Aspen: 140–47.

Lockwood, Michael. 1987. "Qualite de la vie et affectation des resources." *Revue de Metaphysique et de Morale* 92 (July–September): 307–28.

Loewy, Erich H. 1980. "Cost Should Not Be a Factor in Medical Care." *New England Journal of Medicine* 302 (March 20): 697.

———. 1987. "Drunks, Livers, and Values: Should Social Value Judgments Enter into Liver Transplant Decisions?" *Journal of Clinical Gastroenterology* 9 (August): 436–41.

Lomasky, Loren E. 1981. "Medical Progress and National Health Care." *Philosophy and Public Affairs* 10 (Winter): 65–88.

Longman, Phillip. 1987. *Born to Pay.* Boston: Houghton Mifflin.

Lubeck, Deborah P., and John P. Bunker. 1982. "The Artificial Heart: Costs, Risks, and Benefits." In Barbara J. McNeil and Ernest G. Cravalho (eds.), *Critical Issues in Medical Technology.* Boston: Auburn House: 371–79.

———. 1984. "Considering an Artificial Heart Program." In Stanley Reiser and Michael Anbar (eds.), *The Machine at the Beside.* Cambridge: Cambridge University Press: 247–51.

Lubitz, James, and Ronald Prihoda. 1984. "The Use and Costs of Medicare Services in the Last Two Years of Life." *Health Care Financing Review* 5 (Spring): 117–31.

Lundberg, George D. 1983a. "Rationing Human Life." *Journal of the American Medical Association* 249 (April 22/29): 2223–24.

———. 1983b. "License to Plunder or to Paint." *Journal of the American Medical Association* 250 (December 2): 2966–67.

Luthy, David. 1975. "A Survey of Amish Ordination Customs." *Family Life* (March): 13–17.

Lyon, Jeff. 1983. *Playing God in the Nursery.* Chicago: Chicago Tribune.

———. 1986. "Organ Transplants: Conundra Without End." *Second Opinion* 2 (March): 40–64.

Lyons, Catherine. 1970. *Organ Transplants: The Moral Issues.* Philadelphia: Westminster Press.

Lyons, David. 1976. "Mill's Theory of Morality." *Nous* 10 (May): 101–20.

Macek, Catherine. 1983. "Cyclosporine's Acceptance Heralds New Era in Immunopharmacology." *Journal of the American Medical Association* 250 (July 22/29): 449–55.

Mackenzie, Richard. 1986. "Lottery Madness." *Insight* (March 17): 6–16.

Macklin, Ruth. 1984. "Ethical Issues in Treatment of Patients with End-Stage Renal Disease." *Social Work in Health Care* 9 (Summer): 11–20.

———. 1985a. "Ethical Problems in Rationing Medical Care." *Infection Control* 6 (September): 375–76.

———. 1985b. "Are We in the Lifeboat Yet? Allocation and Rationing of Medical Resources." *Social Research* 52 (Autumn): 607–23.

———. 1987. *Mortal Choices.* New York: Pantheon.

Mailick, Mildred D., and Alice Ullmann. 1984. "A Social Work Perspective on Ethical Practice in End-Stage Renal Disease." *Social Work in Health Care* 9 (Summer): 21–31.

Maitland, David J. 1987. *Aging: A Time for New Learning.* Atlanta: John Knox.

Mandel, Stanley R. 1986. "Setting the Record Straight on Organ Sales." *Hastings Center Report* 16 (August): 48–49.

Manes, Penny. 1986. "Organ Transplantation—Selecting the Recipients." Paper presented at A.H.A. Conference on Ethics, Values, and Rights; Chicago, IL, November 17.

Manne, Henry G. 1985. "U.S. Should Allow Sale of Organs for Transplants." *Atlanta Journal and Constitution* (October 20): B1, 7.

Manroe, Barbara L. 1979. "Ethical and Legal Considerations in Decision-Making for Newborns." *Perkins Journal* 32 (Summer): 1–9.

Margolis, Joseph. 1985. "Triage and Critical Care." In John C. Moskop and Loretta Kopelman (eds.), *Ethics and Critical Care Medicine.* Boston: D. Reidel: 171–89.

Maritain, Jacques. 1944. *The Rights of Man.* London: Geoffrey Bles.

Massachusetts Task Force on Organ Transplantation. 1984. *Report.* Boston: Boston University Schools of Public Health and Medicine (October).

Matas, Arthur J., and Vivian A. Tellis. 1987. "Selection of Kidney Recipients." *Journal of the American Medical Association* 258 (September 11): 1328.

Mathieu, Deborah. 1988. "Introduction." In Deborah Mathieu (ed.), *Organ Substitution Technology.* Boulder, CO: Westview.

Mavrodes, George I. 1984. "Choice and Chance in the Allocation of Medical Resources: A Response to Kilner." *Journal of Religious Ethics* 12 (Spring): 97–115.

May, William F. 1986. "The Virtues and Vices of the Elderly." In Thomas R. Cole and Sally A. Gadow (eds.), *What Does It Mean to Grow Old?* Durham: Duke University Press: 41–61.

Mbiti, John S. 1966. *Akamba Stories.* Oxford: Oxford University Press.

———. 1969. *African Religions and Philosophy.* London: Heinemann.

———. 1970. *Concepts of God in Africa.* London: S.P.C.K.

———. 1971. *New Testament Eschatology in an African Background.* Oxford: Oxford University Press.

Mburu, F. M. 1977. "The Duality of Traditional and Western Medicine in Africa: Mystics, Myths and Reality." In Philip Singer (ed.), *Traditional Healing: New Science or New Colonialism.* New York: Conch Magazine Limited Publishers: 158–85.

McClish, Donna K., et al. 1987. "The Impact of Age on Utilization of Intensive Care Resources." *Journal of the American Geriatrics Society* 35 (November): 983–88.

McCormick, Richard A. 1978. "The Quality of Life, the Sanctity of Life." *Hastings Center Report* 8 (February): 30–36.

———. 1988. "'A Clean Heart Create for Me, O God': Impact Questions on the Artificial Heart." In John Monagle and David Thomasma (eds.), *Medical Ethics.* Rockville, MD: Aspen: 122–26.

McGrath, William R. 1977. "Mountaineer Commentary." *The Budget* (October 19): 7.

McIntyre, Kevin M., and Robert C. Benfari. 1982. "Two Cardiac Arrests, One Medical Team: Commentary." *Hastings Center Report* 12 (April): 24–25.

McKevitt, Patricia M., et al. 1986. "The Elderly on Dialysis: Physical and Psychosocial Functioning." *Dialysis and Transplantation* 15 (March): 130–37.

McKinlay, John B. 1981. "From Promising Report to Standard Procedure: Seven Stages in the Career of a Medical Innovation." *Milbank Memorial Fund Quarterly/Health and Society* 59 (Summer): 374–411.

"M.D.'s, Clergy Discuss Prolonging Life." 1966. *A.M.A. News* (May 9): 9.

Mechanic, David. 1976. "Rationing Health Care: Public Policy and the Medical Marketplace." *Hastings Center Report* 6 (February): 34–37.

———. 1978. "Ethics, Justice, and Medical Care Systems." *Annals of the American Academy of Political and Social Science* 437 (May): 74–85.

————. 1979a. "How Should Medical Care Be Rationed?" *American Journal of Medicine* 66 (January): 8–9.

————. 1979b. *Future Issues in Health Care: Social Policy and the Rationing of Medical Services.* New York: Free Press.

————. 1980. "Rationing of Medical Care and the Preservation of Clinical Judgment." *Journal of Family Practice* 11 (September): 431–33.

————. 1986. *From Advocacy to Allocation.* New York: Free Press.

Mehlman, Maxwell J. 1985. "Rationing Expensive Lifesaving Medical Treatments." *Wisconsin Law Review* 1985 (No. 2): 239–303.

Meissner, Joseph. 1986. "Legal Services and Medical Treatment for Poor People: A Need for Advocacy." *Issues in Law and Medicine* 2 (July): 3–13.

Meltzer, Stephen J. 1981. "The New Medical-Industrial Complex." *New England Journal of Medicine* 304 (January 22): 232.

Menzel, Paul T. 1983. *Medical Costs, Moral Choices.* New Haven, CT: Yale University Press.

Merriken, Karen, and Thomas D. Overcast. 1985. "Patient Selection for Heart Transplantation: When Is a Discriminating Choice Discrimination?" *Journal of Health Politics, Policy and Law* 10 (Spring): 7–32.

Meyer, Eugene L. 1984. "Tax Money for Transplant Operations: Who Pays?" *Washington Post* (September 12): C1 + .

Meyers, David W. 1977. "California Natural Death Act: A Critical Appraisal." *California State Bar Journal* 52 (July–August): 326–28 + .

Michael, Jonathan. 1981. "Audit in Renal Failure." *British Journal of Medicine* 283 (August 22): 556.

Michael, Jonathan, and D. Adu. 1982. "Dialysis, Cuts, and District Policy." *Lancet* 2 (October 30): 990.

Middleton, John, and Greet Kershaw. 1965. *The Central Tribes of the North-Eastern Bantu,* rev. ed. London: International African Institute: 67–97.

Midwest Organ Bank (Kansas City, MO). 1986. "Organ Sharing Procedures." Official statement of policy.

Miles, Steven H., et al. 1988. "The Total Artificial Heart: An Ethics Perspective on Current Clinical Research and Deployment." *Chest* 94 (August): 409–13.

Mill, John Stuart. 1863. *Utilitarianism.* In *The Utilitarians.* Garden City, NY: Anchor Press, 1973: 399–472.

Miller, David. 1976. *Social Justice.* Oxford: Clarendon Press.

Miller, Frances H. 1985. "Reflections on Organ Transplantation in the United Kingdom." *Law, Medicine and Health Care* 13 (February): 31–32.

Miller, Norman N. 1980. "Traditional Medicine in East Africa." American Universities Field Staff Reports No. 22. Hanover, NH: American University Field Staff.

Minnesota Coalition on Health Care Costs. 1984. *The Price of Life: Ethics and Economics.* Minneapolis: M.C.H.C.C. (December).

Moody, Harry. 1978. "Is It Right to Allocate Health Care Resources on Grounds of Age?" In Elsie L. Bandman and Bertram Bandman (eds.), *Bioethics and Human Rights*. Boston: Little, Brown: 197–201.

Mooney, Gavin. 1984. "Medial Ethics: An Excuse for Inefficiency?" *Journal of Medical Ethics* 10 (December): 183–85.

Moore, Gordon L. 1971. "Who Should Be Dialyzed?" *American Journal of Psychiatry* 127 (March): 1208–09.

Morgan, Ted. 1976. "The Good Life (Along the San Adreas Fault)." *New York Times Magazine* (July 4): 18–21+.

Morgan, W. T. W. 1967. "Kikuyu and Kamba: The Tribal Background." In W. T. W. Morgan (ed.), *Nairobi: City and Region*. Nairobi: Oxford University Press: 57–66.

Morillo, Carolyn R. 1976. "As Sure as Shooting." *Philosophy* 51 (January): 80–89.

Moskop, John C. 1987a. "Organ Transplantation in Children: Ethical Issues." *Journal of Pediatrics* 110 (February): 175–80.

———. 1987b. "The Moral Limits to Federal Funding for Kidney Disease." *Hastings Center Report* 17 (April): 11–15.

Mulley, Albert G., Jr. 1983. "The Allocation of Resources for Medical Intensive Care." In President's Commission for the Study of Ethical Problems in Medicine and Biomedical and Behavioral Research, *Securing Access to Health Care,* vol. 3. Washington, D.C.: U.S. Government Printing Office (March): 285–311.

———. 1984. "The Triage Decision." In Stanley Reiser and Michael Anbar (eds.), *The Machine at the Bedside*. Cambridge: Cambridge University Press: 221–26.

Munson, Ronald. 1983. *Intervention and Reflection,* 2d ed. Belmont, CA: Wadsworth.

Murray, J. S., et al. 1962. "A Community Hemodialysis Center for the Treatment of Chronic Uremia." *Transactions of the American Society for Artificial Internal Organs* 8: 315–18.

Murray, Thomas H. 1985. "Why Solutions Continue to Elude Us." *Social Science and Medicine* 20 (November 11): 1103–07.

Muthiani, Joseph. 1973. *Akamba from Within: Egalitarianism in Social Relations*. New York: Exposition Press.

Mutungi, O. K. 1977. *The Legal Aspects of Witchcraft in East Africa*. Nairobi: East African Literature Bureau.

Nabarro, J. D. N. 1967. "Who Best to Make the Choice?" In "Selection of Patients for Haemodialysis." *British Medical Journal* 1 (March 11): 622.

Nagelbach, Michael A. 1978. "Justice and Medical Care." Ph.D. dissertation. Chicago: University of Illinois.

Najman, J. M., et al. "Patient Characteristics Negatively Stereotyped by Doctors." *Social Science and Medicine* 16 (No. 20): 1781–89.

National Academy of Sciences, Board on Medicine. 1968. "Cardiac Transplantation in Man." *Journal of the American Medical Association* 204 (May 27): 805–06.

National Council of Senior Citizens. 1986. "For-Profit Hospital Care: Who Profits? Who Cares?" Washington: N.C.S.C., March.

National Heart and Lung Institute, Artificial Heart Assessment Panel. 1973. "The Totally Implantable Artificial Heart: Economic, Ethical, Legal, Medical, Psychiatric, and Social Implications." Washington, D.C.: U.S. Department of Health, Education, and Welfare.

National Heart Institute, Ad Hoc Task Force on Cardiac Replacement. 1969. "Cardiac Replacement: Medical, Ethical, Psychological and Economic Implications." Washington, D.C.: U.S. Department of Health, Education, and Welfare.

National Heart Transplantation Study. 1984. Seattle: Battelle Human Affairs Research Centers.

National Kidney Dialysis and Kidney Transplantation Study. 1986. Seattle: Battelle Human Affairs Research Centers, esp. chs. 1, 2.

Ndeti, Kivuto. 1969. "The Role of Akamba Kithitu in Questions of Human Justice." *Proceedings of the Fifth Annual Conference.* University of East Africa, Social Science Council, Nairobi: 1183–90.

———. 1972. *Elements of Akamba Life.* Nairobi: East Africa Publishing House.

———. 1978. "The Relevance of African Traditional Medicine in Modern Medical Training and Practice." In Magoroh Maruyama and Arthur Harkins (eds.), *Cultures of the Future.* The Hague: Mouton: 179–93.

Nelson, James B., and Jo Anne S. Rohricht. 1984. *Human Medicine,* rev. ed. Minneapolis: Augsburg.

Neu, Steven, and Carl M. Kjellstrand. 1986. "Stopping Long-Term Dialysis." *New England Journal of Medicine* 314 (January 2): 14–20.

Neuspiel, Daniel R. 1985. "On Rationing Organ Transplantation." *American Journal of Public Health* 75 (August): 893.

Nichols, Andrew W. 1981. "Ethics of the Distribution of Health Care." *Journal of Family Practice* 12 (March): 533–38.

Nickel, James W. 1986. "Should Undocumented Aliens Be Entitled to Health Care?" *Hastings Center Report* 16 (December): 19–23.

Nida, Eugene A. 1962. "Akamba Initiation Rites and Culture Themes." *Practical Anthropology* 9 (July–August): 145–55.

Norman, Geoffrey R. 1985. "Objective Measurement of Clinical Performance." *Medical Education* 19 (January): 43–47.

Norman, Geoffrey R., et al. 1982. "A Comparison of Resident Performance on Real and Simulated Patients." *Journal of Medical Education* 57 (September): 708–15.

Novak, Nina. 1984. "'Natural Death Acts' Let Patients Refuse Treatment." *Hospitals* 58 (August 1): 71–73.

Novello, A. C., and D. N. Sundwall. 1985. "Current Organ Transplantation

Legislation: An Update." *Transplantation Proceedings* 17 (February): 1585–91.

Nozick, Robert. 1974. *Anarchy, State and Utopia.* New York: Basic Books.

Oberdiek, Hans. 1976. "Who Is To Judge?" *Ethics* 87 (October): 75–86.

O'Curry, Eugene. 1873. *On the Manners and Customs of the Ancient Irish,* vol. I. Dublin: W. B. Kelly.

Oden, Thomas C. 1976. *Should Treatment Be Terminated?* New York: Harper and Row.

O'Donnell, Michael. 1986. "One Man's Burden." *British Medical Journal* 293 (July 5): 59.

O'Donnell, Thomas J. 1960. "The Morality of Triage." *Georgetown Medical Bulletin* 14 (August): 68–71.

Office of Health Economics (London). 1979. "Scarce Resources in Health Care." *Milbank Memorial Fund Quarterly* 57 (Spring): 265–87.

Office of the Inspector General. 1986. *The Access of Foreign Nationals to U.S. Cadaver Organs.* Boston: U.S. Department of Health and Human Services.

Office of Organ Transplantation. 1985. "Organ Transplantation Background Information." Rockville, MD: U.S. Department of Health and Human Services.

Office of Technology Assessment, U.S. Congress. 1984. "Intensive Care Units: Clinical Outcomes, Costs and Decisionmaking." *Health Technology Case Study* 28 (November).

———. 1987. *Life-Sustaining Technologies and the Elderly,* OTA-BA-306. Washington, D.C.: U.S. Government Printing Office.

Ogden, David A. 1987. "Organ Procurement and Transplantation." In Gary Anderson and Valerie Glesnes-Anderson (eds.), *Health Care Clinics.* Rockville, MD: Aspen: 91–108.

Ogg, Chisholm. 1973. "Society Should Be Better Informed." In "Priorities in Medicine." *British Medical Journal* 2 (June 16): 649 + .

Oglesby, William B., Jr. 1975. "Life or Death—Whose Decision—Theological Aspects." *Virginia Medical Monthly* 102 (September): 710–13.

Oliver, Symmes C. 1965. "Individuality, Freedom of Choice, and Cultural Flexibility of the Kamba." *American Anthropologist* 67 (April): 421–28.

Olshan, Marc A. 1983. "Casting Lots: From Revelation to Randomization." Paper presented at the Society for the Scientific Study of Religion Annual Meeting, Knoxville, TN (November 4–6).

O'Neil, Richard. 1978. "Killing, Letting Die, and Justice." *Analysis* 38 (June): 124–25.

Opelz, G. 1987. "Effect of HLA Matching in 10,000 Cyclosporine-Treated Cadaver Kidney Transplants." *Transplantation Proceedings* 19 (February): 641–46.

Oregon Health Decisions. 1984. "Preliminary Survey Results." Portland, OR: Oregon Health Sciences University.

Oreopoulos, Dimitrios G. 1982. "Should We Let Them Die? The Moral Dilemmas of Economic Restraints on Life-support Treatments." *Canadian Medical Association Journal* 126 (April 1): 745–46.

———. 1983. "Should We Let Them Die?" In F. M. Parsons and C. S. Ogg (eds.), *Renal Failure—Who Cares?* Lancaster, England: MTP: 65–73.

Orient, Jane M. 1983. "Equity in Medical Care: Are the Deserving Poor Eligible?" *Perspectives in Biology and Medicine* 26 (Spring): 411–16.

O'Rourke, Kevin D., and Dennis Brodeur. 1986. *Medical Ethics: Common Ground for Understanding.* St. Louis: Catholic Health Association of the United States.

Outka, Gene. 1974. "Social Justice and Equal Access to Health Care." *Journal of Religious Ethics* 2 (Spring): 11–32.

Oyer, P. E., et al. 1981. "Cardiac Transplantation: 1980." *Transplantation Proceedings* 13 (March): 199–206.

Ozar, David T. 1981. "Justice and a Universal Right to Basic Health Care." *Social Science and Medicine* 15F (December): 135–41.

Pacific Presbyterian Medical Center. 1987. "Who Lives, Who Dies, Who Decides?—National Poll Results." San Francisco: P.P.M.C.

Page, Benjamin B. 1977. "The Right to Health Care." *Current History* 73 (July–August): 5–8+.

Palmer, Lon W. 1980. "Commentary on Belliotti's 'Allocation of Resources.'" *Values and Ethics in Health Care* 5: 265–70.

Palmore, Erdman B. 1982. "Attitudes Toward the Aged." *Research on Aging* 4 (September): 333–48.

Papper, Solomon. 1983. *Doing Right: Everyday Medical Ethics.* Boston: Little, Brown.

Parfit, Derek. 1978. "Innumerate Ethics." *Philosophy and Public Affairs* 7 (Summer): 285–301.

Parsons, Arthur. 1985. "Allocating Health Care Resources: A Moral Dilemma." *Canadian Medical Association Journal* 132 (February 15): 466–69.

Parsons, F. M. 1967. "A True 'Doctor's Dilemma.'" In "Selection of Patients for Haemodialysis." *British Medical Journal* 1 (March 11): 623.

———. 1983. "Five Years Since Stirling—A Progress Review." In F. M. Parsons and C. S. Ogg (eds.), *Renal Failure—Who Cares?* Lancaster, England: MTP: 5–15.

Parsons, Victor. 1978. "The Ethical Challenges of Dialysis and Transplantation." *Practitioner* 220 (June): 871–77.

Parsons, Victor, and P. M. Lock. 1980. "Triage and the Patient with Renal Failure." *Journal of Medical Ethics* 6 (December): 173–76.

———. 1981. "Audit in Renal Failure." *British Medical Journal* 283 (August 22): 556.

———. 1983. "The Selection and De-Selection of Patients for Dialysis and Transplantation." In F. M. Parsons and C. S. Ogg (eds.), *Renal Failure—Who Cares?* Lancaster, England: MTP: 41–47.

"Patient Selection for Artificial and Transplanted Organs." 1969. *Harvard Law Review* 82 (April): 1322–42.

Paule, Verne. 1975. "San Francisco Gets Ready." *Foresight* (March–April): 24–29.

Paulus, Sharon M. 1986. "Suit Filed in Oklahoma Alleging Twenty-Four Infants Died after Being Denied Beneficial Medical Treatment." *Issues in Law and Medicine* 1 (January): 321–30.

Pearlman, Robert A., and Albert R. Jonsen. 1985. "The Use of Quality-of-Life Considerations in Medical Decision Making." *Journal of the American Geriatrics Society* 33 (May): 344–52.

Pearlman, Robert A., and James B. Speer. 1983. "Quality-of-Life Considerations in Geriatrics Care." *Journal of the American Geriatrics Society* 31 (February): 113–20.

Pearlman, Robert A., et al. 1982. "Variability in Physician Bioethical Decision-Making: A Case Study of Euthanasia." *Annals of Internal Medicine* 97 (September): 420–25.

Peel, John. 1973. "Doctors' Dilemmas." *Ulster Medical Journal* 42: 105–15.

Pellegrino, Edmund D. 1980. "Medical Economics and Medical Ethics: Points of Conflict and Reconciliation." *Journal of the Medical Association of Georgia* 69 (March): 174–83.

———. 1988. "Rationing Health Care: The Ethics of Medical Gatekeeping." In John Monagle and David Thomasma (eds.), *Medical Ethics*. Rockville, MD: Aspen: 261–70.

Pennock, John L., et al. 1982. "Cardiac Transplantation in Perspective for the Future: Survival, Complications, Rehabilitation, and Cost." *Journal of Thoracic and Cardiovascular Surgery* 83 (February): 168–77.

Penwill, D. J. 1951. *Kamba Customary Law*. London: Macmillan.

Perkins, Henry S. 1986. "A Comparison between Western and Nonwestern Providers' Attitudes about Patient Autonomy." Paper presented at the annual meeting of the Society for Health and Human Values. New Orleans, LA (October 25).

Perkins, Rollin M. 1957. *Criminal Law*. Brooklyn: Foundation Press.

Perkoff, Gerald, et al. 1976a. "Long-Term Dialysis Programs: New Selection Criteria, New Problems." *Hastings Center Report* 6 (June): 8–13.

———. 1976b. "Decisions Regarding the Provision or Withholding of Therapy." *American Journal of Medicine* 61 (December): 915–23.

Peterson, Daniel T. 1985. "The Rationing of Medical Care." *New England Journal of Medicine* 312 (May 16): 1330–31.

Petuchowski, Jacob J. 1975. "The Limits of Self-Sacrifice." In Marvin Fox (ed.), *Modern Jewish Ethics*. Columbus: Ohio State University Press: 103–18.

Picton, J. Allanson. 1882. *Oliver Cromwell: The Man and His Mission*. New York: Cassell, Petter, Galpin.

Piettre, André. 1977. "Aspects of Economics, Ethics and Civilisation." *Intensive Care Medicine* 3 (December): 253–56.

Pizzulli, Francis C. 1975. "'Ain't Nobody Gonna Cut on My Head.'" *Hastings Center Report* 5 (February): 50–51.

Platt, Robert. 1966. "Ethical Problems in Medical Procedures." In G. E. W. Wolstenholme (ed.), *Ethics in Medical Progress: With Special Relevance to Transplantation*. Boston: Little, Brown: 149–53.

Pledger, H. G. 1986. "Triage of Casualties after Nuclear Attack." *Lancet* 2 (September 20): 678–79.

Plough, Alonzo L., and Susanne Salem. 1982. "Social and Contextual Factors in the Analysis of Mortality in End-Stage Renal Disease Patients: Implications for Health Policy." *American Journal of Public Health* 72 (November): 1293–95.

"A Policy of Despair." 1976. *British Medical Journal* 1 (April 3): 787–88.

Pope John XXIII Medical-Moral Research and Education Center. 1984. "How Should Catholic Hospitals Allocate ICU Admissions? *Hospital Progress* 65 (July–August): 80, 82.

Porter, Susan. 1985. "Ethics and the Elderly—Care at What Cost?" *Ohio State Medical Journal* 81 (June): 400–07.

Potter, Brian. 1981. "A Solution to the Resource Allocation Debate?" *Journal of Medical Ethics* 7 (September): 162–63.

Potter, Charles F. 1949. "Eeny, Meeny, Miny, Mo." In Maria Leach (ed.), *Dictionary of Folklore, Mythology, and Legend*. New York: Funk & Wagnalls, vol. I: 339–40.

Potter, Ralph B. 1977. "Labeling the Mentally Retarded: The Just Allocation of Therapy." In Stanley Reiser et al. (eds.), *Ethics in Medicine*. Cambridge: MIT Press: 626–31.

President's Commission for the Study of Ethical Problems in Medicine and Biomedical and Behavioral Research. 1983a. *Deciding to Forego Life-Sustaining Treatment*. Washington, D.C.: U.S. Government Printing Office.

———. 1983b. *Securing Access to Health Care*. Washington, D.C.: U.S. Government Printing Office.

Preston, Thomas A. 1985. "Who Benefits from the Artificial Heart?" *Hastings Center Report* 15 (February): 5–7.

Price, R. Arlen. 1987. "Genetics of Human Obesity." *Annals of Behavioral Medicine* 9 (Summer): 9–14.

"Prolonging 'Low Life.'" 1985. London *Times*. (January 9): 11.

Prottas, Jeffrey M. 1986. "In Organ Transplants, Americans First?" *Hastings Center Report* 16 (October): 23–24.

Prottas, Jeffrey M., et al. 1983. "Cross-National Differences in Dialysis Rates." *Health Care Financing Review* 4 (March): 91–103.

Pryor, J. S. 1983. "Comparison of Facilities in the United Kingdom and in Europe for Dialysis and Transplantation." In F. M. Parsons and C. S. Ogg (eds.), *Renal Failure—Who Cares?* Lancaster, England: MTP: 17–23.

Purtilo, Ruth B. 1982. "Justice in the Distribution of Health Care Resources:

The Position of Physical Therapists in the United States and Sweden." *Physical Therapy* 62 (January): 46–50.

Purtilo, Ruth B., and Christine K. Cassel. 1981. "Allocation of Scarce Life-Saving Resources." *Ethical Dimensions in the Health Professions.* Philadelphia: W. B. Saunders: 183–91.

Pyeritz, Reed E. 1978. "The Last Bed in the ICU: Correspondence." *Hastings Center Report* 8 (June): 50.

Rabinovitch, Nachem L. 1973. "Random Mechanisms." *Probability and Statistical Inference in Ancient and Medieval Jewish Literature.* Toronto: University of Toronto Press: 21–35.

Rabinowitz, Stanley, and Hermanus I. J. van der Spuy. 1978. "Selection Criteria for Dialysis and Renal Transplant." *American Journal of Psychiatry* 135 (July): 861–63.

Rabkin, Mitchell, et al. 1976. "Orders Not to Resuscitate." *New England Journal of Medicine* 295 (August 21): 364–66.

Rajakumar, M. K. 1984. "Ethical Consequences of Technological Change." *Singapore Medical Journal* 25 (February): 1–5.

Ramsey, Paul. 1962. *Nine Modern Moralists.* Englewood Cliffs, NJ: Prentice-Hall.

———. 1970a. "Choosing How to Choose: Patients and Sparse Medical Resources." *The Patient as Person.* New Haven: Yale University Press: 239–75.

———. 1970b. *Fabricated Man.* New Haven: Yale University Press.

———. 1978. *Ethics at the Edges of life.* New Haven: Yale University Press.

Randal, Judith. 1982. "Coronary Artery Bypass Surgery." *Hastings Center Report* 12 (February): 13–18.

Rapaport, Elliot. 1982. "An Overview of Issues [in coronary bypass surgery]." *Circulation* 66, Suppl. 3 (November): 3–5.

Rapaport, Felix T. 1987a. "Living Donor Kidney Transplantation." *Transplantation Proceedings* 19 (February): 169–73.

———. 1987b. "A Rational Approach to a Common Goal: The Equitable Distribution of Organs for Transplantation." *Journal of the American Medical Association* 257 (June 12): 3118–19.

Rashdall, Hastings. 1948. *The Theory of Good and Evil,* 2d ed. London: Oxford University Press.

"Rationing of Health Care." 1985. *Perspective* 20 (Summer): 1–9.

Rawls, John. 1968. "Distributive Justice: Some Addenda." *Natural Law Forum* 13: 51–71.

———. 1971. *A Theory of Justice.* Cambridge: Harvard University Press.

———. 1978. "Primary Goods and Responsibility for Ends." Unpublished paper on file in the Robbins Philosophy Library, Harvard University.

Reed, William G., et al. 1986. "The Effect of a Public Hospital's Transfer Policy on Patient Care." *New England Journal of Medicine* 315 (November 27): 1428–32.

Reemtsma, Keith. 1964. "Moral Problems of Artificial and Transplanted Organs." *Annals of Internal Medicine* 61 (August): 357–59.

Reidy, Maurice. 1979. "Distribution and Choice." *Foundations for a Medical Ethic.* New York: Paulist Press: 71–81.

Reines, Chaim W. 1978. "The Self and the Other in Rabbinic Ethics." In Menachem Kellner (ed.), *Contemporary Jewish Ethics.* New York: Sanhedrin Press Book, Hebrew Publishing Co.: 162–74.

Reinhold, Robert. 1986. "Treating an Outbreak of Patient Dumping in Texas." *New York Times.* May 25: 4E.

———. 1988. "Crisis in Emergency Rooms: More Symptoms than Cures." *New York Times* (July 28): A1, 20.

Reiser, Stanley J. 1977. "Therapeutic Choice and Moral Doubt in a Technological Age." *Daedalus* 106 (Winter): 47–56.

Reiser, Stanley J., et al. 1977. *Ethics in Medicine.* Cambridge: M.I.T. Press.

Reiss, John B., et al. 1982. "Costs and Regulation of New Medical Technologies: Heart Transplants as a Case Study." In Barbara J. McNeil and Ernest G. Cravalho (eds.), *Critical Issues in Medical Technology.* Boston: Auburn House: 399–417.

Relman, Arnold S. 1985. "Economic Considerations in Emergency Care: What Are Hospitals For?" *New England Journal of Medicine* 312 (February 7): 372–73.

———. 1986. "Texas Eliminates Dumping: A Start Toward Equity in Hospital Care." *New England Journal of Medicine* 314 (February 27): 578–79.

"Remember the Alamo." 1982. *Newsweek* (June 21): 42.

"Renal Failure—Who Cares?" 1982. *Lancet* 1 (May 1): 1011–12.

Rennie, Drummond, et al. 1985. "Limited Resources and the Treatment of Endstage Renal Failure in Britain and the United States." *Quarterly Journal of Medicine* 56, n.s. (July): 321–36.

Rescher, Nicholas. 1966. *Distributive Justice.* New York: Bobbs-Merrill.

———. 1969. "The Allocation of Exotic Medical Lifesaving Therapy." *Ethics* 79: 173–86.

Retan, J. Walden, and Harvey Y. Lewis. 1966. "Repeated Dialysis of Indigent Patients for Chronic Renal Failure." *Annals of Internal Medicine* 61 (February): 284–92.

Rettig, Richard A. 1976a. "Valuing Lives: The Policy Debate on Patient Care Financing for Victims of End-Stage Renal Disease." Rand Paper Series P-5672 (March).

———. 1976b. "The Policy Debate on Patient Care Financing for Victims of End Stage Renal Disease." *Law and Contemporary Problems* 40 (Autumn): 196–230.

———. 1976c. *Health Care Technology: Lessons Learned from the End-Stage Renal Disease Experience.* Santa Monica: Rand Corporation (November).

———. 1979. "End-Stage Renal Disease and the 'Cost' of Medical Technology."

In Stuart H. Altman and Robert Blendon (eds.), *Medical Technology: The Culprit behind Health Care Costs?* Hyattsville, MD: U.S. National Center for Health Services Research: 88–115.

Rettig, Richard A., and Ellen Marks. 1983. "The Federal Government and Social Planning for End-Stage Renal Disease: Past, Present, and Future." Rand Note N-1922-NCHSR (February).

Rey, Michel. 1980. "Measles and Measles Vaccination in India." Report to the World Health Organization, South-East Asia Region, on WHO Project IND SPI 001 (January 21).

Rhoads, Steven E. 1980. "How Much Should We Spend to Save a Life?" In Steven E. Rhoads (ed.), *Valuing Life: Public Policy Dilemmas*. Boulder, CO: Westview Press: 285–311.

Rhodes, Philip. 1973. "Primary Concern Is Comfort." In "Priorities in Medicine." *British Medical Journal* 2 (June 16): 648–49.

Richards, Glenn. 1984. "Technology Costs and Rationing Issues." *Hospitals* 58 (June 1): 80–86.

Richards, Toya. 1986. "Donor Heart Is Being Sought for Frankfort Girl." *Lexington [KY] Herald-Leader* (June 27): C1+.

Rickham, P. P. 1976. "The Swing of the Pendulum: The Indications for Operating on Myelomeningoceles." *Medical Journal of Australia* 2 (November 13): 743–46.

Rivin, Arthur U. 1978. "Rights and Responsibilities in Health Care." *Forum on Medicine* 1 (November): 43–44.

Roach, Thomas A. 1980. "Allocation of Scarce Medical Resources." In Marc D. Basson (ed.), *Ethics, Humanism, and Medicine*. New York: Alan R. Liss: 153–59.

Robb, J. Wesley. 1981. "The Allocation of Limited Medical Resources: An Ethical Perspective." *Pharos* 44 (Spring): 29–35.

Robbins, Christopher. 1984. "The Ethical Challenge of Health Care Rationing." In Jean de Kervasdoue et al. (eds.), *The End of an Illusion: The Future of Health Policy in Western Industrialized Nations*. Berkeley, CA: University of California Press: 110–33.

Robbins, Jhan, and June Robbins. 1967. "The Rest Are Simply Left to Die." *Redbook* (November): 80–83+.

Roberts, J. Deotis. 1974. *A Black Political Theology*. Philadelphia: Westminster Press.

Robertson, John A. 1987. "Supply and Distribution of Hearts for Transplantation: Legal, Ethical, and Policy Issues." *Circulation* 75 (January): 77–87.

———. 1989. "Age, Lifestyle, Social Network of Support, Incarceration, and Other Controversial Considerations." Paper presented at conference on patient selection criteria in organ transplantation, Transplant Policy Center, University of Michigan (March 14). Forthcoming in *Transplantation Proceedings*.

Robin, Eugene D. 1964. "Rapid Scientific Advances Bring New Ethical Questions." *Journal of the American Medical Association* 189 (August 24): 624–25.

Rodgers, Joann. 1984. "Life on the Cutting Edge." *Psychology Today* (October): 58–67.

Rodin, G. M., et al. 1981. "Stopping Life-Sustaining Medical Treatment: Psychiatric Considerations in the Termination of Renal Dialysis." *Canadian Journal of Psychiatry* 26 (November): 540–44.

Roe, Benson B. 1981. "Treatment Decisions and Triage: The Physician's Burden." In Cynthia B. Wong and Judith P. Swazey (eds.), *Dilemmas of Dying.* Boston: G. K. Hall: 89–94.

Rogers, Edward. 1975. "The Right to Live." *The Ecumenical Review* 27 (April): 128–33.

Roper, Elaine. 1975. "Dilemma Lingers On: To Select or Not to Select." *Journal of the American Association of Nephrology Nurses and Technicians* 2: 71–74.

Rosenblatt, Rand E. 1983. "Rationing 'Normal' Health Care: The Hidden Legal Issues." In President's Commission for the Study of Ethical Problems in Medicine and Biomedical and Behavioral Research, *Securing Access to Health Care,* vol. 3. Washington, D.C.: U.S. Superintendent of Documents: 395–411.

Rosner, Fred. 1983a. "Allocation of Scarce Medical Resources." *New York State Journal of Medicine* 83 (March): 353–58.

———. 1983b. "The Rationing of Medical Care: The Jewish View." *Journal of Halacha and Contemporary Society* (Fall): 21–32.

Roth, Julius A. 1972. "Some Contingencies of the Moral Evaluation and Control of Clientele: The Case of the Hospital Emergency Service." *American Journal of Sociology* 77: 839–56.

Rothman, David J. 1987. "Ethical and Social Issues in the Development of New Drugs and Vaccines." *Bulletin of the New York Academy of Medicine* 63 (July–August): 557–68.

Roxe, David M. 1983. "Is Patient Rationing in Our Future? Hidden Issues." *Dialysis and Transplantation* 12 (December): 830–32.

Royal College of Physicians Medical Services Study Group. "Deaths from Chronic Renal Failure Under the Age of 50." *British Medical Journal* 283 (July 25): 283–87.

Rubin, Milton E., et al. 1966. "An Analysis of a Veterans Administration Dialysis Unit." *Transactions of the American Society for Artificial Internal Organs* 12: 376–85.

Ruchlin, Hirsch S. 1984. "The Public Cost of Kidney Disease." *Social Work in Health Care* 9 (Summer): 1–9.

Rund, Douglas A., and Tondra S. Rausch. 1981. *Triage.* St. Louis: C. V. Mosby.

Russell, Avery. 1980. "Applied Ethics: A Strategy for Fostering Professional Responsibility." *Carnegie Quarterly* 28 (Spring/Summer): 1–7.

Rutherford, Ward. 1978. *The Druids and Their Heritage.* London: Gordon & Cremonesi.

Sage, William M., et al. 1986. "Is Intensive Care Worth It?—An Assessment of Input and Outcome for the Critically Ill." *Critical Care Medicine* 14 (September): 777–82.

———. 1987. "Intensive Care for the Elderly: Outcome of Elective and Non-elective Admissions." *Journal of the American Geriatrics Society* 35 (April): 312–18.

Samet, Jonathan, et al. 1986. "Choice of Cancer Therapy Varies with Age of Patient." *Journal of the American Medical Association* 255 (June 27): 3385–90.

Sanders, David, and Jesse Dukeminier, Jr. 1968. "Medical Advance and Legal Lag: Hemodialysis and Kidney Transplantation." *UCLA Law Review* 15 (February): 366–80.

Sanders, John B. 1986. "ICU Admission and Discharge Screening Criteria." *Nursing Administration Quarterly* 10 (Spring): 25–31.

Sanfilippo, Fred, et al. 1984. "Benefits of HLA-A and HLA-B Matching on Graft and Patient Outcome after Cadaveric-Donor Renal Transplantation." *New England Journal of Medicine* 311 (August 9): 358–64.

San Francisco Emergency Medical Service Agency. 1987. "Medical Operations." San Francisco Dept. of Public Health.

Saqueton, A. R. 1982. *In Defense of Life.* Stockton, CA: ARS Publishing.

Sawyer, Tom. 1968. Written text of interview by authors of "Scarce Medical Resources," on file at Columbia Law Library (August 29).

"Scarce Medical Resources." 1969. *Columbia Law Review* 9 (April): 620–92.

Schambeck, Herbert. 1974. "The Ethical and Moral Basis of Human Rights." In Simon Btesh (ed.), *Protection of Human Rights in the Light of Scientific and Technological Progress in Biology and Medicine.* Geneva: World Health Organization.

Scharschmidt, Bruce F. 1984. "Human Liver Transplantation: Analysis of Data on 540 Patients from Four Centers." *Hepatology* 4 (January–February, Suppl.): 955–1015.

Schiff, Robert L., et al. 1986. "Transfer to a Public Hospital: A Prospective Study of 467 Patients." *New England Journal of Medicine* 314 (February 27): 552–57.

Schiffer, R. B. 1977. "The Last Bed in the ICU: Commentary." *Hastings Center Report* 7 (December): 21–22.

Schmeck, H. M., Jr. 1962. "Panel Holds Life-or-Death Vote in Allotting of Artificial Kidney." *New York Times* (May 6): 1, 83.

Schmidt, R. W., et al. 1983. "The Dilemmas of Patient Treatment for End-Stage Renal Disease." *American Journal of Kidney Diseases* 3 (July): 37–47.

Schneider, Andrew, and Mary P. Flaherty. 1985. "The Challenge of a Miracle: Selling the Gift." *Pittsburgh Press* (November 3–10).

Schneider, Edward L., and Jacob A. Brody. 1983. "Aging, Natural Death, and the Compression of Morbidity: Another View." *New England Journal of Medicine* 309 (October 6): 854–55.

Schreiner, George E. 1966. "Problems of Ethics in Relation to Haemodialysis and Transplantation." In G. Wolstenholme and M. O'Connor (eds.), *Ethics in Medical Progress.* Boston: Little, Brown: 126–33.

———. 1968. "There Is a Third Way." *Archives of Internal Medicine* 121 (May): 463–65.

Schreiner, George E., and John F. Maher. 1965. "Hemodialysis for Chronic Renal Failure: III. Medical, Moral and Ethical, and Socio-Economic Problems." *Annals of Internal Medicine* 62 (March): 551–57.

Schroeder, John S., and Sharon Hunt. 1987. "Cardiac Transplantation: Update 1987." *Journal of the American Medical Association* 258 (December 4): 3142–45.

Schuckit, Marc A. 1985. "Genetics and the Risk for Alcoholism." *Journal of the American Medical Association* 254 (November 8): 2614–17.

Schupak, Eugene, et al. 1967. "Chronic Hemodialysis in "Unselected' Patients." *Annals of Internal Medicine* 67 (October): 708–17.

Schwartz, Leroy. 1976. "Resource Allocation in Health Care" (Title Provided). *Medical World News* 17 (October 18): 104.

Schwartz, Robert, and Andrew Grubb. 1985. "Why Britain Can't Afford Informed Consent." *Hastings Center Report* 15 (August): 19–25.

Schwartz, William B. 1987. "The Inevitable Failure of Current Cost-Containment Strategies." *Journal of the American Medical Association* 257: 220–24.

Schwartz, William B., and Henry J. Aaron. 1984. "Rationing Hospital Care: Lessons from Britain." *New England Journal of Medicine* 310 (January 5): 52–56.

Scitovsky, Anne A. 1986. "Medical Care Expenditures in the Last Twelve Months of Life." Final Report to the John A. Hartford Foundation (March).

Scitovsky, Anne A., and Alexander M. Capron. 1986. "Medical Care at the End of Life: The Interaction of Economics and Ethics." *Annual Review of Public Health* 7:59–75.

Scribner, Belding H. 1964. "Ethical Problems of Using Artificial Organs to Sustain Life." *Transactions of the American Society for Artificial Internal Organs* 10 (1964): 209–12.

Seibert, Sam, and Theresa Waldrop. 1988. "Kidneys for Sale: The Issue is Tissue." *Newsweek* (December 5): 38.

"Selection of Patients for Dialysis and Transplantation." 1978. *British Medical Journal* 2 (November 25): 1449–50.

Seligmann, Jean, et al. 1980. "Saving New Hearts." *Newsweek* (January 7): 39.

Shackman, Ralph. 1967. "Surgeon's Point of View." In "Selection of Patients for Haemodialysis." *British Medical Journal* 1 (March 11): 623–24.

Shannon, Thomas A. 1977. "What Guidance from the Guidelines?" *Hastings Center Report* 7 (June): 28–30.

Shapiro, H. A. (ed.). 1969. "Experience with Human Heart Transplantation: Proceedings of the Cape Town Symposium, July 13–16, 1968."

Shapiro, Michael H., and Roy G. Spece. 1981. "Organ Transplantation." *Cases, Materials and Problems on Bioethics and Law.* St. Paul, MN: West: 740–875.

Shatin, Leo. 1966. "Medical Care and the Social Worth of a Man." *American Journal of Orthopsychiatry* 36: 96–101.

Shaw, Anthony. 1978. "Who Should Die and Who Should Decide." In Marvin Kohl (ed.), *Infanticide and the Value of Life.* Buffalo, NY: Prometheus Books: 102–11.

Shaw, George B. 1950. *Doctor's Dilemma.* New York: Penguin Books.

Sheagren, John N., and Meredith Eiker. 1980. "Allocation of Scarce Medical Resources in the Intensive Care Unit." In Marc D. Basson (ed.), *Ethics, Humanism, and Medicine.* New York: Alan R. Liss: 161–63.

Sheehan, John C. 1982. *The Enchanted Ring: The Untold Story of Penicillin.* Cambridge, MA: MIT Press.

Sher, George. 1983. "Health Care and the 'Deserving Donor.'" *Hastings Center Report* 13 (February): 9–12.

Shevory, Thomas C. 1986. "Applying Rawls to Medical Cases: An Investigation into the Usages of Analytical Philosophy." *Journal of Health Politics, Policy and Law* 10 (Winter): 749–64.

Shragg, Thomas A., and Timothy E. Albertson. 1984. "Moral, Ethical, and Legal Dilemmas in the Intensive Care Unit." *Critical Care Medicine* 12 (January): 62–68.

Sidel, Victor W. 1978. "The Right to Health Care: An International Perspective." In Elsie Bandman and Bertram Bandman (eds.), *Bioethics and Human Rights.* Boston: Little, Brown: 341–50.

Siegler, Mark. 1984. "Should Age Be a Criterion in Health Care?" *Hastings Center Report* 14 (October): 24–27.

Silva, Mary. 1986. "Theoretical Foundations of Ethical Decision Making in Nursing Administration: Allocation of Scarce Resources, Program 9" (video). Fairfax, VA: George Mason University.

Simmons, Roberta G., and Richard L. Simmons. 1972. "Sociological and Psychological Aspects of Transplantation." In J. S. Najarian and R. L. Simmons (eds.), *Transplantation.* Philadelphia: Lea and Febiger: 361–87.

Simmons, Roberta G., and Susan K. Marine. 1984. "The Regulation of High Cost Technology Medicine: The Case of Dialysis and Transplantation in the United Kingdom." *Journal of Health and Social Behavior* 25 (September): 320–34.

Singer, Daniel E., et al. 1983. "Rationing Intensive Care—Physician Responses to a Physician Shortage." *New England Journal of Medicine* 309 (November 10): 1155–60.

Singer, Peter. 1977. "Utility and the Survival Lottery." *Philosophy* 52 (April): 218–22.

———. 1985. "Can We Avoid Assigning Greater Value to Some Human Lives Than to Others?" In Ronald Laura and Adrian Ashman (eds.), *Moral Issues in Mental Retardation.* Dover, NH: Croom Helm: 91–100.

Skillman, John S. 1974. "Ethical Dilemmas in the Care of the Critically Ill." *Lancet* 2 (September 14): 634–37.

Smeeding, Timothy M. 1987. "Artificial Organs, Transplants and Long-Term

Care for the Elderly: What's Covered? Who Pays?" In Timothy M. Smeeding (ed.), *Should Medical Care Be Rationed by Age?* Totowa, NJ: Rowman & Littlefield: 140–55.

Smirnow, Virgil. 1984. "Patient Selection: Has Orwell's 1984 Arrived?" *Dialysis and Transplantation* 13: 237–38.

Smith, Alwyn. 1987. "Qualms and QALYs." *Lancet* 1 (May 16): 1134–36.

Smith, David H. 1981. "Deciding for the Death of a Baby." *Progress in Clinical and Biological Research* 50: 49–55.

Smith, George P. 1985. "Triage: Endgame Realities." *Journal of Contemporary Health Law and Policy* 1 (Spring): 143–51.

———. 1987. "Death Be Not Proud: Medical, Ethical and Legal Dilemmas in Resource Allocation." *Journal of Contemporary Health Law and Policy* 3 (Spring): 47–63.

Smith, Harmon L. 1979. "Distributive Justice and American Health Care." In William M. Finnin and Gerald A. Smith (eds.), *The Morality of Scarcity: Limited Resources and Social Policy.* Baton Rouge: Louisiana State University Press: 67–79.

Smith, James P. 1980. "The Ethics of Resource Allocation in Health Care." *Journal of Advanced Nursing* 5 (November): 559–60.

Smith, Kent. 1980. "Commentary on Ackerman's Meningomyelocele and Parental Commitment." *Man and Medicine* 5: 308–10.

Smurl, James F. 1980. "Distributing the Burden Fairly: Ethics and National Health Policy." *Man and Medicine* 5: 97–125.

Society for the Right to Die. 1986. *Handbook of 1985 Living Will Laws.* New York: Society for the Right to Die.

Soltan, Karol E. 1982. "Empirical Studies of Distributive Justice." *Ethics* 92 (July): 673–91.

"Some Kidney Patients over 45 'Not Treated.'" 1977. London *Times* (May 19): 4.

Somerville, Margaret A. 1981. "Ethics and the Nephrologist." *Lancet* 1 (May 16): 1109–10.

———. 1986. "Should the Grandparents Die?: Allocation of Medical Resources with an Aging Population." *Law, Medicine and Health Care* 14 (September): 158–63.

Sommers, Christina H. 1986. "Once a Soldier, Always a Dependent." *Hastings Center Report* 16 (August): 15–17.

Sorensen, Thorkild I., et al. 1984. "Prospective Evaluation of Alcohol Abuse and Alcoholic Liver Injury in Men as Predictors of Development of Cirrhosis." *Lancet* 2 (August 4): 241–44.

Spector, William D., and Vincent Mor. 1984. "Utilization and Charges for Terminal Cancer Patients in Rhode Island." *Inquiry* 21 (Winter): 328–37.

Spicker, Stuart F., and John R. Raye. 1981. "The Bearing of Prognoses on the Ethics of Medicine: Congenital Anomalies, the Social Context and the Law."

In Stuart F. Spicker et al. (eds.), *The Law–Medicine Relation: A Philosophical Exploration.* Boston: D. Reidel: 189–216.

Spitzer, W. O., et al. 1981. "Measuring the Quality of Life of Cancer Patients." *Journal of Chronic Diseases* 34 (December): 585–97.

Stacey, James. 1983. "Name of 'New Game': Allocation of Resources." *American Medical News* (January 7): 1+.

Starr, T. Jolene, et al. 1986. "Quality of Life and Resuscitation Decisions in Elderly Patients." *Journal of General Internal Medicine* 1 (November/December): 373–79.

Starzl, Thomas E. 1987. "Selection of Kidney Recipients." *Journal of the American Medical Association* 258 (September 11): 1328–29.

Starzl, Thomas E., et al. 1987a. "Liver Transplantation in Older Patients." *New England Journal of Medicine* 316 (February 19): 484–85.

———. 1987b. "A Multifactorial System for Equitable Selection of Cadaver Kidney Recipients." *Journal of the American Medical Association* 257 (June 12): 3073–75.

———. 1988a. "Equitable Allocation of Extrarenal Organs: With Special Reference to the Liver." *Transplantation Proceedings* 20 (February): 131–38.

———. 1988b. "Orthotopic Liver Transplantation for Alcoholic Cirrhosis." *Journal of the American Medical Association* 260 (November 4): 2542–44.

Staveley, E. S. 1972. *Greek and Roman Voting and Elections.* Ithaca, NY: Cornell University Press.

Stein, Jane J. 1978. *Making Medical Choices.* Boston: Houghton Mifflin.

Steinbrook, Robert, and Bernard Lo. 1984. "Decision Making for Incompetent Patients by Designated Proxy." *New England Journal of Medicine* 310 (June 14): 1598–1601.

Stickel, D. L., et al. 1967. "Human Renal Transplantation with Donor Selection by Leukocyte Typing." *Southern Medical Journal* 60 (July): 730–35.

Stiller, C. R. 1985. "Ethics of Transplantation." *Transplantation Proceedings* 17 (No. 6, Suppl. 3, December): 131–38.

Stoddard, Michael M. 1969. "American Conscription: A Policy Evaluation." Ph.D. dissertation. Los Angeles: University of California, Los Angeles.

Strauss, Michael J. 1984. "The Political History of the Artificial Heart." *New England Journal of Medicine* 310 (February 2): 332–36.

Strauss, Michael J., et al. 1986. "Rationing of Intensive Care Unit Services: An Everyday Occurrence." *Journal of the American Medical Association* 255 (March 7): 1143–46.

Suleiman, Abu B., et al. 1982. "Living Related Renal Transplantation in Kuala Lumpur." *Medical Journal of Malaysia* 37 (September): 273–75.

Sullivan, Ronald. 1982. "More Hospitals Refusing Emergency Cardiac Cases." *New York Times* (May 2): 1+.

———. 1987. "Doctors' Quandary: Picking Who Gets a Heart." *New York Times* (December 16): B1, 5.

Sutherland, D. E. R., et al. 1982. "The High-Risk Recipient in Transplantation." *Transplantation Proceedings* 14 (March): 19–27.

Swales, J. D. 1982. "Medical Ethics: Some Reservations." *Journal of Medical Ethics* 8 (September): 117–19.

Tancredi, Laurence R. 1982. "Social and Ethical Implications in Technology Assessment." In Barbara J. McNeil and Ernest G. Cravalho (eds.), *Critical Issues in Medical Technology.* Boston: Auburn House: 93–112.

Task Force on Organ Transplantation. 1986. *Organ Transplantation: Issues and Recommendations.* Rockville, MD: U.S. Department of Health and Human Services.

Taube, David H., et al. 1983. "Successful Treatment of Middle Aged and Elderly Patients with End Stage Renal Disease." *British Medical Journal* 286 (June 25): 2018–20.

Taurek, John M. 1977. "Should the Numbers Count?" *Philosophy and Public Affairs* 6 (Summer): 293–316.

Taylor, T. R., et al. 1975. "Individual Differences in Selecting Patients for Regular Hemodialysis." *British Medical Journal* 2 (May 17): 380–81.

Telfer, Elizabeth. 1976. "Justice, Welfare, and Health Care." *Journal of Medical Ethics* 2 (September): 107–11.

Tempels, Placide. 1959. *Bantu Philosophy,* trans. Colin King. Paris: Presence Africaine.

"10,000 Win Rare Lottery to Stay in U.S." 1987. *Lexington [KY] Herald-Leader* (February 23): A4.

Teres, Daniel. 1984. "Rationing Intensive Care." *New England Journal of Medicine* 310 (April 19): 1059.

Tessler, A., and J. Kroll. 1982. " 'Not Admitted' at Four Hospitals, Woman Dies." Saginaw (MI) *News* (March 10).

Teuber, Andreas. 1981. "The Relevant Reasons for Distributing Health Care." *Southern Journal of Philosophy* 19 (Winter): 517–30.

"The Ethical Challenge: Four Biomedical Case Studies" (video). 1975. White Plains, NY: Science and Mankind.

"The Heart of a New Medicine." 1982. *New Scientist* 94 (May 13): 398.

"The Life-and-Death Choices Created by Medical Technology." 1984. *Business Week* (October 15): 144–45.

The Queen v. *Dudley and Stevens.* 1884. 14 Q.B.D. 273.

"The Right to Live: Who Decides?" (video). 1972. New York: Learning Corporation of America.

"The Sale of Human Body Parts." 1974. *Michigan Law Review* 72 (May): 1182–1264.

Thibault, G. E., et al. 1980. "Physicians' Ability to Predict Outcome of Medical Intensive Care." *Clinical Research* 28: 301A.

Thielicke, Helmut. 1970. "The Doctor as Judge of Who Shall Live and Who Shall Die." In Kenneth Vaux (ed.), *Who Shall Live?* Philadelphia: Fortress Press: 146–94.

Thiroux, Jacques P. 1977. *Ethics: Theory and Practice.* Encino, CA: Glencoe Press.

Thomas, Anthony E. 1975. "Health Care in *Ukambani* Kenya: A Socialist Critique." In Stanley R. Ingman and Anthony E. Thomas (eds.), *Topias and Utopias in Health.* The Hague: Mouton: 267–81.

Thomas, Gwyn. 1986. "QALYs or Short Straws." *British Medical Journal* 293 (August 2): 338.

Thomasma, David C. 1982. "An Apology for the Value of Human Lives." *Hospital Progress* 63 (April): 49–52 + .

———. 1984a. "Ethical Judgments of Quality of Life in the Care of the Aged." *Journal of the American Geriatrics Society* 32 (July): 525–27.

———. 1984b. "Freedom, Dependency, and the Care of the Very Old." *Journal of the American Geriatrics Society* 32 (December): 906–14.

———. 1986a. "Social Triage of the Elderly." *Contemporary Philosophy* 11 (January): 5–7.

———. 1986b. "Quality of Life Judgments, Treatment Decisions and Medical Ethics." *Clinics in Geriatric Medicine* 2 (February): 17–27.

Thomasma, David C., and Andrew Griffin. 1983. "Critical Care of Children: The Ethics of Using Contested and Expensive Medical Resources." *Linacre Quarterly* 50 (February): 64–74.

Thompson, Mark E. 1983. "Selection of Candidates for Cardiac Transplantation." *Heart Transplantation* 3 (November): 65–69.

Thurow, Lester C. 1984. "Learning to Say 'No.'" *New England Journal of Medicine* 311 (December 13): 1569–72.

Tizes, Reuben, and Bruce R. Tizes. 1977. "The Rights of Mentally Incompetent and Senile Patients to Emergency Hospital Care." *Journal of Legal Medicine* 5 (April): 8AA–8DD.

Tobin, Richard S. 1980. "Should Cost Be a Factor in Personal Medical Care?" *New England Journal of Medicine* 303 (July 31): 288.

Toledo-Pereyra, Luis H. 1983. "Is Patient Rationing in Our Future? Who Shall Decide?" *Dialysis and Transplantation* 12 (December): 830.

Torriero, E. A. 1986. "Donor Heart Found for Baby." Knight-Ridder News Service (e.g., in *Lexington [KY] Herald-Leader,* June 11): A1 +).

Touche Ross. 1986. *U.S. Hospitals: The Next Five Years.* New York: Touche Ross.

Towers, Bernard, et al. 1984. "Kidney Failure and Hemodialysis: Should Everyone Be Treated?" (video). Los Angeles: UCLA Media Center.

Trachtman, Leon E. 1985. "Why Tolerate the Statistical Victim?" *Hastings Center Report* 15 (February): 14.

Trammell, Richard L., and Thomas F. Wren. 1977. "Fairness, Utility and Survival." *Philosophy* 52: 331–37.

"Transplant Conference Probes Medical Need and Suitability." 1987. *Update* (Loma Linda U. Ethics Ctr.) 3 (January): 1.

"Transplant Groups Defend Allocation Based on Need." 1987. *Medical Ethics Advisor* (July): 89–92.

Transplantation Society (Council). 1985. "Commercialisation in Transplantation: The Problems and Some Guidelines for Practice." *Lancet* 2 (September 28): 715–16.

Treaster, Joseph B. 1978. "Shortages at Elmhurst Hospital Are Forcing Some Life and Death Decisions." *New York Times* (March 17): B1+.

Tulpius, Nicolaus. 1641. *Observationum Medicarum*. Amsterdam, 1641. Summarized in *The Queen v. Dudley and Stevens*: 276–77.

Uddo, Basile J. 1986. "The Withdrawal or Refusal of Food and Hydration as Age Discrimination: Some Possibilities." *Issues in Law and Medicine* 2 (July): 39–59.

Uhlmann, R. F., and W. J. McDonald. 1982. "An Empiric Study of Non-Resuscitation." *Clinical Research* 39 (February): 45A.

"Unfunded Patients Have Few Costly Procedures." 1984. *American Medical News* (April 20): 22.

UNICEF. 1987. *The State of the World's Children 1987*. New York: Oxford University Press.

———. 1988. *The State of the World's Children 1988*. New York: Oxford University Press.

United Nations, Secretary-General. 1975. "Human Rights and Scientific and Technological Developments." 30th Session, Item 70 of the Provisional Agenda (July 28).

United Nations. 1948. "Universal Declaration of Human Rights."

United States. 1776. "Declaration of Independence."

United States v. Holmes. 1842. 26 F. Cas. 360 No. 15, 383 (C.C.E.D. Pa.).

UNOS. 1988. "Memorandum on UNOS Policy Regarding Utilization of the Point System for Cadaveric Kidney Allocation." November 11.

———. 1989a. "The Nursing Shortage." *Transplant Perspectives* (February): 1–3.

———. 1989b. "Memorandum on Kidney Allocation Policy: Final Policy Statement." April 7.

U.S.A.I.D. 1980. "Kitui Feasibility Study Report." Nairobi.

U.S. Bureau of the Budget. 1967. *Report of the Committee on Chronic Kidney Disease*. Washington, D.C.: U.S. Government Printing Office. Summarized in Welt.

U.S. Congress. 1972. *Congressional Report* 118 (September 30): 33003–09.

U.S. Department of Commerce, Bureau of the Census. 1988. *Statistical Abstract of the United States*. Washington, D.C.: U.S. Government Printing Office.

U.S. Department of Health and Human Services. 1986. *HHS News* (July 29).

U.S. Department of Health and Human Services, Task Force on Organ Transplantation. 1985. "Report to the Secretary and the Congress on Immunosuppressive Therapies." Rockville, MD: U.S. Dept. of H. H. S., October.

U.S. Health Care Financing Administration. 1981. "Medicine Program; Solicitation of Hospitals and Medical Centers to Participate in a Study of Heart Transplants." *Federal Register* 46 (January 22): 7072–75.

U.S. House of Representatives, Committee on Science and Technology, Sub-Committee on Investigations and Oversight. 1983. "Procurement and Allocation of Human Organs for Transplantation" (November 2 and 9 hearings). Washington, D.C.: U.S. Government Printing Office.

U.S. House of Representatives, Select Committee on Aging, Subcommittee on Health and Long-Term Care. 1984. "Technology and Aging: Rationalizing or Rationing." Washington, D.C.: U.S. Government Printing Office, March 15.

U.S. House of Representatives, Committee on Ways and Means, 92d Congress. 1971. *National Health Insurance Proposals Hearings, 1st Session* (November 3 and 4). Washington, D.C.: U.S. Government Printing Office.

U.S. House of Representatives, 97th Congress. 1982. *Conference Report No. 97-765, Communications Amendments Act of 1982* (August 19). Washington, D.C.: U.S. Government Printing Office.

"U.S. Puts Landing Slots of Braniff Into Lottery." 1982. *New York Times* (May 23): 26.

"Utilitarianism." 1984. *Journal of Medical Ethics* 10 (September): 115–16.

Van Rood, J. J. 1981. "Prospective HLA Typing is Helpful in Cadaveric Renal Transplantation." *Transplantation Proceedings* 19 (February): 139–43.

Varga, Andrew C. 1984. *The Main Issues in Bioethics,* rev. ed. New York: Paulist.

Veatch, Robert M. 1975. "Medical Ethics in a Revolutionary Age." *Journal of Current Social Issues* 12 (Fall): 4–19.

———. 1976. "What Is a 'Just' Health Care Delivery?" In R. M. Veatch and R. Branson (eds.), *Ethics and Health Policy.* Cambridge, MA: Ballinger: 127–53.

———. 1977a. "Death and Dying: The Legislative Options." *Hastings Center Report* 7 (October): 5–8.

———. 1977b. *Case Studies in Medical Ethics.* Cambridge: Harvard University Press.

———. 1977c. "Ethical Foundations for Valuing Lives: Implications for Life-Extending Technologies." In The Futures Group, *A Technology Assessment of Life-extending Technologies* (Supplementary Report, vol. 6). Glastonbury, CT: The Futures Group: 196–242.

———. 1979. "Justice and Valuing Lives." In R. M. Veatch (ed.), *Life Span.* San Francisco: Harper and Row: 197–224.

———. 1981. *A Theory of Medical Ethics.* New York: Basic Books.

———. 1985a. "From Fae to Schroeder: The Ethics of Allocating High Technology." *Spectrum* 16 (April): 15–18.

———. 1985b. "Distributive Justice and the Allocation of Technological Resources to the Elderly." Contract report prepared for the Office of Technology Assessment, U.S. Congress, Washington, D.C. (December).

———. 1985c. "The Ethics of Critical Care in Cross-Cultural Perspective." In John C. Moskop and Loretta Kopelman (eds.), *Ethics and Critical Care Medicine*. Boston: D. Reidel: 191–206.

———. 1986. *The Foundations of Justice*. New York: Oxford University Press.

Velez, Ramon, et al. 1981. "Treatment of End-Stage Renal Disease." *New England Journal of Medicine* 304 (February 5): 356–57.

Verwilghen, R. L. 1981. "Audit in Renal Failure." *British Medical Journal* 283 (August 22): 556.

Vincent, Richard H. 1977. "The California Natural Death Act—Some Help with Antidysthanasia." *Journal of the Medical Association of Georgia* 66 (January): 38–40.

Vinogradoff, Paul. 1917. "Ordeal (Christian)." In James Hastings (ed.), *Encyclopedia of Religion and Ethics,* vol. 9. New York: Charles Scribner's Sons: 519–20.

Von Stetina v. Florida Medical Center. 1982. 1 Fla. Supp. 2d 55 (Fla. 17th Cir. 1982), 436 So. Rptr. 2d 1022 (1983).

Waldholz, Michael. 1981. "Cost of Using Kidney Device Sparks Debate." *Wall Street Journal* (February 5): 23, 32.

Wallis, Claudia. 1982. "Which Life Should Be Saved?" *Time* 120 (November 22): 100–01.

———. 1986. "Of Television and Transplants." *Time* 127 (June 23): 68.

Walters, James W. 1987. "Larger Issues of Justice Are Still Troublesome." *Update* (Loma Linda U. Ethics Ctr.) 3 (January): 2.

"Wanna Win a Piece of Wyoming?" 1981. *Economist* 280 (August 22–28): 25.

Ward, Elizabeth. 1984. "Death or Dialysis—A Personal View." *British Medical Journal* 289 (December 22/29): 1712–13.

———. 1986. "Dialysis or Death? Doctors Should Stop Covering Up For an Inadequate Health Service." *Journal of Medical Ethics* 12 (June): 61–63.

Warmbrodt, Jane. 1985. "Who Gets the Organs?" *Midwest Medical Ethics* 1 (Summer): 3–4.

Washington Health Choices. 1986. *Executive Report.* Seattle, WA: Puget Sound Health Systems Agency.

Waterfall, Wallace K. 1980. "Dialysis and Transplant." *British Medical Journal* 281 (September 13): 726–27.

Watts, D., et al. 1984. "Psychiatric Aspects of Cardiac Transplantation." *Heart Transplantation* 3 (May): 243–47.

Wauters, J., et al. 1983. "Selection Criteria and Physician Bias in the Treatment of End-Stage Renal Failure: Results of a National Survey." Report presented at the 4th Congress of the International Society for Artificial Organs (Kyoto, Japan).

Weale, Albert. 1979. "Statistical Lives and the Principle of Maximum Benefit." *Journal of Medical Ethics* 5 (December): 185–95.

Weckman, George, and Richard W. Willy. 1987. "Descriptive Medical Ethics and Allocation." *Listening* 22 (Winter): 12–21.

Wehr, Elizabeth. 1984. "National Health Policy Sought for Organ Transplant Surgery." *Congressional Quarterly* 42 (February 25): 453–58.

Weir, Robert F. 1984. *Selective Nontreatment of Handicapped Newborns.* New York: Oxford University Press.

———. 1985. "Selective Nontreatment—One Year Later: Reflections and a Response." *Social Science and Medicine* 20 (No. 11): 1109–17.

Weller, John M., et al. 1982. "Analysis of Survival of End-Stage Renal Disease Patients." *Kidney International* 21 (January): 78–83.

Welt, Louis G. 1968. "Dialysis and Transplantation." *New England Journal of Medicine* 278 (March 14): 622–23.

West, Charles. 1975. "Justice within the Limits of the Created World." *The Ecumenical Review* 27 (January): 57–64.

Westervelt, Frederic B. 1970. "A Reply to Childress: The Selection Process as Viewed from Within." *Soundings* 53 (Winter): 356–62.

Westlie, L., et al. 1984. "Mortality, Morbidity and Life Satisfaction in the Very Old Dialysis Patient." *Transactions of the American Society for Artificial Internal Organs* 30: 21–30.

Wetle, Terrie T. 1985. "Ethical Aspects of Decision Making for and with the Elderly." In Marshall B. Kapp et al. (eds.), *Legal and Ethical Aspects of Health Care for the Elderly.* Ann Arbor, MI: Health Administration Press: 258–67.

———. 1987. "Age as a Risk Factor for Inadequate Treatment." *Journal of the American Medical Association* 258 (July 24/31): 516.

Wetle, Terrie, and Sue E. Levkoff. 1984. "Attitudes and Behaviors of Service Providers Toward Elder Patients in the VA System." In Terrie Wetle and John Rowe (eds.), *Older Veterans: Linking VA and Community Resources.* Cambridge: Harvard University Press: 205–30.

White, Charles H., and John F. Monagle. 1982. "Ethics and Economics: Making 'Lifeboat' Decisions." *Hospital Progress* 63 (November): 8–10.

"Who Is Worth Saving?" 1962. *Newsweek* 59 (June 11): 92.

"Who Shall Be Dialyzed?" 1984. *Lancet* 1 (March 31): 717.

"Who Shall Die?" 1980. *Journal of Medical Ethics* 6 (December): 171–72.

Wikler, Daniel I. 1982. "Persuasion and Coercion for Health: Ethical Issues in Government Efforts to Change Life-Styles." In John B. McKinlay (ed.), *Law and Ethics in Health Care.* Cambridge: MIT Press: 297–332.

———. 1987a. "Comments on Battin's 'Age Rationing.'" In Timothy M. Smeeding (ed.), *Should Medical Care Be Rationed by Age?* Totowa, NJ: Rowman and Littlefield: 95–98.

———. 1987b. "Personal Responsibility for Illness." In Donald VanDeVeer and Tom Regan (eds.), *Health Care Ethics.* Philadelphia: Temple University Press: 326–58.

———. 1988. "Ought the Young Make Health Care Decisions for Their Aged Selves?" *Journal of Medicine and Philosophy* 13 (February): 57–71.

Wilensky, Gail R. 1985. "Making Decisions on Rationing." *Business and Health* 3 (November): 36–38.

"Will the U.S. Ration Health Care?" 1979. *Perspective* 14 (Winter): 1–5.

Willard, L. Duane. 1980. "Scarce Medical Resources and the Right to Refuse Selection by Artificial Chance." *Journal of Medicine and Philosophy* 5 (September): 225–29.

Williams, Alan. 1986. "QALYs or Short Straws." *British Medical Journal* 293 (August 2): 337–38.

Williams, Bernard. 1971. "The Idea of Equality." In H. A. Bedou (ed.), *Justice and Equality.* Englewood Cliffs, NJ: Prentice-Hall: 116—37.

———. 1973. "A Critique of Utilitarianism." In Bernard Williams and J. C. C. Smart, *Utilitarianism: For and Against.* Cambridge: Cambridge University Press: 75–155.

Williams, G. Melville, et al. 1984. "Reasons Why Kidneys Removed for Transplantation Are Not Transplanted in the United States." *Transplantation* 38: 691–94.

Wilson, M. A. 1967. "Doctor's Duty to His Patient." In "Selection of Patients for Haemodialysis." *British Medical Journal* 1 (March 11): 624.

Wineman, Robert J. 1982. "End-Stage Kidney Disease: Trends in Statistics." In Barbara J. McNeil and Ernest G. Cravalho (eds.), *Critical Issues in Medical Technology.* Boston: Auburn House: 289–300.

Wing, A. J. 1983a. "Medicine and the Media: A Lottery for Life." *British Medical Journal* 287 (August 13): 492.

———. 1983b. "Why Don't the British Treat More Patients with Kidney Failure?" *British Medical Journal* 287 (October 22): 1157–58.

Wing, A. J., et al. 1978. "Combined Report on Regular Dialysis and Transplantation in Europe VIII, 1977." *Proceedings of the European Dialysis and Transplant Association* 15: 2–76.

Winslade, William J., and Judith W. Ross. 1986. *Choosing Life or Death.* New York: Free Press.

Winslow, Gerald R. 1982. *Triage and Justice.* Berkeley: University of California.

———. 1986. "A Test of Ethical Principles." *Business and Health* (April): 11–16.

———. 1987. "Rationing and Publicity." In G. J. Agich and C. E. Begley (eds.), *The Price of Health.* Boston: D. Reidel: 195–211.

Wojcik, Jan. 1978. *Muted Consent.* West Lafayette, IN: Purdue University Press.

Wolff, Robert Paul. 1969. *The Ideal of the University.* Boston: Beacon Press.

Woodland, James F. 1981. "Why the Numbers Count." *Southern Journal of Philosophy* 19 (Winter): 531–40.

Woolley, F. Ross. 1984. "Ethical Issues in the Implantation of the Total Artificial Heart." *New England Journal of Medicine* 310 (February 2): 292–96.

Working Group on Mechanical Circulatory Support; National Heart, Lung and Blood Institute. 1985. *Artificial Heart and Assist Devices: Directions, Needs,*

Costs, Societal and Ethical Issues. Bethesda, MD: National Institutes of Health.

World Bank. 1986. *Poverty in Latin America.* Washington, D.C.: World Bank.

Wrenn, Keith. 1985. "No Insurance, No Admission." *New England Journal of Medicine* 6 (February 7): 373–74.

"Young Mother Wants Transplant for Baby." 1986. Associated Press News Service (e.g., in *Lexington [KY] Herald-Leader,* June 5: A7).

Young, Robert. 1975. "Some Criteria for Making Decisions Concerning the Distribution of Scarce Medical Resources." *Theory and Decision* 6 (November): 439–55.

Zawacki, Bruce F. 1985. "ICU Physician's Ethical Role in Distributing Scarce Resources." *Critical Care Medicine* 13 (January): 57–60.

I N D E X